BUSINESS, NOT POLITICS

Between Men ~ Between Women

BUSINESS, NOT POLITICS

The Making of the Gay Market

KATHERINE SENDER

Columbia University Press　　New York

COLUMBIA UNIVERSITY PRESS
Publishers Since 1893
NEW YORK   CHICHESTER, WEST SUSSEX

Library of Congress Cataloging-in-Publication Data
Sender, Katherine.
  Business, not politics : the making of the gay market / Katherine Sender.
      p. cm. — (Between men—between women)
  Includes bibliographical references and index.
  ISBN 0–231–12734–0 (cloth : alk. paper)
  1. Gay consumers—United States.   2. Lesbian consumers—United States.   3. Marketing—United
States.   I. Title.   II. Series.
  HC110.C6S46   2004
  658.8'0086'64—dc22

                                                                                          2004055119

c 10 9 8 7 6 5 4 3 2 1

Chapter 6 appeared in somewhat different form as "Neither Fish nor Fowl: Feminism, Desire, and
Lesbian Readers," *Communication Review* 7.4 (2004); chapter 7 appeared in somewhat different form
as "Sex Sells: Sex, Taste, and Class in Commercial Gay and Lesbian Media," *GLQ (Gay and Lesbian
Quarterly)* 9.3 (2003): 331–65.

Between Men ~ Between Women
LESBIAN, GAY, AND BISEXUAL STUDIES
Terry Castle and Larry Gross, Editors

Between Men ~ Between Women is a forum for current lesbian and gay scholarship
in the humanities and social sciences. The series includes both books that rest within
specific traditional disciplines and are substantially about gay men, bisexuals, or lesbians
and books that are interdisciplinary in ways that reveal new insights into gay, bisexual, or
lesbian experience, transform traditional disciplinary methods in consequence of the
perspectives that experience provides, or begin to establish lesbian and gay studies as a
freestanding inquiry. Established to contribute to an increased understanding of lesbians,
bisexuals, and gay men, the series also aims to provide through that understanding a
wider comprehension of culture in general.

To my mother,
Judith Olivia Sender

CONTENTS

ACKNOWLEDGMENTS

As with all processes of cultural production, this book does not emerge from a vacuum but is the result of much kind assistance. As I review the long and often lonely seeming progress of this project, I am struck by the openheartedness of the many people who have supported me in myriad ways—some at pivotal moments, others consistently throughout.

This project rests largely upon the generosity of my interviewees, who made time in their very busy lives to share their thoughts on the gay market; their contributions give life to this work and I thank each of them for this. I am particularly grateful to Dan Baker, Stephanie Blackwood, Howard Buford, and Sean Strub for repeatedly offering details of their experiences and their contact information, for passing on relevant articles, and—in Dan's and Sean's case—for hosting me on research trips to New York and Milford, Pennsylvania. Bob Witeck's friendship and generous collegiality have been a great pleasure, and he was also an invaluable reader at a crucial stage of the manuscript. Additionally, Jason Heffner and Michael Kusek passed on the names of gay marketers to me, and Michael Bronski gave me advice, opinion, reading suggestions, and his collection of gay merchandise catalogs.

I thank my dissertation adviser Lisa Henderson for bringing her awesome intellect, the breadth of her knowledge, and the thoroughness of her methods to our working together. Her input is present in every page of this work. Thanks to my dissertation committee members Sut Jhally and Kathy Peiss for their expertise, advice, and ongoing enthusiasm for this project. Thanks also to Justin Lewis, who left the United States before I completed the dissertation.

I appreciate my friends and colleagues in Massachusetts, who offered their intellectual, affective, and practical support. James Allan, Lynn Comella, Neil

Hartlen, Susan McKenna, Laurie Ouellette, and Heather Thompson have thought, talked, read, and otherwise engaged with me in the research and writing of this book. Vincent Doyle has been my dear friend and intellectual coconspirator throughout this process and was a generous reader of a late draft of the book. I am deeply grateful to Laurel Shortell, who generously shared her love, intelligence, sense of perspective, and income with me while I was writing the dissertation.

I thank the faculty and staff at the Department of Communication at the University of Massachusetts—Amherst, especially Carolyn Anderson, Michael Morgan, Pearl Simanski, and April Tidlund for helping me to navigate departmental life. Thanks also to Lee Badgett and Carol Heim in the Economics Department for sharing sources, ideas, and work in progress with me.

Thanks to my friends and colleagues at the Annenberg School for Communication, the University of Pennsylvania, including Carolyn Marvin, Joe Turow, Barbie Zelizer, and especially Larry Gross, whose support and encouragement with the completion of this book has been invaluable. I greatly appreciate Bethany Klein's expert research and editing assistance, and Jason Tocci's help with finding and scanning images. I give heartfelt thanks to Joe'l Ludovich for encouraging, distracting, and loving me through the final stages of the project.

Thanks to the Department of Communication at the University of Massachusetts for twice awarding me dissertation support funds, to the University of Massachusetts Graduate School for a student fellowship in 1997, and to the Gay and Lesbian Alliance Against Defamation (GLAAD) for support to write a commissioned paper on the topic in 2001. Thanks also to Kathleen Hall Jamieson, who provided funds for research assistance in the summer of 2003.

While geographically distant, my family is present in this work: I thank my mother Judith, my father Michael, and my brother Richard for their love, confidence, pride, and financial support. I also thank my uncle Nick Hedley for his loving wisdom. I appreciate my grandmother Patricia Hedley, who died in January 2003, for her enduring fascination for what I would get up to next.

I hope that each of you see your presence in these pages and know that insofar as this project is successful it is so as a result of your contributions. To all of you I offer my deepest thanks.

BUSINESS, NOT POLITICS

CHAPTER 1

THE BUSINESS AND POLITICS OF GAY MARKETING

Since the early 1990s, the United States has seen a rapid increase in the visibility of a new consumer niche: the gay market. A growing number of national corporations, including Subaru cars, Tanqueray gin, Abercrombie & Fitch menswear, and American Express Financial Advisors, court readers of the gay press, and commercials from the travel Web site Orbitz, and insurance company John Hancock, feature gay and lesbian couples on prime-time television. Within a year of its debut, *Out* magazine—a stylish lifestyle publication for lesbians, gays, and bisexuals—received $271,000 in advertising revenue for a single issue (December 1993), and in the early 1990s gay-owned advertising agencies such as Prime Access and Mulryan/Nash produced campaigns for AT&T's long-distance service and Alizé liqueur, respectively. In the spring of 2000, the *Advocate*'s publishing company, Liberation Publications, Inc., bought its main competitor for gay readers—*Out*—and then proposed (though later withdrew from) a merger with PlanetOut, an online service for gay, lesbian, bisexual, and transgender Internet users. In January 2002, Viacom subsidiaries MTV and Showtime considered the viability of a gay cable channel, and Bravo, owned by NBC, produced the hit makeover show *Queer Eye for the Straight Guy* in 2003. Collectively, these initiatives suggest that gays and lesbians are now considered a sufficiently large and profitable group to warrant marketers' attention, and signal a mature phase of the gay market.

Advocates and critics have looked at the boom in gay marketing with both excitement and trepidation, speculating about its cultural significance. Yet whatever these marketing efforts may portend for the lives of gay, lesbian, bisexual, and transgender (GLBT) people, corporate representatives and media executives have been careful to circumscribe these developments within a discursive framework of sound business practices. Trade and popular press articles abound with claims that marketing appeals to gay and lesbian consumers are a matter of "business, not politics." As a spokesperson from Naya water said, "This is not a political decision to go after the gay niche. It was a business decision."[1] Similarly, commenting on his company's lesbian-themed television commercial, a John Hancock vice president said that whether the ad "ultimately causes social change is for others to decide. . . . For us, it's simply a business decision" to represent a lesbian couple.[2] Or as a Miller beer representative claimed, "We market to gays and lesbians for business reasons because we want to sell our product to consumers. It doesn't get more complicated than that."[3] Yet in the realm of gay and lesbian marketing, it does indeed get more complicated than that: the business opportunities that gay politics offers have structured the gay market just as much as the politics of gay-targeted business practices have. Far from aligning with *either* business *or* politics, marketers, many of whom identify as gay, lesbian, and bisexual, have actively produced the gay market from a mutually dependent but not necessarily civil union between the business imperatives and political stakes of gay marketing.

An episode of Showtime's gay soap opera *Queer as Folk* from 2002 neatly summarizes some of these frictions. The show's bad boy, Brian Kinney, is an advertising executive commissioned by a homophobic client, Clayton Poole, to develop a new campaign for a beleaguered beverage. Repositioning the product from the young women's market to the gay market, Brian changes the product's name from Poolside to Poolboy and puts a photo of a muscular man in tight Speedos on the label. Yet Brian's lesbian friend, Lindsey, takes him to task for pandering to homophobes, asking, "Poole Beverages: do you know who that guy is?" Brian responds, "What he does with his money is his business." Lindsey counters, "Except when it hurts us—then it's our business." "*That*," according to Brian, "is my business." The gay-inflected Poolboy campaign is an instant success, and Clayton Poole is made to eat humble pie (and to donate generously to gay marriage initiatives) when he realizes the power of the gay market. Here the joke is at the homophobe's expense: You homophobes may not like us, but you can't ignore us any longer, at least not as consumers.

Viewers might read this *Queer as Folk* episode as a thinly veiled reference to gay beer drinkers' long-standing boycott of Coors beer because of the Coors family's contributions to antigay groups. The show does not simply extol the virtues of gay consumption, but instead engages with some of the debates that have underpinned the development of the market since the early 1970s. In the process, the episode offers predictable (and predictably gendered) stereotypes of lesbian and gay consumers: *Queer as Folk*'s partyboys just wanna have fun with beefcake in Speedos, while the lesbians have their eyes on the political prize of gay civil rights gains. Yet however much Brian asserts that Clayton Poole's homophobia is none of Brian's business, and Brian's targeting of gay consumers on behalf of this homophobe is none of Lindsey's business, the politics of gay marketing permeates this episode. Are corporate moguls' political views relevant in the marketing sphere? Is helping homophobes capitalize on gay consumption a political issue? What role do gay-identified people play in courting the gay market?

The Business of Politics, the Politics of Business

With the claim that gay marketing is a matter of "business, not politics," marketers have attempted to establish a commonsense idea that the business of gay marketing can be considered independently of the politics of gay rights, identity, and visibility, a view that *Queer as Folk* clearly contests. Italian political theorist Antonio Gramsci has written about how "commonsense" beliefs become naturalized, taken for granted as "the way things are," and thereby obscure their own ideological foundations.[4] The common sense of "business, not politics" simultaneously asserts a particular idea of both business and politics, and argues for their independence. Here *business* implies a rational system in which "economic action is separated from cultural and social relations and is carried out in a separate sphere, the economic."[5] This system is disinterested, equilibrium-seeking, and inherently fair: citizens come to the marketplace with, in theory, equal chances of competing successfully for the resources being offered. In contrast, *politics* conjures an image of activities that are irrational, out of control, biased toward the interests of one group, and utterly incompatible with—even damaging to—the needs of a healthily functioning economy. By separating business from politics, marketers appeal to a liberal-utilitarian economic model in which financial decisions can be made free of political motivations or ramifications, and where marketers can reach new consumers and generate increased profits independently of any impact this activity might have on social relations or cultural politics.

Yet the division of business from politics disavows the extent to which all economic activity has political effects, from the macroeconomic impact of the North American Free Trade Agreement to the daily microeconomic decisions householders make in the distribution of their weekly paychecks. In his critique of the idea of the self-regulating free market, economics scholar Robert Kuttner argues that economic decisions are always political. Market deregulation that endeavors to remove economics from the realm of government and policymakers has political consequences: "A decision to allow markets, flaws and all, free reign is just one political choice among many. *There is no escape from politics*."[6] The political implications of consumption have been ignored by neither governments nor private corporations: historian Lizbeth Cohen shows how two competing images of consumption have dominated marketing discourses since the Great Depression: the citizen consumer who demands government regulation of the marketplace, and the purchaser consumer who asserts political power directly through that marketplace.[7]

Even a cursory look at contemporary marketing activity reveals that the separation of business endeavors from their political effects is spurious. Consumers have been told that certain kinds of consumption are "patriotic," and that "spending creates jobs and prosperity."[8] The cumulative impact of advertising on the economy in terms of generating ad revenues and stimulating consumption, the circulation of an ethos of consumption as part of the American Dream, and the affirmation of ideologies about gender, class, and race in advertising illustrate some of the profound effects marketing has on the political life of a citizenry.

Although press coverage of the gay market obsessively revisits the division of business from politics, it is by no means only with this market that the distinction is made: comparisons with the African American market reveal that white business leaders played down the political consequences of target marketing on racial politics.[9] As with the gay market, this disavowal is not borne out by the historical record. Business scholar Lisa Peñaloza shows that the African American and gay civil rights movements were both constituted in part through consumer activism. She asserts that "issues such as identity, subjectivity, and agency, which are central to studies of social movements, are also critical in understanding the place gays and lesbians occupy in the contemporary market economy."[10] Peñaloza draws from the history of black civil rights activism in consumer contexts to observe that "many civil rights gains were and continue to be manifest in the marketplace—at the lunch counters, in bus and retail service, in hotel accommodations, and in socially acceptable standards of dress. In this sense, the marketplace may be viewed as an important domain of social contestation whereby disenfranchised groups engage in ongoing struggles for social and political incorporation."[11] The deployment of consumer boycotts to pressure antigay business owners is limited neither to black civil rights activism nor to strategies of a bygone civil rights era: in the summer of 2003, GLBT groups advocated withdrawing support from Urban Outfitters, whose owners, Richard and Margaret Hayne, had contributed $13,150 to notoriously homophobic Pennsylvania senator Rick Santorum's campaign funds.[12]

The particular contours of the gay market have been forged through and respond to a history of gay invisibility, homophobia, and heterosexism. Like

Peñaloza, lesbian activist and critic Alexandra Chasin recognizes the power of consumer identifications in terms of political leverage and community formation. Chasin argues that gay people believed themselves to be part of a national community for the first time in 1977 as a result of a popular, nationwide gay boycott of oranges and juice from the Florida Citrus Commission, whose spokeswoman, Anita Bryant, led a campaign against a gay rights ordinance in Dade County, Florida. This sense of a gay community based on a nationally connected activist movement was facilitated by the burgeoning gay press:

> The national U.S. gay community came into being through the imagined comradeship of gay men and lesbians reading an increasingly commercial gay press. In that press, gay men and lesbians read for news of the growth of the movement, they read for news of consumption opportunities that reinforced their belonging in the community, and they read vernacular language that helped delineate the boundaries of the community.[13]

Chasin's example shows that the gay community, on a national scale at least, is not a preexisting entity that marketers simply need to appeal to, but is a construction, an imagined community formed not only through political activism but through an increasingly sophisticated, commercially supported, national media. Marketing has thus been instrumental in the very formation of groups, including politically inflected groups.

Marketing activity has been pivotal in the constitution of GLBT community and identity, but has also had a significant impact on the visibility of gays and lesbians (less so of bisexual and transgender people) beyond queer subcultures and media. The increase in gay visibility is perhaps the most hotly contested aspect of gay marketing, both by groups hostile to GLBT people and causes, and by GLBT-identified commentators themselves. Right-wing religious groups have suppressed national companies' open appeals to GLBT consumers, as when the Southern Baptists, among other groups, successfully pressured AT&T to drop a gay-themed campaign in 1994, and less successfully boycotted Disney enterprises over the company's progressive policies for GLBT employees and for supporting Ellen DeGeneres's coming out as both a character and a celebrity on its subsidiary, ABC, in 1997. Large media corporations have correspondingly been wary of being seen as overly supportive of openly gay or lesbian marketing: the ABC television network refused to run an ad for the lesbian-oriented Olivia Cruises during the landmark coming-out episode of *Ellen* in April 1997 because network executives saw the ad as politically motivated. An ABC executive told Olivia, "It is our position that discussion about same-sex lifestyles is more appropriate in programming" than in ads.[14] This forced Olivia to negotiate with individual affiliates for spots during the show. Large retailers have also been nervous about being associated with public acknowledgments of homosexuality, as when Chrysler and JC Penney withdrew their commercials from the same episode of *Ellen*.

What is contested here is not that GLBT people are consumers, but that they are increasingly openly recognized, organized, measured, and appealed to as such in mainstream contexts. Historical research on gay and lesbian communities in New York City and in Buffalo, New York, suggests that even before gay market segmentation was imagined on a national scale, gays and lesbians consumed in distinctly identity-related ways. In his study of New York gay male subcultures, George Chauncey quotes a late 1930s historian who recalls "green suits, tight-cuffed trousers, flowered bathing trunks, and half-length flaring top-coats" as distinctively homosexual attire.[15] In a similar vein, Elizabeth Lapovsky Kennedy and Madeline Davis argue that lesbian subcultures in Buffalo since the early twentieth century coalesced in part through the "increasing eroticization of the public realm through the development of consumer society, which promoted sexual pleasure and leisure to sell products, [and] created a culture that separated sex from reproduction and valued the pursuit of leisure interests."[16]

In both accounts, the visibility that gay consumption afforded was limited largely to subcultures: gays and lesbians used clothes, furnishings, and gifts to signal their sexuality to other gays and lesbians. The rise of a national gay market demands a consideration of the implications of gay visibility beyond those subcultures. Those who welcome gay and lesbian themes in advertising applaud appeals to GLBT consumers as validating their existence. As one marketing professional I interviewed said, "I hate to admit it, but if AT&T perceives that it's okay for me to be a gay man, then hey, everybody must. Which isn't true, but there's this sense, 'Wow! There must be more acceptance out there than I thought, and that's a good thing.'"[17] For GLBT people unaccustomed to seeing images of themselves, let alone being taken seriously as explicitly gay or lesbian, national corporate appeals to the gay market can seem profoundly affirming.

Other commentators express optimism that this increasing visibility facilitates a wider acceptance of gay and lesbian people among heterosexuals. Such a view positions gay rights developments firmly within the economic sphere, comparing marketers with early gay entrepreneurs. According to one gay-identified marketer, "Like the first gay business pioneers who saw their new enterprises as a way of serving and helping to create a newly conscious gay community, today's marketers are still fighting the battle to gain acceptance for gay

men and lesbians in our society."[18] This excitement reflects the belief that seeing gay and lesbian people in all walks of life—in marketing, media images, political life, and as celebrities—demonstrates that "we are everywhere" and nor-
malizes gayness for a hitherto fearful and ignorant heterosexual population. The
ongoing invisibility of bisexuals and the comic or pitiable presence of transgender people in mainstream media does not permit a "we are everywhere"
optimism beyond images of gender-normative gays and lesbians, however.

The "battle for acceptance" is fought within the national imagination,
through media images and legal debates, but it is also fought within corporations themselves. As marketer and journalist Grant Lukenbill writes, "Gay and
lesbian consumerism . . . is already affecting much of America's commercial
media imagery. It is impacting corporate hiring practices in the workplace and
even the commercial buying habits of heterosexual Americans."[19] He argues
that courting the gay market forces corporations to demonstrate an awareness
of gay issues, including instigating nondiscrimination and domestic partnership policies, if these are not already in place. Appeals to the gay market also
provide vital funds to nonprofit groups and fund-raising events. Some companies complement their advertising campaigns in gay media with event sponsorship: for example, Absolut vodka has offered long-term support to the
GLAAD (Gay and Lesbian Alliance Against Defamation) Media Awards.[20]
Other companies that are reluctant to openly advertise in gay and lesbian
media find sponsoring civil rights groups a less risky alternative.

Yet even with its beneficial effects, some GLBT critics have contested the
overall value of the visibility that gay marketing affords. They are concerned
that marketing misrepresents "real" communities, that it has a negative effect
on GLBT politics, and that it has a mainstreaming effect on GLBT subcultures. Writer Michael Bronski offers one of the earliest critiques of "the myth
of the gay consumer," constructed narrowly as white, male, professional, urban,
with an abundance of good taste and discretionary income.[21] Subsequent critics have taken up Bronski's observations and have focused on two related
themes: overestimations of gay affluence and stereotypes of the ideal gay consumer.[22] Relying on gay-publication readership surveys and other nonrepre-
sentative market research, marketers have extrapolated to the larger population
gay respondents' higher-than-average incomes. According to one journalist,
GLBT spending was estimated to be $451 billion in 2002.[23] However, econo-
mist Lee Badgett finds that lesbian and gay incomes are on average *lower* than
those of heterosexuals, and lesbians are at a particular disadvantage by not
being allied with the generally higher incomes of men.[24] The affluent images
of lesbians and gays that unrepresentative research methods produce are combined with a generally conservative strategy in advertising to show only the

most "desirable" members of the market. Economists Amy Gluckman and Betsy Reed argue that gay-focused advertising is only a "limited victory" because "the real contours of the multicultural, class-stratified gay populations are languishing in the closet, while images of white, upper-middle-class lesbians and gay men become increasingly conspicuous."[25]

Inflated figures of gay wealth and narrowly conceived images of gay people not only obscure the variety of GLBT experience; they have also been used by reactionary lobbyists as a justification for working *against* gay, lesbian, and bisexual civil rights. The antigay group, the Concerned Women for America, asks:

> Are homosexuals economically, educationally, or culturally disadvantaged? Any homosexual claims to that effect seem clearly bogus in light of emerging marketing studies that show homosexuals to be enormously advantaged relative to the general population—and astronomically advantaged when compared to the truly disadvantaged minorities.[26]

This conservative group pits the "real" claims of "truly disadvantaged minorities"—who are, apparently, people of color and implicitly straight—against the "bogus" claims of an already privileged homosexual elite, a phantom constituency invoked by gay marketers, among others.

Antigay activists' use of inflated income figures suggests that the political advantage offered by increased marketing visibility is a double-edged sword, particularly when the image produced is based on skewed data. Other concerns about the effects of gay marketing have also preoccupied GLBT critics. Some see gay consumerism as closely linked to an assimilation of gays into mainstream culture, posing a direct threat to gay political activism on both a local and a national scale. Writer Sarah Schulman considers efforts to market to gays and lesbians alongside current debates about homosexual monogamy and campaigns for gay marriage.[27] She argues that aligning gay consumption with a specifically domesticated, monogamous model of gay relationships increases the respectability of those relationships, because straight neighbors see gay consuming couples as "just like them." Yet Schulman suggests that the model of privatized gay consumption that both homosexual conservatives and marketers offer threatens the community-based activism of lesbians and gays: "Gay monogamy should remain a personal decision based on an individual's emotional, sexual, and pragmatic needs. To sacrifice this in order to help straight consumers identify with a normative gay model is good marketing but a bad argument for social change."[28] Indeed, national advertising has had a significant impact on the political and sexual content of gay magazines. Communication scholars Fred Fejes and Kevin Petrich argue that as "the economic logic of national advertising begins to drive publications aimed at the lesbian and gay community, the only voice being heard is that of an upper-income, urban, de-sexed, white male."[29] Although they may somewhat overstate the case here, Fejes and Petrich nevertheless make a compelling argument for the relationships between whiteness, wealth, a lack of overt sexuality, and national corporate advertising in gay and lesbian magazines.

Alexandra Chasin also perceives gay consumerism to be closely aligned with an assimilationism that runs counter to a progressive gay activism because "the slippage between politics and the market conspire to feature consumption as the chosen, the ideologically elect, act of choice."[30] She finds corporate sponsorship of gay rights groups worrying because groups that successfully court donations and sponsorship tend to be national in scope, centrist in political goals, and run by white, professional people—that is, people who are most likely to be able to successfully raise funds among other white, professional, and wealthy people. Like Schulman, Chasin worries about the effects of identity-based marketing on the rights-based identity politics advocated by mainstream gay civil rights groups and wants to "dislocate the myth that private consumption can ever do the work of progressive political action."[31]

Whereas Chasin and Schulman are concerned about the fate of grassroots activism in gay consumer culture and see gay assimilation as available only to privileged and respectable gay people, other critics fear for the survival of an authentically gay subculture. Both author Daniel Harris and journalist Daniel Mendelsohn are concerned that increasing acceptance by mainstream society robs gay subcultures of their distinctiveness. Harris laments the demise of "aristocratic ideals of aestheticism" that gay invisibility fostered.[32] Mendelsohn argues that "gay sensibility is now indistinguishable from the mainstream or has been pasteurized into total consumer-culture irrelevance—Ru Paul selling makeup for MAC."[33] He concludes, "Oppression may have been the best thing that could have happened to gay culture," because without it, gay identity becomes "a set of product choices. 'I am what I am' is increasingly becoming a matter of 'You are what you buy.'"[34] For Schulman, Bronski, and Chasin, consumer culture threatens to replace community-based politics and sexual radicalism with an image of affluent homonuclear families and domesticated desires; for Harris and Mendelsohn, what is at stake is the survival of an aesthetic, gay highbrow.

GLBT critics of gay consumer culture, then, see the visibility afforded to gay and lesbian people through marketing and media as a mixed blessing, at best. Media scholar Suzanna Danuta Walters acknowledges that although increased media attention has made the lives of many GLBT-identified people easier, "this new visibility creates new forms of homophobia (for example, the good, marriage-loving, sexless gay vs. the bad, liberationist, promiscuous gay) and lends itself to a false and dangerous substitution of cultural visibility for inclusive citizenship."[35] Similarly, Eric Clarke argues that gay and lesbian visibility has

> become the privileged sign of what is deemed an increasingly successful fight for lesbian and gay justice, legitimacy, and inclusion. . . . In its quest to secure inclusion, mainstream lesbian and gay politics in the United States has sought to reassure straight America that lesbians and gay men are "just like everyone else" and in this sense it seems to have restricted itself to a phantom normalcy.[36]

Walters, Clarke, and others argue that within this bargain, only the most sanitized, privileged, accommodationist, apolitical aspects of gay existence are made visible, at great cost for the real diversity and necessary offensiveness of a queer politics that is unconcerned with—indeed balks at the very idea of—being "just like everyone else."

Debates about the stakes of gay visibility undermine marketers' anxious refrain that gay marketing is a matter of "business, not politics," neutral economic exchange, not messy GLBT activism. Marketers distance their appeals to the gay market from politics because their companies do not want to be seen endorsing gay civil rights claims, promoting gay visibility, or funding political groups or media. It is clear, however, that neither GLBT commentators nor antigay critics of gay marketing are seduced by this distinction. Rather than assume that gay marketing activity can be disentangled from its political effects, they recognize that marketing, especially to a group that remains controversial, cannot help but have political ramifications. Yet frequently in these debates, politics tends to be defined in terms of increased social acceptance and consequent civil rights gains for GLBT people. I want to expand this sense of politics to consider the impact of marketing on the cultural politics of sexuality, to argue that what is at stake is not only acceptance and civil rights but the very meaning of GLBT sexual identification.

Marketing Sexuality

The description of "the gay market" shows how definitions of sexuality can be applied strategically, depending on what marketers find expedient at a given time. For although marketers and journalists refer to "the gay market" and, more recently, "the GLBT market" to encompass all members of this "class" of non-

heterosexual people, their interest and investment are mainly focused on affluent gay men. There is some interest in lesbians, but mostly marketers hope that
lesbians will interpret ads to gay men as appealing to them as well. Marketers
occasionally acknowledge bisexuals and transgender people in their consideration of the gay market, but most believe these groups to be too small to warrant marketing attention. To reflect the predominant focus on gay men, and to
remain consistent with marketers' terminology, I refer to "the gay market"
throughout, unless I want to indicate specific other groups. The recent shift to
include the Ls, Bs, and Ts in references to the GLBT market appears to be a
somewhat disingenuous inclusivity that exists in name only: by far the dominant target of market research and advertising appeals remains gay men.

Even when some marketers acknowledge that the current construction of
the gay market offers an unsatisfactorily narrow view of GLBT people, they
tend to take for granted that there are essentially homosexual persons to whom
they can appeal in advertising. Correspondingly, debates among GLBT critics
about the value of gay marketing commonly assume a gay or lesbian (sometimes bisexual or transgender) subject who can be "made visible" or damaged
by false or co-opted representations. Yet cultural studies reminds us that social
life—texts, artifacts, lived experience—does not reflect a natural state of being,
but is produced and constantly must be reaffirmed through myriad practices.
Meaning is constructed, not merely represented. Even our identities are not
given but are fashioned through practices that suggest who we are like, from
whom we are different, and what of our infinitely complex selves we profile to
say: "This is who I am." Cultural studies scholars and historians have explored
consumption not simply as a domestic and trivial (if necessary) endeavor but,
rather, as a social and cultural activity fundamental to identity formation. The
most fruitful analyses look at how marketing strategies intervene in the social
uses of goods, how marketers "make their product integral to, part of, the meaningful reproduction (or production) of a social relation through particular social practices."[37] A nuanced approach to studying the gay market, therefore,
must consider how marketing does not merely represent gay and lesbian people, but produces recognizable—and sellable—definitions of what it means to
be gay or lesbian. Such an approach is situated at the intersection between marketing as a set of historically and socially specific practices, and consumers who
are engaged in those practices in the course of sexual identification. Three
premises underpin this perspective on gay marketing: that sexuality is produced, not given; that marketing constitutes a primary discourse through which
sexual and other identities are constructed; and that identities and social formations are produced through a complex relationship among media producers, marketing texts (including ads), and audiences.

Media researchers have long been preoccupied with portrayals of women in advertising.[38] Yet whereas women have been a repeated focus, few scholars consider "Mrs. Consumer" to be anything but heterosexual. Some feminist and queer theorists have offered much to a reformulation of sexual representation, going beyond content analysis that documents the scarcity, or limitations, of roles for women and GLBT people in media to suggest how gender and sexuality are produced through institutional discourses and media representations.[39] Michel Foucault argues that there is no "natural" sexuality; gender, sex, and sexuality are instead natural*ized* in layers of medical, pedagogical, legal, religious, and other discourses through which citizens collectively locate and experience sex.[40] He traces the nineteenth-century development of new, or newly expanded, social institutions in France—medicine, law, education, psychiatry—as they took what had hitherto been considered only aberrant *acts*, such as sodomy, and created an aberrant physical and psychic *identity*: the homosexual. If authoritarian discourses constructed, and pathologized, this newly identified sexual person in the nineteenth century, how might discourses of consumption similarly construct nonnormative sexualities in the twentieth and twenty-first centuries? Are the discourses of marketing more benign, since they adopt the liberal mantle of consumer sovereignty, or do they merely replace repressive institutional authority with an internalized system of self-management through which subjects produce themselves as gays and lesbians, in part through consumption?

Consumer discourses do not only guide people in the construction of a coherently gay self, but assist in distinguishing those gay selves from their heterosexual neighbors. Queer theorist Eve Kosofsky Sedgwick argues that the distinction between homosexuality and heterosexuality is a central organizing principle of modernity.[41] She concludes that the "minoritizing view" of gayness—that there is a "distinct population of persons who 'really are' gay," who are essentially different from the heterosexual majority, and who have unique qualities, attributes, ways of talking, of acting, and so on—has achieved ascendancy over the "universalizing view" that sees homoerotic desires as experienced (and largely repressed) potentially by anyone. Sedgwick counters that "apparently heterosexual persons and object choices are strongly marked by same-sex influences and desires, and vice versa for apparently homosexual ones."[42] How far do advertising images flirt with a slippage between gay and straight and, conversely, how does the logic of target marketing reinstate the minoritizing view to distinguish "real" gay people from "real" heterosexuals?

One way in which GLBT and heterosexual people are distinguished is through moral sanctions associated with particular forms of sexuality. Anthropologist Gayle Rubin shows how legal, social, psychological, and media discourses distinguish abject desires from "normative" sexuality, that of the "charmed circle of sex."[43] The charmed circle includes monogamous, private, vanilla, procreative, same-generation, and heterosexual sex. She suggests a process whereby nonnormative sex is ejected from the charmed circle and where some delegitimized practices are subject to even tighter constraints than others, with queer sex requiring specific restrictions. Rubin acknowledges that "some forms of homosexuality are moving in the direction of respectability"—those that are vanilla, coupled, and monogamous—but that "most homosexuality is still on the bad side of the line."[44] In the production of the gay market and its personification of the ideal gay consumer, marketers struggled with the stereotype of the hypersexual, promiscuous gay man and attempted to displace this with "charmed" (or at least, less stigmatized) manifestations of homosexuality that have become the public face of gayness.

Whereas Foucault and Rubin focus mainly on state-supported discourses (law, medicine, and so on) and Sedgwick looks at sexual boundary-making in literature, it is a short step to investigate how normative and aberrant sexualities are not merely reflected by, but are rendered intelligible in, marketing. And whereas both mainstream images of and theories about gays and lesbians commonly take for granted that sexuality can be filtered out from other forms of identification, some feminist and queer theorists have argued that identities are produced in multiple, interacting configurations.[45] To dislodge debates about gay marketing that are entrenched in a struggle between the enabling and damaging effects of "gay visibility" demands an investigation of how that visibility is produced not just in terms of sexuality, but through gender, race, and class as well. The history of gay visibility reveals the tensions between invisibility and limited visibility, between typification and stereotyping, and between needing to find telegraphic ways of representing gayness and doing so at the expense of gay people. How has the construction of a gay market reified gay and lesbian "identity"? Given both the dominance of the minoritizing view of sexuality and the demand of niche marketing to imagine discrete, identifiable market segments, how have gay market practices affirmed a "natural" boundary between people who "really are" gay and lesbian, as distinct from those who are "really" heterosexual? What space is there for bisexual and transgender people within this distinction? Further, how do advertising routines, impelled to represent the most "desirable" face of any niche market, rework negative stereotypes of homosexuality to recoup gays and lesbians within Rubin's charmed circle of sex?

Sexual identity is produced in the spaces between subjects and discourses, readers and texts, consumers and things. As cultural studies scholar Stuart Hall writes, "Identities are thus points of temporary attachment to the subject positions which discursive practices construct for us all."[46] Pierre Bourdieu's work on class identity and taste offers an empirical approach to the relations between social position and cultural practices.[47] He rejects a rigid, linear class structure based solely on economic wealth in favor of more complex ways in which social hierarchies are cultivated, reflected, and struggled over, in part by legitimating some tastes more than others. Taste is not arbitrary, but rather reflects class-specific training or "cultural capital" engendered through family upbringing and education, in particular. As cultural scholar Sarah Thornton summarizes, "Cultural capital is the linchpin of a system of distinction in which cultural hierarchies correspond to social ones and people's tastes are predominantly a marker of class."[48] Taste does not only refer to food and aesthetics, however, but extends to what Bourdieu calls the habitus: home furnishings, grooming, clothing, reading preferences, forms of transportation—indeed, all interactions in the consumer sphere—involve a naturalized assessment and deployment of taste.

Bourdieu introduces the idea of "habitus" to describe how tastes shape the relationship between the body and its symbolic and material contexts. Habitus embodies the lived conditions within which social practices, hierarchies, and forms of identification are manifested through an individual's choices, but signals that those choices are already predisposed by an existing social position. Bourdieu's use of habitus extends the term *lifestyle* by developing it beyond its trivializing connotations (as in "the gay lifestyle") to suggest intimate connections between ways of living and one's sense of class, gender, race, and other forms of cultural belonging. Habitus is constructed through myriad displays of taste that structure lived environments, more or less comfortably "reflect" our social and cultural position, and maintain boundaries between those environments one feels "naturally" at home in (that is, those that are class or gender appropriate) and those that feel uncomfortable (those that are class or gender transgressive). Through habitus, Bourdieu offers us a way of looking at how taste is structured by a consumer's position within social hierarchies—in embodied practices, in lived environments.

Bourdieu focuses on occupation, education, and gender as dominant variables in the formation of habitus, yet lived environments also include practices and sensibilities that are organized around other forms of identification, including sexuality. Class identification enables and requires members to cultivate a particular habitus: so too does identifying as gay or lesbian. Indeed "gaydar," a GLBT person's heightened ability to recognize others through subcultural cues—the placement of a pocket, the shape of a vase, whether and what to shave—points to a shared understanding of gay habitus. The gay habitus is not structured solely by an economic relation to taste, but also by established (and changing) aspects of gay sensibility. Extending Bourdieu's notion of cultural capital, Thornton argues that *sub*cultural capital may function in a semiautonomous relation to more established hierarchies of cultural capital. Thus camp, kitsch, dress and grooming, awareness of gay-relevant current affairs, and star gossip all function as gay-specific subcultural capital, producing consumer tastes that collectively form a gay habitus.

It is clear, however, that there is no single gay habitus. At the very least, gender, gender identity, race, class, and generation segment the "gay community," and its tastes and practices, into a number of discrete and overlapping clusters. Yet each of these clusters does not have equivalent opportunity to appear as— and speak for—the gay community. A race-, class-, and to some extent gender-limited constituency forms the most visible and socially sanctioned gay collectivity. This constituency is identified in part by its participation in a dominant gay habitus. I use "dominant" here not to suggest that this habitus overpowers a putatively heterosexual mainstream, but that the gay habitus constructed through marketing and in gay publications makes visible people who tend to be otherwise already empowered. Gay marketing practices profile members of a dominant gay habitus, obscuring the less "respectable" (i.e., marketable) members of the GLBT communities: lesbians, bisexuals, people of color, poor and working-class gays, transgender people, and sex radicals.

Bourdieu focuses on the family and schooling as the primary mechanisms for the transmission of cultural capital, but advertising, marketing, and the media also transmit taste hierarchies and habitus. In his study of the rise of monthly "family" magazines at the turn of the twentieth century, Richard Ohmann offers a fascinating analysis of the relationship between magazine readership, consumption, and the emergent professional-managerial habitus. He argues that magazines such as the *Ladies' Home Journal*, *Munsey's*, and *McClure's* offered guidance and training that helped to consolidate readers' sense of their newfound status: "The implicit offer the magazines made to their readers was of *socially correct participation*—reading the right fiction, seeing the new paintings, knowing who counted as a celebrity, having sophisticated (if second-hand) views on the current theatrical season, and so on."[49] What could be considered merely "entertainment"—magazine reading—had a more direct pedagogical function: instructing readers on the appropriate cultivation of tastes and knowledge for their class position. Just as family magazines guided the formation of the new professional-managerial classes in the early twentieth century, gay media and marketing have cultivated sexually situated readers as members of an increasingly visible post-Stonewall community, offered GLBT people instruction in "socially correct participation," and promoted gay subcultural capital as central in an increasingly marketable version of the gay lifestyle. Further, the Bravo makeover show *Queer Eye for the Straight Guy* demonstrates that gay subcultural capital is not only relevant to GLBT subcultures but is also increasingly marketable to the heterosexual mainstream (see fig. 1.1). The series is a celebration of gay tastes and the transformative powers of consumption as it turns schlubby straight men into presentable romantic partners. In the process, it assists the formation of a new consumer niche, "metrosexual" men: "straight urban men willing, even eager, to embrace their feminine side," not least through abundant consumption of high end shoes, jeans, and men's cosmetics.[50]

In order to look at the relationships among marketing, media, and gay habitus, it is not enough to look only at media texts and to impute from these the intention of their producers and the impact on their audiences. Ohmann is one of a growing number of scholars who considers the methods by which texts are produced; some, including Thomas Frank and Roland Marchand, have augmented their focus on advertisements with historical documents, company reports, minutes, and autobiographies.[51] Others have observed the processes of creating ads and campaigns firsthand.[52] These researchers analyze the culture of agencies and the routines, assumptions, and stereotypes invoked, largely unconsciously, by advertising agents in the production of easily interpretable appeals. Consumer culture scholar Don Slater looked at the institutional arrangements of British ad agencies, arguing that "whereas the advertising agent *par excellence* is generally thought to be the 'creative person,' the real centers of power in most agencies are the account handlers."[53] Account executives, after all, not only act as gatekeepers between clients and the creatives but also control "the brief," the blueprint on which each campaign is founded. Advertising scholar Karen Shapiro investigated ad-making at four large agencies, concluding that advertisements are produced in highly unstable and unpredictable environments, with volatile accounts, frequent staff and role changes, and involving multiple organizations.[54] As a result, agency decision-making processes are designed to stabilize relations between the agency, the client, and other organizations to protect the creative workers and to offer them maximum flexibility. Both Slater and Shapiro stress the importance of institutional constraints in the production of ads. Agency practices take on particular significance in gay marketing because they must accommodate both the routine and the exceptional—the normal production of advertising that appeals to nonnormative, sexually constituted groups.

Media professionals produce not just texts but their own professional identities through taste, subcultural capital, and specific forms of expertise. In her work on the Book-of-the-Month Club, Janice Radway looks in part at how the club's editors constituted themselves as professionals.[55] She argues that the

FIGURE 1.1 THE FAB FIVE MAKE OVER THE STRAIGHT WORLD, ONE SLOB AT A TIME (*ENTERTAINMENT WEEKLY*, AUGUST 8, 2003).

editors' book reviews were "not unmediated transcriptions of acts of reading" but were personal, idiosyncratic, subjective, even biased readings of each book. These reports not only conveyed whether editors found a book engaging, but were also demonstrations of the editors' cultural capital, and as such were "highly accomplished presentation[s] of self."[56] The Book-of-the-Month Club's editors thus produced not only a list of reviewed books for purchase by (aspiring) professional-managerial class readers but also continually reproduced their own membership in a highly literary fraction of that professional-managerial class. Similarly, gay and lesbian marketing executives construct a specifically gay or lesbian professional-managerial class identity, an identity somewhat precarious in work environments still structured if not by outright homophobia, then at least by heterosexism. Yet the increasing recognition of the gay market among corporate marketers and in advertising agencies makes gay and lesbian professionals' sexuality less a liability than an asset: their gay-specific subcultural capital may become a marketable commodity.

Media production also yields a particular view of the audience.[57] In the 1920s, the Book-of-the-Month Club, among other middlebrow projects, produced not only cultural products but also cultural subjects: subjects who, because of their nascent and precarious class position, both bought products and bought *into* a set of cultural values, tastes, and practices that positioned them as particular kinds of consumers. Book-of-the-Month Club readers crossed cultural capital borders to appropriate knowledge from another, more powerful class to fortify a literate, middle-class sense of self. The formation of consumers' sexual identities is as important as that of class, gender, and race: just as family magazines and middlebrow books cultivated a "respectable" professional-managerial class reader, so have gay media and marketing aided the formation of a "respectable" gay consumer since the early 1970s.[58] Marketers build on their own identities and aspirations for an ideal (and marketable) view of gayness to produce a sexually specific and class-specific gay consumer, and conversely, gay and lesbian consumers buy into these cultural values when they respond to gay-specific marketing.

In his discussion of television talk shows, Joshua Gamson suggests that acknowledging the relatively disempowered position of guests in that genre should be the *beginning* of a discussion about the place and value of talk shows, not its conclusion.[59] Similarly, the fact that gay marketing misrepresents gay people and subcultures should be the beginning of an analysis of gay marketing and consumer culture, not its end. No pristine GLBT culture existed before, or outside of, consumer culture, nor are gay people free of the need or desire to use products and services in socially meaningful ways. Critics who suggest that gay marketing is inevitably assimilationist ignore the complexities and contradictions of what gay marketers do, say they do, and believe about what they do. A more useful approach investigates how marketers have structured the gay niche from a history of invisibility and negative stereotyping to produce gay and lesbian "socially recognizable person[s],"[60] how gender, class, race, and sexuality intersect with consumption in such social recognition; and how GLBT politics and queer sex intersect within gay consumer culture. All marketing, whatever the target niche, both creates and distorts the cultural identities it represents; gay and lesbian marketing is not unusual in this sense. What is significant, however, are the distinctive ways by which marketing makes available, misrepresents, and influences the meaning of gayness in a history of invisibility, homophobia, and heterosexism. If, as cultural studies scholar Larry Gross suggests, advertising shows life not "as it is but as it should be—life and lives worth emulating," what ways of living does gay marketing suggest are worth emulating?[61]

Researching the Gay Market

To look at how marketing processes have helped to produce both sexual identity and a vision of gay lives worth emulating, I focused on people involved in producing gay advertising, marketing strategies, market research, and even the idea of the gay market itself. Since January 1998, I have interviewed forty-five professionals who work in gay marketing and media, including gay, lesbian, and bisexual magazine publishers, ad directors, marketers, sales representatives, and editors; advertising agency creatives and account executives; corporate marketers; public relations consultants; and journalists. (For a detailed account of my methods, see appendix 1; for a list of each interviewee's name, gender, sexual orientation, occupation, company, and the method and date of each interview, see appendix 2.) Twenty-six interviewees were men, eighteen were women, one was transgender. Thirty-four identified as gay, lesbian, or bisexual, four identified themselves as heterosexual, and seven did not disclose their sexual identity. I acknowledge the complications of interviewees identifying themselves as "gay," "lesbian," "bisexual," or "heterosexual" and that these terms can suggest an overly reductive, essential, or stable sexual identity. For my purposes, however, these identifications proved valuable in making claims about the investments of marketers in their gay-specific work.

In follow-up interviews with thirteen openly gay, lesbian, and bisexual interviewees, eleven identified their current socioeconomic status as "professional," "upper middle class," or "bourgeois," one identified as "educated working class," and another as "Class X" (that is, with much educational capital but little economic security).[62] One interviewee identified himself as

African American, the only person of color in the sample. Five described their family backgrounds as working class; the remainder said their upbringing was middle or upper middle class. Most interviewees' current socioeconomic status corresponds to what cultural critics Barbara Ehrenreich and John Ehrenreich call the professional-managerial class: marketing, advertising, and public relations professionals are all "cultural workers" who facilitate the circulation of products, revenues, and ideology through marketing.

With the exception of journalist Patrick Califia (formerly Pat Califia), I call these professionals "marketers," insofar as they have all been involved in producing the gay market in some way—by creating ads that represent gays or lesbians, making ad-supported gay and lesbian media, conducting market research, and/or writing about the gay market and thus bringing it to readers' imaginations through the advertising trade and popular press. Each interviewee's occupational position required that she or he construct and respond to gay marketing in specific ways. Yet although these marketers occupied very different points in the circuit of marketing—from working in corporations interested in courting gay consumers to publishing ads in gay and lesbian magazines, for example—the differences between them were in many ways less significant than what they shared. There was a high level of consensus among them; overall I found remarkably little friction between their commonsense views of gay and lesbian marketing, regardless of their specific occupational expertise or obligations. They occasionally talked about the contradictions between this common sense—what was professionally possible—and their own preferences, but this was unusual. Marketers' similar class positions may have contributed to their shared understanding of the business demands of their work. The underlying class demands of marketers' professional roles raise interesting questions for those interviewees who identified as gay, lesbian, or bisexual, because the demand for respectability placed on the professional-managerial class is potentially undermined by their less "respectable" (because it is nonnormative) sexual identity. How they negotiate between this identity and their dominant professional identity guides the strategies of sexual representation that gay marketers pursue.

In addition to conducting the interviews, I attended nine presentations that addressed different aspects of the gay market, such as how gay and lesbian magazines court national advertisers and how marketers advertise to gay and lesbian consumers on the Internet. I examined ads and consumer-related content from gay, lesbian, bisexual, HIV-positive, pornographic, and other magazines since 1967, as well as from local gay papers.[63] Ad pages and ad content were counted in three issues each of the *Advocate*, *Curve*, *Girlfriends*, and *Out* magazines from the fall and winter of 2002–2003.[64] I repeatedly reviewed ads and content on three Internet sites with gay, lesbian, and bisexual content,[65] and collected more than two hundred newspaper and trade press articles on gay marketing that have appeared since 1972.[66] These data were supplemented by other corporate documents such as press kits, market research reports, and marketing proposals. By focusing on marketers and their production routines, I analyzed the business and politics of gay marketing beyond the dichotomy of exploitation or celebration, to look instead at how gay marketing both circulates and limits GLBT images, ideas, and aspirations. These combined data enabled me to investigate how the routines of gay marketing intersected with the contested position of homosexuality to produce an image of the ideal gay consumer.

The book is organized in eight chapters. Chapter 2 traces the development of the gay market since the early 1970s in the context of the gay civil rights movement and the increasing sophistication of market-segment techniques. I consider gay- and lesbian-identified marketers' and publishers' roles in fostering the market, the development of a gay and lesbian publishing industry supported by advertising, and the necessity of market research and trade press coverage in piquing the interest of national corporations. What is striking in this history is the similar processes of market formation to those of the African American niche development decades earlier. It would be a mistake to overplay the similarities between African American and gay market formation, however, both because racism and homophobia function differently and because such a comparison falls into the trap of niche marketing itself, which assumes that all people of color are straight and all gays are white. With these cautions in mind, such a comparison nevertheless offers insight into the routinized practices of market formation and suggests some of the strategies by which marketers produce a desirable market from a stigmatized group.

In chapter 3, I study the people involved in producing the gay market. I consider the role marketers' sexual identity plays in their professional lives and in the work they produce. Marketers who are gay or lesbian occupy an especially interesting position because they must promote themselves both as professionals and as possessing distinct skills and expertise by virtue of their gayness. Importantly, both their professionalism and their expertise are constituted in part by their identifications as politically aware individuals and by their commitments to gay marketing as a form of political or cultural progress. Yet in their role as educators of the "straight" business world and in creating gay imagery, they must negotiate constantly between professional demands (to be "businesslike") and community demands (to be aware of the political stakes of visibility).

Chapter 4 is concerned with the means, products, and venues through which a visible gay consumer culture is produced. Can marketers "show" gayness while avoiding GLBT stereotypes and, if so, do they want to? Marketers must engage with the challenge of representing gayness not just in advertising in glossy magazines, local papers, general-market media, and on the Internet but also through direct mailings, event and nonprofit sponsorship, and in extratextual coverage in the gay, trade, and mainstream press. This chapter also looks at the range of products seen to be appropriate to advertise to gay and lesbian people and the textual strategies used to do so, what a "gay" or "lesbian" product is, what products are articulated to gayness, and how such an articulation may be made. I investigate the production of an advertorial (which looks like editorial copy but sells like an ad) for Dockers khakis in *Out* magazine to consider how marketing can be articulated with a polite form of politics to maximize a product's appeal for gay consumers.

In chapter 5, I address how marketers and advertisers have imagined gay and lesbian consumers and how this image has been adapted to accommodate increasingly accurate data on the affluence, size, and diversity of the gay market. This chapter investigates the ontological impossibility of identifying the true boundaries of the gay market, not only because of the challenges of finding a representative group of openly gay market-research respondents but also because sexual identity is neither discrete nor stable. These challenges mean that marketers can only, at best, work with a necessary fiction of an identifiable body of gay consumers, a fiction that offers only a narrow image that bears little resemblance to the "true" GLBT population.

I address, in chapter 6, marketers' struggles to imagine and organize lesbians as a viable target niche. Appealing to lesbians is marked by paradox: as women, lesbians might be seen as ideal consumers, yet they have proven hard to imagine as agents of desire, whether erotic or acquisitive. I address some of the practical considerations that make lesbians less attractive as a market: they have a lower average household income than gay male and heterosexual couples, and they are hard to reach for market research purposes and with ads. I also address the popular image of lesbians as anticonsumption, parsimonious, unsexy feminists who resist marketers' interest in them as consumers. (Whether Showtime's *The L-Word* displaces this stereotype remains to be seen.)

Although lesbians may be difficult to imagine as agents of desire, gay men have been hard to imagine as anything else. The problem of constructing a respectable gay consumer in the face of long-standing stereotypes of the hypersexual gay man is the topic of chapter 7. Because of social anxiety about public sexual expression generally, and gay men's sexuality in particular, gay marketers, advertisers, and publishers have been hypervigilant about maintaining boundaries on images of gay sex in ads and in editorial content. Although glossy magazine publishers, for example, consistently maintain that they reject "sex ads," in fact some sex-related advertising appears on their pages. I investigate the "dimensions of taste" that publishers apply to sexual content and ads, to argue that these dimensions are as much structured by class concerns as they are by sexual explicitness.[67]

In my concluding chapter, I return to the trope of "business, not politics" to argue that, despite this disclaimer, tracing a history of gay- and lesbian-themed marketing reveals a complicated and contradictory relationship between these apparently discrete imperatives. I revisit the discussion among gay critics and supporters about the limits and opportunities of gay marketing, especially on the issue of assimilation. Counter to the claim that gay marketing encourages gay assimilation, I argue that marketers are invested in producing and maintaining gay *difference*. The real dangers of marketers' constructions of gayness lie in how they produce this difference, limiting what is imaginable as a recognizably gay citizen: usually white, male, affluent, discreetly sexual, apolitical, gay subjects.

The questions raised by the episode of *Queer as Folk* at the beginning of this chapter warrant a consideration of the tensions between the business and politics of gay marketing. Gay consumer culture is neither necessarily exploitative nor liberatory, but produces a complex relationship between people, products, identities, and communities. Like many other GLBT readers and viewers, I have watched with fascination as advertisers have begun to produce gay and, occasionally, lesbian images, thrilled at the glimpse of a nonnormative sexual presence in increasingly mainstream venues. I have welcomed the possibilities that consumer culture offers—at least to those with the resources to pursue them—for subcultural participation, recognition, eroticism, and fun. Yet these moments of opportunity are undercut by the sense that something is amiss: there may be more images of gay people on television and in ads, but there are not images of more *types* of gay people. So, my engagement with gay consumer culture is tempered by an ambivalence that underscores this project: gay marketing may make gayness visible, but the gayness it produces is a woefully narrow one, stripped of most of its erotic radicalism, activist impertinence, and identificatory complexities. This view of gayness is not inevitable, but is the product of the social and historical circumstances of the past thirty years in which the gay market has been produced. How did marketers interested in appealing to gays use these circumstances to produce a gay market?

CHAPTER 2

EVOLUTION, NOT REVOLUTION

> Advertising clearly isn't treating the gay movement as a viable market, deserving of special campaigns and special treatment, as it is now beginning to do with blacks and women and has done for years with teenagers.[1]

So declared *Advertising Age* in 1972, under the headline: "No Gay Market Yet, Admen, Gays Agree."[2] Yet within three decades, the gay market and gay and lesbian media were sufficiently established for Viacom subsidiaries MTV and Showtime to explore the development of a gay cable channel, Outlet.[3] MTV executive Matt Farber described this progression as "an evolution, not a revolution," contrasting the image of a revolution—a politically motivated, violent upheaval—with a Darwinian ideal, where natural selection by an intrinsically fair, equilibrium-seeking free market facilitates an inexorable march toward increasingly progressive images of GLBT people. "Evolution, not revolution" is the cousin of "business, not politics": it suggests that gay marketing, and the media it supports, simply evolved through rational development within the entrepreneurial sphere, and disavows the efforts of marketers, media publishers, journalists, market researchers, and consumers themselves toward actively producing this market. Yet despite marketers' claims that they are interested in gay and lesbian consumers for dispassionate reasons of "business, not politics," the history of the gay market shows that this consumer niche was forged out of an intimate meeting of the entrepreneurial search for ever-expanding sources of revenue and the political quest for sexual equality.

As Richard Ohmann observes, "markets are shaped, not discovered."[4] Marketers do not simply begin to offer images of and sell products to preexisting niches, but shape the contours of those groups in order to present a credible, desirable, and viable target market. The development of the gay market is only one such process of niche-formation that dominated marketing in the twentieth century: before gays garnered marketers' attention, youth, women, African Americans, and other groups had already been courted as coherent target markets.[5] To question the evolutionary model of market development requires a consideration of the processes through which markets are produced from existing cultural stereotypes and social movements. How was the gay market shaped, propelling gay and lesbian consumers from the obscurity of market invisibility in the late 1960s to the glare of attention from global corporations such as Saab, Pepsi, and Viacom in the early 2000s?

The history of the gay market reflects complex relations among GLBT media and advertisers, niche and mainstream media, unflattering images of GLBT people and their new incarnation as desirable consumers. These relations structure the growth of the gay market from the 1960s, a period when gays and lesbians were largely ignored or reviled by mainstream media and marketing, to the present day, when gays and lesbians are increasingly courted in niche media, and occasionally appear in general market print and television ads. The history of the gay market reveals a number of struggles over the meaning and definition of gayness in the public sphere, where political imperatives clash with business demands, where the desire for civil rights coverage and sexual content in gay media conflict with the need to produce a palatable vehicle for national advertisers, and where advertisers, market researchers, and publishers wrestle over who, exactly, constitutes the "gay market."

Before Stonewall: The 1960s

Before the Stonewall riots of June 1969, gays and lesbians were largely invisible in mainstream media, openly gay-owned businesses serving gay and lesbian clientele were few, and the idea of a "gay market" was embryonic at most. Yet since the late nineteenth century, gay men had congregated in urban centers such as New York and San Francisco, freed by industrialization from their obligations to rural families and farms. As historian John D'Emilio asserts, capitalism facilitated the development of gay *identity*, distinct from same-sex sexual *activity*, by relieving men of their duty to marry upon which agrarian life had hitherto depended.[6] This process was accelerated for both gay men and lesbians by the geographical and social upheaval of World War II. According to historians George Chauncey, Elizabeth Lapovsky Kennedy, and Madeline Davis, growing communities of gay men and lesbians in the mid-twentieth century began to consume in distinctly homosexual ways, signaling their sexual identities to each other through such accoutrements as red ties for men and men's suits for butch women.[7] Urban businesses serving a gay clientele (whether intentionally or inadvertently) included brothels, bathhouses, bars, restaurants, and residential hotels such as the YMCA.[8] Although queer theorist Jeffrey Escoffier estimates that after the Second World War 25 to 30 percent of gay bars in San Francisco were owned by gay men and lesbians, even into the 1960s gay and lesbian entrepreneurs tended not to be open about their sexuality. The Mafia—being somewhat more protected from legal and social sanctions than were aboveboard, but openly gay, businesspeople— commonly owned bars and nightclubs that were patronized by gays and lesbians.[9] As activist Karla Jay remarks, in the late 1960s Craig Rodwell's Oscar Wilde Memorial Bookshop was one of the earliest publicly gay commercial spaces owned by a gay person.[10]

The postwar period was also notable for the rapid growth of the gay and lesbian press. In 1958 the U.S. Supreme Court ruled that gay publications were not necessarily "obscene, lewd, lascivious and filthy," as Wisconsin's Postmaster General had claimed; the decision facilitated the circulation of publications such as *ONE* and the *Ladder*.[11] Early gay and lesbian politically inflected publications tended to be noncommercial, were funded by sponsoring groups such as the Mattachine Society and the Daughters of Bilitis, and had few, if any, ads. Men's "physique" publications tended to achieve larger circulations, and a few of these contained at least somewhat openly gay, erotic advertising.[12]

Inaugurated in 1967, the *Los Angeles Advocate* was "the country's first, true, gay newspaper";[13] it contained nonfiction material in tabloid format, had a full-time paid staff, and was the first openly gay newspaper to actively court national advertisers. Between 1967 and 1974 the paper carried out its mission, as publisher Dick Michaels stated in the first issue, "to publish news that is important to the homosexual—legal steps, social news, developments in the various organizations—anything that the homosexual needs to know or wants to know."[14] What the homosexual readership was assumed to need and want to know in this and other early issues had primarily to do with legal cases and political developments pertaining to civil rights for gays: who had successfully overturned cases of "obscenity"; which states upheld antisodomy laws; and how politicians viewed homosexual issues.

Advertising in the first issue of the *Advocate* was sparse. There were ads for a men's clothing store, a homosexual night at a local bar, and *Barfly*, a printed guide to euphemistically labeled "interesting, friendly places." Joe Landry, the magazine's current publisher, related that of the $24 of advertising space sold, only $7 was ever collected.[15] Within a year, advertising revenues would grow to more than $200 per issue.[16] The first issue of the *Advocate* also included a classifieds column ("Trader Dick's") with eight ads—for gay books, cards, a dating service, and items for sale. By December 1968, "Trader Dick's" had grown to a full page, much of which contained personal ads from men looking for other men for sexual encounters.

In addition to personal ads, retail ads for sexual goods and entertainment quickly became a significant category. These included ads for mail-order pornography, and bookstores, some of which exhorted potential patrons not to be "chicken" (either fearful or underage) and encouraged "browsers." An ad from Anvil offered "a shattering new concept in male physique [photography]" (fig. 2.1).[17] The early publishers of the *Advocate* were not squeamish about including sexually explicit ads alongside their editorial content, which contributed to its eventual profitability. In contrast to journals that were funded by homophile organizations, such as the *Ladder*, which was produced by the Daughters of Bilitis, the *Advocate* was the first openly gay news publication in the United States to be supported entirely by advertising and the cover price. In the newspaper's first year, publisher Dick Michaels recognized that in order to be taken seriously by national advertisers, the *Advocate* would

FIGURE 2.1 PORNOGRAPHY ADVERTISEMENTS APPEARED REGULARLY IN THE *ADVOCATE* FROM ITS EARLY ISSUES (*LOS ANGELES ADVOCATE*, JUNE 1969).

need to offer the same circulation and readership data that other magazines could. He commissioned the Walker Struman research firm to conduct the first market research of gay readers, and soon after hired an independent auditing firm to verify circulation figures.[18] Yet despite Michaels's hopes of creating a national gay newspaper with corporate advertising, it would be many years before the *Advocate* would achieve this aim.[19]

Through the 1950s and 1960s no ads that openly showed gay men or lesbians appeared in the mainstream media. There are a couple of "gay window" or "gay vague" examples, however, where advertisers subtly coded ads with gay subcultural cues that were probably opaque to heterosexual readers.[20] A 1958 Smirnoff ad appearing in *Esquire* magazine showed two men in close proximity, and declared "mixed or straight, it leaves you breathless."[21] Whether this ad read as gay to gay or heterosexual audiences in the 1950s, history does not relate.

Despite the dearth of open appeals to gay consumers through the 1960s, a range of cultural and advertising trends that marked the latter half of this decade as one of nonconformity, defiance, and self-chosen identity set the stage for the earliest attempts to imagine a gay market. Increasing sexual freedoms afforded some tolerance for alternative sexual and relationship choices and made youth culture and sexuality attractive to mainstream America, including advertisers. Young adults, at least in the middle classes, "embodied the unspoken fantasies of a consumer society extended to the sphere of sex."[22] This relative sexual liberalism echoed the social nonconformity of the black civil rights, antiwar, women's liberation, and gay liberation movements.[23] In 1969 the Stonewall riots, conventionally held as inaugurating the contemporary gay rights movement, precipitated a period in which gay people were perceived as a community with similar aims and a shared purpose. The post-Stonewall gay liberation movement brought GLBT people, and especially gay men, into public view and focused much more on visibility than on accommodation as a goal.[24]

These political movements, in turn, made identity groups more visible to mainstream marketers. The development of African American, youth, and other consumer niches shows that in the 1960s marketers were already familiar with attributing distinguishing characteristics to a group for the purposes of segmentation. Rejecting an earlier emphasis on conformism, safety, and popularity, advertising messages began to encourage rebellion, individualism, and authenticity.[25] The increased visibility of a nonconformist gay liberation movement and marketers' developing skill at harnessing identity movements to products prepared the way for the formation of the gay market.

The Gay Playboy: The 1970s

The energy that inspired the Stonewall riots and subsequent gay rights activism achieved a number of civil rights gains in the late 1960s and early 1970s. The most significant of these was the removal of homosexuality from DSM-II, the American Psychiatric Association's manual of mental disorders, in 1973.[26] These gains, in turn, were reflected in the greater visibility of gays and lesbians in both news and entertainment programming. Advertising trade press articles about the potential for a gay market began to appear in 1972, even though national marketers remained apprehensive about associating their products with gay consumers who, for their part, seemed less than interested in petitioning for marketers' attention. As one journalist surmised,

> Unlike those larger segments of the population that can cite discriminatory practices [in advertising] because of race, color, gender or creed, the gay movement's leaders appear to be less concerned with advertising and more concerned with winning legal sanctions for their activities and raising the consciousness of the media. Perhaps at some later date they will turn their attention to advertising; perhaps advertising will turn its attention to them first.[27]

When advertisers did turn their attention to gay consumers in the mid-1970s, the gay market was imagined almost universally as made up of fashionable, "young, educated, and affluent" men. Yet some gay commentators expressed fear that "we would see a lot of 'silly queens' dancing around in ads directed to a homosexual consumer."[28] Despite the scarcity of market research data at this time, the tension between the stereotypes of the trendsetting, free-spending gay man and the immature, flaming homosexual became quickly entrenched in marketing discourses.[29] Lesbians were not mentioned in the trade press, and lesbian publications carried little advertising beyond small-business ads for lesbian-specific products and services.

If advertisers wanted to approach gay consumers they needed to look to the gay press to do so, because mainstream venues for advertising to gay consumers were limited; in the early 1970s the *New York Times*, the *New York Daily News*, and *Esquire* magazine, among others, refused ads that mentioned the words *gay* or *homosexual*.[30] Some magazines, such as the arts and entertainment magazine *After Dark*, were seen as "subtextually gay" by many readers, and included ads for records, theater, films, and books that covertly appealed to gay men.[31] There were few, if any, openly gay appeals in ads on television, although there is an early example of the "Gasp! It's a man!" genre of cross-dressing ads in a 1974 pantyhose commercial that slowly pans along a fabulous pair of legs, ultimately revealing that they belong to athlete Joe Namath. His voice-over reassures us, "Now, I don't wear pantyhose, but if Beautymist can make *my* legs look good, imagine what they'll do for yours." The emphatic kiss between Namath and a woman at the end of the commercial restores viewers' confidence in his heterosexuality.

The *Los Angeles Advocate* remained a news-focused, tabloid-format paper supported by increasing numbers of display and classified ads through the early 1970s. Retail advertising expanded from less than one page in 1967 to more than twenty pages in 1972, and the classifieds grew from less than half a page to more than five pages in the same period. Within two years, the circulation increased from its original press run of 500 to 23,000 copies, which were distributed every two weeks in urban centers nationwide. This was in marked contrast to the fate of many other gay publications in the early 1970s: the *Gay Liberator*, the *Gay Times*, and even the venerable *Ladder* folded. The explicit critique of capitalism and consumption in radical gay and lesbian feminist magazines was one reason these magazines halted production after relatively short lives, because such a critique precluded the development of sufficiently strong relationships with the more lucrative advertisers. In contrast, the *Advocate* continued to grow, although advertising revenue still came predominantly from baths, bars, pornographers, and bookstores.

In 1974, Dick Michaels sold the *Advocate* for a staggering $1 million to David Goodstein, the son of a wealthy Denver family and a financial entrepreneur who had been fired when his employers discovered that he was gay.[32] Goodstein was pivotal in the circulation of a desirable image of the gay male consumer, an image that came to personify the "gay market." He quickly transformed the *Advocate* from a politically oriented newspaper into a lifestyle magazine, reducing its sexual content and distancing editorials from the more militant factions of the gay civil rights movement. He also dropped "Los Angeles" from the name to stress the *Advocate's* national appeal. In the first issue under new ownership Goodstein flattered his audience with an idealized image of the *Advocate's* reader: male, employed, "responsible," with a "meaningful lifestyle . . . an attractive body, nice clothes and an inviting home."[33] He emphasized the most positive stereotypes of gay men—that they were stylish, trendsetting, and affluent—to displace the less palatable caricatures, including that of the "immature" homosexual that the American Psychiatric Association had only recently dropped from DSM-II. This was not the first time that publishers had struggled to produce a desirable image of the male consumer: as scholar Kenon Breazeale outlines, the founders of *Esquire* in the 1930s worked

to position a sufficiently masculine, virile, male consumer against the feminiz-
ing associations of a consumer magazine, countering the common assumption
that "men produce and women shop."[34] The *Esquire* editors achieved this by
insisting that consumption was something men do *better* than women, particularly in the pursuit of high-culture tastes, and by compulsively reaffirming
heterosexual masculinity. *Esquire* thus laid the groundwork for *Playboy* in the
1950s. As Hugh Hefner gloated, "We enjoy mixing up cocktails and an *hors
d'oeuvre* or two, putting a little mood music on the phonograph and inviting
in a female acquaintance for a quiet discussion on Picasso, Nietzsche, jazz,
sex."[35] Cultural scholar Barbara Ehrenreich notes that the unmarried heterosexual man of the 1950s risked being seen as frivolous and immature because
he was unfettered by the responsibility for a wife or children. The urbane playboy lifestyle that emphasized a sophisticated model of male consumption and
plentiful (straight) sex helped offset the taint of immaturity.

Goodstein took Hefner's model of male consumption and reworked a
specifically homosexual version of it. Like unmarried men in the 1950s, gay
men were seen as immature in the popular imagination of the 1970s. Estab-
lishment psychiatrists had long framed male homosexuality as a stunted version of a "normal" desire for women: gay men remained too attached to their
mothers and unable to mature into heterosexual relations. In the pages of the
Advocate, the gay playboy was encouraged to emulate the successful route out
of immaturity established by his heterosexual counterpart of an earlier era by
constructing a tasteful, luxurious, and sexually satisfying lifestyle. Goodstein
thus established the gay playboy as central to the identity of the magazine and,
beyond its pages, as a viable market for forward-looking advertisers. The familiar stereotype of the psychologically unhealthy, immature homosexual per-
sisted, however, in both the trade press and in the pages of the *Advocate* itself.
Editorials distanced the magazine from associations with drag queens, trans-
vestites, and transsexuals by casting them as pathetic misfits: "The most flamboyant, nelliest 'queen,' if one takes the time to try to know him, is revealed as
a very unhappy individual."[36] The *Advocate* distanced the image of the gay
playboy from the effeminate connotations of consumption by emphasizing his
masculinity.

The shift in the *Advocate*'s content from political news to address the reader
as a consumer, first and foremost, also necessitated a shift in the placement of
sexual commodities in the paper. By the second issue under new management, the classified section and most other sex-related advertising had been
removed from the magazine proper into a newly designed pull-out section
which was easier to both find and identify (the photo on the front made the

section more attractive—it looked like another, 'free' magazine—and alluded to its sexual content).[37] Readers who were most interested in this content had quick and easy access to it, while those who might be offended could more easily discard it. Most importantly, however, Goodstein excluded sexually explicit material from the main body of the magazine so that mainstream advertisers might find the *Advocate* a more hospitable context for national ads: in an interview with the *New York Times*, he said "we've come a long, long way. . . . We are being desleazified."[38] Ironically, the exclusion of sexually explicit ads from the main pages of the magazine precipitated an expansion of explicit pornographic advertisements for goods and services in the classifieds supplement.

In 1976 the *Advocate* was one of the country's fastest-growing magazines, with a biweekly distribution of 60,000, yet advertising revenues did not grow correspondingly, and ads remained limited to bars, hotels and travel services, discos, and theater shows. However, the late 1970s saw increasing gay visibility in mainstream media and a rapid expansion of marketing to gay people in the gay press. Images of gays on television, including coverage of Anita Bryant's 1977 Dade County antigay campaign and the 1979 gay and lesbian rally in Washington, D.C., alerted marketers to a sizable cluster of potential consumers. As journalist Karen Stabiner notes, Bryant's campaign "was what drove many homosexuals out into the open, into the business community's line of sight."[39] National advertising in the local gay press was also made much easier by the formation of Rivendell Marketing in 1979, a media sales company that places ads in gay publications across the country. Rivendell's sales staff courted advertisers for the local publications they represented, and schooled agencies and their clients in how to appeal to the gay market. Gay marketers' and activists' growing visibility was reflected in mainstream advertisers' increasing interest in gay consumers. The huge crossover success of disco led many record companies to gay publications, making these the first ads from national corporations, soon to be followed by ads for beer and liquor, entertainment, hi-fi equipment, financial services, personal care items, clothing, and rental cars.

The Gay Market "Deep Freeze": The 1980s

The 1980s opened with promise for the gay market. Mainstream corporations showed continued interest in reaching readers of gay media; Boodles Gin, for example, produced the first openly gay ads by a national company that appeared in gay publications, featuring Walt Whitman and other famous (and famously gay) men (fig. 2.2). Although not openly gay, other ads appearing in the *Advocate* seemed tailored toward an ironic gay sensibility; a Gitanes cigarette ad "quoted" the Marquis de Sade: "it hurts me to say it, but I love them." Liquor companies bought ad space for Tuaca liqueur, Smirnoff, and most famously, Absolut vodka (fig. 2.3). As an editor of *Genre* magazine commented, "When Absolut took the risk of placing ads in gay magazines, no gay man would serve anything but Absolut. Those ads took Absolut from fifth place to the number-one selling premium vodka in the country."[40] The story of Absolut's success may be largely responsible for gay people's legendary loyalty to those brands advertised openly and directly to GLBT people.

The trade press continued to characterize gay male consumers as white, highly educated, gainfully employed, trendsetting, and free of the financial burden of wives, children, and mortgages.[41] One gay commentator assured advertisers that gays were very concerned with conspicuous consumption in

FIGURE 2.2 BOODLES GIN COURTS GAY DRINKERS BY INVOKING "FAMOUS [GAY AND BISEXUAL] MEN OF HISTORY" (*ADVOCATE*, APRIL 16, 1981).

FIGURE 2.3 ABSOLUT VODKA APPEALED TO GAY READERS' SEARCH FOR "ABSOLUT PERFECTION" (*ADVOCATE*, JANUARY 21, 1982).

order to signal that they were "finally . . . in the 'in' group [and] no longer the outsiders [they] were in high school."[42] Peter Frisch, then publisher of the *Advocate*, listed a gay man's "must-haves: 'A convertible. A sports car, a foreign sports car. Believe me, that imported sports car shows up in our demographics. It's incredible. Some fabulous wardrobe. You take umpteen vacations and weekend trips a year. You have a second home.' "[43] The image of the affluent homosexual did not circulate without some concern by gay commentators, however; in the same article, sociologist and activist Laud Humphries expressed concern that this affluent image would work against employment rights activism. He commented, "I can imagine a lot of people reading about the gay market and saying 'we should give them their rights? We're starving. They're buying a Mercedes.' "[44]

In contrast to the dominant image of the desirable gay consumer as white and male, people of color and lesbians remained almost completely invisible. As Stabiner commented, lesbians "are discounted so completely, when it comes to consumer power, that most people who talk about the 'gay market' make the implicit assumption that it is a male market."[45] She argued that significantly lower income levels contributed to marketers seeing lesbians as a less attractive consumer segment: In 1982 women earned only 59 cents for each dollar earned by men, a wage differential that was compounded in households of two women. Gays and lesbians of color were so disregarded that not even the trade or popular press commented on their invisibility in the market.

Representing only a limited view of the gay market demographic—affluent white men—did not completely reassure marketers about the wisdom of approaching the niche, however. National corporate advertisers remained nervous about making openly gay appeals in mainstream media through the early 1980s. First, they were concerned that their merchandise might be branded a "gay product," thereby alienating their heterosexual customers. Second, advertisers were worried that approaching gay consumers might provoke retribution from what was then a relatively new phenomenon: Moral Majority boycotts. Third, corporate advertisers expressed anxiety over explicitly sexual advertising in gay publications: "A vice-president of Transamerica Corp.'s Budget Rent a Car [*sic*] subsidiary notes that his company had some reservations about advertising in the *Advocate* because of the personal ads in the magazine's midsection."[46] But, the article continues, the company managed to overcome its squeamishness because " 'for very little money we reach a potentially large audience that travels a lot, has high disposable income, and feels more loyalty to the advertiser.' " National advertisers interested in openly courting the gay market at the beginning of the decade frequently constructed a rhetorical quandary over the sexual content of the gay press before they could posit the profit rationale as the reason for taking the "risk" of advertising there. Indeed, most articles in the trade and mainstream press from the mid-1970s onward posed the dilemma confronting advertisers interested in the gay market as a struggle between the desirability of an affluent, loyal market niche, and the distastefulness of gay magazines' sexual editorial content and advertising.[47] Publishers responded by removing most or all sexual content: Goodstein pulled all the remaining sex ads from the *Advocate*, printing them only in the pull-out section. He was not alone in seeing gay sexual content as antithetical to national advertising: the short-lived, covertly gay magazine *Bicoastal* launched with "no nudity, no sexually explicit personal ads, nothing to upset a mainstream advertiser."[48] Editor Charles Codol explained that, "You can appeal to advertisers with discriminating tastes . . . if you don't visualize, pictorially, any activity that goes against the grain of American society."[49]

Finally, sex was not the only topic editors of gay publications avoided in order to court national advertisers: political coverage, especially when sympathetic to gay activists, was also seen as creating a hostile environment for corporate advertisements. According to *Advertising Age*, increased political visibility led some marketers to feel that "more advertisers would be trying to reach the emerging gay minority market if it would quiet down some of its enthusiasts."[50]

With these accommodations, national corporate advertisers increasingly looked toward gay consumers as a new, desirable target market, and toward the gay press as a means to reach them. The more open cultivation of the gay market would prove short-lived, however: the AIDS epidemic put gay-themed appeals back into the "deep freeze."[51] The years 1984 to 1989 were marked by the rapid withdrawal of many advertisers from gay media as they realized the extent of the health crisis; only Absolut vodka remained a consistent advertiser in the gay press through the 1980s, consolidating gay consumers' loyalty to the product. Publishers at the *Advocate* responded by filling the gap left by national advertisers with profitable classified and phone sex advertising, bringing back into the magazine those "questionable" ads that had only recently been moved to the pull-out section. The withdrawal of national advertising was reflected in press coverage: in the mid- to late-1980s the advertising and marketing trade press stopped covering the gay market altogether.

Although marketers responded to the AIDS epidemic with a near-total moratorium on open appeals to gay consumers, advertisers nevertheless still made implicit "gay window" appeals to the gay market in mainstream media.[52] More explicitly gay images in ads dropped out of sight in the mid- and late-1980s, in dramatic contrast to the massive increase in gay visibility in the news and elsewhere in mainstream media. This new visibility was dominated by the twinned images of the sexually promiscuous, diseased gay man and the angry, anarchic ACT UP activist—images from which most advertisers fled. In 1987 a new category of ads appeared in the gay press, those marketing AIDS-related services and products. An ad from the San Francisco AIDS Foundation, for example, showed a mustachioed, muscular man wrestling with the question "Should you take the AIDS antibody test?" (fig. 2.4). Although early AIDS-related ads were funded by charities and public health services, they prefigured a plethora of advertising that appeared in the late 1980s and 1990s to market drugs, health supplements, counseling, and financial programs to people with HIV and AIDS. The meaning of the "gay market" was to take a tragic—but nevertheless still profitable—turn.

Although the gay press in the early 1980s made occasional references to lesbians and GLBT people of color, the dominance of AIDS issues from mid-decade on narrowed the editorial focus largely back to white, gay male concerns. A new publication for gay African Americans, *BLK*, offered an alternative to the overwhelming whiteness of the gay press, but remained underfunded into the 2000s. The focus on AIDS issues also legitimated the ongoing marginalization of women within gay media, because lesbians were not considered a desirable audience for AIDS-related advertising dollars. This coverage failed to address risks of HIV infection for lesbians, risks that the lesbian pornography magazine *On Our Backs* took care to educate its readers about;

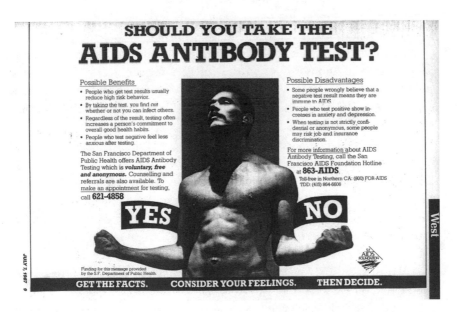

FIGURE 2.4 STRUGGLING WITH THE DILEMMA OF HIV TESTING IN AN AD FOR THE SAN FRANCISCO AIDS FOUNDATION (*ADVOCATE*, JULY 7, 1987).

as one feature headline urged:"Let's Go Safe Sex Shopping!"[53] Many gay publications also ignored both the very large numbers of lesbians involved in
AIDS awareness and political action, as well as the extent to which mobilization of lesbian and gay men's communities in response to the epidemic went
a long way in healing some of the traditional antipathy between them.

The Market of the Decade: The 1990s

The 1990s were distinguished by renewed interest in the gay market from both
the trade press and from advertisers themselves. Greater numbers of national
advertisers bought space in existing national and local gay publications than
ever before: advertising in gay media rose throughout the 1990s to a record
$120.4 million in 1999, a 20.2 percent rise from the previous year.[54] The
growth in revenues for gay and lesbian media led to an expansion of gay publishing, especially of glossy magazines: the early 1990s saw the debut of *Out*
and *Deneuve*, the first glossy magazines to seriously challenge the *Advocate's*
dominance; the mid-decade saw the addition of magazines such as *Girlfriends*,
a sexy lesbian lifestyle magazine, *Hero*, a desexed magazine for gay men, *Victory!*, a publication for gay entrepreneurs, *Alternative Family*, for lesbian and gay
parents and their children, and *AIDS Digest*, *POZ*, and later *POZ en Español*,
for HIV-positive people and people with AIDS. The *Advocate's* owner, Liberation Publications, Inc. (LPI), also diversified, publishing a number of new
pornography titles, including the *Advocate Classifieds*, *Big Daddies*, *Big Men on
Campus*, *Street Trash*, *XX Men*, as well as their existing *Advocate Freshmen*.[55]

In addition to a rapid expansion of print media, advertisers also looked toward direct mail, sponsorship, and the Internet to gain access to gay consumers. Direct-mail efforts were informed by the strategies developed by Sean
Strub and other fund-raisers during the 1980s in response to the AIDS crisis.
Trade press articles heralded the arrival of catalogs sent to gay and lesbian
direct-mail lists, such as Shocking Gray, Tzabaco, and International Male, and
then quickly announced their demise.[56] Gay consumer expositions also proliferated since 1993, with expos for HIV-positive people following in 1996.[57]
But the Internet proved to be the most significant development in gay marketing through the 1990s; affinity sites such as PlanetOut and gay.com rapidly
reached more consumers than all gay and lesbian magazines combined; some
data suggested that GLBT people, many of whom may not be reachable
through other gay and lesbian media, were more likely than heterosexuals to
subscribe to online services.[58]

Both trade articles and my interviewees offered similar explanations for the
renewed interest in marketing to gays in the early 1990s. Commentators argued

that the AIDS crisis led to the mobilization of the gay community, more people coming out to family and colleagues, and increasing professional visibility for openly gay marketers. Stuart Elliott, advertising columnist at the *New York Times*, commented that with "the response to the AIDS epidemic, . . . you tended to get a solidarity among gay men and lesbians which made them somewhat easier for marketers to find as a target market."[59] Increased visibility from AIDS activism made marketers more aware of gays as a potential target reachable through the gay press, as the mobilization of gays against Anita Bryant's Dade County antigay initiatives had in the 1970s.

Journalists suggested that the recession at the beginning of the 1990s sent marketers in search of new groups of consumers, a move that affirmed the rationale that marketing to gays was a question of "business, not politics." Stuart Elliott quoted Doug Alligood, vice president of special markets at BBD&O New York: "For a lot of people, the main concern right now is surviving in a tough economic climate. . . . When that happens people get liberal in a hurry." So if marketers can "find a market that's educated, affluent and can be reached through targeted media . . . there's no reason to be concerned about politics."[60]

Marketers also attributed shifts in marketers' attention back toward gays to improved research and statistics on gay consumption. From the late 1980s and into the early 1990s, Overlooked Opinions, Simmons, and other market research companies circulated data about "the gay market" based on readership surveys from the *Advocate*, other gay publications, and charity mailing lists:

> Research reveals the USA's estimated 20 million to 25 million gay men and women to be demographically desirable—affluent and well-educated. A survey by Simmons Market Research Bureau shows gays with an average household income of $55,430, vs. a national average of $32,144; 59% are college graduates vs. 20.3% of all Americans.[61]

By the mid-1990s these market research reports were increasingly criticized, primarily for their unrepresentative sampling methods, with critics observing that readership surveys that relied on respondents' willingness to self-disclose their sexual identity were bound to be skewed toward those more financially and professionally secure. Data from a more representative sample in a 1994 Yankelovich study suggested that although spending patterns for gays and heterosexuals were a little different, income and other demographic factors were more similar between these groups than research had found previously.[62] Other attempts to gain representative data included Greenfield Online's Internet study with the Spare Parts marketing group, and surveys by large corporations such as IBM, American Express, and Subaru that hoped to get reliable information before launching expensive campaigns.

Another factor in the growth of the gay market was that gay visibility in news and entertainment media was higher than ever. The battles over same-sex marriage in Hawaii and gays in the U.S. military were regularly featured in the news in the early 1990s. The 1993 gay and lesbian March on Washington brought gay people into public view: not coincidentally, the trade and popular press produced a flurry of articles on the gay market in the months leading up to the march.[63] Some writers made explicit links between a political presence and a target market. One journalist observed, "Two months from now, when nearly 1 million gays, lesbians and their supporters are expected to come to Washington in a massive march of unity, many participants might be surprised by who else will be joining them in force. Marketers."[64] Many articles continued to endorse the perspective that gay marketing was a matter of business, not politics, but a few did express a progressive impulse in their appeals to the gay market. A spokesperson from Carillon Importers, marketers of Absolut, commented: "We're not encouraging or discouraging [homosexuality], we are just making a statement. It's very important in [the] nation and civilization we are living in to be accepting of people."[65] Yet some marketers were nervous about their products becoming associated with political activism. A spokeswoman from Naya water, which did not advertise but did distribute water at the march, said: "I don't need to have my banner up next to people who may be throwing eggs at Vice President Gore. . . . It's not our image. And it's not controllable."[66] The relationship between the march and marketing complicates the discourse of "business, not politics," because political visibility makes the market more available to advertisers, both conceptually (amassing an organized, apparently cohesive community) and practically (giving sponsors access to many people congregated in one place).

President Clinton's willingness to acknowledge gay people from the beginning of his first term was also seen as a watershed in public acceptance of homosexuality. Celebrities too embraced gay causes or came out, further increasing marketers' awareness of GLBT people. Many of the marketers I spoke with mentioned the positive impact of greater numbers of gay and lesbian television characters (not least Ellen DeGeneres's character, Ellen Morgan), and tended to see the increase in such characters as creating the circumstances for, rather than as responding to, increased gay marketing. Stuart Elliott suggested that shows with gay characters were vehicles for corporations to reach a large gay viewership, implying that television producers may have such advertising aims in mind during program development.[67]

The 1990s also saw more openly gay people in the workplace. Gay advertising professionals established gay-specialized agencies such as Mulryan/Nash (which folded in 1999) and Prime Access (which also specializes in the African American and Latino markets), as well as gay-focused public relations and marketing firms such as Spare Parts and Witeck-Combs Communications. A parallel move occurred with gay and lesbian professionals in general-market agencies; the New York Advertising and Communications Network formed alongside other gay and lesbian professional groups, including the Bankers' Group, the Publishing Triangle, and the Wall Street Lunch Club.[68] Employees also formed groups within large corporations such as Apple, Digital Equipment, AT&T, and Coors. The organization of gay professionals emphasized the presence of gays and lesbians not only within the workforce but also as customers, and afforded gay and lesbian personnel more security in suggesting gay marketing strategies. An increased enthusiasm for gay marketing was not matched by improved conditions for gay professionals in ad agencies, however. A survey of fifty top agencies' policies on gay staff garnered responses from only seven, showing a disappointing view of agency life for gays in terms of antidiscrimination protection, partner benefits, diversity training, and the presence of openly gay management. According to *Advertising Age* journalist Michael Wilke, the Hill, Holiday, Connors, Cosmopulos agency in Boston had the best record, probably because Jack Sansolo, an openly gay man, had been president of the company at one time.[69]

The threat of boycotts by right-wing and religious antigay activists also became somewhat less pressing in the mid-1990s. Although AT&T's 1994 "Let Your True Voice Be Heard" direct-mail campaign to gay and lesbian consumers was suppressed by a religious right boycott, other antigay efforts to pressure companies proved far less successful (fig. 2.5).[70] Some companies remained more vulnerable to right-wing boycotts, but religious fundamentalists tend not to be frequent (or, at least, open) consumers of many products that are advertised to gay people: alcoholic beverages, cigarettes, designer clothes, and other "image" products.

With a rapid increase in coverage from 1993 onward, trade and popular press journalists encouraged the sense that advertising to gays was respectable and profitable. Their opinion and guidance was supplemented by *Quotient*, a monthly newsletter developed by gay marketing specialists Dan Baker, Harold Levine, and Sean Strub. Although only six monthly issues were published (December 1994 to May 1995), the publication both helped marketers think through diverse ways of approaching gay consumers (such as sponsorship, catalogs, and direct mail, in addition to advertising) and aimed to rectify some of

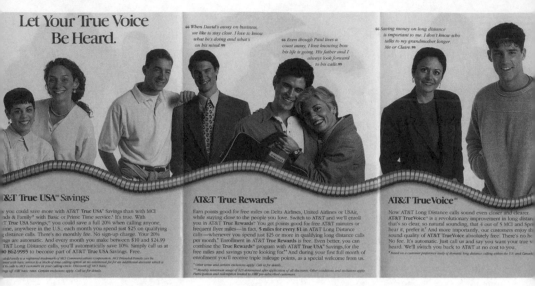

FIGURE 2.5 COMMUNICATING DIVERSITY IN AT&T'S "LET YOUR TRUE VOICE
BE HEARD" DIRECT MAIL CAMPAIGN (PRIME ACCESS, 1994).

the grossest distortions of the gay consumer market. *Quotient*'s writers advocated a more sober approach to marketing than did some other gay marketing professionals, by circulating more representative demographic data and reminding readers that an estimated total annual gay income of $202 billion per year "isn't all spent on Don't Panic T-shirts, rainbow keychains and fabulous vacations in Palm Springs."[71]

All these influences combined to boost the visibility of gay and lesbian consumers and the apparent profitability of marketing to them. Throughout the 1990s, gay market formation was characterized most strongly by processes of diversification: in media, marketing strategies, products, and in target audiences. As more magazines entered the field, each needed to differentiate its content and readers from its competitors. Interviewees from *Out* and the *Advocate* were most careful to distinguish the other publication from their own: *Out*'s president, Henry Scott, commented, "I say to people who [ask], 'don't you compete with the *Advocate*?,' . . . 'does *Vanity Fair* compete with *U.S. News*?' They do different things, they are different magazines."[72] Within two years of this interview, however, LPI owned both titles. Another interviewee said that publishers of local papers felt ambivalence about the proliferation of gay glossies such as *Out*, *Girlfriends*, and *Genre*: they loved the magazines for making the market as a whole more attractive to advertisers, but were also worried that the glossies would take business away from local and regional gay publications.[73]

As marketing efforts toward gays and lesbians intensified in the 1990s, advertisers and sponsors needed to work harder to distinguish themselves in an increasingly crowded market. Some used more explicitly gay images in their ads in order to stand out from advertisers of similar products, and in response to research that gay consumers want to see ads that "address gay and lesbian themes."[74] Others looked to event and community sponsorship to place their logo in contexts beyond magazines or papers. As *Advocate* publisher Joe Landry said, "Through sponsorship of gay fund-raisers or political organizations or sporting events and other events, sponsors reap the rewards of the emotional connection that the community has with these events."[75] Indeed, the late-1990s produced intensified efforts to create such an emotional connection with gay consumers as a way of capitalizing on gay consumer loyalty. Articles emphasized the need for advertisers to demonstrate that they are able to form a deeper relationship with their gay consumers than with others. For example, a Miller Brewing Company spokeswoman said that gay people "really want to see that we understand them."[76] Other advertisers went beyond advertising or sponsorship to create marketing approaches designed to "get under the skin" of the consumer.[77] *Out* magazine collaborated with a long-standing advertiser, Seagram's, on a cocktail and entertainment guide, "Out to Party," inserted in the July 1998 issue. Seagram's spokesman described this shift in advertiser-editorial relations: "[Magazines] are not in the business of selling ad space, but of building relationships with advertisers."[78] In their November 1998 issue, the *Out* staff also produced a 12-page advertorial with Levi's for its Dockers line, "Inside Out," which blended advertising with editorial copy that advocated for gay youth and education organizations (figs. 2.6 and 2.7). This stylish fashion-spread combined consumption and politics to intensify the ways in which marketers make "authentic," "emotional" appeals to gay consumers.

The diversification of advertising venues and approaches mirrored a huge proliferation of products and services advertised to gay people. Notable new ads included television commercials for Ikea furniture and Mistic beverages, and print ads for increasing numbers of travel companies, HIV and other pharmaceuticals, viatical (or "life settlement") companies, automobiles, apparel, home furnishings, airlines, online services, car and health insurance, and a few packaged goods such as vegetarian burgers, toothpaste, and pet food. Advertisers left open, and even encouraged, debates about possible gay appeals in ambiguous ads appearing in mainstream media such as Volkswagen's "da-da-da" commercial ("Sunday Afternoon") and Abercrombie & Fitch's ads by photographer Bruce Weber.

Not all products and services found a welcome corner in the newly blossoming gay media, however. Continuing the trend from the 1970s, sex ads

Dockers® Khakis invites you to
take a look at 10 extraordinary
people and how their lives are
making a difference, for all of us.

Photographed by Carter Smith

inside
OUT

FIGURES 2.6 AND 2.7 EXTRAORDINARY PEOPLE IN AN EXTRAORDINARY
PROJECT: LEVI STRAUSS'S ADVERTORIAL COLLABORATION WITH *OUT*
(NOVEMBER 1998).

WILSON CRUZ
ACTOR

No one who saw *My So-Called Life* will ever forget Ricky, an unhappy, introspective youth who nonetheless embraced life—and his sexuality— with a sweet-natured candor that took our breath away. Recently awarded a Dramalogue Award for his performance in *Rent*, Wilson returns to the movies in the futuristic setting of *Supernova*, opposite James Spader and Angela Bassett, out next spring.

were all but eliminated from national gay lifestyle publications in the mid- to late-1990s. In 1992 the *Advocate* moved the classified section of the magazine out of its newsstand version altogether as part of what publisher Niles Merton called a two-year "mainstreaming plan."[79] Interested readers had to purchase the *Advocate Classifieds* independently: it had a cover price of $1.95, but subscribers to the main magazine could receive it free of charge. Editor Jeff Yarbrough reflected on the removal of sex ads from the newsstand *Advocate*: "We needed to clean up our act and get a little more happy and shiny to attract advertisers."[80] It was not only national advertisers who were attracted: as large corporations became increasingly willing to advertise in the pages of the *Advocate*, sexual advertising in the *Classifieds* mushroomed, expanding from a 12-page pullout in 1990 to a 66-page separate publication in 1992.

Although local publications in general could not afford to remove sex ads altogether, most shunted them to the back pages in order to encourage national advertisers in the front pages. The *Washington Blade* reportedly made it "difficult" for sex-oriented businesses to advertise, in order to attract "Mom and Pop businesses in Du Pont Circle" that might be squeamish about appearing next to sex ads.[81] Internet sites such as PlanetOut and gay.com similarly distanced themselves from sexual advertising: a gay.com spokesperson said, "'That's not the business we're going to be in. We're in the business of community, news' and other services."[82] Such comments reinforce assumptions that gay sexual content is inherently incompatible with a marketing-friendly sense of gay community.

In the 1990s the gay market diversified not only in terms of media and products but also beyond the stereotype of the young, affluent, white gay man. Although some journalists continued to circulate inflated household income statistics and hyperbole about gays as "advertising's most elusive, yet lucrative, target," the "market of the decade," and a "goldmine," others began to recognize that "the gay market" as previously imagined was only a slice of an otherwise economically disparate population.[83] As an editor at *Genre* magazine explained, "Targeting the gay male population rather than a segment of the market is as ill-conceived as targeting all straight men."[84] Michael Wilke suggested that, because the market is not as affluent as once thought, packaged goods, over-the-counter drugs, and other more general products could join luxury products such as Gucci and Waterford Crystal in *Out* and other magazines.[85] However, *Out*'s president, Henry Scott, responded to Wilke that there is a misconception that Gucci and other upscale companies are targeting "the 'gay market' any more than they're pursuing the heterosexual market. The truth is those brands are in logical pursuit of only the most affluent segment of the gay market"—an affluent segment that *Out* could deliver.[86]

Income was not the only criterion marking an increasingly diversified conception of the gay market. A spokesman for the National Gay and Lesbian Task Force cautioned "marketers who think there is only one way to reach gays: . . . It's very different trying to reach gay men in West Hollywood than, say, lesbians in Columbus, Ohio."[87] Journalists and marketers made more concerted efforts to address lesbian readers' issues: the *Advocate* included "lesbian" in its header, and *Deneuve* and *On Our Backs* put a sexy, worldly, fun image of lesbians into the publishing and marketing sphere. Specific references to lesbians in the trade press also began to appear more often, such as the article "Economics Holds Back the Lesbian Ad Market," in a 1993 *Advertising Age* special feature on marketing to gays and lesbians.[88] These articles attempted to account for the time lag in marketing to lesbians, suggesting that marketers' beliefs about anticonsumerist politics, lower average annual incomes, and lower visibility compared with gay men made lesbians, in *Deneuve* publisher Frances Stevens's words, "the invisible of the invisible."[89] The rise in attention to "lipstick lesbians" and more openly lesbian celebrities heightened marketing attention somewhat, but lesbians remained "on the fringe of the gay marketing movement."[90]

During the 1990s, ads began to appear in both mainstream and gay and lesbian media that showed images of people with AIDS.[91] Benetton notoriously pushed the boundaries of public taste in 1992 with its "David Kirby 'a pietà'" print ad showing the dying AIDS activist with his family (fig. 2.8). As protease inhibitors and combination therapies came on the market, images of people with AIDS shifted from the emaciated AIDS "victim" that dominated the news to representations of increasingly robust-looking people living, exercising, and loving with AIDS (fig. 2.9). The transformation of the public image of people with AIDS led to the first national commercial showing an HIV-positive person advertising a product that was not AIDS related: Ric Muñoz, an openly gay, HIV-positive athlete, appeared in a Nike ad in 1995. This transformation of images of people with AIDS has been received ambivalently, however. For example, Sean Strub, an HIV-positive man and the publisher of *POZ* magazine, traced the trajectory of images in HIV-related ads through the 1990s:

> The first ones invariably would have somebody alone, very thoughtful with a long face and looking at the moon and walking alone along the beach and clearly contemplating life and death issues. . . . So then, the next wave were ads where they were saying [*cheerful tone*]: "Joe, who has HIV . . ." You know, a white man and he would be looking, if not cheerful, somewhat more alive than the guy walking along the beach. And

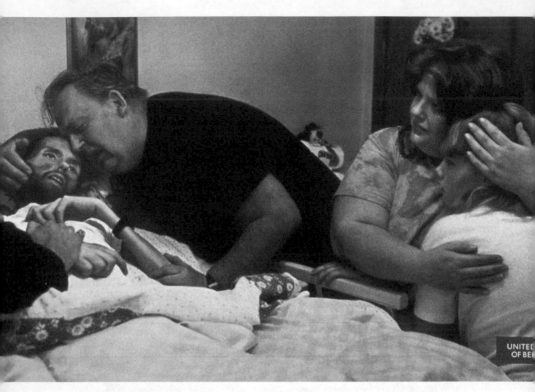

FIGURES 2.8 AND 2.9 DEATH AND REDEMPTION IN IMAGES OF HIV:
BENETTON'S "DAVID KIRBY 'A PIETÀ'" (WWW.BENETTON.COM, RETRIEVED
MAY 14, 2004) AND MERCK'S CRIXIVAN AD (*POZ*, OCTOBER 1998).

then the wave after that was bringing some diversity into those ads,
showing situations where there's a relationship, either a couple or a family situation or whatever, and there's gender or racial diversity and so
on. . . . But then it went from there to body builders and people climb-
ing mountains and ridiculous extreme stuff like advertising does.[92]

Strub's comment raises thorny issues concerning the representation of people
with AIDS, which are reminiscent of debates over the benefits and limits of
positive images of gays, lesbians, and other groups that have been dogged by
negative stereotypes. People with AIDS might feel great relief both that their
image is not solely associated with sickness and sadness, and that there is less
stigma for HIV-positive people appearing in ads. However, Strub and others
are concerned that the most recent incarnation of people with AIDS in medication advertising encourages unrealistic expectations of life on HIV drugs
and minimizes their less attractive side effects.[93]

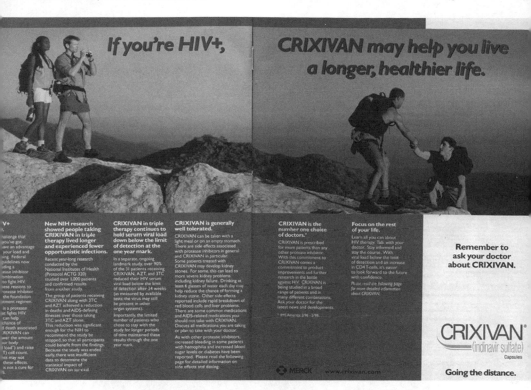

The 1990s nevertheless stand as a watershed for marketing to gays, lesbians, and people with HIV. Increased media visibility and the GLBT community's response to the AIDS epidemic brought advertisers in droves to gay and lesbian consumers and provided an infrastructure to appeal to them. As advertisers explored this potential and as the national media landscape became somewhat more tolerant of openly gay and lesbian images, advertisers used these images to appeal to queers and straights alike. Yet despite more representative data showing the diversity of gay people among the U.S. population, and excepting some HIV-related ads, images targeted at gay consumers largely continued to recirculate long-held notions of gays as white, male, affluent, body-conscious, and trendsetting (figs. 2.10 and 2.11).

Putting Power into Fewer Hands: The 2000s

The early 2000s built upon the increasing presence of gay and lesbian people in mainstream advertising and other media, and on the growing interest in gay and lesbian consumers from national corporations. This interest provided

FIGURE 2.10 LOVE—AND TOYOTA—MAKE A FAMILY (*ADVOCATE*, OCTOBER 6, 1992).

FIGURE 2.11 CAMPING IT UP WITH VERSACE (*OUT*, JANUARY 1999).

more revenue for gay media, facilitating a growth in the number of gay publications and Web sites which, in turn, led to increased competition for readers and advertisers. As gay and lesbian publishing became more profitable, media companies began to merge into larger conglomerations that were then faced with the challenge of prospering in a faltering economy.

In 2000, gay media continued to be dominated by ads for apparel, alcohol, cigarettes, entertainment and music, financial services, and HIV-related pharmaceuticals. With the debut of the travel magazine *Passport* in 2001, and a gay and lesbian microsite on Orbitz's Internet travel site in 2002, gays and lesbians were courted as tourists with unprecedented openness (fig. 2.12). Orbitz estimated that U.S. gays and lesbians spent $1.2 billion on travel in 2001 (although where this figure comes from, journalist Jim Kirk does not relate).[94] The early years of the twenty-first century also saw some expansion into the gay market of more traditionally conservative advertisers: Crest "Whitestrips" (Procter & Gamble's teeth-whitening product) appeared in *Out* magazine in the summer of 2001 (fig. 2.13). *Out* and *Advocate* publisher Joe Landry saw this as a breakthrough in the hitherto reluctant packaged goods market: to get an ad from Procter & Gamble "opens the door to more packaged goods."[95] Also new on the market were a number of automobile manufacturers: in 2001, Jaguar, Volkswagen, and Volvo joined Saab, Saturn, and Subaru, which had been advertising in gay publications since the 1990s. Subaru had distinguished itself by aligning its product with the "civic-mindedness of the gay and lesbian community," creating gay-punning print ads such as: "It's not a choice. It's the way we're built."[96]

Recognition of gays and lesbians as consumers and as part of the television audience also led to a few ads in mainstream media. Subaru expanded its pro-gay campaign from gay and lesbian print publications to television. In Subaru's "What do we know?" commercial, Martina Navratilova, dumped by mainstream advertisers when she came out as a lesbian, joined two other female athletes to demonstrate the virtues of the Subaru Forester. The ad explained "what they know" about the vehicle's control, handling, and performance, and Navratilova delivered the punch line: "What do we know? We're just girls." A more explicit lesbian reference came in a commercial from John Hancock, the insurance company, which featured a lesbian couple adopting a baby. The company had to change the spot after its initial airing to downplay that it showed a lesbian couple, and to announce the arrival of the flight—and thus the baby—from Cambodia, not China, since China had banned adoption by openly gay couples in 1998. This ad debuted during the 2000 Summer Olympics, demonstrating a shift toward using affirming gay and lesbian images to appeal to mainstream audiences. However, a spokesperson distanced the

FIGURE 2.12 DROPPING THE POUNDS COURTESY OF THE LONDON TOURIST BOARD (*OUT*, JANUARY 1999).

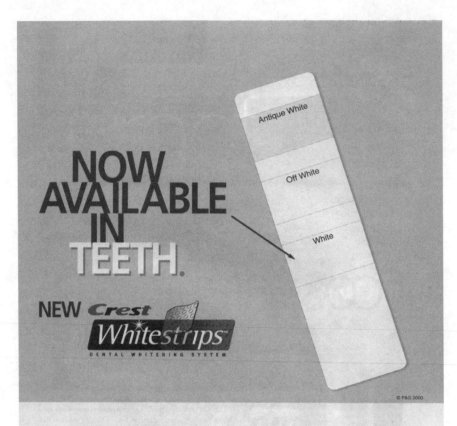

FIGURE 2.13 PROCTER & GAMBLE NIBBLES ON THE GAY MARKET WITH CREST WHITESTRIPS (*OUT*, APRIL 2001).

company from its lesbian and gay customers by claiming that it was "not so much targeting a specific audience" as making a more general appeal to "diversity" by showing a gay couple.[97]

An increasingly common theme in television commercials involved heterosexual women cruising men who turn out to be gay: Miller Lite's "Switcheroo" showed two women sending a beer to a handsome man at the other end of the bar, only to watch as his boyfriend shows up. The ad concludes, "Well, at least he's not married." With this ad Miller could get the best of all worlds: in testing, gay men appreciated the ad because it represents them; heterosexual women enjoyed it because it shows them as sexually assertive; and heterosexual men found it amusing and unthreatening because it suggests that when women *are* sexually assertive—that is, when they usurp straight men's conventional role—they mess up. Further, the product avoided the risk of becoming known as "the gay beer" because it's the women who order Miller Lite, not the gay men. Nevertheless, Stuart Elliott saw this commercial as

> really a watershed because in this country it's been that beer companies were perfectly willing to do stuff targeted to the [gay] market as long as it never got out, never sees the light of day in the general market. So that was a real change. And it's driven by the fact that they think their target market for [beer] thinks it's perfectly okay. Or it's cool, or whatever.[98]

Although mainstream audiences may be beginning to think that gay male couples are "okay" or "cool," the same cannot be said for transgender images. Those rare appearances of transgender people in general market ads continued to exploit the "mistaken identity" joke; a print ad for TheStreet.com warned: "Mail-order bride, transsexual, Internet stock. It never hurts to do a little research before bringing one home." This ad repeated the assumption that deception (and a later, nasty revelation) is at the center of transgender identity, and that readers would necessarily rather avoid the shock of finding out that their one-night stand (like their bride or their stock) is other than advertised.

Still, gender-normative gays and lesbians were of growing interest to national advertisers, an interest that continued to support efforts for increasingly accurate data on them as a market. Two market research projects dominated the first years of the decade: one from OpusComm with Syracuse University and Gsociety, Inc; the other from Witeck-Combs Communications with Harris Interactive. Although both used online surveys, which offer relative anonymity but not representative samples, each took a distinct strategy for recruiting respondents and analyzing data. Calling its project the "Gay/Lesbian

Consumer Online Census," OpusComm advertised for subjects on the Internet, with such slogans as "Stand up and be counted!: Take pride in knowing that you are affecting [*sic*] a change in the world for yourself and the future of the GLBT community."[99] Over a six-week period they collected data from more than 6,000 respondents: 55 percent were male, 92 percent were living in the United States, and the sample had an average household income of $65,000. At a recent panel, one of the researchers admitted that the sample was not representative, and the data were therefore "not projectable" to the GLBT population as a whole.[100]

In contrast, Witeck-Combs Communications' collaboration with Harris Interactive is based on a 20,000 member, GLBT-identified subset of a sample of three million consumers who regularly give information on their behaviors and attitudes. None of the GLBT participants is recruited from gay-specific sites or venues. Although this sample is necessarily self-selected and has access to the Internet, skewing the overall data toward people with both time and money, Witeck-Combs and Harris attempt to get a diverse sample by recruiting not only online but by mail and telephone as well. They also weight their data according to U.S. Census information and by using a statistical technique known as "propensity weighting" to reduce the effects of selection bias in their results. Witeck-Combs found that 39 percent of GLBT consumers preferred to purchase products from companies that advertise in gay media, and that 46 percent would patronize companies that support GLBT nonprofit organizations. Because of the statistical techniques employed by Witeck-Combs Communications and Harris, this market research offers perhaps the most representative and projectable GLBT market research to date.[101]

Better market research helped gay and lesbian media win lucrative national advertising, and these media's increased profitability led to further expansion and consolidation in the early 2000s. In particular, the Internet emerged as the premiere route to access gay consumers: in 2002 PlanetOut and gay.com, both owned by PlanetOut Partners, Inc., together boasted 5.2 million members, reaching more GLBT people than the gay print media combined. After six consecutive quarters of increasing income, the company announced its first profitable quarter in October 2002, with a 15 percent rise in ad revenue.[102] The early part of the decade also saw a diversification of print media directed toward gay and lesbian people of color: *Noodle*, for Asian American gay men; *Tentaciones*, a bilingual publication for GLBT Latino/as; *2lips*, for Latina lesbians; and *Trikone*, a quarterly magazine for GLBT South Asians.[103] Although most of these are produced using personal financial investments and rely on voluntary labor, it nevertheless suggests that GLBT people of color are responding to a need for media that address not only their sexual but their racial and ethnic identities too. Yet the challenge for GLBT print media in an increasingly competitive environment is reflected in the fate of many lesbian publications; Todd Evans, whose company, Rivendell, sells advertising space for GLBT publications, reported that the number of lesbian publications they represent declined from eleven in 1994 to only three in 2002.[104]

The profitability and consequent diversification of gay (if not lesbian) media suggests a mature phase in gay marketing. This phase has two manifestations: the consolidation of existing media, and expansion into new—and more expensive—media forms. As more media vehicles enter the market, each is subject to increased competition; one consequence of this is a move toward conglomeration of the more successful titles. In the early 2000s the *Advocate*'s parent company, LPI, bought *Out* magazine; Windows Media, which already owned the *Southern Voice*, bought the *Washington Blade* and the *New York Blade News*; America Online bought a 12 percent share of the gay Web-site portal, PlanetOut; PlanetOut negotiated a merger with LPI (a deal that was dropped as a result of the dotcom crash of 2001); and PlanetOut and gay.com merged.[105] Such activity did not come without concern, however. One headline asks: "Will Mergers Quiet the Voice of the Gay Press? Many Fear Takeovers Will Put Power into Fewer Hands and Put Diversity at Risk." Henry Scott, who left as president of *Out* magazine shortly after it was acquired by LPI, expressed concern that the PlanetOut–gay.com merger "threatens to further diminish the opportunity for vigorous debate over issues of politics and culture and style that is our community's greatest strength."[106]

Dedicated GLBT Internet and print media have also been supplemented by cable television. In January 2002, MTV and Showtime announced a new joint project: Outlet, a cable channel devoted to GLBT content and audiences.[107] Following the success of television shows on network and cable television such as *Will & Grace* and *Queer as Folk*, these Viacom subsidiaries joined forces on the project of bringing "all gays, all the time" to cable subscribers in the United States. According to a leaked memo, Outlet was scheduled for launch in the spring of 2003 and was subsequently shelved. In May 2004, MTV announced it would go ahead and launch the channel, now called Logo, in 2005. Logo's developers face the challenges of persuading enough cable distributors to carry the channel, of providing sufficiently diverse content to attract large enough audiences, and of funding the development of original programming, a very expensive proposition. Canada's 24-hour GLBT channel PrideVision announced in 2002 that it was scaling back on original programming after subscriptions had not grown as fast as expected. It may be that Bravo becomes the de facto "gay cable channel," with its hit makeover show *Queer Eye for the Straight Guy* and its queered version of the dating show, *Boy*

Meets Boy. It remains to be seen how the dynamics of gay marketing will intersect with cable channel marketing and programming: the attention given to
youngish white men in U.S. GLBT print and Internet media may dominate
television too, as both Bravo's and PrideVision's programming suggests.

The challenge to become and remain profitable in an increasingly competitive media environment was exacerbated by the overall decline in advertising budgets in the tight economic climate of the early 2000s. The Gay Press
Report, published by Prime Access, Inc., and Rivendell Marketing, related that
after a period of rapid growth in the late 1990s, 2001 saw a decline in advertising in gay media of 1.9 percent, with the local gay press taking the biggest
hit. Circulation figures for all print media were down, perhaps because of
growing GLBT Internet use. On a more positive note, the report found that
there was an expansion of gay-themed (rather than generic) ads in gay and lesbian media. Although it is hard to predict the effects of the recession on gay
marketing, the marketers I interviewed were optimistic about an ongoing diversification of products advertised to gay consumers, particularly in the packaged goods and automobile categories.[108] The *New York Times*'s Stuart Elliott
mentioned that the slump might have a positive impact on gay marketing, because it was a similar economic climate in the early 1990s that sent mainstream
marketers in search of gay consumers: "People said, 'Oh God, nobody's spending money—oh wait! Those people [gays] are spending money, maybe we
should advertise to them!' "[109] In the hard times brought on by economic instability, the doctrine of "business, not politics" may be particularly persuasive
as demands for new consumers overshadow trickier questions of if and how
to market to gays and lesbians.

Race, Sexuality, and Market Segmentation

Tempting as it might be to see the development of the gay market as a process
of natural evolution, the formation of the gay market reflects a growing tendency throughout the twentieth century to segment potential consumers into
ever more narrowly defined niche markets. As Richard Tedlow and Joseph
Turow describe, market segmentation was made possible by increasingly sophisticated manufacturing, media, research, and distribution technologies that
both led to a proliferation of goods and allowed for more precise means of di-
viding, measuring, and appealing to consumers.[110] And although niche marketing is most associated with identity-based movements since the 1960s, the
linkage of target marketing with identity began early in the twentieth century,
when marketers appealed to women, Jewish immigrants, and people of color,
even if market segments were only roughly drawn and lacked the statistical so-

phistication of contemporary demographics. When marketers became interested in gay consumers they were therefore already familiar with the processes
required to cultivate niche markets, and many large companies already had
personnel in their marketing departments skilled in appealing to identity
groups.

Looking at the development of the African American market since the
1930s suggests some interesting parallels with the development of the gay market decades later, especially in terms of the strategies marketers deployed to
produce a desirable market from a stigmatized social group. At the turn of the
twentieth century, white business-owners largely ignored African Americans,
considering this often poor and largely rural population insignificant and undesirable as consumers. Black people were mainly served by black business-
owners, who began to form associations such as the National Negro Business
League in 1900. Massive migration to northern cities by rural black South-
erners during the First World War increased the incomes of many and led to a
pouring of African American dollars into black-owned businesses, including
those producing "race" records and films, and cosmetics.[111] As African American consumers became more affluent and more visible to both black- and
white-owned businesses, the National Negro Business League and other
groups began to carry out small-scale market research.

By the beginning of the Second World War, black consumers were increasingly likely to be recognized and appealed to by both black- and white-
owned businesses as a result of increased incomes, market research, trade press
coverage, and a recognition of black spending. The Second World War also saw
another large migration of black workers from the South to northern cities,
raising many black families' standard of living, and 1946 marked the first attempt at a representative survey of African American consumers, paid for by
interested corporations and Interstate United Newspapers, Inc., a consortium
of black-owned papers. Trade press coverage reflected increased market research efforts. David Sullivan, an African American market researcher and expert on black consumption, published articles with such titles as " 'Don't Do
This—If You Want to Sell Your Products to Negroes!' " that offered advice to
white business-owners: " 'Don't exaggerate Negro characters, with flat noses,
thick lips, kinky hair, and owl eyes.' "[112]

As African American consumers began to be considered a desirable market, so too were black publications recognized as a route to reaching them.
From 1940, companies could buy ad space through the Interstate United
Newspapers that placed ads in a large number of geographically disparate regional papers. The 1940s saw the beginning of ad-sponsored glossy magazines
for African American readers, such as *Ebony*, which debuted in 1945. By the

1950s, Hoover, Schlitz beer, and Pillsbury Mills began advertising in the magazine, despite Pillsbury's fears that its product would become known as "the nigger flour."[113]

The 1950s also saw the recruitment of African American marketing specialists by white-owned agencies such as BBD&O. Often isolated from white colleagues in these companies, these executives formed professional associations such as the National Association of Market Developers to provide information, professional training, and social contact with other African American marketers. Black-owned advertising agencies began to flourish, such as the UniWorld Group, founded in 1969. Yet as general-market agencies employed more black personnel, agencies specializing in African American marketing struggled for business and many collapsed. Since the early 1980s the number of black employees in senior positions at advertising agencies has significantly declined, despite ongoing claims that racially diverse agency teams add expertise to broadly targeted campaigns.[114] Some general-market agencies accommodated the shift in expertise away from black agency professionals by minimizing the differences between black and white consumers, calling (affluent) black consumers "dark-skinned white people."[115] Historian Robert Weems holds a bleak view of African American market development and the incorporation of black consumerism into mainstream American culture, arguing that although this process affords some visibility and leverage for black people, the cost to autonomous black businesses has been too high.

The development of the African American market offers a useful comparison for the later development of gay marketing, revealing commonalities in ideologies and technologies of segmentation. Both groups have suffered invisibility and stereotyping in mainstream media. Yet in compensating for these earlier images, marketers helped to consolidate new stereotypes, often under the guise of "positive images": black men appear as athletes and musicians; gays as affluent, desexualized white men. Market research and trade press coverage were instrumental in the dissemination of (sometimes questionable) information about each market to national advertisers and "legitimized" each segment. Minority media expanded and diversified as advertising dollars bolstered circulation revenues and as publishers further segmented each group (black and gay entrepreneurs, for example, with *Black Enterprise* and *Victory!*, respectively). African American and gay professionals were instrumental in forming, organizing, and providing "insider" expertise about each community, seeing the development of a niche market as offering gains in visibility and reflecting a general sense of progress. Advertising appeals to African American and gay consumers have been interpreted by some commentators as a sign of acceptance and validation on a broader cultural level, and by others as merely a co-optation of an authentic subculture by corporations in search of further profits.

Consciously or otherwise, marketers redeployed those tactics that had enabled them to imagine and produce the African American market in the formation of the gay market. The similarities in the development of each market were not lost on gay marketers, who made frequent comparisons between the groups when discussing the gay market. An early article in *Business Week* reported that at least one apparel company "monitors the gay community for clues to fashion trends the way it monitors young urban Blacks—to spot fashion trends that may move into the majority community."[116] This links gays with blacks not just through how minority markets are formed, but in terms of assumptions about each group as trendsetters. Journalists also compared the value of gay marketing for GLBT and African American communities by locating marketing centrally in the advancement of civil rights. Stuart Elliott described what he saw as the significance of the appearance of a person of color in an ad: "In a lot of ways there was as much progress in the civil rights era when the civil rights bills were signed as when the first ad ran showing a black man in a suit and a tie standing in a phone booth making a phone call, or a national commercial [aired] with a black woman telling her child to take Anacin."[117] Elliott went on to suggest that for people of color and GLBT people, civil rights changes come from recognition within the consumer sphere: "That's the kind of culture we live in. So we define ourselves a lot by that, so the fact that advertisers are trying to chase after you to take your money from you is perceived as a sign of progress." Marketers thus not only applied similar strategies to the formation of each group but assumed similar gains from consumer visibility.

The easy comparisons marketers made between African American and gay markets are only possible, however, while these consumer categories are seen as mutually exclusive: that "all the blacks are straight and all the gays are white." Howard Buford, the openly gay, African American president of Prime Access advertising agency, articulated a notable exception to this. He considered it his social responsibility to challenge this artificial split: "we [at Prime Access] very much think of people of color being very much part of the gay market, very much think of Spanish-speaking people being part of the gay market, and I don't think that's true anywhere else."[118] Such a view is unusual, however, because the logic of niche marketing mitigates against such complex perceptions of consumer identities. The lack of recognition of GLBT people of color as consumers in *both* markets reveals that markets are normally constructed within unitary notions of identity. Marketers, like media producers, can think only in terms of what cultural scholar Lisa Henderson terms "one-dimensional diversity":[119] "minority" markets may be black or gay, but for the most part cannot encompass a version of identity produced from more than one of these positions, not to mention myriad others.

The simplistic comparison between markets also obscures the specific ways in which marketers have had to transform negative stereotypes into positive attributes: just because both African Americans and GLBT people have been demonized in mainstream media does not mean they have been demonized in the same way. Each identity group struggles with a different history of both offensive and ostensibly "positive" stereotypes, requiring marketers to compensate for particularly negative associations with more flattering characteristics associated with each group. To displace the homophobic stereotype of the flaming sissy, marketers constructed an image of the ideal gay consumer as gender-normative and displaying a decidedly masculine standard of good taste. Similarly, marketers interested in African American consumers were advised to replace images of pickaninnies, minstrels, cannibals, and people eating watermelon with more "respectable" characters: entertainers, athletes, and musicians.[120] Racism and homophobia play out in specific ways in the mainstream imagination, and other social factors such as gender and class further complicate the process of transforming negative stereotypes into more "positive" images of each group. All are stereotypes, however, but some are more welcome than others.

Overemphasizing the similarities between the *process* of African American and gay market formation obscures the specific *conditions* of representation, the different struggles in which marketers had to engage, and the specific representational strategies they deployed to resolve some of the most problematic associations with each market. The similar methods marketers deployed to produce the African American market and, decades later, the gay market suggest the extent to which markets, no matter what their target niche, do not simply "evolve" but are produced from specific technological, economic, demographic, and cultural contexts, contexts that markets and marketers then influence. Yet their differences remind us that these conditions are distinct for each market. The conditions in which the gay market was shaped, and the challenges of producing an image of an ideal gay consumer within a homophobic culture, meant that specific pressures were brought to bear on this image. Marketers maximized gay consumers' ideal characteristics—their tastefulness, trendiness, and affluence—and played down their political commitments and sexual desires. Despite the costs this limited view exacted from the GLBT community, this history shows that we cannot claim that the gay market—like the African American market—was simply imposed on the community from "above" by cynical heterosexuals in mainstream corporations.

It was instead produced largely by members of the GLBT community itself: gay-, lesbian- and bisexual-identified marketers, publishers, and entrepreneurs who saw something to gain—financially, certainly, but also in terms of gay visibility, recognition, and cultural leverage. These professionals, with their business and political investments, populate the following chapter.

CHAPTER 3

PROFESSIONAL HOMOSEXUALS

The tensions between business and politics not only shape the history of the gay market but also structure the ongoing, lived experience of gay marketing professionals. Lee Badgett argues that gay consumer culture has not been foisted upon unwitting, GLBT-identified people, nor has a gay sensibility simply been co-opted by mainstream advertisers, but "this latest stage of commercialization is the result of a complex interaction between market forces, corporate marketing practices, gay collective action, less homophobic public policies, and the rise of the 'professional homosexual.'"[1] "Professional homosexuals" describes openly GLBT people who work in professional-managerial status occupations and whose sexuality constitutes part of their professional expertise. Not all those involved in producing gay marketing are GLBT-identified, but those who are must negotiate between their professional and sexual identifications. The display of personal identity—especially one that is sexually and politically marked—tends to be seen as "unprofessional," yet the experience gained by identifying as gay, lesbian, bisexual (and, possibly, transgender) constitutes a significant part of the expertise of "professional homosexuals." Consequently, GLBT marketers' professional credibility both rests upon and risks being undermined by their sexual identity. The strategies these marketers employ to ease the strain between occupational and identity demands not only influence gay marketers' individual and professional cultures, but have broader implications for the formation of the gay market itself; gay marketers both construct their own professional culture and produce cultural products, such as ads, articles, and press releases. Gay marketers are by no means the only "professional homosexuals": openly gay lawyers, health workers, academics, fund-raisers, and others working in response to the AIDS crisis paved the way by making their sexual identities salient in their work life. Gay marketers, however, occupy a pivotal role in shaping gay consumer culture and, beyond gay marketing, help to circulate ideas about gayness in the national imagination.

Consumer Engineers

Gay marketers' professional culture has been produced from two occupational developments: the century-long professionalization of marketing, publishing, public relations, and advertising, and the more recent rise in the number of openly GLBT employees. The early twentieth century in the United States witnessed a crisis for the burgeoning industrial age: the shift from artisan production techniques to mass production necessitated a shift from a producer-oriented economy to one in which consumption became a problem to be solved. Government and business leaders were faced with potentially explosive social upheaval: industrial expansion led to a massive increase in the production of goods, creating a desperate need for accelerated consumption; a huge influx of workers to cities from both rural America and Europe produced urban overcrowding and allowed racial, ethnic, gender, and class interaction; and business mergers formed large corporations that were perceived to be unresponsive to employees' and consumers' needs. These combined influences consolidated moves toward a consumption- rather than a production-based society. Historian of consumer culture Don Slater writes, "Mass consumption kills two capitalist birds with the single stone of a rising standard of living: firstly, it secures the markets necessary to absorb mass output; secondly, it secures industrial and political peace."[2]

Mass consumption did not come naturally to people, however; consumers needed to be educated about the usefulness and desirability of the electric wash boiler (eventually, our washing machine), the vacuum cleaner, and the iron.[3] New professions, including advertising, public relations, and magazine publishing, facilitated mass consumption on an unprecedented scale. William Leiss, Stephen Kline, and Sut Jhally, Roland Marchand, Michael Schudson, and others describe the advertising agent's progress from the nineteenth-century hawker of patent medicines to the respectable professional of the mid- to late-twentieth century.[4] Until the late 1800s, advertising agents worked for newspapers, earning commission on space they sold to businesses interested in reaching consumers. Gradually, agents realized they could increase their revenues by buying larger amounts of space and selling it in small portions for higher rates to those businesses. As advertising agents distanced themselves from publications and developed closer, longer-term ties to the advertisers, they also began to experiment with illustrations and writing copy. With this came efforts to position advertising as a specialized, scientific profession, to develop market research techniques, to form professional associations, and to improve its reputation. Despite these efforts, even into the 1920s the professional status of advertising agents remained tainted. As Marchand writes,

> Patent medicines had loomed large in nineteenth-century American advertising. The lingering effects of that association continued to fuse images of the modern advertising man with recollections of carnival barkers, snake-oil salesmen, and such celebrated promoters of ballyhoo and humbug as P. T. Barnum. Advertising leaders chafed under public suspicion of their craft.[5]

The industry's attempts to reconstruct itself as a respectable profession atrophied by mid-century, according to some critics: "Madison Avenue was 'Ulcer Gulch,' the preserve of the famous 'Man in the Gray Flannel Suit'; it was the archetypal destination for look-alike commuters from Westchester; it was slow-moving, WASPy and serious."[6] This stuffy, pseudoscientific advertising culture was transformed by the so-called "creative revolution" in the 1960s, leading to discourses of nonconformism, authenticity, and individualism both in agency environments and in ads: a 1966 Young & Rubicam handbook for creatives exhorted, "the first rule for copywriters is to be suspicious of rules."[7]

As advertising developed throughout the twentieth century to meet the needs of a modern, industrialized economy, so public relations developed in parallel. To counter early twentieth-century muckraking journalism, public hostility to increasingly consolidated corporations, and worker unrest, business owners and governments alike looked for means to reestablish social order. PR developed to manage this potential crisis in two ways: to make businesses more responsive to public opinion, and to "plead the cause of a client or organization in the free-wheeling forum of public debate."[8] Media historian Scott Cutlip calls this a two-way model of public relations, in which PR consultants use research "not only to shape messages but also to position the organization in rapport with its constituent publics, [forging a] mutual understanding."[9] Scholar of consumer culture Stuart Ewen suggests that according to the cultural climate of each decade, PR responded either by offering a public service function, where public opinion about employee, consumer, or citizen dissent was fed back to corporations, or a manipulative function, where corporations were more concerned to "stroke and cajole the public psyche" in ways favorable to the owning classes.[10] He argues that since the 1970s, research technologies have become so sophisticated that consumer market segments have produced fragmented, lifestyle niches that enable corporations to respond most effectively to the public opinion of only a narrow set of valued consumers, and thus leave many citizens unheard and unaddressed.

Another, related profession that developed rapidly in the late nineteenth century was advertiser-supported magazine publishing. Instead of competing with the expensive monthly magazines such as *Harper's* and *Atlantic Monthly*, in 1893 Frank Munsey set out to "identify a large audience that is not hereditarily affluent or elite, but that is getting on well enough, and that has cultural aspirations; give it what it wants [in terms of editorial content]; build a huge circulation; sell lots of advertising space at rates based on that circulation; sell the magazine at a price *below* the cost of production, and make your profits on ads."[11] *Munsey's* sold for a dime and was quickly joined by the *Ladies' Home Journal*, *McClure's*, and *Cosmopolitan* (in its pre–Helen Gurley Brown incarnation) in serving a then unique function: instructing their "not hereditarily affluent or elite" readers in appropriate class behavior, dress, and leisure pursuits.[12] These magazines appealed to the members of a newly legitimated, increasingly suburban, professional-managerial class, who wanted to acquire "culture" in order to signal their class belonging:

> Having eliminated much home production and streamlined the rest, these [middle-class] families were filling some of the newly available time and space with socially correct leisure activities and displays, drawn from the historical repertory of the class above them. Advertisers both fed and fed upon this aspiration, in an upscale movement characteristic of mass culture from its earliest phase.[13]

Together, advertisers, ad agents, magazine publishers, and public relations specialists forged new relations between consumption and class, relations that would diversify in the increasingly segmented markets of the twentieth century.

Marchand describes advertising agents as "liaison officers, interpreters of the consumer viewpoint, experts on consumer reaction, ambassadors of the final consumer, consumption engineers."[14] Like other members of the professional-managerial class, such as social workers, educators, and managers, marketers emerged from the social upheaval of the late nineteenth and early twentieth centuries to facilitate relations between large corporations and a volatile workforce.[15] Professional-managerial employees worked for industrial corporations, for burgeoning social management sectors, and for companies whose primary function was to oil the cogs between industry and workers and, in the

case of advertising agencies, publishers, and public relations, between the production and consumption of goods. As Bourdieu suggests,

> The emergence of this new petite bourgeoisie . . . can be understood
> only in terms of changes in the mode of domination, which, substitut-
> ing seduction for repression, public relations for policing, advertising for
> authority, the velvet glove for the iron fist, pursues the symbolic inte-
> gration of the dominated classes by imposing needs rather than incul-
> cating norms.[16]

Through higher-than-average incomes and a newly professional image, advertisers, public relations consultants, and magazine publishers became members of the new class they were simultaneously helping to form. They were
pivotal in the transformation from a producer- to a consumer-oriented economy, in part by cultivating new social norms, tastes, and cultural capital that
required correct consumption for the growing middle classes. They simultaneously fashioned their own professional identities, transforming the disrep-
utable image of the snake oil salesman into the technically sophisticated consumer engineer. Almost a century later, gay marketers must construct their
identities not only as members of the professional-managerial class but as
openly GLBT-identified members of that class. Marketers thus face the additional project of cultivating the cultural capital that pertains to a gay-specific
taste fraction of that class.

Dignifying Difference

In a cultural environment of proliferating media images of gays and lesbians,
it is easy to forget the ongoing discrimination against GLBT people, including in employment. According to a report from the National Gay and Lesbian
Task Force (NGLTF), in 2001 only ten states banned employment discrimination based on sexual orientation, and two more, plus Washington, D.C.,
banned job discrimination based on sexual orientation and gender identity.[17]
Thus the majority of GLBT workers in the United States face the possibility
of being fired, demoted, and harassed because of their sexual identification. A
primary issue, then, is how open GLBT employees can be about their sexuality: a 1989 survey found that 62 percent of gay men but only 33 percent of lesbians had come out to colleagues.[18] Business scholars Annette Friskopp and
Sharon Silverstein have since found that increasing numbers of gay and lesbian
Harvard Business School graduates chose to be open about their sexuality
with at least some of their colleagues, some of the time.[19] None of Friskopp

and Silverstein's interviewees was either entirely closeted or totally out, however, but was more or less open depending on context.

Communication scholar James Woods identifies a variety of identity-
management strategies that gay male professionals used to handle their sexuality in their professional lives.[20] Some counterfeited a heterosexual identity
by fabricating opposite-sex dates, for example; others avoided conversations
about their private life; still others integrated their gay identity into their professional personae. Woods argues that although closeted professionals tend to
think in binary terms, that one is either closeted or openly gay, "there are at
least as many ways of shaping a gay identity as there are of trying to evade one,
and while the man who reveals his homosexuality no longer finds it necessary
to hide, his change in strategy brings with it a new set of obligations. . . . He
now faces decisions about where, when, and how often his sexuality is to be
displayed."[21] His subjects' integrative strategies included minimizing the importance of their sexual identity by allowing a tacit understanding of being
gay, and normalizing what others perceived as an "abnormal" sexual identity
by, for instance, calling their partner a "spouse." Sometimes, gay professionals
would "dignify" their nonnormative sexuality: "Rather than emphasize how
normal homosexuality is, assimilating it to the mainstream, [dignifying] tactics
preserve its marginality. Differences are transformed into assets."[22] More confrontational strategies Woods calls "politicizing marginality": if being gay could
not be absorbed by making it normal or an advantage, gay professionals would,
for example, form professional groups within companies to push for greater
acceptance and equal benefits. Gay professionals did not necessarily consistently deploy one strategy over others, however, but moved between them as
the situation demanded. Significantly, however, many of his interviewees believed that to remain professional meant they must present an asexual persona.

Many of Woods's gay-identified subjects did not work in gay-friendly environments, which meant that they were more likely to employ counterfeit-
ing, avoidance, and minimizing strategies to lessen the possible impact of their
sexuality on their professional lives. By contrast, the majority of my interviewees (thirty-four of forty-five) explicitly identified themselves to me as gay, lesbian, or bisexual, and constituted part of their professional expertise through
that very identification. They were, therefore, "gay marketing professionals"
both in the sense that they openly identified as gay, lesbian, or bisexual, and
that they were professionals active in marketing to gays. This is not to say, however, that their gayness was unproblematic and needed no managing: after all,
many of these GLBT marketers worked in mainly straight agencies or corporations and regularly interacted with heterosexual colleagues and clients. As a
result, this group needed to adopt identity-management strategies that pro-

filed the advantages of their sexuality, while containing its more threatening aspects.

My use of these identifications is not meant to designate the "fact" of their sexuality in an essentialized sense, but is nonetheless useful in terms of marketers' own self-definitions and the relationship between these and their professional and political commitments. Indeed, responses from a couple of interviewees demonstrated the inadequacies of both sexual and gender identifications; these boundary cases suggest how even gay marketing and media professionalism is structured by normative ideas of gender, on one hand, and an essentialist perspective on sexuality, on the other. Patrick Califia told me that since he openly identified as a female-to-male transgender person (FTM), his status as a regular contributor to the gay press had been compromised by editors pigeonholing him into a narrow, transfocused niche: "Because I've come out and said that I am doing this gender transition, it really affects the way I am positioned in gay literature and gay journalism, which is still driven a lot by identity politics. So what happens is I get invited to write things about transgender stuff, which is incredibly, after a while, limited and boring."[23] As is routine in the dynamics of marginalization, writers who don't conform to the normative binaries of gender are only invited to contribute as a marked "other," where the source of their difference—here a transgender identity—becomes the only valid perspective from which to write.

A normative binary also structures sexual identification. Sean Strub told me:

> I have always considered myself bisexual. Yet, since I was 17, I have always identified myself publicly as gay. Why? It was easier. I was brainwashed into thinking that my bisexuality, or non-defined sexuality as I prefer to think of it, was a cop-out, or an excuse, a symptom that I was not sufficiently evolved.[24]

Even gay media and marketing contexts maintain a tenacious grip on gender and sexuality binaries; you are either male or female, straight or gay, and little space is available for professionals who don't conform to either axis of identification. Nonconformity brings with it either marginalization, in Califia's case, or a self-chosen but nonetheless painful silence, in Strub's.

Radway shows that maintaining a professional identity is an ongoing project that takes work; Woods emphasizes that the strategies gay professionals used to manage their sexuality in work contexts took far greater effort than those of their heterosexual colleagues. Professional homosexuals' personae are thus formed in the interstices between their professionalism and their sexuality, where the former is always potentially undermined by the latter. Yet for GLBT marketers, their professional status was also *produced* by their sexuality. I asked thirteen GLBT-identified marketers to talk about their upbringing, schooling, and current socioeconomic status or class identification. Five described their status while growing up as working class or blue collar, four as middle class, and four as upper middle class. In contrast, eleven of the thirteen described their current status as professional or upper middle class, one as "class X" (that is, with much cultural capital but little economic security), and one as "educated working class." I was struck by the high degree of class mobility among this group; although it is by no means a representative sample, that over one third shifted from working-class origins into a significantly higher class position (even if this was not reflected in income) is significant. Such mobility may be profession-specific: partly because of their less reputable origins, marketing and media work may offer more flexible career structures than the traditional professions such as medicine and law, and thus may afford workers from less privileged backgrounds better opportunities for upward mobility. This fluidity may have been one reason my interviewees chose their professions, yet they tended to play down the conditions inherent to their profession when they talked about class mobility.

The marketers articulated various narratives to describe the intersections of class and sexuality in their career trajectories. MTV consultant Matt Farber grew up "very middle class," "was always an overachiever," and was expected to become a doctor, but felt that his sexual identity compromised his career prospects: "[I] knew inside that I was drawn to boys more than girls so I felt different. [I] couldn't share that with anyone as that did not fit with my wonderboy profile."[25] Farber feared that being openly gay would undermine his upward mobility and believed he had to choose between a successful career and a stigmatized sexuality, only coming out at the age of 29. Others saw success as a way to compensate for parental and social disappointment about being gay, where the pressure to be "good" had a galvanizing effect on their career aspirations. When I noted *New York Times* advertising columnist Stuart Elliott's upward class mobility from his working-class origins, he commented:

> I think it's that whole "best little boy in the world" syndrome, where you feel you have to excel, whether it's because you feel it's for self-worth issues or self-validation issues or "I'll show them" kind of a thing, or maybe the whole idea that you sublimate all your energy into your career.[26]

For Elliott and others, career success offset queer stigma.

Some working-class marketers explained that realizing they were gay leveraged them out of what would otherwise have been the life of their parents, and into a self-made world of professional status. Joe Landry described his trajectory from "a small dilapidated mill town" in Massachusetts to publisher of Liberation Publications, Inc., in Los Angeles as propelled by desperation, hard work, and good luck. As a teen he realized he was gay, "freaked out, and ran to Boston to explore [his] sexuality."[27] He put himself through school, then began working one day a week for a now defunct gay publication on a commission-only basis. When one of the full-time sales staff went into the hospital, Landry was hired to replace him. Landry went on to work for Don Tuthill, first at *Genre* and later at the *Advocate*, moving up the ranks to become LPI's publisher.

Stephanie Blackwood told a similar story of upward mobility from a blue-collar family in a small Kansas town, but her narrative suggests that although being GLBT-identified may have helped her envision a future different from her upbringing, it also placed some limits on it:

> It is interesting to me that my brother and I come from the same family, have all the same influences and stepped into the world with completely different ways of being in that world: . . . he toed the line, . . . just doing what he had to do, following all the rules, and then there's someone who somehow managed to do all the same things in terms of academic success, but who could not, to save her life—that would be me—do the thing of corporate dress codes, of doing what I was told, of being able to keep my mouth shut about who I am: I always needed to let people know that I was gay. Because in every other way I was perfectly acceptable: I am attractive, I am intelligent, I don't do outrageous things, I show up, I've always been so responsible about work, I am an overachiever, and I had to blow off my mouth about that.[28]

In contrast to her brother, who now holds a senior position at a large high-tech company, Blackwood saw that there were limits on her success in mainstream companies by virtue of her outspokenness about being a lesbian. Although Friskopp and Silverstein found that lesbians might be better positioned than heterosexual women for professional success, there may be a "lavender ceiling" that limits openly GLBT-identified employees' socioeconomic potential in large corporations.[29] Blackwood's solution, like that of many others, was to become self-employed and to start various marketing-related businesses, including the gay-market consultancy firms Spare Parts and Double Platinum. As Sean Strub hypothesized,

I think gay people are more likely to go into business for themselves, people who have an identity around being gay. First of all, to get that identity they are more self-reliant, . . . they have more self confidence to be able to accept that identity, or embrace it, which is somewhat in parallel with people who go into business for themselves. I think that because certain kinds of career paths are not open to openly gay people it makes them more likely to go in other directions.[30]

Entrepreneurship does not guarantee upward mobility, however. Don Tuthill, a self-employed gay magazine publisher, grew up in a "bourgeois" home with independently wealthy parents. When I asked how he would identify his class position now, he joked he felt always potentially "homeless": although his background allowed him to identify as upper middle class, he felt that his entrepreneurial status meant that his economic security was always precarious.[31]

When I asked this subset of interviewees if they felt their class background had an effect on their work, Joe Landry believed that coming from a working-class background made him "scrappier" than his upper-middle-class colleagues, and meant he could "relate to anyone, whatever level they are on."[32] Michael Shively felt that his working-class background allowed him to question sexual mores: "In the United States, as you progress up the ladder of class you don't talk about any of these things [i.e., sex] and can't be rude and crude."[33] At the other end of the spectrum, some marketers believed that upper-middle-class privilege made GLBT people more likely to be activists. Califia described former *Advocate* editor Robert McQueen as "a very cultured person who came from a pretty prosperous family; it was outrageous to him that he would be denied anything just because he was queer. So some of his activism came out of his outrage about losing his class privilege."[34] For the most part, however, interviewees responded awkwardly to my questions about their class identification and how this played out in their work as gay marketers. As Strub argued, "In America it's drilled into you that we're a classless society, and as an adult you realize how far from the truth that is, but subsequently you become uncomfortable talking about things in class terms. So looking at and thinking of things in that way is not easy."[35] His comment affirms Friskopp and Silverstein's findings that when interviewing Harvard MBA graduates in a range of professions, "sex, race, religion, health, or politics were not taboo topics. Money and class were."[36]

GLBT professionals are not only required to minimize the impact their sexual identity might have on their professional aspirations, but to accommodate gender and race factors too. Friskopp and Silverstein found that lesbians and people of color across a range of professions were less likely to be open about their sexual identification than were white gay men, largely because they already suffered workplace sexism and/or racism and believed that to also be known as gay would result in a double dose of discrimination.[37] Although it is impossible to reliably measure the number of openly lesbian marketing and advertising professionals, my research suggests that this group is fairly small. Jack Schlegal, board member of the New York Advertising and Communications Network (NYACN), said that women made up approximately 15 percent of their members.[38] This compares with estimates by Ivy Kazenoff and Anthony Vagnoni that although 39 percent of advertising students are women, this percentage drops rapidly at each level of seniority in agencies.[39] From interviews with current and former agency creatives, Kazenoff and Vagnoni suggest that some women may be put off by agency life perceived to be " 'a boy's club where women have to adapt,' and 'a big boy gangbang' " (19). Others found the "men's locker room humor," sexism, prejudice toward women perceived to be "girly-girl[s]," and the pressure to fit in by being "one of the guys" stifling (19—20). In addition, women in advertising agencies may find themselves guided or gravitating toward account management positions, conforming to expectations that they be "mommies who simply take care of [creatives' and clients'] every need" (19).

If advertising agencies are perceived to be inhospitable places for women, especially in creative departments, there are additional challenges for lesbian agency workers. Friskopp and Silverstein note that lesbians in a variety of professional roles expressed anxieties about being associated with the "negative stereotypes" of lesbians that both arose from and reproduced an internalized homophobia: "the big dykes with the big breasts hanging out in the parade, with no hair on their head and hair everywhere else."[40] The authors argue that lesbians' reluctance to come out denies them access to emotional and professional support systems. In contrast, gay male professionals tend to network very effectively, exploring possibilities for career development and advancement. As Sarah Schulman notes,

> Because of the lack of power networks, lesbians at all social levels tend to be more closeted and less visible than gay men. Lesbians, therefore, would be less likely to fill an expressly stated professional position as a niche marketer in the way that a gay man or a straight woman might.[41]

Although 40 percent of my interviewees were women, none of my lesbian interviewees worked at ad agencies. If openly lesbian professionals are rare in agencies, they appear to be more present in other aspects of gay marketing, particularly in public relations and in marketing departments of corporations. As marketing consultant Stephanie Blackwood commented,

I think that there are fewer women in marketing than men. There are fewer women in everything than men, except social services, social work. . . . That's why they are involved in things like diversity issues on a corporate level and consulting, but not the hard business side. For instance, of the lesbians I know who are in corporate marketing, one was—until she got promoted—the brand manager on Diet Pepsi. Another is the marketing VP for the four premium brands at Philip Morris. You know, they have really excelled, but I don't know a lot of them. At all.[42]

Blackwood suggests here that when women, including lesbians, excel in corporations, they tend to do so in implicitly "softer," "social" positions concerned with "diversity issues," not in "hard business" roles. Feminist-identified lesbians may struggle with ideological questions about being in the lion's den of patriarchal capitalism as marketers. As Friskopp and Silverstein suggest, "While lesbian cultural norms are changing, the expectation that lesbians should be politically correct—that is, anticapitalist, downwardly mobile do-gooders—remains an obstacle for those who wish to pursue careers in business."[43] The tensions for lesbians working in advertising, epitomized within some feminist critiques as exploitative, manipulative, and oppressive of women in particular, may further mitigate against their pursuing careers there.

Friskopp and Silverstein found that, like women, GLBT people of color were less likely to be openly gay at work than were white male professionals.[44] Howard Buford, president and CEO at Prime Access advertising agency, which specializes in marketing to black, Latina/o, and gay consumers, was the only participant who identified as a person of color among forty-five interviewees. He grew up in an upper-middle-class African American household: his father was a surgeon and his mother a social worker. When I mentioned that some interviewees had described their coming out as potentially compromising their class status, Buford exclaimed, "No, no, it wasn't like that for me." He went on to say that he had always felt like an outsider from childhood, because of his race, so coming out as gay felt familiar to him. He likened it to already being bilingual, familiar in the languages of the white dominant culture and his African American familial culture, and learning a new language—that of gay culture. When he started an agency that specializes in advertising to both sexual and racial minorities, Buford forged a professional niche by making an asset of his double marginality.

GLBT-identified marketers' sexuality was certainly a central factor in their professional identity, but not the only identity of significance. The strategies observed by Woods and Friskopp and Silverstein that enable gay and lesbian professionals to function successfully are as class-, gender-, and race-inflected as they are shaped by their nonnormative sexual identifications. Yet all GLBT-identified marketers had to negotiate a complex set of demands posed by occupational professionalism, a nondominant sexual identification in more or less gay-friendly work environments, and GLBT cultural politics. Marketing routines and practices common to the profession intersect with the identity-management strategies that Woods elicited: thus gay marketers dignified their sexuality by making an asset of their gay subcultural capital, and politicized their marginality by vouching for the gains offered by increased gay and lesbian visibility and claimed (to a greater or lesser extent) an activist identity. Marketers also deployed normalizing strategies, arguing that gay consumers are "just like" heterosexual ones. However, they tended not to apply normalizing strategies to themselves, because their professional reputations depended upon the distinctiveness of their skills. My interviewees thus dignified and politicized their roles by positioning themselves as experts, as members of a professional community, and as political progressives. As such, they did not situate themselves as *either* professionals *or* as political activists, but as both: their activism enhanced their professional expertise, and their work advanced the politicized project of GLBT visibility.

Experts

We most often think of marketing as involving the production and dissemination of advertising, direct mail, promotions, and sponsorship. In addition, my interviewees were more generally involved in cultivating the conditions necessary for a thriving gay market: "conquer[ing]" and educating prospective marketers;[45] doing market research; directing diversity training videos; liaising with the national press; handling relations between corporations, gay consumers, and antigay critics; helping companies establish fair employment practices such as nondiscrimination clauses and domestic partner benefits; and turning events from "marketing, presentation, and media problem[s]" to "marketing and sales opportunit[ies]."[46] Each task requires a high degree of professional expertise, but interviewees repeatedly asserted that effective marketing to gay consumers required expertise that professional training alone could not offer. Most GLBT-identified marketers suggested that gay people were most likely to produce effective gay appeals because of the experience that only living as a gay person could provide. As activist and writer Sarah Schulman observes, many gay-specific advertising campaigns are

> increasingly created by design teams that include at least one representative individual from the particular consumer category in question,

who works inside the industry. Their job is to take their knowledge of the source community, to engage its sensibility and wrap that around the desire for specific products, presented in such a way as to acknowledge the codes of the particular niche.[47]

In the early to mid-1990s large corporations sought out gay agencies and free-lancers because, according to Dan Baker, former editor of the gay marketing newsletter *Quotient*, these companies "didn't know—and their advertising agencies didn't know—anything about the gay market, and . . . they wanted to deal with people they felt could tell them something that they didn't know."[48] Bob Witeck recounted that his PR firm had been hired by an international airline because it employed openly gay public relations specialists who were integrated into gay and ACT UP communities, had previous experience dealing with gay public relations issues, and could offer expertise not developed in the airline's general-service PR firm. Baker argued that gay people make better marketers because they have gay-specific tastes: "If you are using images that are supposed to be erotic or supposed to appeal to gay men as sexual, it probably helps to have a gay man who's doing it."[49]

Kurt DeMars suggested that gay-specific cultural capital is as important for magazine sales staff as for producers of advertising: "you've got to make sure that whoever's selling for [*Out*] really knows what we're talking about, has close connections [with the gay community], and is a natural reader. Because they are much more passionate about it if they really understand and are part of this movement."[50] His comment suggests that hiring gay employees has two advantages: their taste affinities are likely to help in selecting potential adver tisers and ads; and their being part of the "movement" is assumed to produce greater passion and thus commitment to their work.

Recently, some general-market agencies have utilized the skills and sub-cultural knowledge of their openly gay employees on gay-themed ads. Michael Wilke commented,

> As more gay-specific ads come along, the mainstream agencies are going to try and suit those needs. They may do a medium job on that unless they start becoming more specialized and up front about appealing to the market and bringing on people who will do a good job in that area and will specialize in it within the mainstream agencies.[51]

Bob Witeck talked about a client's agency that had put young, heterosexual creatives on a gay-themed campaign, and the problems that a lack of gay-specific expertise and research produced. His marketing and PR agency took on a mission of meeting with [the client's] advertising agency, and their straight staff who were doing it . . . well, we imputed that they were straight, we don't know one way or the other—but they put it in the hands of a very junior group of people, which I thought was actually very insightful, because they were of an age, twentysomethings, who have just not as much baggage, and also a lot more openness to the idea of what to say. But we brainstormed with them on some ideas that they were eager to talk about, and the thing we were puzzled by [was that] they didn't know about basic things about imagery in the gay community—what was appropriate, what was inappropriate imagery, or what are appropriate messages and what's inappropriate. There are certain things you can say that talk about being special or unique that can connote being ghettoized, and some that can talk about it in a way that is refreshing and appropriate. And they would come up with some that were not quite right at all, and some that could have been downright offensive.[52]

This quote suggests how fine the distinctions are between "unique" and "appropriate" or "offensive" ways of talking about gays. However, although Witeck naturalized these distinctions, he was not clear about how to adjudicate between them: the boundaries were set by an indefinable, but necessarily gay, judgment. Insider knowledge is positioned as key to navigating the murky waters between appropriateness and inappropriateness, legitimating marketers' gay expertise in the production of successful advertising to gay consumers.

Almost all the GLBT-identified marketers I spoke to assumed that GLBT people do better gay-targeted advertising than heterosexuals, by virtue of possessing knowledge and tastes particular to a subculture not easily accessible to nonmembers. Bourdieu imagines cultural capital predominantly in socioeconomic terms; the value of what you know increases as you climb the social ladder. However, cultural capital is not only class-based but is also organized around other forms of identification, including sexuality. Sarah Thornton develops Bourdieu's notion of cultural capital, arguing that subcultural capital may function in a semiautonomous relation to more established hierarchies of cultural capital: "subcultural capital confers status on its owner in the eyes of the relevant beholder."[53] For gay marketers, the subcultural capital afforded by their sexual identification and participation in largely urban GLBT enclaves equips them with an expertise that becomes professionally marketable. Although Thornton found that her subjects—young, British club ravers—used their subcultural capital to deflect class, occupation, and income differences among their peer group, my interviewees augmented their professional roles with gay subcultural capital. As *Out* marketer Caitlin Hume put it, the gay male sales representatives at the magazine embodied advertisers' ideal audience: "a trendy, stylish, jet-set guy saying 'talk to me, I'll listen'—I think that's an incredible strength that they have."[54] Their subcultural capital, present even in the way they dressed, showed advertisers the kind of audience they could gain access to through the magazine.

Although necessary, gay subcultural capital may not be sufficient to create a successful campaign. Howard Buford argued that simply identifying as gay did not offer specific enough expertise, but that a gender-specific sensibility was required on some campaigns. When Prime Access was commissioned to develop a campaign for a lesbian dating service,

> They asked us to design the logo and treatment and that kind of thing for it. And at the time they asked, in house we didn't have a lesbian designer, so I contracted outside to make sure that it was really right, because I wasn't confident, you know—a gay man can't design something specifically for lesbians, . . . unless he's really, really, incredibly sensitive, you know what I mean? Yes, white people can do some of the stuff for African Americans and sometimes it can be incredibly authentic-looking, but usually that's not the case.[55]

According to Buford, appeals based on identifications—gay, straight, lesbian, African American—require the particular knowledge of that identification to be successful.

Other marketers complicated the idea of a unified gay expertise in regard to regional and urban specificity. Like advertising agents in the 1920s who worried that their urban experience meant that they were "soaked in big-city consciousness," and were therefore unable to relate to the majority of the population who lived in small towns, gay marketers eighty years later expressed concern that their experience as urban dwellers put them out of touch with a large proportion of the gay market.[56] Witeck said, "One concern I have, and I think of this as a New York, L.A., maybe Washington [D.C.] problem, is that . . . when you are open as can be, you forget that not everybody lives the way we do. And that we can be out there far more than somebody else."[57] Witeck and others argued that urban gays (and the marketing they produce) take it for granted that people can be openly gay at work, in their neighborhoods, in consumer contexts, and so on, and worried that advertising appeals so framed would not resonate with gays who do not live in major (coastal) cities. Marketers frequently made urban-coastal, rural-heartland comparisons, and displayed what seemed to me a false modesty along the lines of "this is what *we* do (think, feel, wear) in the city, but we don't really know what goes on *there*," but have few intentions of going "there" to find out. Claiming a lack of knowledge about the heartland may actually elevate gay marketers' subcultural capital, because it suggests their immersion in a particularly hip urban subculture. Yet marketers also mentioned that expanding beyond urban markets may help advertisers, however, because "heartland" GLBT consumers are assumed to be less cynical and not saturated with gay marketing. As Stephanie Blackwood related, "[What] we have often recommended to our clients is: 'get off the coasts, go to the heartlands if you want to have an impact, if you want to test what the general gay and lesbian consumer might think of your product, your ad, your campaign. Get off the coasts, because New York, Los Angeles, San Francisco, Washington, D.C., Boston, are inundated with marketing efforts by companies that want to reach this segment.'"[58] Insofar as the gay subcultural capital that dominates marketing is a product of coastal urban environments, this expertise may be necessary but too specific to produce a broad-reaching campaign for the gay market.

Yet to talk about differences between urban and rural lives for GLBT people is not to suggest that all urban gays share the same views on the best way to produce gay-themed ads. At an NYACN event, an attendee criticized Howard Buford for a Prime Access ad in the group's newsletter, *Newsbreaks*. The ad showed a naked, muscular, male torso, with the words "Specs," "Buys," and "Ads" over clearly defined pectoral, biceps, and abdominal muscles, respectively.[59] The attendee argued that the ad reinforced the stereotype of the buff gay man as desirable, and told Buford, "I was surprised to see your ad in the NYACN newsletter: I don't think it reflects your best work." Buford responded graciously, saying that there had been much debate about the ad among his agency staff, and he had ultimately decided to run it because it was intended as an ironic play on words. Gay marketers, therefore, struggle among themselves with their own and others' perceptions of ads, and with questions of gay-inflected irony and stereotyping. This conversation took place in April 1999; in subsequent *Newsbreaks* issues, the debated ad was replaced by a text-dominated one emphasizing Prime Access as "The Leading Edge in Multicultural Marketing," suggesting that Buford took this conversation to heart.

The question of gay subcultural capital was especially problematic for those marketers who identified as heterosexual (four of forty-five interviewees). Only one interviewee, gay advertising agent David Mulryan, commented that gay people don't necessarily do the best gay advertising. By way of comparison, he asked, "Do you think women are the only people who can do good advertising to women?" Yet interviewees stressed that if marketers were not themselves gay, they needed to acquire knowledge about gay culture and concerns in order to make successful appeals to the gay market. Patrick Sullivan, account supervisor for a large brewing company, recalled the process of learning how to appeal to gay consumers: "I am not gay, so I have had to put aside my own stereotypical perceptions and really go out to a lot of gay bars and try to learn about this marketplace, and there's no way a straight person can market to gays and lesbians without getting out there—you know, you can't do it from a desk."[60] Sullivan's comments suggest that gay subcultural knowledge cannot be fully shared by straight-identified marketers, but only understood vicariously by looking in on the gay world.

In some circumstances, however, identifying as heterosexual was an advantage. Caitlin Hume found that as a heterosexual woman she was much more successful selling ad space for *Out* to some alcohol beverage companies than were her gay male colleagues because she could respond less defensively to corporate executives' homophobia:

> I don't walk around thinking "Oh, I'm straight" . . . [but] I am very conscious of it when I am championing the magazine with conservative advertisers. . . . I really let them voice all their concerns in a way that if it was closer to home and if someone was picking on my family or attacking South Africa—and believe me, as a South African during the '80s it wasn't a popular thing to be! . . . I think I have the power, people say, especially the booze clients, some of them are really good ol' boys. Wild Turkey wouldn't see anyone [even though *Out*'s sales representatives] called and called and called. Booze isn't my category, and I called through and [they said] "sure, come on in." They didn't know what my story was, maybe it was just the fact that I was a woman. . . . If there's a conservative good ol' boy, they'll say "Cate, [get down there]" and I'll say "okay."[61]

In some cases, then, the advantage that GLBT-identified marketers' subcultural expertise offers is overshadowed by prospective customers' discomfort in dealing with openly gay sales representatives. Hume exploits her heterosexuality by appealing to the problematic assumption that people who are not members of a stigmatized group do a better job at representing that group because they are not "personally involved" with the issue, an assumption that has, for example, prevented openly gay journalists from reporting on gay rights issues.[62] This common sense also assumes that only members of a stigmatized group may be personally sensitive to hostile or degrading speech about that group, rather than considering it a political responsibility to take "personally" hostile or degrading speech about any group.

Considerations of who does the best gay marketing therefore raise interesting and sometimes contradictory perceptions of subcultural knowledge and expertise. Most of the time, gay marketers' deployment of this expertise in their professional lives demonstrates Woods's "dignifying difference" strategy, turning their marginal status into an asset. Dignifying strategies mark a bold move by openly gay professionals to neither hide nor minimize their sexual identifications, and help gay marketing professionals distinguish their skills and expertise, offering advertising agencies and corporations access to gay media, communities, and consumers not easily available to heterosexual marketers. Gay-specific agencies and openly GLBT personnel have a vested interest in protecting the boundaries of this expertise, especially as more general-marketing agencies formulate appeals to gay consumers, and heterosexual marketing professionals feel equipped to carry out such appeals. Dignifying strategies, therefore, reaffirm the specific expertise of gay marketing professionals in part to ensure ongoing employment.

Employees

Even as a growing number of openly gay employees in companies and marketing agencies protect their employment by offering their gay subcultural expertise, these employees are usually in the minority in corporations and agencies. This status offers them leverage, assuming their expertise is in demand, but also leaves them vulnerable to antigay hostility and marginalization. GLBT marketers have straddled this often uncomfortable position by making the most of their gay subcultural capital while gaining social and professional support from other GLBT employees within and beyond their place of employment, forming GLBT employee groups such as the Lesbian, Bisexual, Gay, and Transgender United Employees at AT&T (LEAGUE), and gay professional associations such as Out Professionals. These groups have had a pivotal role in the improvement of gay employees' working conditions and in courting gay consumers. Many groups started from what Woods calls a "politicizing marginality" strategy—organizing in the face of discrimination or harassment, with or without the company's approval.[63]

Ginny Schofield, engineer and cochair of her high-tech company's gay and lesbian employee group, related that her company had banned such groups for years out of fear they would function as trade unions.[64] However, in the mid-1990s her employer initiated the formation of a gay and lesbian employee group, along with groups representing African Americans, disabled people, women, Native Americans, Latina/os, and white men. I was surprised at the company's decision to form a group for white men, because it suggests that all identities are equal in the need for organized representation. I joked to

Schofield that white heterosexual men needed a group "in case they felt left out," and she chided me, saying, "They're part of our constituency, too." However expansive a model of their constituencies this response might suggest, the company's view of sexual minorities at the time of the interview was a narrow one: after I mentioned the "GLBT" employee group, Schofield corrected me, saying, "Actually, it's GL . . . No Bs, no Ts," a nomenclature that has since expanded.

The function of these groups is not only to provide support for gay and lesbian (sometimes bisexual and transgender) employees, however. A number of my interviewees referred to the role of employee groups in encouraging corporations to initiate and sustain marketing to gay consumers. For example, Blackwood told me that "in some cases our lead into corporations has come because the gay-lesbian employee group has started saying 'hey, wait a minute, there are gay and lesbian consumers out there.'"[65] Schofield's employee group was charged with the task of suggesting measures to improve the recruitment, training, retention, and productivity of gay and lesbian employees, which led to the company's adopting a nondiscrimination policy based on sexual orientation and domestic partnership benefits. In addition, however, the group was asked to provide specialized expertise on marketing to gay consumers: "The chairman asked [the gay and lesbian employee group] to go answer questions about what makes gay and lesbian people feel welcomed and valued at [the company]. . . . How can we reach your target constituency and sell more products to them?" Schofield related that cochairing the employee group, including having input into gay-specific ad campaigns, was "one of the more fun things that I have done, because I don't normally touch advertising—it was fun to actually give opinions on things."[66] In this way, gay subcultural expertise supersedes profession-specific expertise, as an engineer becomes an (unpaid) advertising consultant, at least temporarily.

Although some client companies encourage the organization of gay groups, most advertising agencies do not offer similarly open environments. Despite claims by Thomas Frank, Woods, and Friskopp and Silverstein that advertising is one of a number of "gay-friendly industries," the overwhelming view offered by the trade press and my interviewees was that advertising agencies are not generally sympathetic to, or supportive of, their openly gay employees.[67] *Adweek* journalist Betsy Sharkey argued in 1993 that although more advertising professionals were openly gay than in previous decades, gay and lesbian ad executives had plentiful stories about ongoing homophobia, closetedness, and stalled careers:

> Agencies like to consider themselves as progressive and forward-thinking places, always ready to anticipate or respond to social trends.

The gay market has become increasingly desirable for certain clients, with ads directed at or depicting gays now appearing in mainstream publications. And yet for years, many gay men and lesbians have chosen complete silence, either avoiding the issue entirely or trying to pass for straight, sometimes creating elaborate fictions of wives, husbands, children, dates, sometimes actually marrying and leading a double life.[68]

Sharkey acknowledges that there were some age-related differences among her 100 interviewees, where younger agency personnel "have, for the most part, made their sexual orientation clear from the moment they started their job."[69] Further, given the rapid expansion of the gay market through the 1990s and consequent demand on general-market agencies to capitalize on the gay subcultural expertise of their employees, homophobia and closetedness in ad agencies may have diminished. But Michael Wilke wrote that even in the late 1990s he did not "believe that [gay agency personnel] have been encouraged to be out, because at this point the advertising business among agencies is still fairly closeted, to many people's surprise."[70] Stephanie Blackwood said that although agency life was "as closeted as the individual decides to make it, surprisingly there are very few—*very* few—agencies that offer nondiscrimination policies, [or] domestic partner benefits."[71] Wilke suggests that the fact that only seven of the top fifty ad agencies responded to an *Advertising Age* survey on their nondiscrimination and domestic partnership policies for gay and lesbian employees shows a lack of commitment to the issue.[72] Those agencies that did respond reported some pro-gay policies (three offered same-sex health insurance benefits, five had gay-inclusive nondiscrimination clauses), but the low response rate suggests that agencies are unmotivated or unwilling to disclose their policies (or lack thereof) regarding gay employees. Howard Buford said that general-market agencies "have no investment in hiring [GLBT] people; they may by accident get someone good for a year or two, but they don't go anywhere inside that agency. So we have a wonderful talent pool looking for a place to go: really good people, but unable to be who they are and to really express themselves [elsewhere]."[73] Niche agencies such as Prime Access capitalize on this, gaining access to talented staff with gay subcultural expertise by offering a congenial work environment, if not large salaries. Further, some general-market agencies were seen as more gay-friendly than others. Deutsch, for example, was frequently mentioned as one of the best agencies for openly gay employees and, not unrelated, has produced gay-themed television commercials for Ikea furniture and Mistic beverages.

Although gay agency workers might have limited opportunities to organize within their companies, the growth of gay professional associations offers interorganizational networking opportunities. Journalist Thomas Stewart recalls that gay professional groups "mushroomed" in New York alone in the late 1980s and early 1990s, when the advertising association NYACN was joined by the Bankers' Group, the Publishing Triangle, and the Wall Street Lunch Club.[74] These groups often functioned as social meeting places as well as professional networking contexts, and Stewart's description of them offers insight into their class-specificity. He explains that "together [the New York gay professional associations] are simply called the Network," whose annual dinner was such an event that "you'd have thought you were at a corporate dinner for US Steel."[75] One agency employee told him: "I've brought in business through this network. And I've grown. I've been exposed to normal people—people with ambition, not people in bars."[76] Stewart's article suggests the conservative tenor of gay professional groups, at least in the early 1990s, and hints that members have in mind distinguishing, maintaining, or elevating their professional class position through membership.

NYACN was the primary professional organization for advertising, public relations, and communications personnel in New York, the city that produces more gay marketing than any other. Formed in 1983 with ten lesbian and gay members, the group grew rapidly to 200 members by 1985, to more than 950 in the late 1990s, and reached 1,200 members after it changed its name to Out Professionals in 2000.[77] The rapid increase of membership during these years reflects larger numbers of people who were openly gay at work, a parallel increase in gay marketing in the same period, and the growing reputation of such organizations, if not their clout. Out Professionals offers members professional benefits, including access to a membership directory, a monthly newsletter, a Web site, and frequent e-mails publicizing job opportunities. It additionally offers workshops on managing finances with domestic partners, notices of book readings, plays, ballet, and other cultural events, and dating, health, dress, and home furnishing advice, such as "Return to Romance: Male Dating Strategies," "Is Natural Alternative Medicine for You?" and "How Feng Shui Helps You Free Your Energies."[78] Through these "extracurricular" programs, Out Professionals guides members not just in the professional aspects of their lives, but in refining their social and cultural capital as well.

Despite the rapid increase in membership in the 1990s, the gender distribution of NYACN's members remained consistently unequal: women made up only 15 percent of members, and lesbians' attendance at NYACN events tended to be even lower. On the "testimonials" page of the group's Web site, only two of thirty-five quotes came from people with (recognizably) female names. One related: "I have been to seminars [at Out Professionals] where I was the only woman in the room. This does not bother me because the subject and information I came away with was so valuable."[79] Women's low membership and attendance rates reflect in part the lower numbers of women than men in gay marketing, and may also reflect differentials in the value of what Pierre Bourdieu calls "social capital." In addition to how much one owns (economic capital) and what one knows (cultural capital), *who* one knows (social capital) contributes to one's position on social hierarchies.[80] Professional organizations institutionalize the cultivation of social capital, offering members opportunities to elevate their status by shrewd networking. Yet the benefits for lesbians and bisexual women in these contexts may be minimal because women tend to have fewer resources to tap into than do men, both in terms of other women with whom to network, and fewer material benefits—jobs, contracts, leads—to offer. Stephanie Blackwood confessed, "I was one of the dykes who hung around with the boys; now when I see other women doing it I know it's because that's where the power is. When I see women not having time for other lesbians, not giving to lesbian organizations, . . . I draw back because that's who I was."[81] Blackwood's comment suggests ambivalence about professional networking: networking with men increases women's social capital, but betrays women's solidarity. Women instead should be working for other women's empowerment by capitalizing on social contacts with other women. Yet in an employment culture increasingly negotiated through networking, lesbians and bisexual women may be at a significant disadvantage, with less to gain from professional organizations where the "old boys' club" has been replaced by the "gay boys' club."

Other marketers I spoke to questioned the benefits of membership in gay-specific professional associations. David Mulryan said,

> NYACN just doesn't make any sense to me. . . . There's no good work that comes out of there. It's sort of like a little social club. . . . It's kind of interesting because there's all these associations—gay doctors, gay lawyers, gay bank tellers, and all this—and yet the mission and the charter of them all is sort of fuzzy, you know? What is it [they] do exactly? I don't belong to any of those, I belong to all of the regular advertising things.[82]

Thus by no means were all my interviewees, or even all the men I interviewed, members of gay professional organizations. However, many of them mentioned less formal associations with other gay marketing professionals. Interviewees living and working in New York and in Los Angeles knew or knew of each other. Many had worked together at publications: Stephanie Blackwood and Grant Lukenbill were colleagues at the *Advocate*, and Blackwood and Don Tuthill were both at *Genre*, for example. Some had circulated information throughout the gay marketing community: Michael Wilke and Stuart Elliott were in frequent contact with many of my interviewees in their work as journalists with a gay "beat." Others knew each other through the Gay and Lesbian Alliance Against Defamation (GLAAD) and business events. Some interviewees also mentioned having initially met through AIDS-related activism, including ACT UP, and Out Professionals' "history" page (on its Web site) relates that in the early 1980s professional groups "were just beginning to form, primarily in response to the AIDS crisis."[83]

GLBT associations, both within companies and in professional groups, offer solidarity and social opportunities to personnel who might otherwise feel in the minority and potentially stigmatized. They give employees leverage with corporations to treat GLBT staff equitably, and in turn, they provide employers access to gay expertise, an expertise that may be honed by professional associations beyond the company. It was striking to me, however, that corporate employee groups tended to adopt a more expressly political agenda than did Out Professionals. There was no mention in the Out Professionals literature of the possibility that the group might organize on behalf of members at a particularly inegalitarian agency, for example, or campaign for more, or more representative, images of gays in advertising. Members may have seen this latter function as being the domain of GLAAD, the GLBT media watchdog group, and some interviewees talked about being members of both GLAAD and Out Professionals. Nevertheless, Out Professionals' more personalized approach to GLBT professionalism and subcultural capital contrasts with the political agenda of groups such as GLAAD. In the tension between business and politics that structures this niche, marketers' associations stress professional development and elide the political potential of their organizations.

Activists

Even though NYACN and Out Professionals did not take a particularly activist role toward the production or circulation of gay marketing images, the interviewees I spoke to frequently commented on what they saw as the progressive aspects of their work. Yet these discussions revealed a tension between the activist possibilities of their roles and the potential damage that being seen as an activist might have on their professional reputations. The two main political frames they employed were seeing their work as promoting gay and lesbian visibility, and educating potentially homophobic corporate employees, advertising executives, and mainstream America.

Sean Strub rejected a simplistic division between activism and entrepreneurship by arguing that gay marketing was started by direct mail marketers, such as himself, who appealed to potential donors to gay and AIDS-related causes:

> Joe DiSabato and a few others were working in the market, but it was the nonprofit fund-raising efforts for NGLTF, HRC [Human Rights Campaign], etc., that politicized people, identified them on lists, etc., and made a viable market of significant size. . . . Just as politics was a critical factor in the establishment of most of the early gay press (other than porn, there was no gay press that didn't have political content and a strong pro gay rights point of view), politics also was the critical factor in creating lists.[84]

Most marketers, however, played down activism in their current role. Some, like Walter Schubert, argued that activism was a state of being: "when you are openly gay you are considered an activist and you are automatically making a political statement."[85] Others saw their activism outside of their professional roles. When I asked Howard Buford if he saw himself as an activist, he initially listed all the GLBT organizations he was involved with, such as GLAAD and the HRC, and only later talked about some of the more progressive aspects of his work. Conversely, Matt Farber described his activism as arising much more from the work he did on developing the gay cable channel than from political activity in a more conventional sense:

> I'm not historically at all an activist. . . . So it's kind of strange for me to be in the spotlight around the [gay channel]. . . . My partner and I live in the suburbs . . . and it's not like we're living in West Hollywood or the Village or Chelsea. . . . So I guess part of what I think about is that [in] the very entertainment people see, they'll see all shapes and sizes [of GLBT people] and we're just the same, and I think that's entertaining and empowering.[86]

Farber describes here what I would call an "accidental activism," a role not unusual among my interviewees; gay marketers commonly see themselves as activists, even if only because of their work. Indeed part of their status as "professional homosexuals" may rely upon an activist identification, if a tempered one. But the common sense of marketing that separates business from politics requires that marketers distance their professional activities from their expressly activist ones. With very few exceptions, my interviewees framed their activism within respectable boundaries that emphasized the progressive and pedagogical aspects of their work over the radical and confrontational.

Marketers articulated a generally progressive perspective on gay marketing that associated visibility with validation: advertisers' recognition of gay consumers was taken as evidence of increasing political or social recognition of gay people, even if such visibility also raised the profile of antigay responses. Patrick O'Neil, a former Deutsch creative who developed a gay-themed Ikea commercial in 1994, commented that he watched gay appeals with interest, anticipating "the influence, and what's going to happen with it, and how's it going to change people's opinions: the more you see, the better off we are, the more visibility."[87] Marketers positioned themselves as central in proliferating gay and lesbian visibility through advertising and other media and sponsorship efforts.

Part of achieving greater gay and lesbian visibility required teaching mainstream companies that gay consumers were a desirable and acceptable market. Catherine Draper, Kurt DeMars, and others acknowledged that getting some corporations to advertise was still an "uphill battle" because of homophobia, the risk of antigay boycotts, and anxieties about conservative investors' protests.[88] Magazine sales staff saw advertising agencies as the route to persuading large companies about the value of the gay market, although Caitlin Hume lamented the agencies'

> lack of understanding about what a powerful market [gays represent], then you get them over that bump and you suddenly realize that it pays to advertise to gays, and then they're scared to go and talk to their clients about it. Quite often because they don't know how to. We've got to educate them on that until they get there, and then you've got to say "Go and tell the client" and then the client may respond—and we're talking about a worst-case scenario now—so [our role is] hand-holding all the way.[89]

Marketers educate prospective advertisers and their agencies about the market in three main ways: its size, its spending power, and its tastes. *Out's* sales and editorial executives, for example, not only distributed data about the magazine's circulation figures but also its readers' higher-than-average household incomes, positioning the "premium, upscale, bold and beautiful" publication as an ideal vehicle to reach affluent gay consumers.[90] As head of an agency that specializes in marketing to black, Latina/o and gay consumers, Howard Buford saw his role as not only educating prospective advertisers about the demographics of these groups but also as presenting a sophisticated, respectful, and nuanced view of those communities to prospective advertisers, a view not readily available from other agencies.[91]

Marketers also saw the progressive potential of educating the general public about the existence and respectability of gays and lesbians (if not bisexuals or transgender people). Elliott said that "people perceive it as, quote-unquote, 'progress' when Ford or Chrysler runs an ad for a car in a gay magazine, or runs an ad in a mainstream magazine showing two women in flannels and Birkenstocks driving away in a car."[92] Showing gay people in ads—especially those that appear in general-market media—was seen as progressive, on par with earlier commercials showing underrepresented populations in ads: "The working woman in advertising was a new idea once too . . . or women who smoked, or . . . black couples, whatever. All those things had their taboos and to greater or lesser degrees they were overcome in advertising."[93]

A further role for gay marketers is to educate GLBT consumers about companies that appeal to them and that have progressive corporate policies. In a statement strikingly reminiscent of Cutlip's two-way model, in which PR consultants liaise between corporations and consumers, Stephanie Blackwood explained that her PR and marketing agency was "in the business of providing consultation on the gay and lesbian market, marketing, and communication to corporations that are interested not only in enhanced business transactions with the market but with increasing their understanding and communications. . . . And trying to do that in both directions, helping the [gay] market understand what corporate America's all about."[94] Gay marketers can thus help GLBT consumers learn how to consume and which companies to patronize, while simultaneously educating corporations about the gay market.

Marketers' activism is largely expressed through their roles as educators; as such, they see themselves as progressives, rather than as radicals, in an industry perceived as very conservative. This conservatism placed limits on how far the marketing industries could further gay visibility and civil rights. Andrew Beaver commented that "advertising is just a very knee-jerk reaction to what the culture is, . . . a very superficial interpretation of the culture";[95] while the broader culture retains narrow-minded views of sexuality, advertising can do little to change it. Interviewees tended to blame institutions other than their own for maintaining the conservatism of advertising: publishers blamed advertising agencies; advertising agents blamed corporations; corporations blamed public opinion. Eschewing a radical agenda for marketing, interviewees were generally anxious to play down the potential of advertising for social *change*, in favor of the more moderate concept of social *responsibility*. As Buford stated,

> Advertising is not about social change, it's about marketing. And we
> don't lose sight of that. But we also can't lose sight of the fact that right

now we're at a stage when people are forming their opinions and impressions and defining things they had no definition for before, and we do have a role in that, we do have a responsibility in that.[96]

Liz Gumbiner also suggested that while hoping for social change through advertising naively disregarded the industry's generally conservative climate, it was possible to aim for some social good, as when the lesbian-themed Mistic commercial was seen as having an affirmative and educative function.[97] Thus some marketers suggested that although they worked within narrow constraints placed upon them from the outside (by clients, media, and audiences), they could still aim for a progressive outcome from individual campaigns.

Not all marketers were so cautious, however. Sean Strub, direct marketer and publisher of *POZ*, straddled the line between activism and entrepreneurship in complex ways, including some that troubled his relations with potential advertisers. As a very vocal member of New York ACT UP, Strub went head-to-head with pharmaceutical companies by strongly advocating in *POZ* that HIV-positive people delay taking medication unless or until they became sick. Around 1990 he rejected an ad from a drug company that purported to be a public service notice recommending that readers take the HIV antibody test, but was actually an ad for treatment. Drug companies, however, were the magazine's primary sponsors. Strub told me:

> We've been critical of ads, highly critical, in fact sometimes when we've run the issue [with the ad in]. Agouran [Pharmaceuticals], when their protease [inhibitor] came out, Viracept, were going on about how it had a unique resistance profile, implying that you could take Viracept and if you failed on that you still had all the other drugs in the class to do it. And the research was not nearly as clear as they presented, and we did a huge article on it that made them livid. Their stock dropped about 10 percent within the few days after the article came out. We had people, Wall Street analysts, dropping by the office for copies of the magazine. And they were really angry with us. Almost every company at one time or another has been furious with us.[98]

Strub later told me that "three or four months prior to the publication of the first issue of *POZ*, a friend at Ogilvy Adams and Rinehart [Burroughs Wellcome's PR agency] leaked me an internal memo from them to their client, Burroughs Wellcome, analyzing BW's 'relationship' with Sean Strub and his companies and what the new AIDS magazine would mean for them."[99] Strub's criticism of the company for pushing its HIV medication, AZT (azidothymidine), was perceived to be incompatible with advertising in his magazine. On another occasion he visited a pharmaceutical company to pitch *POZ* as an advertising venue, and quipped to marketing staff, "The last time I was here I was demonstrating outside your gates on the highway."[100] He told me that they laughed, but he did not relate whether he won an advertising contract from them: Strub's activism meant that some drug companies continued to boycott *POZ*.

Strub acknowledged that his status as a publisher and entrepreneur afforded him more flexibility in straddling activism and professionalism than other jobs permit. Potential corporate employers had been wary of hiring him because they saw him as "too political, and they couldn't be certain that [his] politics wouldn't get in the way." Openly GLBT employees in mainstream companies have much stricter limits placed on their political initiative. Yet the limits of these roles, he suggested, might suit those employees well:

> More often than not, people who are hired as a gay liaison or to deal with the community are hired because the company has confidence that they won't make waves. I know some of these people and like them, and even respect them, so I hesitate to call them Uncle Toms, but it's that kind of thing—they are being used to co-opt the community. A lot of the PR firms that have dealt with the difficult issues, or companies that have awful policies or that have an incident of some kind, that's what they are being hired to do. Now in some cases that does result in some change at the company, in the culture or the policies of the company; even caring about what the gay community thinks about them is better than not caring at all, even if it's in a callous or bottom-line kind of way.[101]

Strub thus acknowledged that even in those limited environments, GLBT employees can have some beneficial impact. In a professional culture that deflects the tensions between business and politics by framing marketing efforts within a pedagogical context, Strub was in a minority, working to make those tensions as productive as possible. For the most part, however, marketers were content to claim that their work had modest social value—at the very least, increasing gay visibility and educating mainstream America—even if this value was constrained by corporate conservatism.

Normal People with Ambition

In her analysis of WHYY's *Storyline*, a radio call-in show based on a reading group format and featuring books by women authors, communication scholar

Lisa Henderson looks at the friction between the producers' feminist politics and their professional practices. She argues that the show's female personnel were "self-consciously professional producers in a bureaucratic and hierarchical network organization, whose senior managerial appointees are men and many of whose professional standards, while not expressly commercial, remain concerned with ratings, production values and mainstream appeal."[102] The focus on women writers and the all-female staff suggests that gender-specific experience and expertise were important. However, the senior producers played down the feminist potential of the show and made programming decisions designed to offset the impression that a feminist show would seem "preachy, unappealing, and only narrowly relevant to women."[103]

Like Henderson's *Storyline* producers, gay marketers must negotiate complex social and professional contexts in constructing their occupational identities. Advertising executives, journalists, public relations consultants, and publishers who both appeal to the gay market and are themselves GLBT-identified are among a small group of professionals for whom a nonnormative sexuality is less a liability than an asset, even a necessary attribute of the work they do. They must simultaneously navigate the standards of their profession and the demands placed upon them by the still contested status of homosexuality in the United States. The marketers I interviewed were aware that gay marketing is always contradictorily and at least implicitly political, and believed that the meaning of GLBT images in a mainstream culture of inequity and homophobia had a significant impact on the welfare of GLBT people. In contrast to the claim that marketing to gays was a matter of "business, not politics," all of my interviewees couched at least some of their approaches to gay marketing in political terms. In many cases, moreover, their involvement in progressive causes contributed to both their subcultural capital and their professional credibility. Woods's distinction between the "dignifying" and "politicizing" strategies employed by gay professionals may be overdrawn, then, because gay marketers both cultivate their gay-specific expertise and use it for political ends. I found the prevalence of a political perspective reassuring, as it suggests that gay marketers were invested in influencing heterosexual colleagues' and clients' perceptions of GLBT people. However, I also felt that many of my interviewees complacently equated consumer visibility with political progress. This is problematic for two reasons: it suggests that their work alone constitutes a sufficient level of activism to effect social change, and it positions the free market economy and its popular manifestations—advertising, advertiser-supported publishing, and public relations—as the rightful place of social struggle. Marketers maintained their professional status by distancing themselves from a more confrontational image of the GLBT community; they were "normal . . . people with ambition," not "people in bars," "silly queens," or "dykes on bikes showing their breasts."[104] This contrast between normal and stigmatized people distinguishes two worlds: one of adult, decorous responsibility, the other of sexual and playful excess, making unimaginable the prospect that gay marketers could be dykes on bikes with professional ambitions.

GLBT–identified marketers thus negotiate the tensions inherent in being openly gay in a potentially hostile work and cultural environment by emphasizing a gay-specific professional identity that maximizes the "desirable" elements of gay subcultural capital, and contains a more irascible activist identity, manifested especially in queer politics. This has consequences both for the small group of "professional homosexuals" employed in gay marketing and for their work: gay marketers produce and reproduce not only their own professional culture but also marketing texts and, more broadly, a visible, gay, consumer culture. The contours of this consumer culture are the topic of the following chapter.

CHAPTER 4

How Gay Is Too Gay?

Gay marketers are faced with two primary challenges. The first is common to all marketing: how to create credible and desirable connections among people, products, and well-being, as communication scholars William Leiss, Stephen Kline, and Sut Jhally trace in their study of advertising.[1] The second challenge is specific to gay marketing: how to produce recognizably "gay" texts that interpellate gay-identified consumers. As film professor Richard Dyer observes, "A major fact about being gay is that it doesn't show. . . . There are signs of gayness, a repertoire of gestures, expressions, stances, clothing, and even environments . . . that bespeak gayness, but these are cultural forms designed to show what the person's person alone does not show: that he or she is gay."[2] Since gayness doesn't necessarily show in marketing (as with anywhere else), gay marketers must deploy gestures, expressions, stances, clothing, and environments to make compelling connections between products and consumers. Not only must gayness be made visible, but that visibility comes burdened with political weight, since it is produced in a contested cultural context. Marketers must therefore deploy the prosaic routines of marketing in exceptional circumstances, facilitating the consumption of goods while accommodating the distinguishing features of the gay market.

In the late 1970s, Karen Shapiro investigated the routine stages of advertising in four agencies in order to understand why commercials showed women primarily in domestic roles, disavowing their rapid integration into occupational and public life. Although each of the campaigns she studied had unique features, she identified a number of stages that remain relatively consistent across clients, products, and media. Each case involved, first, isolating the "problem" that the product should solve. This included researching the product's attributes and uses, identifying existing or prospective markets, and specifying how the product did, or could, meet the target consumers' needs or desires. Second, agencies devised a campaign strategy to link target consumers to the product. Third, agency creatives executed this strategy in a number of iterations, suggesting copy, image, sound, and media placement. This stage is seen as the quintessentially creative moment in advertising folklore, research, and criticism, yet it in fact represents only one moment in a continuous process by which advertisers attempt to make meaningful links between products and consumers. Next, agency workers and clients negotiated how the ads should look and sound, whether the strategy has been adequately communicated through the ads, and so on, until the client was satisfied with and approved the campaign. Fifth, agencies worked with (usually) out-of-house production companies to produce a 30-second commercial. Finally, each agency undertook an evaluation of the ads, looking at feedback from focus groups, telephone interviews, and trade and popular press articles. Other studies affirm Shapiro's outline of the production process, and all suggest that while campaigns differ in their products, target audiences, media vehicles, strategies, and results, a level of routinization is required in order that the various personnel function efficiently for each campaign.[3]

Through her analysis of outmoded gender norms in commercials, Shapiro concludes that the routines of advertising, more than any individual's conscious intent, were responsible for reproducing stereotypes of women. Similarly, Gayle Tuchman addresses how the routines of cultural production—in her case, the production of news—are not merely functional but have ideological consequences.[4] Production routines repeatedly shaped particular events and people as "news," letting others slip through the news "net" into oblivion. Her analysis of the *New York Times*'s coverage of the women's movement in the mid-1970s, for example, suggests some of the ways in which the routines of news production did not, could not, or would not accommodate issues and events outside male-dominated conventions of news production, except in conditional and marginalizing ways.

Taking a lead from Shapiro's and Tuchman's studies, I look at how marketing routines produce a visibly gay consumer culture. In contrast to gender, however, which for most people is readily identifiable, GLBT identity is not necessarily apparent to others: both gay-identified people and the texts that interpellate them must signal their gayness in some way. In her study of the rise of gay visibility in the United States, cultural studies scholar Suzanna Danuta Walters argues,

> Most of the time, difference is not marked on our bodies. . . . Gays can
> hide, be overlooked, be mistaken for heterosexual. Thus, for lesbians and

gays, issues of visibility and "coming out" are centrally and inextricably linked to the process of acquiring civil rights, in a way I think quite different from other minority groups for whom *mis*representation has often been a more driving concern than simple *rep*resentation.[5]

Representation, however, is no simple thing. Because invisibility has been at the expense of GLBT people, even if it is presented as a privilege (you, too, can choose the closet), struggles over visibility, representation, and the meaning of positive images have dominated gay civil rights discourse and activism since the early 1970s, at least. Indeed, many of the marketers I interviewed asserted that their work had political value if only because they made images of gays and lesbians visible to GLBT communities and the mainstream.

Yet Walters and others have challenged the assumption that visibility is simply good for gays. Because gayness itself is not something that a person's person can show, gay marketing must depend to some extent, at least, on typification. Ads need to produce a recognizable gayness while also negotiating the continued, embattled status of gay subcultures within the dominant culture, engaging the most conventionally "positive" stereotypes (the trendsetting gay man, for example) and suppressing other, long-standing negative images of gays and lesbians (silly queens, perverts, and ugly, anticonsumer lesbians). Some critics, like Michael Wilke on his commercialcloset.org Web site, suggest that all stereotypes have negative consequences, insofar as they limit what is imaginable as a GLBT person. Others, including representatives from GLAAD, take issue only with those stereotypes generally thought of as negative, and battle for "positive" images to displace homophobic ones. Yet even positive images might have negative consequences, since these tend to show GLBT people who are already otherwise privileged by status (they are white, affluent, young) or by behavior (they are sexually discreet and politically acquiescent). In contrast, people of color, poorer people, activists, sex radicals, transgender people, older GLBT people, and others who don't fit with this image languish in obscurity. Such conditional visibility has implications for how GLBT people are seen, occluding the diversity of GLBT communities and limiting the choices GLBT people can make without forfeiting their visibility. Other commentators question whether being visible as consumers has any necessary impact on political participation: as communication scholar Danae Clark puts it, "capitalists welcome homosexuals as consuming subjects but not as social subjects."[6]

These analyses tend to focus more on the effects of visibility than on the routines by which gay visibility must be constructed. Taking visibility at face value presumes the authenticity of the gay body, an essential gay self that media and marketing practices simply reveal to other GLBT people and to the public at large. Such a perspective disavows the productive aspects of a constructed homosexuality: like markets, sexualities "are shaped, not discovered."[7] Gay marketing routines do not reveal people or products as inherently gay so much as construct gay-inflected connections among the different nodes of marketing—companies, their products, media venues, and marketing texts. Gayness resides in none of these nodes, but in the relations between them. Products are understood to be relevant to gay consumers because other gay consumers have used them before; conversely, consumers can be read as gay because the products they consume have gay associations. Ads are assumed to appeal to gays because they appear in gay media; some media, in turn, are assumed to be intended for a gay audience because of their gay-specific content, including ads. Fabricating such relationships between products, media, and people is the task of all marketing routines. What is specific to gay marketing, however, is that connoting gayness is especially challenging, both because it is not flagged by any incontrovertible physical marker, and because the stakes of gay connotations are high. Representational routines never transparently reproduce a real world, but frame that world within highly coded ideological parameters. The demand for ideological containment is especially pressing with an issue as culturally contested as gayness, so corporations, and the marketers they employ, use representational routines that allow them to explore their business interests in the gay market, while minimizing the political flak that this interest might provoke.

This chapter and the next are both concerned with how marketers adapt their professional routines to the gay market, navigating between their business interests and political risk to produce a contained gay visibility. In the chapter that follows I address the narrow view of GLBT people that contemporary gay marketing routines produce, and how this imagined constituency is constantly challenged both by the real diversity of GLBT communities and by a homophobic right wing's attempts to erase a public GLBT presence altogether. Before looking at the contained visibility of the ideal gay consumer, however, I look at how generic marketing routines intersect with the challenge of representing gayness to produce a visibly gay consumer culture. In this chapter I investigate the routines of marketing that articulate people, products, and images of well-being with particular kinds of gay sensibility; marketers more easily or willingly articulate gayness to some products than others, in some venues over others, and use a selection of signs and significations from a plethora available to connote gayness. The chapter concludes with a case study of a Dockers khakis advertorial that appeared in *Out* magazine in 1998, which demonstrates how a not necessarily "gay" product, a hip gay-oriented magazine, GLBT readers, and a political sensibility were all framed within the imperatives of a marketing mission. The Dockers campaign shows that rather

than assuming that one is either visible or invisible as gay, or even that visibility exists on a continuum between total invisibility and complete openness,
marketers construct desirable and relevant connections among people, products, media, and gay visibility. This approach allows a view beyond debates
about visibility to investigate how "visibility" as a discourse is brought into the
commercial sphere, containing what becomes imaginable as "gay."

Drugs, Booze, and Sex: Gay Products

Describing his decision to market hotels to gay men, Keith Ferrazzi, former
vice president of a large hotel chain, claimed, "It's not difficult to envision marketing to gays and lesbians if you are selling drugs, booze, or sex, and that's really where marketing started with the GLBT community; it was the alcohol
companies, the pharmaceutical companies and the travel industry."[8] Yet
Roland Barthes argues that, in the language of marketing, even the most
obvious-seeming affinities between products and consumers are arbitrary:[9] that
families "need" minivans is as culturally constructed a relationship as playboys
"needing" Porsches. Consumer culture scholar Don Slater plays down the
commonsense distinction between material needs and symbolic ones, insofar
as modern subjects must necessarily use goods for identity-formation and display. He writes, "The eminently modern notion of the social subject as a self-
creating, self-defining individual is bound up with self-creation through consumption: it is partly through the use of goods and services that we formulate
ourselves as social identities and display these identities."[10] Marketers and manufacturers have responded to the role of consumption in identity-formation
both by producing products and services that meet the signifying needs of
GLBT people, and by articulating products, usually "image goods," with the
positive aspects of gay sensibility. Thus the association between gays and products is not a natural one: while some products may seem to be born gay, others
achieve gayness, and some have gayness thrust upon them.

Products that are "born gay" include those that are produced with the intention of allowing the owner to signal her or his sexuality, such as products
with rainbow flags, pink triangles, or queer slogans on them. *Out* president
Henry Scott rather dismissively reported that a number of the magazine's regular advertisers "want to reach gay and lesbian people because they have products that will specifically appeal to them. . . . The most, I guess, trite example
is somebody who's trying to sell a rainbow flag item. You know, we have a
bunch of that."[11] Other common gay-specific appeals are for those services
that offer access to gay-populated spaces or groups: circuit parties, one-off
events like the Millennium March on Washington, and vacation resorts and

cruises. The International Gay and Lesbian Travel Association, invested in stimulating gay-focused marketing, estimates that gays and lesbians around the globe spend $55 billion annually on travel.[12] Encouraged by these figures, gay-owned companies such as Olivia Cruises and Resorts and RSVP Travel offer packaged deals that guarantee GLBT tourists can "immerse themselves in the humor, camaraderie, and romantic attentions of the like-minded."[13]

Recent years have seen a rapid increase in companies offering specific expertise to gay people, such as financial services equipped to respond to the unique tax, property, and inheritance circumstances of gay people who cannot legally marry (such as Christopher Street Financial Services and gfn.com, the Gay Financial Network). The pages of national and local publications were at one time dominated by gay-specific sexual services, including phone sex lines and escort companies, but since the mid-1990s publishers have turned away explicitly commercial sex ads. Ads for sex stores such as San Francisco's Good Vibrations and Stormy Leather and New York's Toys in Babeland still offer their GLBT clientele same-sex sexual merchandise, however. An ad that appeared in the lesbian press for the Instead menstrual cup capitalized on the challenge of negotiating not one but two menstrual cycles in lesbian relationships. Showing two women in a passionate embrace, the ad warns, "A period can ruin a romantic moment. Yours doesn't have to" (fig. 4.1).

National media and entertainment companies use gay media to advertise books, music, films, videos, and TV shows that are not intended exclusively for the gay market but have a good chance of appealing strongly to GLBT audiences. These may be gay-themed (*The Birdcage*), feature a gay character (*As Good As It Gets*), or present an actor or star who is either openly gay (Rupert Everett) or has a large gay following (Whitney Houston). Premium cable television channels have courted gay audiences in both the gay press and the mainstream: Showtime spent $10 million in a range of media promoting the U.S. version of *Queer as Folk* in 2000.[14] Three years later HBO appealed to gay subscribers with an ad insert playing on the metaphor of the closet: "OUTRAGEOUS. OUTSPOKEN. OUTSTANDING. OUTRIGHT HBO."[15] This reminded viewers of the channel's GLBT-relevant offerings, with shows including *Six Feet Under* and *The Wire*, and films such as *The Deep End*.

At the local level, gay-identified merchants and professionals offer services to readers of the gay press: car dealerships with gay-identified or gay-friendly staff, realtors, tax advisers, bars, stores, restaurants, gyms, and clubs. One estimate suggests that 90 percent of local and regional publications' ad dollars comes from local advertisers.[16] According to Grant Lukenbill, a journalist and gay market consultant, "most products [advertised in local papers] are probably from small businesses in localized geographic areas: that's probably where

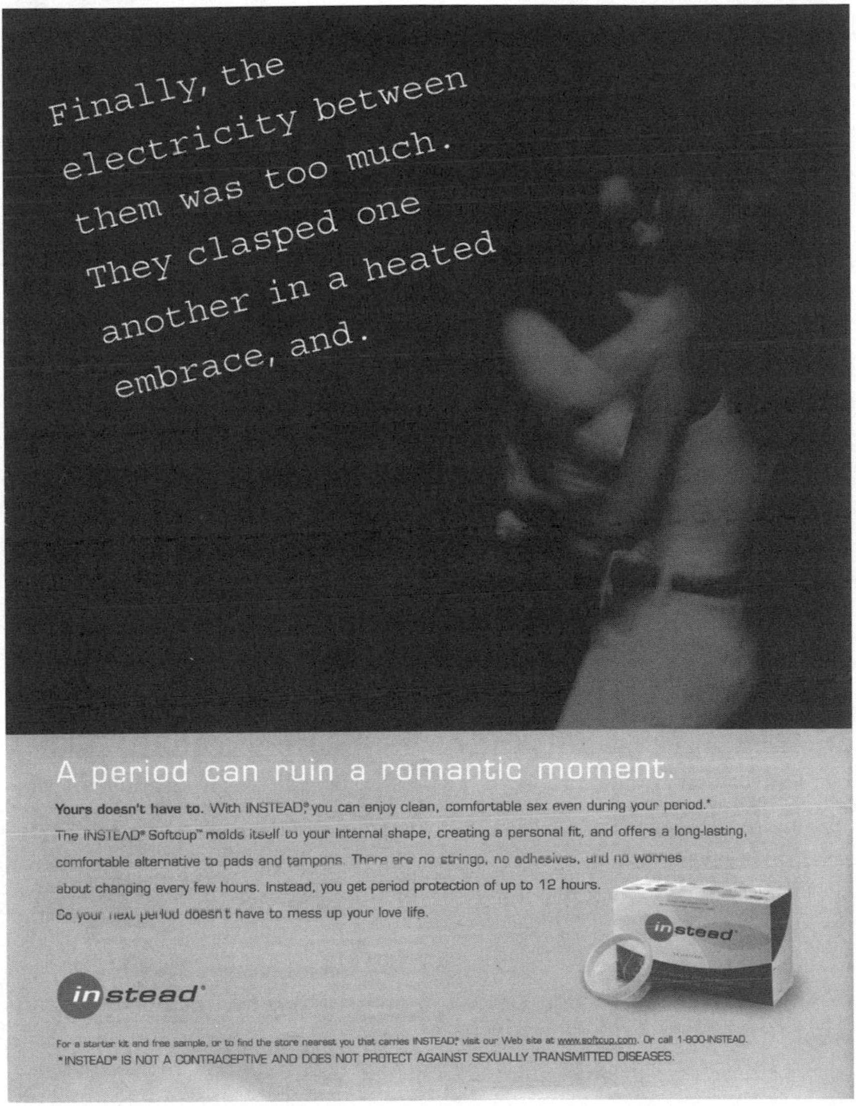

FIGURE 4.1 THE INSTEAD MENSTRUAL CUP SIGNALS A NEW PERIOD OF LESBIAN-TARGETED ADVERTISING (*GIRLFRIENDS*, JANUARY 2003).

the lion's share of the money is being made."[17] These businesses know that most or all of their clientele are gay-identified, and that the most efficacious method of reaching them is through local, often free, newspapers.

HIV-related pharmaceuticals are also commonly advertised in gay media; although these are not only for gay-identified consumers, gay men nevertheless make up a disproportionate number of people with HIV and AIDS.[18] Publisher Sean Strub conveyed how hard his staff found it to entice other advertisers to buy space in *POZ*, even for products well suited to their readers, such as vitamins or health foods. He lamented, "I hate all the advertising [currently dominating *POZ*] because it so narrowly defines the lives of our readers, [and] some of it is depressing. And there are lots of incredible products out there that are useful to people, even things that are specific around treatment and health conditions, but I don't think [an expansion of advertised products] is going to happen any time soon."[19] Strub suggested that while it is advantageous to link some products—HIV drugs and viaticals—to HIV-positive people, other advertisers fear being "contaminated" by an association with AIDS.

In contrast, some goods and services have no "natural" link with gayness but become gay-inflected through use by gay consumers, or have gayness thrust upon them by advertisers keen to capitalize on the more desirable stereotypes of gay consumers. Interviewees explained why marketers increasingly advertised "image products" or "badge brands," such as fashion, home furnishings, and upscale brands of alcohol, to gay consumers. Bob Witeck, a gay public relations specialist, said, "If you want to give [a product] a special upscale sort of branding, gay people would be good for doing that because there's a certain snob appeal" associated with advertising to gays.[20] In 1999, for example, 30 percent of *Out* magazine's advertising revenue came from apparel manufacturers looking both to appeal to gays and to associate gay men's trend-setting reputation with their product. Henry Scott explained why gay men, in particular, have been targeted by fashion and other lifestyle advertisers in recent years:

> Part of the appeal is—because [*Out* has] a style-conscious audience—the notion is if you can get particularly gay *men* to adopt the product, the rest of the world eventually follows. . . . So if you reach that gay market and it adopts your product, you not only sell to that market, which has tremendous spending power, but you also have a chance at establishing this particular product as fashionable to a larger group of people. Those kinds of advertisers come to *Out*. We might not have big numbers, but we have the right audience: an audience that can afford to buy the prod-

uct, that has an inordinate interest in style—perhaps an unhealthy interest in style . . .—and tends to influence a larger population.[21]

Here Scott acknowledged that marketers do not simply advertise gay-specific products to gay consumers, but work to get gay people to adopt products for the prestige that such adoption brings to the product.

While some marketers wanted to associate their product with the gay market to bring image products an upscale, trendy cachet, others forged associations between same-sex eroticism and young, urban trendiness. Rachel Fox, account executive for Disaronno Amaretto, suggested that their 1998 ambiguously lesbian-themed campaign was designed to make their product seem "younger, hipper: we needed to move away from where it was to a much fresher, more contemporary look."[22] The Disaronno campaign showed lesbian intimacy in the service of a more general appeal to sexy glamour: "Our core desire for Disaronno was to make women or men feel glamorous, desirable, the center of attention. And our selling idea was that Disaronno causes the consumer to feel alluring at any time. . . . So taking that brief and giving that to the creative teams, . . . it's quite easy to come up with something very sexy and sensual."[23] Despite the erotic exchange between women in the commercial, Fox never used the word *lesbian* in relation to the campaign or to the market, claiming, "our intention was to advertise to everyone and not alienate anyone." The commercial appeared only on Canadian television, while the "lesbian" version of their print ad appeared in both the lesbian press and in men's publications, including *Playboy* (see fig 6.5, p. 193). The appearance of the lesbian ad in both lesbian venues and a heterosexual men's upscale, mainstream pornography magazine speaks to a common disparity: ads can show sexiness between two straight-looking women and be read as alluring, glamorous, and sexy, but it would be hard to imagine such explicit images of men together connoting a similar theme. Indeed, the commercial suggests that when the women's behavior encourages a man to come on to his male friend, this gesture is met with incredulity and offense.

Lesbian sexiness comes in part from its nonconformism; other marketers also capitalized on the positive aspects of lesbians' outsider status by showing them as individualists. Deutsch copywriter Liz Gumbiner recounted that the impetus for a lesbian-themed Mistic beverages television commercial came from a liberal appeal to "being true to yourself": "the whole point of Mistic is that Mistic has all these different colors and flavors and they're very strong in urban environments. It's less mainstream than Snapple was at the time, and [we] wanted to say to people . . . 'we're smaller and we're about individualism and our flavors are really unusual, and it lets you show your colors.'"[24] Advertisers of "sin" products such as cigarettes and liquor similarly use GLBT people's outsider status, along with their reputation as partygoers, as a basis for their pitch. Catherine Draper, advertising director for two lesbian magazines, suggested that alcohol and cigarette companies tend to be more "open-minded" and gay-friendly than others, explaining why they were some of the earliest advertisers in gay media in the late 1970s and early 1980s.[25] *New York Times* ad columnist Stuart Elliott argued that this more open-minded approach may result from cigarette and alcohol companies' reduced vulnerability to antigay consumer boycotts:

> If Absolut vodka got a letter from Mississippi saying "we're going to stop buying your product" what would happen? Their sales would go down from four cases a year in Mississippi to two! It was a risk that marketers like that determined was worth taking, in terms of the balancing act between the intended consumer they were hoping to find in the gay market versus whatever fallout or loss they would have suffered from conservative consumers.[26]

Yet entry into the gay market has not been without incident for tobacco companies, according to *Advocate* publisher Joe Landry:

> In 1992, Philip Morris ran their first ad in a gay magazine for Benson & Hedges Special Kings, which is a brand extension of B&H. It was the largest and most conservative company to run in gay media at the time. The *Wall Street Journal* ran a front-page story lambasting the ad campaign and implied that Philip Morris [had] stooped so low to target the gay audience, and also implied that they were creating a gay brand. I don't think Philip Morris liked that story! The brand did not succeed, and to this day ads from Marlboro are conspicuously missing from gay media while all their competitors are walking away with the market share.[27]

Cigarette ads now frequently appear in gay media, as do ads for liquor, but not without publishers' ambivalence. Sean Strub refused cigarette ads outright, and would take alcohol ads in only limited circumstances, such as if the company also sponsored AIDS causes. Publisher Dan Mullen reported that the bisexual magazine *Anything That Moves* would not accept alcohol or cigarette ads because of addiction and health concerns in the bisexual and queer communities, and because *ATM*'s editorial board believed alcohol and cigarette companies merely "exploit" rather than "support" these communities.[28] Former *Advocate* publisher Michael Shively remembered debates about letting alcohol companies sponsor *Advocate*'s fund-raising parties: "There was a lot of conflict and hand-wringing behind the scenes because alcohol is an issue, there are a lot of alcoholics in the gay community. And we're taking all this money from people who made alcohol. And, obviously, we took the money [*laughs*], but it wasn't because [the *Advocate* staff] didn't fret about it."[29] Despite the legendary allegiance gay consumers have shown brands such as Absolut vodka that are seen as loyal to the gay community, alcohol distributors' interest in the gay market may have less to do with a humanitarian impulse than with the legal and venue-specific limits placed on their advertising in other contexts (television, Web sites, other publications) that send them in search of more permissive (or advertising-desperate) outlets such as gay and lesbian magazines.

While some advertisers sell gay-specific products, then, others who offer products that seem to have an affinity with gay consumers shy away from advertising in gay venues for fear of "contamination"; negative associations with gayness bring an unwanted visibility to their products. This fear of contamination might explain the absence of athletic apparel advertisers in gay media, even though gay readers are potentially a large market. Deutsch advertising executive Andrew Beaver said,

> I think that sports is an area that there's still just too much machismo in the whole athletics area . . . you don't necessarily create . . . something aspirational with gay people right now, or gay messages. It really has to be jock-oriented. And whereas there's a tremendous amount of latent homosexuality in sports, that's about as far as it goes. And, quite honestly, you can take it there, but you just can't be explicit about it.[30]

Beaver's comment suggests that the danger of association with explicit, same-sex eroticism keeps sporting goods manufacturers out of gay publications. Although he was referring to the "machismo" of men's athletics, marketers may also avoid courting lesbian consumers of sporting goods out of fear that the stereotype of the butch lesbian athlete might contaminate the product.

The fear of being associated with gay sex also hovers over another notably scarce category: condoms. Not until the summer of 2003 did a condom ad—for Lifestyles condoms and lubricant—enter the gay press (see fig 7.2, p. 211). Trojan had begun to advertise its lubricant in the gay press, along with other lubes such as KY lotion, Wet, and Astroglide, but condoms were for a long time notably absent. Joe Landry suggested that there were two theories to explain this:

> One is that there is no clinical proof that condoms—because they were not designed for anal intercourse—will work for anal intercourse. So

they need clinical proof, because they were designed and manufactured for vaginal intercourse. . . . And another one is that [condom company executives] are hugely, hugely conservative, and their buddies on the golf course will laugh at them if they are advertising in a gay magazine.[31]

It strikes me as suspicious that, in more than twenty years of health workers and educators promoting condoms for safer sex, condom manufacturers have not tested their efficacy for anal intercourse. Such neglect suggests condom companies are anxious that their product could suffer from an association with gay men's sexual practices and from becoming known as the "gay condom." This anxiety may be specific to the United States, however: at the 1998 Gay Games in Amsterdam, Durex distributed 75,000 condoms to an expected 200,000 attendees.[32]

Some advertisers stay away from gay marketing not only because of the risk of being associated with gay male sex but also out of fear that their product might become associated with gay consumers, thereby alienating heterosexual customers. Others don't advertise in gay media more for reasons of scale: Henry Scott explained that very large companies demand higher circulation figures than gay magazines can offer, even if the readers' demographics are more desirable and the cost per page is lower in gay magazines: "It's inefficient for Proctor & Gamble if they want to advertise Tide—just the cost of producing the advertising materials that they have to send to us, making the phone calls and processing the paperwork makes no sense for them if you are talking to a 133,000 circulation magazine. So we don't get that kind of advertising."[33] Yet packaged goods companies also tend to be notoriously conservative and thus anxious about being associated with the gay market. Further, these companies may perceive their products to be particularly vulnerable to antigay consumer backlash; although fashion, alcohol, tobacco, and entertainment companies can advertise products that benefit from an association with gay consumers by appealing to their trendsetting, party-going reputation, everyday products from more conservative companies may have less to gain and a great deal more to lose. As gfn.com's CEO Walter Schubert said, even in the early 2000s, "corporate America . . . is somewhat timid, sheepish, about projecting their brand into the gay community. They don't want hundreds of letters and e-mails coming from the extreme conservative Right talking about boycotting their product because they are patronizing the gay community."[34]

One product that Proctor & Gamble has advertised in gay media, however, is Crest Whitestrips, their teeth-whitening product. This campaign is endorsed by media and marketing consultancy Witeck-Combs Communications' findings that gay men are more concerned with their appearance and its modification than are heterosexual men, and are twice as likely to have laser vision-correction surgery and seven times as likely to have laser hair-removal treatments.[35] The company's willingness to court the gay market for Whitestrips suggests that conservatism and fear of antigay backlash are not deterrents if a product is seen as sufficiently appropriate for the gay market. Indeed, the president of Prime Access agency, Howard Buford, explained that advertisers make shrewd judgments about whether their product can be made relevant to gay identity or lifestyle. For the most part,

> Packaged goods just aren't leveragable to gay identity. . . . Travel absolutely is, financial services are: being gay influences where you go on vacation, who you go with, and you want to know you are going to be accepted. With your toothpaste, there's nothing leveragable about gay identity through that. . . . That's why you get companies who wouldn't be in the gay market at all, that are very conservative, but that are in there because their product is very leveragable to the gay identity. Proctor & Gamble would not be in there, but there's Whitestrips, [because for gays] appearance is very important. Hair care, skin care, it's right up there in terms of spending. So it's not a question of how much money you make, it's how much you spend in the category.[36]

When I asked Buford how companies try to make products leveragable, he explained,

> To the extent that your product is need-specific, or can be marketed through lifestyle, you can do something with the gay market. Toothpaste is not marketed through lifestyle. High-image products are marketed to lifestyle. And particular need products like financial services: I want to know about shared access for nonmarried couples, that's a need I have based on my identity. That's leveragable.[37]

Companies offering gay-specific products, services, or expertise have more obvious leverage with gay consumers; others—those selling image goods, in particular—attempt to establish leverage between their goods and gay consumers. As with other advertising that semiotically links products with desirable connotations (Chanel No. 5 with Catherine Deneuve and, by extension, with sexy Frenchness, as Judith Williamson demonstrates),[38] some companies aim to articulate the attractive features of the gay male stereotype—trendsetting, stylish, urban—to their product. There is no natural relationship between, say, Prada clothes and *Out*'s readers, but advertisers, publishers, and marketers more generally encourage such relationships. By doing so, they hope to construct an association between image products and gay people to suggest a particular kind of well-being for gay consumers and, by association, for the heterosexual majority who want to cash in on gay cachet. As Michael Bronski writes,

> Some gay men have been happy to be placed in the position of trendsetters and taste purveyors because it has accorded them a measure of social status and conformity. Ironically, when gay sensibility is used as a sales pitch, the strategy is that gay images imply distinction and nonconformity, granting straight consumers a longed-for place outside of the humdrum mainstream.[39]

In our discussion of gay-themed ads from Deutsch, Liz Gumbiner attempted to naturalize this relationship between products and a gay sensibility. She said that she would not do a gay-themed ad unless it was "right": "We do what's right for our clients, and we don't say 'let's go to gay-themed ads' or 'let's do ads directed at women'; we do what's right for everybody. And what's right for Mistic and Tanqueray and Ikea, and if it's right for someone else, we'll do it, and if it's not, it's not." I asked, "How do you—and who decides—what's right?" Gumbiner responded: "If it's right strategically, if it's the right campaign for them to be doing and, conceptually, if it's relevant to them."[40] Gumbiner's emphasis on what is "right" and "relevant" supposes a commonsense association between a product and its marketing, rather than acknowledging that new products are developed with particular constituencies in mind, or that new campaigns actively forge "right" relationships with new consumers. Visibility thus intersects in complex ways with products: some, like the proverbial rainbow flag, bestow gay visibility upon those sporting them; others will (manufacturers hope) become symbols of gay sensibility that will produce for them a hip visibility; still others are popular with gays but avoid an association with the gay market because of a negative image this may project on the product or company.

Getting the Message Out: Gay Marketing Venues

Advertisers' choice of marketing venue depends upon a range of factors that influence all media campaigns, including budget, creative considerations, client, target market, and the function of an ad (augmenting a brand's image versus a special offer, for example). Yet the unique conditions of the gay market pose both opportunities and risks to advertisers. Once marketers have decided to appeal to gay consumers, they must choose a media vehicle—or range of vehicles—with which to do so. At one level this decision appears pragmatic, involving costs per page, circulation and pass-on figures, unique visitors per month, and other data gleaned from media kits. Yet placement for gay marketing also demands attention to the question of visibility: although advertisers want to maximize access to gay consumers, they are often simultaneously concerned that antigay backlash will negatively affect their profits. As a result, marketers carefully choose venues for appealing to gays in order to balance out the benefits and costs of such appeals. Buying space in gay lifestyle magazines is only one approach to gay marketing, even if it has had the highest profile. Other venues include the Internet, local gay papers, sponsorship of gay groups and events, direct mail, general-market media, gay cable channels, and public relations communication.

The exponential rise in gay marketing during the 1990s has been attributed in large part to "the emergence of national magazines that are less political and more lifestyle oriented."[41] *Advertising Age* reported that advertising revenues for gay magazines increased 150 percent to $21.8 million in 1997 alone, and these publications have proven remarkably resilient to the economic recession of the early 2000s, increasing their total number of ad pages by 34 percent between 2001 and 2002.[42] High-quality paper stock, full-color printing, and high production values have increasingly drawn national advertisers to the pages of gay glossies. Indeed, most gay magazines are dependent on advertisers for the majority of their revenues: for example, *Q San Francisco*'s publisher Don Tuthill told me that advertising accounts for 90 percent of his magazine's income.[43]

Growing revenue for gay magazines encouraged their rapid diversification and proliferation throughout the 1990s, with titles designed to appeal to men, women, entrepreneurs, parents, and tourists, among other segments. This proliferation required each to be distinguished from its competitors, and necessitated a segmentation of both audiences and advertisers. Throughout the 1990s, staff at the two largest gay glossies, *Out* and the *Advocate*, worked to differentiate the publications. Because the demographics of both publications' readers were similar in age, income, education, and geographical region, each magazine used editorial content, design features, and style to distinguish its publication from the nearest rival. *Advocate* publisher Joe Landry described the *Advocate* as "*Time* meets *Entertainment Weekly*";[44] John Finco, director of marketing at *Out*, suggested that while the *Advocate* was more like *Newsweek*, *Out* resembled *Vanity Fair*.[45] *Out*'s president, Henry Scott, acknowledged that some vehicles were more appropriate for certain advertisers than others: "Our publisher will kill me for saying this, but there are some advertisers who I think belong in a news magazine more than in a style-oriented magazine like *Out*."[46] *Out* may be ideal as an "upscale" context to improve a product's image, but not so fitting for retail ads—promotions, price offers, coupons—that tend to be seen as more prosaic and that require shorter production schedules. Henry Scott further distinguished the advertisers coming to *Out* from those at the *Advocate*, saying that *Out* "appealed to those advertisers who were nervous about the gay and lesbian community because [the magazine] was not as political as the *Advocate* needs to be, necessarily, because it's a news magazine."[47] This rivalry took an ironic turn in 2000 when the *Advocate*'s parent company, Liberation Publications, Inc., bought *Out*. Since then, LPI has adjusted the editorial content of each to further facilitate differentiation between the titles.

Howard Buford and Henry Scott both described the segmentation of gay magazine publishing as reflecting an "evolution" common in media serving increasingly established communities. Buford compared race and gay niche publishing:

> In the gay market there's not as much segmentation because the evolution of the market just isn't at the same point yet as the African American market or the Hispanic market. But you are starting to see more segmentation—the real issue in the gay market in terms of media is who is going to find the formula that is going to get the kind of readership like *Ebony* magazine [did] with the African American market.[48]

Scott suggested that the segmentation of gay media reflected not just marketers' and publishers' sophistication, but an increasing complexity of gay communities that warranted diverse media:

> It's actually been an interesting thing in the development of *Out* and the development of media for the gay and lesbian community, and I liken it a lot to immigrant communities because I think in some ways it's the same. As more of us have come out, as we have arguably become more sophisticated and complicated, and we have more institutions and subdivisions and we are now communi*ties* rather than a community, I think what's happened is that the media world has changed too, and there's now room for different media that are more narrowly focused.[49]

Magazine segmentation does not award all its various members with advertising revenue, however. Megan Ishler, ad director at *On Our Backs*, said that getting national advertisers was so hard that she could not even give away the back cover—usually a publication's most desirable advertising page—to non–sex industry advertisers, even to tobacco or alcohol companies, which are normally less squeamish about advertising in "adult" magazines. For different reasons, ads are notably sparse in *Gay Community News*, Boston's nationally distributed, expressly "queer progressive quarterly," which covers community and political issues from a critical perspective. The magazine currently survives on grants from foundations that buoy this nonprofit publication. The lack of national ads in publications with sexual content or a critical perspective reveals the incompatibility between flourishing mainstream marketing and erotic and political environments, suggesting that sex and politics are forms of a visible gay culture less appealing to advertisers than is the trendy, urban, "lifestyle" version.

Gay glossies such as the *Advocate* and *Out* offer advertisers a relatively visible means of accessing gay consumers. In contrast, advertising on the Internet offers more discretion, both for advertisers who believe that the Internet is less monitored by the antigay right wing and for users who may welcome the Web's relative anonymity. Since the mid-1990s the Internet has blossomed as a means to reach gay consumers.[50] PlanetOut, gay.com, and gfn.com, among others, have effectively courted advertisers, including many who do not advertise to gay consumers in other venues; after six consecutive quarters of increasing revenue, PlanetOut Partners announced its first profitable quarter in September 2002.[51] Advertisers have been drawn to the Internet partly because market research reports that gay people spend more than average amounts of time online: a Harris Poll found that 25 percent of gays and lesbians spend more than twenty-one hours per week online, compared with only 18 percent of heterosexuals.[52] PlanetOut Partners reported that gay.com and PlanetOut combined had 5.2 million members and 6 million unique visitors each month, with almost half their revenue coming from personal ads (together they host 1.8 million personal profiles).[53] These sites thus offered advertisers access to more gay consumers than all the national gay publications together, whose combined circulation figures have been estimated at 200,000 to 250,000.[54] Further, gay Web sites attract more women than do gay print media, offering a particularly effective way of appealing to lesbians.[55]

Marketers also believe that the Internet is a particularly good way of getting access to people who do not feel safe buying a gay paper or attending a sponsored gay event. One journalist explains, "Both Gay.com and PlanetOut say they can help marketers solve what PlanetOut calls the 'Closet Paradox': reaching gays who might still be in the closet and might never go to a bar or rally—or even subscribe to a gay publication—but who might look for information or conversation from the privacy that a modem affords."[56] Many advertisers also believe that advertising to gays on the Internet reduces the risk of discovery by antigay groups. As Stuart Elliott surmised, Internet advertising is "a way to market under the radar: if you are a packaged goods company and you are concerned that people in Alabama are going to get mad if you're targeting gay consumers, you could run it on the PlanetOut Web site and who the heck is going to be on the PlanetOut Web site except gay people!"[57] An information technology analyst similarly suggested that "now there's really no risk to advertising to [the gay] niche because you have dedicated sections online that are for this community."[58] This suggests there is a widespread, if erroneous, belief among advertisers that some media reach only gay people, offering protection from reactionary backlash.

When marketers tout the Internet as a means of gaining access to unprecedented numbers of gay and lesbian consumers, they tend to ignore the fact that not all GLBT people have computers, modems, Internet service providers, and the skills to use them. This excludes the less affluent, people who are not technologically confident, and those who do not have the privacy to surf the Web (for example, people whose computer access is at work, not at home). Assumptions about the value of the Internet for marketing thus reproduce existing stereotypes of ideal gay consumers, because those who are more likely to have Internet access are also more likely to be privileged in other ways valued by marketers.[59]

Further, the privacy of the Internet has recently come into question. Sites such as gay.com and PlanetOut ask members to divulge a great deal of private information in order to "personalize" their accounts, bartering the details of their identifications, choices, and practices in return for free membership.[60] While all the major GLBT Internet portals have explicit privacy statements that agree not to disclose personal information even to their advertisers, they nevertheless collect IP and cookie information to accumulate data if not on individuals, on trends in Internet activity among their users. A greater risk to personal privacy comes from recent efforts to link anonymous online activity with individual surfers' information. By linking direct mail databases and placing identifying cookies on an Internet user's hard drive, DoubleClick offers advertisers a means to track online activity and link it with users' personal information (name, address, workplace, and so on).[61] In response to opposition from privacy advocates, DoubleClick established a consumer privacy advisory board, including a representative from PlanetOut.[62] Nevertheless, it seems that truly anonymous, untraceable Web activity is an unachievable ideal for gay users, as with other populations, but the stakes for gay Web surfers may be higher: gay-specific Internet activity may bring to surfers an unwanted visibility.

If Internet surfing is dogged by questions of anonymity, local gay newspapers in contrast offer GLBT readers often free and untraceable access to information, news, and mostly local advertisers. Rivendell Marketing's president and CEO, Todd Evans, explained that with an estimated cumulative reach of five million monthly readers, he can place an ad in only ten local papers and still reach as many readers as he would in the *Advocate* and *Out*.[63] According to Evans, national magazines "stole the show" in the early to mid-1990s in terms of trade press attention, but local publications had their own advertising boom during that decade, mostly in increased local business advertising. *Advertising Age* reported that local gay newspaper revenue rose 23.9 percent to $56.2 million in 1997, almost double that of national gay glossies.[64] This revenue, however, is divided among many more local than national publications: Evans estimated that there are more than 200 local gay publications, compared with fewer than twenty national publications.[65]

Although national magazines successfully built a lucrative advertising base from national corporations, less than 10 percent of ad revenues in local and regional gay and lesbian publications comes from high-paying national advertisers.[66] National advertisers in gay media, as with general-market media, prefer the production values glossy magazines offer over black-and-white printing on lower-quality newsprint stock.[67] Those national corporations that advertise in local gay publications may be looking for what Evans called a "backdoor into the gay market," a route by which nervous advertisers can reach gay consumers without attracting attention from trade magazines and antigay organizations.[68] Yet as Anheuser-Busch found when it ran an ad for Bud Light in *EXP*, a gay biweekly publication in St. Louis, Missouri, Jerry Falwell has his eye on local publications too (fig. 4.2).[69] Falwell complained that the ad "presents two Bud-drinking homosexual men in a hand-holding posture"—scandalous indeed—and encouraged readers of his "Falwell Confidential" e-mail newsletter to call the brewing company to complain.[70] This event suggests that antigay groups are fully aware of marketing activity in a range of gay media, and that the fantasy of the discreet "backdoor" may be more a gay marketer's reassuring gesture to encourage nervous advertisers than a real protection against religious fundamentalist ire.[71]

Corporate sponsorship of nonprofit organizations and events is another relatively discreet method of approaching the gay market. Many advertisers see this approach as projecting a positive image of sponsors who, in one marketer's words, "want to be able to somehow build brand loyalty within the [gay] community or increase the number of impressions that they make within the community."[72] Donations to events, groups, community centers, and other organizations are a highly targeted means to raise an advertiser's profile and consumer loyalty. Sponsorship can be simply financial or in-kind, such as the donation of airline tickets for a nonprofit organization's use. In

FIGURE 4.2 BUD LIGHT'S "INAPPROPRIATE" DISPLAY OF AFFECTION (*ADVOCATE*, JUNE 8, 1999).

return, groups include the donor's logo on letterhead, in publicity brochures, on Web sites, and so on. Steve DiBruno, sales representative to the gay market for a national airline, argued that in some cases sponsorship was a more effective approach than conventional advertising. His employer sponsored the Human Rights Campaign which, in return, included the airline's ad in every quarterly review they sent out. Because the distribution of this publication exceeds the circulation of the *Advocate* and *Out* combined, the airline's ad may have been seen by far greater numbers of gay people than a magazine could deliver. Market research found that gays and lesbians recognized this airline's logo more than any other, yet at the time of our interview the airline had never paid for an advertisement in a gay publication. However, the airline's expectations that sponsorship is a lower-profile marketing approach were not met: in 1997 the Family Research Council and other antigay religious groups complained that the airline was "promoting homosexuality" by funding charitable groups.[73]

Some companies sponsor events and groups not to minimize backlash, but to augment existing advertising campaigns in gay media. Event sponsorship, such as Absolut vodka's annual support of the GLAAD Media Awards, tends to be high profile and to encourage consumer use at the event itself. Absolut's ad "Absolut GLAAD" appeared in the gay press showing the trademark bottle as a lava lamp with the GLAAD logo rising in blobs (fig. 4.3). According to an Absolut spokesperson, this was the first time they had "customized an ad to fit one of our not-for-profit partners."[74] The ad thus blended their advertising strategy with their sponsorship program, demonstrating to readers of the gay press their commitment to the GLBT community through their support of a major gay organization. Yet sponsorship by liquor companies has not been uncontroversial: both John Finco and DiBruno commented that although sponsorship of circuit parties in the early to mid-1990s had been popular with alcohol beverage companies and airlines, scandals associated with heavy drug use and casual sex had alienated many early sponsors of these events, who subsequently moved toward "a much more responsible approach."[75] Being "more responsible" meant sponsoring high culture and not necessarily gay-specific events: ballet, art exhibits, and opera. Absolut may have seen its GLAAD ad as a way to emphasize a "more responsible approach," distancing the company from the image of the gay party-boy and emphasizing the more serious sphere of gay media activism.

Companies monitor closely, then, what kind of visibility sponsorship produces, welcoming the positive image it solicits from grateful GLBT consumers, while attempting to avoid negative publicity and homophobic retribution. In contrast to advertising and sponsorship, direct mail offers perhaps the most

FIGURE 4.3 A MERGER OF BUSINESS AND POLITICS IN "ABSOLUT GLAAD"
(IMAGES: A JOURNAL OF THE GAY AND LESBIAN ALLIANCE AGAINST
DEFAMATION, SUMMER 2001).

"closeted" form of marketing. Companies send correspondence directly to prospective consumers, hoping that this transaction is invisible to anyone who may potentially be hostile either to the company or to the recipient of the appeal. Direct mail has the added advantage of appealing to consumers who identify as gay but who do not read publications, do not attend sponsored events and, in Sean Strub's words, have "never given to a gay organization, never been part of any kind of movement."[76] Using proliferating lists from gay publications, catalogs, charities, vendors of gay products, Web sites, and so on, Strub and other direct marketers construct a sophisticated "prospecting universe" for gay-targeted mail in order to catch consumers who may not otherwise be exposed to marketing messages. Although marketers might hope to reach every gay-identified person in the United States through this method, direct mail prospectors know that older, more affluent male gays with geographically stable lives tend to be overrepresented on mailing lists, and younger, less well off, geographically transient GLBT people tend not to appear as often.[77]

Direct mail lists not only suffer from the problem of omission but also inevitably include names of people who don't, or don't publicly, identify as gay: as Howard Buford quipped, "Sir, I can't help it if your wife opened your mail and asked you why this was sent to you."[78] Strub recalled some hostile responses to gay direct mail from people whose names had turned up on gay pornography lists: "In 1985 . . . the only lists we could get were erotic product lists and so on, [for] which we got intense hate mail, even from people who were buying gay pornography. That was one thing, but you get something in your mailbox that's talking about having a gay *identity*, it's just really something else."[79] Errors in prospecting for gay consumers suggest that not all people who read gay porn or who donate to gay causes also have same-sex erotic or romantic relationships, and even that those who do may not comfortably self-identify as gay.

Another problem with direct mail concerns the belief that there are any truly private methods by which advertisers can reach gay consumers in a climate where gay marketing is news. Buford developed AT&T's 1994 "Let your true voice be heard" direct marketing campaign, which used gay and AIDS-related mailing lists to appeal to gay and lesbian consumers. Yet his story suggests that antigay groups monitor the gay and trade presses for information about national corporate marketing activity in this as well as other forms; they responded to this campaign by boycotting AT&T and promoting a Christian-owned long-distance company. Buford recalled:

> It was a real chance for [the Christian right wing] to—it was a real stand
> for them to take. They can't hurt Seagram's, they can't hurt liquor com-

panies—they aren't buying their products anyway—they can't hurt the cigarette companies, but they saw a chance there, so they took it. Quite frankly, also, because they have their own long-distance [phone] organization that lines their pockets, it's called Lifeline, I think: "the only long-distance company centered around Jesus Christ," I think it is. So, of course, in those letters of boycotting, [recipients were told] "here's how you sign up for Lifeline." So it was really a marketing effort for themselves, it was a very slick way to get people to sign up for their long-distance [service] and for them to make money personally.[80]

This strategy demonstrates the skill with which antigay groups have not only acted effectively against GLBT initiatives but also profited in the process.

Direct mail can also bring an unwanted visibility to marketers themselves. During the 1990s, Sean Strub's direct mail company, Strubco, distributed packs of advertising cards to a large number of gay and AIDS-related lists:

I had a nightmare for a couple of years in my hometown because my Mom hosted a fund-raiser for [the] AIDS Action Council and a bunch of their friends gave money and got on our [direct mail] database that was also used to send cardpacks to. There was Sean's hello from the card-pack message upfront, with various porn cards scattered throughout (although never highly explicit images). My parents got grief, understandably, and it was not a pretty chapter.[81]

Thus although direct mail may seem a good way to control the visibility marketers offer advertisers, neither the mail system nor list compilation routines are as watertight as direct marketers hope.

At the opposite end of the spectrum of visibility from direct mail is gay marketing that appears in general-market media. Marketers hope that gay appeals in generic contexts will reach consumers not otherwise connected to gay publishing, Internet sites, sponsored events, or direct mailing lists. A small number of gay-specific television commercials have aired for generic and gay products, including Ikea furniture, Mistic beverages, and Olivia Cruises, none of which was nationally broadcast. Ikea's ad, which showed two men buying a table together as a symbol of their romantic commitment, appeared only in those markets where Ikea has stores and aired after 10 P.M., so the company "couldn't be accused of shoving homosexuality down children's throats," explained Patrick O'Neil, the ad's art director.[82] Mistic's ad appeared on youth-targeted cable channels such as MTV. The ABC network assessed Olivia's ad as "politically motivated" and therefore inappropriate for national broadcast, despite the fact that an ad for another cruise company showing greater physical intimacy between male and female actors was aired by ABC at this time and was thus not considered, by the network's standards, "politically motivated." This refusal required Olivia to undertake the time-consuming and costly enterprise of negotiating individually with affiliates to air its ad during the coming-out episode of *Ellen*. Despite these limits on airing gay-themed television commercials, Andrew Beaver nevertheless saw these ads as more effective than ads in gay media, both because more gay consumers watch television than regularly read gay publications and surf the Web, and because the commercials increased gay visibility for heterosexual audiences who would not otherwise see gay commercial images. Ikea and Mistic risked antigay consumer backlash in order to capitalize on the very publicity that gay-themed television commercials would garner in terms of national press interest, and these ads remain famous even among consumers who have never seen the ads themselves. Yet according to O'Neil and Liz Gumbiner, copywriter for the Mistic commercial, both companies suffered backlash as a result of these very public campaigns: an Ikea store received a bomb threat and a Mistic distributor in the South dropped its contract with the company. As a result, both ads aired for only a limited time and subsequent campaigns abandoned their "diversity" strategies.

Describing a more circumspect approach, Stuart Elliott surmised that advertisers who want to covertly attract gay consumers place ads during commercial breaks in television shows with large gay audiences, particularly those with gay characters: "You have Proctor & Gamble advertising on *Will & Grace*. So, you know, they wouldn't have done that four or five years ago. . . . They can probably assume that some of the people watching—some of the people watching *every* show are gay—but you can probably assume that *Will & Grace* has a somewhat larger gay audience than most programs."[83] The question then becomes whether advertisers that want to appeal to gay audiences become interested in shows that happen to have gay characters, or whether program writers include more characters in the hopes that they will draw a sizable gay audience and then use this audience to attract advertisers.

Some marketers also suggested that advertisers reach gay consumers through generic print media with a large proportion of gay readers. Howard Buford asserted that advertising in *Men's Health* is a more "efficient buy" than many gay-specific magazines because *Men's Health*'s circulation is larger and, anecdotally at least, includes a large proportion of gay men.[84] Stephanie Gibbons, marketer at Showtime, explained that advertising for the American version of *Queer as Folk*

> was broad: we were in *People*, in *Vanity Fair*, in the *New York Times*, the *LA Times*. We were also in the *Advocate*, in *Out*, in all of the targeted media. But over 80 percent of our media expenditure was in broad-based media.

> As a lesbian I hate to confess that I do not read the *Advocate*, every single issue. I do not focus my media time on just gay and lesbian media, I focus it on all sorts of media. And we felt from the outset that the best way of reaching the gay and lesbian population was to be in broad media.[85]

Acknowledging her own experience as a lesbian with varied media consumption patterns afforded Gibbons a perspective that proved successful. According to senior vice president Gene Falk, Showtime added "at least a couple of hundred thousand subscribers" to its base of "somewhere in the vicinity of 15 million" when it promoted *Queer as Folk*, which quickly became the channel's top-rated show.[86]

Using a similar strategy, gfn.com placed full-page ads in the *Wall Street Journal, Entertainment Weekly, Time*, and other national, general-market media. Gfn.com's CEO Walter Schubert explained, "I always wanted to get into mainstream media, believing that our target market was people who read things like the *Wall Street Journal*, the *New York Times* and *Vogue*, and whatever. I felt that the market didn't necessarily reside completely in publications like the *Advocate* and *Out*. So in trying to reach the [gay] market [I] felt that the mainstream was definitely a place that shouldn't be ignored."[87]

Feedback to the gfn.com campaign in general-market media suggested that this broad appeal won appreciation from prospective customers. At a panel on gay marketing and the Internet, gfn.com's president Jeffrey Newman read a letter from a *Wall Street Journal* reader who expressed gratitude for the very different kind of visibility that the gfn.com ad offered. The writer identified himself as

> a nearly 60-year-old gay man who has worked in the financial sector for the last thirty years; for most of that time I remained in the closet. When my partner passed away four years ago I could tell no one, certainly not anyone in my company. Two years ago I came out, and today things are much different. Never in my life did I think I'd see the day when a gay company would advertise in the mainstream, or be accepted in the mainstream, much less a financial company, and much less a gay financial company advertising in a paper like the *Wall Street Journal*. I began to cry when I saw this. I never knew your site existed, because I don't read gay publications, and for the first time as a gay man in the financial field I felt proud. Your ad made me realize how far we've come.[88]

This letter suggests that explicit appeals in general-market media may in fact be hugely successful in winning support of gay readers, which is especially valuable if readers are not also reading gay-specific media. Yet despite this appreciation and critical acclaim, and contrary to Showtime's success, Schubert told me that the campaign had not won the site significant new business:

> There were very few responses to these ads. If I had seven million dollars all over again, I promise you, I wouldn't waste it on ads in the *New York Times* or the *Wall Street Journal*. . . . I would be much more grassroots-oriented. I would be spending money at business expositions, cosponsoring seminars and conferences, supporting some of the political groups that are out there campaigning for equal rights for the gay community. I'd spend a great deal of money in that direction, rather than just buying full-page ads in magazines.[89]

Schubert also believed that advertising for Internet products and services should be done on the Internet to maximize click-through rates.

As the example from gfn.com suggests, the strategy of advertising in general-market media is an even less certain advertising prospect than usual. David Mulryan, partner of the gay-specific agency Mulryan/Nash, commented that he would love to help advertisers target gays in national newspapers: "the *Boston Globe* has gay readers, but we don't know how many, we don't know what they are like, we don't know where they live."[90] Questions therefore remain about whether general-market appeals are appropriate for all campaigns. However appreciative gay consumers may be, gratitude does not necessarily correspond to subscriptions or purchases.

The most recent approach to appealing to gay consumers comes from gay-specific cable television channels. U.S. efforts to launch a 24-hour channel dedicated to gay content date back to 1994, when Marvin Schwam founded Gay Entertainment Television. He began by producing three shows a month and bought time on local cable channels in viable markets to air them, paying for this time with advertising slots throughout the show. His intention, however, was to launch a gay cable channel "within two years," a goal that never came to fruition.[91] Canada's gay cable channel PrideVision was launched in 2001 and soon after unsuccessfully attempted to boost subscription figures from 20,000 to the 240,000 necessary to remain profitable.[92] As a result, the channel cut almost all its original programming and laid off staff in December 2002, while plans to launch PrideVision in the American market have languished.[93] Back in the United States, Viacom's subsidiaries Showtime and MTV announced that their premium gay cable channel, Outlet, would launch in the spring of 2003, according to a leaked memo.[94] Outlet was to be supported by a hybrid model that combines subscriptions (predicted to be about

$6 per month) with "non-traditional advertising opportunities: . . . program sponsorships, product placements and other tie-ins," according to the same memo. Outlet was shelved while Viacom waited out the economic recession, reappearing as MTV's Logo, to launch in 2005. Dedicated gay cable is an uncertain economic investment, and faces the multifarious challenges of negotiating distribution contracts with cable carriers, appealing to a sufficient number of subscribers, winning contracts with advertisers, and raising funds for original programming. Of all the basic cable stations currently available, Bravo is arguably the de facto gay channel, offering the hit makeover show *Queer Eye for the Straight Guy* and the gay dating game *Boy Meets Boy*.

Gay marketing visibility is not only produced through gay-specific media and targeted campaigns, however, but also through the efforts of PR executives who work with trade and popular press journalists to generate interest in gay-focused campaigns. Both Patrick O'Neil and Liz Gumbiner reported that their gay-themed commercials garnered a huge amount of publicity that was received ambivalently by Ikea and Mistic beverages. According to O'Neil, Ikea played down the significance of its gay spot, unsuccessfully trying to prevent it from overshadowing the rest of the campaign. Mistic executives became anxious when their lesbian spot received a great deal of press coverage, and so didn't capitalize on it, to Gumbiner's frustration. Andrew Beaver, who oversaw both campaigns, argued that even if the company expressed nervousness about press coverage, this was nevertheless good for them because it raised the campaign's profile through word-of-mouth. He said, "Of all the people that are aware that Ikea did that ad, I would say maybe 10 percent saw it: . . . it got talked up, it was in the *Advocate*, it was a national news story, it was a big deal."[95] Some marketers suggested that certain advertisers cynically produce high-profile, gay-themed spots simply to garner press coverage, without showing a commitment to gay consumers in terms of company policies, sponsorship, or sustained support of gay media. Stuart Elliott complained that Virgin Cola's 1998 television commercial, which showed two men kissing during a commitment ceremony, "never ran. Nobody ran it. A lot of times they'll put a gay theme in an ad because they know it'll be controversial, and they know it won't be accepted and then they get a lot of publicity, . . . you know: 'Virgin Cola redefines cutting edge.' This is baloney. They knew that nobody was ever going to run that ad; to me that's somewhat disingenuous. It's exploitative because they know the ads aren't going to run."[96] Liz Gumbiner worried that Deutsch's use of a lesbian theme in the Mistic ad would be seen as similarly exploiting gay visibility: "We were concerned that people would think we were being gratuitous, like using homosexuality to sell something, and we didn't want it to come across that way at all."[97] In order to offset this charge, Gumbiner explained that the spot aimed to be sincere, genuine, and avoid the shock of revelation. The ad "was trying to show some emotion; it felt more sort of the sensitive side of it as opposed to an easy joke. It wasn't supposed to be a joke, and in fact we didn't want the spot to be revealed, like it's her and then *ta-da*! [She's gay!] . . . I think some people go for the joke like 'Surprise! It's a gay man.' And to me that's like a cheap, easy shot."[98] The belief that advertisers use gay themes to drum up press attention and increase consumer awareness may be well founded: Patrick O'Neil estimated that the Ikea commercial generated "ten million dollars of free publicity, at least" from national press coverage.[99] Yet this strategy may also be seen as taking advantage of the contested visibility of gays simply in order to increase the visibility of the brand across markets.

We can thus see advertisers negotiating a line of visibility in gay marketing. Although they want to maximize their product's profile among gay consumers, they are often ambivalent about, and attempt to contain, the visibility of their gay-themed appeals with the general population. Because these containment strategies attempt to limit gay visibility to gay communities alone, they somewhat undercut marketers' claims that gay marketing is good for gay people because it increases gay visibility to the mainstream. Further, the presence of advertising influences what other kinds of visibility venues will allow: increasingly, gay magazines, papers, and Internet sites refuse sexual content and, in some cases, eschew overtly or antagonistically political perspectives in order to provide a hospitable environment for advertising.

Out, Proud, Gay Rainbows: Gay Significations

Choosing products and venues to appeal to gay consumers constitutes only two of the mechanisms by which marketers produce gay visibility; gay marketing also necessitates representational routines to construct a recognizable gayness. Because being gay does not always show, gay marketers must depend on gay coding, stereotyping, and typification to produce gay-themed ads. Yet to appeal to gay consumers, marketers must negotiate the continued, embattled status of gay subcultures within the mainstream by engaging the most conventionally "positive" stereotypes and suppressing other, long-standing negative images of gays and lesbians. Marketers therefore walk a narrow line between making gayness visible, and making it too visible in ways that alienate people, whether this is gays themselves (through the use of clichéd images, for example), or the antigay right wing which is offended by overtly gay appeals.

For many years, national advertisers have placed generic ads in gay media, avoiding the expense and expertise required to produce gay-specific copy.

There is some debate over whether these ads are sufficiently targeted to appeal to gay consumers, however. *Out*'s Henry Scott suggested that generic ads in gay and lesbian publications were acceptable as long as they were not "flagrantly heterosexual" or, according to Don Tuthill, did not show very sexy women in gay men's magazines such as *Genre*.[100] Other interviewees believed that GLBT audiences see generic advertising as cheap and uncommitted, as "just going after the money."[101] Reviewing developments in gay marketing since the mid-1990s, Howard Buford said:

> It was enough for the consumer to say "Oh wow, they ran an ad in *Out* magazine, [therefore] they must be gay-friendly." But now your competition is doing something a little more direct, and making a stronger relationship, a stronger connection to the consumer. Well, you have to do it too. It's more competitive, and that's how it evolves.[102]

Marketers are increasingly compelled to produce gay-specific ads, which challenges them to find ways to signal to readers that these are intended for gay audiences. Common representational routines include using recognizably "gay" or stereotypical images, showing same-sex couples, using gay iconography, and making appeals to gay subcultural knowledge. Each of these strategies involves a process of encoding by advertising creatives, and a more or less transparent decoding by gay audiences.[103] Yet the processes by which ad creatives devise strategies are notoriously hard to investigate: advertising researchers Karen Shapiro and Randall Rothenberg both comment on the difficulty of gaining access to the creative process whereby agency art directors and writers come up with the "big idea" for an ad.[104] Shapiro regrets that "no complete or even representative listing of the construction principles that abound in the industry is possible here; each creative person uses a slightly different set and most of them are not articulated."[105] Yet she notes some of the ways in which routines of ad production employ stereotypes to facilitate both the production and reading of commercials: the stylists "try to make the characters look typical of whatever they are playing so that there is no confusion in the mind of the audience or their colleagues about who they are supposed to be."[106]

Richard Dyer suggests that typification is employed by GLBT people themselves as an economical means to indicate their sexuality: "Typification, visually recognizable images and self-presentations, is not just something wished on gay people but produced by them."[107] Accordingly, the need for visual cues was not lost on my interviewees. David Mulryan argued that "gay people in general are one of those very strange things in the world that are simply defined by what they are standing next to. They don't exist in isolation. And so how do you portray that? It's impossible, in some ways."[108] In an earlier article, Dyer discusses how stereotypes differ from other forms of social typing: stereotypes are usually imposed on subordinate groups by groups in power, are frequently demeaning, are seen as rigid and unchanging, and are synecdochic (where the stereotyped characteristic—such as flamboyant gayness—is taken to stand for the whole person or group).[109] It is not surprising, then, that the use of stereotypes to signal gayness was one approach recognized—and largely rejected—by my interviewees. *Out*'s ad director Kurt De-Mars recalled an ad "that had a rainbow sticker in the window with some guy in a wife-beater tank top and another guy in cutoff jeans shorts and somebody else wearing freedom rings and it was just trying *so* hard that it was almost offensive."[110] Howard Buford told me that he resisted using the hypersexualized gay man stereotype unless he was working on a campaign that called for this approach: "Until we got a dating service client, we had never done an ad with a guy with his shirt off—I said we just wouldn't do it, you know, we are *not* going to do it! If it's suntan lotion, fine, whatever, but we are not going to do it gratuitously, we are not going to play into [the stereotype]."[111]

Similarly, Patrick O'Neil described wanting to avoid gay stereotyping in the Ikea commercial:

> I think that you can't tell people are gay by the way they look; really, I don't think—unless they are dressed like the Village People, [then] maybe people would go "they look dressed like gay men," or [in] leather, or whatever . . . If they were really buff, wearing super-tight T-shirts and jeans and they were holding hands in the first frame, you'd get they were gay men. But the fact that [the men in the Ikea ad] were shopping and wearing sort of like jeans and Saturday clothes, it didn't tip you off right away.[112]

O'Neil related his anxiety in trying to walk a thin line between offensively stereotyping the gay couple, and "cutting the balls off" the Ikea ad by downplaying their gayness too much:

> I was nervous about it, . . . I felt really responsible for how it was going to work. Because there wasn't a precedent set at all: how gay is too gay? How not gay is not gay enough? . . . When we were casting I knew it was a first and didn't really want to blow it, it would piss off the community. It was the last thing I wanted to do . . . to make people feel like you cut the balls off of this spot. Even when we were editing it together,

I was a little concerned that people would be disappointed that it wasn't gayer, or more overt. Um, but I felt like it was just right.[113]

Through his use of a strikingly emasculating metaphor, O'Neil addresses a fundamental dilemma: how to produce a message readable as gay without using offensive stereotypes. He hoped to avoid stereotyping by casting a "real" gay couple for the Ikea spot, attempts that ultimately resulted in one gay and one heterosexual actor. These casting efforts imply that a real gay couple would automatically and authentically convey "gayness," and that such an authentic gayness could not also appear stereotyped.

O'Neil's and others' solution to the problem of coding a visible gayness while also avoiding overt and potentially offensive stereotypes was to show a same-sex romantic or domestic relationship. Examples interviewees gave of this approach included "two women and a baby in a Subaru"; "boy meets boy" in a hepatitis vaccine ad; "two women . . . one late forties, the other fiftysomething, on a beach together, looking out, probably toward the sunset" in a financial services ad; and two male or two female names on shared travelers' checks.[114] O'Neil's description of the gay couple in the Ikea ad suggests the limits placed on representing couples in order to make them look "normal": "We thought that was a great thing to do, have them shopping together for something, and took their sexuality out of it. It was a couple, any couple, not say[ing] anything about their being gay, they aren't going to come out and say it, they are going to treat it as if it's normal, completely normal."[115] As I discuss more fully in chapter 7, since gay men, in particular, have been demonized as hypersexual, representing an acceptable version of same-sex relationships as "normal" has often led to the decision to present very desexualized images of gay people, to "take their sexuality out of it."

Advertisers have commonly avoided the minefields of stereotyping and sexual intimacy by using gay subcultural knowledge and iconography to signal their address of gay readers, sometimes with the added hope of escaping recognition from heterosexual consumers. Stephanie Blackwood recalled an ad for Naya water that ran in gay publications: "The visual was a very rural, arid land, and the caption was 'West Hollywood, 20 billion years ago.' If you're gay, you get it, if you're not, you don't."[116] This ad demands a knowledge of famously gay neighborhoods in order to get the joke and to make the connection between gayness and Naya water. Other examples of ads appearing in general-market media that allowed for a gay subcultural reading were television commercials for Volkswagen (their "Sunday Afternoon" spot that premiered during the coming-out episode of *Ellen*), and for Quaker Toasted Oat cereal (showing two men bickering over breakfast). *Advertising Age* journalist Michael Wilke described a K-Mart ad with Rosie O'Donnell and Penny Marshall who were

> looking at a tennis bracelet—now tennis is sort of a stereotypical lesbian sport, with Martina Navratilova and that sort of thing, and some other historic stars who are lesbian, and they're looking at it and Penny says— this is sort of the K-Mart line—"K-Mart, who knew?" and Rosie says *"I* knew," and she goes "You never said anything," and then Rosie says "There are lots of things I don't tell you." Then Penny says "What, that thing from last year?" and so it just leaves the viewer going "well, what is that about, what are they talking about?"[117]

This ad invokes gay subcultural knowledge by acknowledging the association between secrecy and gayness, epitomized in the current "Don't ask, don't tell" U.S. military policy on gays, by winking to lesbian fans of the television show *Laverne and Shirley* in which Marshal starred, and by tapping into what were then only rumors concerning O'Donnell's sexual identity.

As self-described "recovering semiotician" Heather Findlay, now editor in chief of *Girlfriends* and *On Our Backs*, writes:

> When it comes to our social lives, lesbians and gay men have compensated for our obscurity by inventing a whole pantheon of "signifiers"— to cite the high-tech jargon used by French literary types to describe any words or symbols that carry meaning—that proclaim our proclivities. The highly touted "gaydar" is simply the name for a well-developed literacy in the signs and signifiers of gay identity.[118]

Findlay summarizes the pantheon of gay signifiers, at least as they stood in 1994: pink and black triangles, rainbow flags, freedom rings, leather, boots, wallets on chains, motorcycles, bandannas, piercings, tattoos, muscles, drag, wigs, boxer shorts, lambdas, labryses, and double-female symbols. She concludes that "the proliferation [of gay signifiers] is itself a sign—this time, of the fact that gay invisibility is fast becoming a modern inconvenience."[119] National corporations have adopted such iconography to identify their gay-specific appeals. One airline representative described his company's upcoming debut into openly gay advertising as showing airplanes flying through rainbows and skywriting a red AIDS ribbon.[120] An agency worker for a brewing company, Patrick Sullivan, described his efforts to employ gay iconography without slipping into cliché or alerting heterosexual audiences:

The rainbow has been used to death by every marketer who has tried to court this group, but we wanted to do the rainbow but do it in a hipper way. So this almost looks like the soft lighting you would see in a disco or something. With a clear [beer] bottle superimposed over it . . . [and] the tagline at the bottom is "OUT"—which is in bold—"in style." So if a straight person looked at that, some who are pretty hip and have gay friends might get it, but the majority wouldn't. They'd be, like, "ah, neat, it has an industrial dance kind of feel to it."[121]

Merely including a word in an ad can signal an advertiser's interest in gay consumers: as Sullivan's example suggests, "OUT" is a popular sign, as is "PRIDE."

The proliferation of gay signifiers has meant both an increase in explicitly gay imagery, and more questions about the sexual sensibility of ads that appear in mainstream publications. In Elliott's words,

Take any issue of *Vanity Fair*—are the ads straight, are they gay, are they bi, what the heck are they? Who knows? I mean, [with] any kind of a hip fashion magazine, or lifestyle magazine aimed at a twenty- or thir-tysomething consumer, you could go through and see dozens of ads, and are they supposed to be mainstream or niche or straight or gay, who the heck knows? . . . There's been a gay sensibility in fashion and a lot of fields for years and years and years. . . . I'm sure it's been there all the time, it's just now that there's quote-unquote, a "gay market," it becomes somewhat more of an issue.[122]

Some interviewees proposed that rather than thinking of some ads as "gay" and others as not, that there are instead levels, or a spectrum, of gay significa-tion. Elliott said, "There are times when clearly the ads are openly gay, and there are times when the ads are in the closet, or when they are just meant to be ambiguous."[123] Andrew Beaver argued that ambiguously gay appeals were beneficial for advertisers because they offer audiences a "message that . . . em-braces them [all]."[124] However, queer media scholar Alexander Doty has called gay connotation the "closet of mass culture" and the "dominant signifying practice of homophobia," allowing media producers to both court and efface gay audiences.[125] Yet, as Doty also recognizes, in the contexts of marketers' ambivalence about stereotyping and of the chaste limits placed on showing same-sex couples, ads that require a campy, subtextual, insider knowledge to "get it" may offer more pleasure to gay audiences than more explicitly gay, po-tentially stereotypical images do.

"Gay visibility" in marketing, as in other media genres, is an ambivalent process: marketers cringe at ads that "try *so* hard" to signal their gay appeal, but must still produce ads that indicate that appeal.[126] The ways in which marketers talk about coding their ads as "gay" suggest a complex set of negotiations among implicit and explicit appeals, typification and stereotyping, romantic yet nonsexualized imagery. Gay signification and typification combine with marketers' choice of products and media vehicles to produce a contained visibility. A 1998 initiative for Dockers khakis shows some of the ways that visibility is produced in a remarkably "out" gay marketing campaign, yet also reveals how marketing norms nevertheless still shape the contours of that visibility.

It's Not About the Pants, It's About the People

The November 1998 issue of *Out* magazine contained an unusual insert titled "Inside Out" (see figs. 2.6 and 2.7, pp. 44 and 45). This 12-page Dockers khakis advertorial, an elaborate advertising section which resembles editorial content, featured ten "gay role models . . . men [and] women who have positively moved the gay culture forward through their unique style, personal action, and independence of spirit," according to Levi's marketing specialist, Mark Malinowski.[127] The advertorial portrayed actors Mitchell Anderson, Wilson Cruz, and Guinevere Turner; good samaritan Thomas Rollerson; youth advocate Rea Carey; gay rights campaigner James Dale; writer Brad Gooch; television producer Max Mutchnick; photographer Eve Fowler; and athlete Bruce Hayes. Grainy black-and-white images on card stock depicted the role models in dramatic lighting, moody poses, and the requisite pair of Dockers flat-front khakis. The images were accompanied by text giving the models' names, professional roles, and short descriptions of their accomplishments. The advertorial exhorted readers to "show personal conviction—and . . . to be true to yourself." Produced by the combined efforts of Levi's and *Out*'s sales and creative staff, the Dockers insert offers an example of gay marketing that is distinct in its form and its collaborative relationships from ordinary advertising. I was interested in whether its atypical production routines disrupted the representational routines of gay marketing, and how the advertorial's producers handled thorny issues of typification and stereotyping, products and people, business and politics.

The advertorial brought together Dockers' parent company (Levi Strauss), *Out*, ten gay and lesbian role models, GLSEN (the Gay, Lesbian, and Straight Education Network), the Hetrick-Martin Institute, and other youth-oriented organizations. It represents a newer trend in marketing that aims to forge especially compelling links between consumers and products by combining advertising with sponsorship. As Caitlin Hume, production coordinator for the advertorial, explained: "People are getting jaded and cynical, and want more, want something that really speaks to who they are, hits them where they live, has emotional resonance which is the key stock-in-trade of the Dockers piece, to give to people who don't have many role models a wonderful array of high-profile and low-profile [people]."[128] Hume and others wanted to shift the emphasis from the product to a broader sense of social justice. As Malinowski said, "It's not about the pants . . . it's about the people."[129]

The impetus for the advertorial came from Levi's long-standing commitment to the GLBT community, and the company's wish to transform the image of their Dockers brand to appeal to a younger market. Over the previous fifteen years, Levi's had donated more than $20 million to AIDS groups, was the first Fortune 500 company to offer domestic partner benefits to unmarried partners of employees, and had withdrawn their support of the Boy Scouts of America over its ousting of an openly gay man, James Dale.[130] According to Stuart Elliott,

> Levi Strauss, which is based in San Francisco, has been for decades on the vanguard in terms of "gay-friendly corporate policy"—nondiscrimination clauses, domestic partnership benefits, so on and so forth—yet until . . . two years ago . . . Levi Strauss had never run advertising, whether a mainstream regular campaign or a specifically tailored campaign . . . with gay and lesbian content, had never run advertising in gay media, yet the company was among the very most—maybe *the* most—progressive, in terms of its own internal policies.[131]

Levi's had resisted entering the market earlier because, according to Malinowski, the company did not want to appear as though they were exploiting their pro-gay employment policies for purely marketing gain and, further, had not yet developed marketing strategies specifically tailored to gay consumers.[132]

In 1998, Levi's began to experiment with placing ads in gay media, spending half a million dollars on gay-targeted advertising even before the advertorial came out. Lou Fabrizio, then *Out*'s publisher, recalled meeting with their West Coast advertising manager and the vice president for marketing at Dockers: together they "discussed the need for Dockers to do a major branding impact on the gay market."[133] Malinowski explained that Levi's was looking to shift the image of Dockers khakis away from an association with "your father's khakis" and "casual Fridays,"[134] toward "25–34-year-olds . . . whom we call urban modernists. When we looked at who made up that group, gay men and lesbians are a large part of it."[135]

The Dockers advertorial was not the first effort of this type; *Out* had already developed in-house "co-branding" productions with other advertisers. The July 1998 issue contained a pull-out advertising supplement, "Out to Party," a cocktail and party guide sponsored primarily by Seagram's, distributor of longtime advertiser Absolut vodka.[136] Similarly, Levi's had already experimented with advertorials elsewhere. Malinowski explained:

> I'd worked on a couple of advertorials with Dockers khakis. One appeared in *Vogue* that focused on women in film and actresses [and] received such a positive response that we sat down with the Dockers team [to develop new ideas]. We were placing these ads in *Out*, but we were like "what can we do that's really untraditional advertising? What can we do that can really speak to the gay consumer in a way that's relevant to him or her, in a way that's going to be truly meaningful . . . to hit that emotional hot button?"[137]

As research by Greenfield Online and others suggest, gay consumers are more likely to look positively on advertising they perceive to be created with them in mind.[138] But according to Malinowski, "it can't just be about advertising" because gay consumers want marketers "to place our brands in front of them in a meaningful, relevant way," what Elliott describes as "cause-related marketing."[139] From the beginning, the project was framed with an emphasis on heroes: Malinowski said that he and the *Out* team had decided "to focus on highlighting gay men and women who have really stuck their necks out there, who have succeeded in whatever field it was—entertainment, being an activist, whatever they did—and look at those people, salute those people."[140] The focus on heroes also linked back to Levi's emphasis on sponsorship. Hitting gay consumers'"emotional hot button" involved recruiting the role models in support of gay youth to show that Levi's was "giv[ing] back" to the gay community.[141] As Fabrizio explained, "GLSEN is an organization that benefits gay youth and it was a perfect tie-in—gay role models as people for the gay youth to look up to and emulate."[142]

As with all advertorials, the Dockers insert stretches the usual routines of marketing. It blurs the boundaries between advertising and editorial content even more than the normal practices of producing an advertising-compatible editorial environment do. In addition, it changed the relationship between the advertiser and the magazine's staff, who became account planners and creatives for the project. Thus, rather than using their usual advertising agency personnel, Dockers worked with Lou Fabrizio, Dan Lori, Caitlin Hume, and Donna Capossela, *Out*'s publisher, creative director, production coordinator, and intern, respectively. Hume described the value of using *Out*'s expertise in appealing to their readers for

> advertisers who'd love to talk to the [gay] market but don't know how to. [They] are scared to farm it out to an agency, because in many places the big, heavy-hitting agencies don't have the research or the knowledge themselves, but [want] to turn the magazine into an ad agency, since we know our world best. We can tell it in a way that's going to apply to readers, [so] it makes a lot of sense.[143]

The selection of heroes for the piece required Malinowski, Fabrizio, Lori, and Scott to decide who was "appropriate and then . . . narrow the list down to make sure the people were available and willing for the shoot."[144] They were looking for a balance between celebrities and activists, and were concerned less with conventional attractiveness than with an embodied, readable quality of "heroism." As Hume said, "I wouldn't say they're glamorous, but they've all got rather an interesting look, and there's a depth of character that comes through in their faces, and it wasn't enough for them to be rather brilliant at what they did, we wanted to see if that showed."[145] Hume also related that some of the more famous people originally shortlisted—including Gus Van Sant, Anne Heche, Ellen DeGeneres, and Ru Paul—were not available at the time of the shoot. From her perspective this turned out to be an advantage because it produced a piece with less "razzle-dazzle" and more "depth."[146]

Hume showed me the lists of possible talent from which final selections were made; these suggest complex negotiations in what constitutes a gay "hero." In the initial lists were many women, some bisexuals (such as Ani Di Franco, musician), Latina/os (José Muñoz, academic), African Americans (Linda Villarosa, journalist), Asian Americans (Gregg Araki, film director), "seniors" (Paul Cadmus, painter), drag queens (Candis Cayne), and sex industry workers (Lukas Ridgeston, porn star, and Chi Chi Larue, porn producer). Yet the final lineup shows seven youngish men, one of whom is a person of color, and three apparently white, also youngish, women. None of these role models works in the sex industry, at least not to my knowledge, and all are conventionally gendered; Ru Paul was the only drag queen invited to the project and declined. No older people were selected to appear, reflecting Hume's notes from one meeting that indicated that Levi's was only interested in "models in the 25–35-year-old range."

Another striking element of the original lists of possible talent is that although all names were identified by profession, only the women, people of color, and older people were identified by gender, race, and age: younger white men were not. "Navratilova, Martina, former tennis champ, female" follows "Muñoz, José, academic focusing on queer theory (NYU), Latino," which in turn follows "Montello, Joe, Broadway director." (None of these people appeared in the final advertorial.) The fact that younger white men are unmarked in this list suggests both that people are assumed to be white, male, and not old, unless identified otherwise, and that race, gender, and age were important factors in the selection process. I asked Hume whether the ratio of seven men to three women intentionally reflected the distribution of *Out*'s readership:

> There has been some talk about the balance of the sexes, . . . there were all sorts of criteria, . . . we had X amount of celebrities that we wanted, and obviously that number shifted. There were X amount of sports people that we wanted, so there were all sorts of criteria before that. . . . And funnily enough it was harder to get women. . . . I know there was a little sense that there should be more of a balance. I suppose the fact that *Out*'s readers are seventy-thirty male made the higher male balance make sense as well.[147]

Hume and her assistant on the project, Donna Capossela, later explained that there had been some contention about the inclusion of Wilson Cruz, the only person of color included in the advertorial, who played a biracial, nascently sexual, feminine young man on the television drama *My So-Called Life*. They told me that either photographer Carter Smith or creative director Dan Lori had resisted Cruz's participation because they didn't like his "look." Malinowski, however, insisted that he be included. I asked if Cruz was the only person of color included, and Hume and Capossela thought about it and said yes. When I suggested that it might be important to represent some racial diversity, they were rather reticent to respond and seemed uncomfortable. Although they had freely acknowledged the gender imbalance, it seemed harder to talk about the racial imbalance, or to reflect on what it was about Cruz's "look" that was—initially, at least—undesirable to some members of the *Out* team.

The talent's reasons for involvement were various. Levi's offered each model $1,000 for their time, paid either to them or to their charity of choice (arguably a paltry sum given the company's profits and advertising budget). They also paid travel and hotel expenses for the couple of days they were in New York for the shoot. Some talent welcomed the free publicity that appearing in the advertorial would offer their causes. For example, Hume recalled that Thomas Rollerson, who runs Dalmatian Dreams (now the Dream

Foundation) that fulfills the last wishes of people dying from AIDS-related ill-
nesses, had missed the deadline to send in application materials for the project. "And then he called me at home . . . and I wouldn't say he was teary, but
he was close to tears:'This would have meant so much to me, I make people
who are terminally ill's dreams come true and I think *Out* is the place where
I'd want to tell that story more than anywhere else.'"[148] After much negotiation with the production team, Hume was able to accommodate him.

Other participants saw the advertorial as generally progressive for gay visibility: James Dale said, "Before this, I would not have worn Dockers. But this
is . . . something that Dockers specifically did for the community, and I like
that."[149] Bruce Hayes argued, "I don't have any illusions . . . it's part of a marketing strategy. But it seems to be a more authentic way to market a product,
to use one of their hallmark words."[150] Whatever the ambivalence of some of
the people involved, Levi's attempt to hit an "emotional hot button" through
the merging of advertising, sponsorship, role models, and community visibility nevertheless offered unprecedented publicity to some good causes.

Hume's notes suggest a whirlwind preproduction-and-shoot schedule familiar to fashion or publishing work. After the production team decided on
the shortlist of desired people, she sent biographical information and sample
photos to Smith, negotiated with possible talent and their agents, and worked
with their schedules. Hume also coordinated the New York shoot, arranging
travel plans and hotels, organizing transportation from airports and to the studio, and making last-minute inclusions and cancellations of talent. Hume
talked of the two-day shoot in a studio-built set in New York with fondness:
"It was a great feeling on the set—Carter's very relaxed, there were lots of
ideas being shared at the table, [the talent] were all there."[151] After the shoot
she also arranged to collect contact sheets and continued to work with Levi's
on its sponsorship of GLSEN and the other groups.

In the resulting advertorial the role models look without smiling at the
camera. Their surroundings are sparse (bare bulbs, exposed pipe) but nonetheless literary and arty, with books open on surfaces and drawings tacked to
walls. The advertorial tells us that they are wearing flat-front khakis, and have
"personalized the look with items from their own wardrobes." The models
are notably not glamorized: the pants are unhemmed, the models' own clothes
are very casual, they wear no obvious makeup and little jewelry. The overall
impression of the piece is of a stripped-down, understated, serious stylish-
ness; through a self-consciously nonglamorized aesthetic, the advertorial honors these individuals' contributions to gay civil rights. Dockers khakis are the
garb of "extraordinary" gay civil rights activists and artists, not nameless corporate employees on casual Fridays. Indeed, the advertorial reminds us that

"style is about more than how you look. It's about how you live your life. In their lives, these 10 subjects show personal conviction—and how to be true to yourself."

Although we may not recognize the models as gay and lesbian from the images alone, the text makes clear that these are "just a small sample of the many gay or lesbian individuals that enrich this nation's life." The brief personal biographies tell us that one is an "Olympian who champions gay rights" and another brings "the gay experience to a wider audience." The advertorial's position as a gay text is also reinforced by the mention of Dockers' sponsorship of GLSEN and other gay youth and education groups working toward "ending homophobia in schools." The advertorial interpellates the reader as part of a politically committed gay and lesbian community, through its reference to "us"—presumably the role models, the staff at *Out*, and the readers. It links this community to a forward-looking, noncomplacent, "true-to-yourself" gay conviction and, in turn, to the product.

The response to the advertorial from consumers, activists, and the trade and popular press was very positive. Elliott called it Levi's "most ambitious marketing campaign aimed at gay men and lesbians."[152] Indeed, press coverage increased the campaign's profile further, with Kurt DeMars relating that "Dockers estimated their additional revenues [at] over a million dollars" from an article on the front page of the business section of the *San Francisco Examiner* alone.[153] *Out* generated its own publicity, as well, by paying for the advertorial to be distributed in *Advertising Age* in order to publicize its marketing skills to other advertisers. Fabrizio recalled:

> Out received a lot of publicity from the section as well as forging a tighter relation with the Dockers brand. *Out* also was able to promote this section to the advertising community at large which helped to underscore its importance as a major fashion advertising vehicle that positioned mainstream brands to the very important trendsetting gay consumer.[154]

Further, both the advertorial itself and Levi's public relations firm dealing with the gay market—Bragman, Nyman, Cafarelli—won GLAAD Media Awards for the campaign. (Bragman, Nyman, Cafarelli also handles PR for the GLAAD Media Awards.)

Consumers too responded positively to the advertorial and associated publicity. Caitlin Hume told me, "I've got lots of e-mails from high school students saying 'I've never seen this before, it's not the usual loser campaign, it's something you can relate to.'"[155] Malinowski recounted:

When we did the piece and when it came out, I did think we were going to get a lot of [negative] responses from consumers saying "you are doing this," and we probably got about five or six calls and a few [letters] in the mail, people saying that they're never going to buy our brand and they can't believe that a company like Levi's was doing this with a brand like Dockers. But interestingly enough we got hundreds and hundreds of positive responses and it totally [outweighed] the negative responses.[156]

As some participants had hoped, the campaign also brought the causes it championed a level of publicity they would not have achieved independently. Youth activist Rea Carey said, "We could never pay for the kind of visibility around the work we do that we have received from this campaign. . . . Young people and youth service providers from around the country are calling us: they want to know more about our work."[157]

The advertorial is an example of a marketing strategy that built on a business-savvy deployment of the ideal characteristics of the gay market as well as a company's best-intentioned commitment to gay civil rights. The selection of role models and the way they are represented emerge from this dual commitment: each person represents a different admirable challenge within gay rights activism and media representation, but all these challenges are safely contained within a "polite politics."[158] Collectively, the conventionally attractive, slim, youngish group reflects the dominant features of *Out*'s largely white, largely male, thirtysomething readership. The text makes frequent references to "gay or lesbian individuals," "coming out," "gay youth," "the gay experience," and so on, but the advertorial signifies a particular *kind* of gayness: respectable, gender normative, attractive and, above all, heroic. As one article explained in its review of the piece:

> The ad appears just days after Matthew Shepard, the gay University of Wyoming student killed in a suspected hate crime, was buried. This is a coincidence [*Out* publisher] Fabrizio found significant. "Gay people are brutalized from the time they are in school right through, sometimes, their death," he said, "and demonstrating successful gay people is an extremely important step taken by Levi [Strauss]."[159]

Indeed, press attention to the advertorial emphasized its focus on "interesting and successful gay and lesbian people," role models who are heroes, not victims.[160] As such, the piece links the product (Dockers khakis), people (gay and lesbian role models and the consumers who want to emulate them), and well-being, where the sense of well-being is bound up with a valorized, heroic, pioneering role in gay civil rights, youth activism, and media representation. Missing from the lineup of heroes are labor unionists, journalists from local gay papers, academic agitators, sex radicals, and others who present an image of gay activism less consistent with *Out*'s and Levi's marketing strategy of polite politics. Although all advertising attempts to forge relationships between products, persons, and well-being, these relationships are distinct according to the target market. In Levi's appeal to the gay market, well-being is tied to an institutionally sanctioned, nonconfrontational gay rights activism.

The advertorial's explicit blurring of the advertising/editorial divide, the use of gay-specific knowledge and commitments, the assertively philanthropic thrust, the political sensibility, and the focus on authenticity set it apart from other, routinized marketing efforts in the general market but also from other forms of gay marketing as well. For these reasons it presents a refreshing form of gay visibility within the marketing sphere, and one that cannot easily be put down as merely a cynical exploitation of gay issues to get consumers' attention. However, the piece was nevertheless subject to some of the routines and constraints of marketing and publishing generally, and these contain the kinds of visibility possible in the advertorial. Even though the advertorial does not use professional models, it nevertheless deploys a routine association between gays (especially gay men) with fashion, reproducing the urban, trendsetting stereotype. Although bypassing the advertising agency may have allowed for greater "authenticity" in the piece, it was nevertheless produced by marketers, publishers, and a photographer, all of whom have personal, professional, and publication standards to uphold. Levi's and the *Out* staff selected from a large and varied collection of possible candidates a group of people who could all be considered conventionally attractive, and who represented the distribution of readers in terms of race and gender. Further, the team rejected people who were "deviant" (my term) within gay marketing standards: bisexuals, lesbians of color, transgender people, older people, less conventionally attractive people, sex workers, and "impolite" activists. As a result, the gay visibility that the advertorial produced is a conditional one in which only the normative qualify as heroic.

The Dockers case study offers an example of perhaps the most laudable form of gay marketing. Socially and politically motivated, reflecting not only business but philanthropic concerns, the advertorial raises gay visibility along with the visibility of the product. The campaign demonstrates that it is too simplistic to collapse a company's commitment to gay civil rights to a purely profit-driven rationale. That businesses appeal to gay consumers as part of their business plan does not mean that it is *only* a business plan. Yet the routines of ad production help explain some of the limits placed on gay visibility. Gay marketers struggle with often competing demands: to make gayness decipherable, to avoid offensive stereotypes, to produce an authentic gayness, to maximize contact with gay consumers while protecting advertisers from antigay backlash, and, ultimately, to make meaningful connections between products, consumers, and a gay-inflected sense of well-being. These competing demands produce a contained visibility evident in the polite politics of the Dockers advertorial. The association between the pants and a heroic gayness, embodied by the attractive, youthful, gender-normative role models, reproduces gay marketing stereotypes that may have unwanted consequences, even if they were fashioned in the pursuit of a larger social good.

Marketers employ professional routines to contain the visibility of their clients' products and services. These routines structure not only a visibly gay consumer culture, however, but also how the participants in that culture are seen both within GLBT communities and beyond. The following chapter addresses the ideal image of the gay consumer, shaped by thirty years of marketers' efforts, and looks at how the contained visibility of this ideal image is challenged by increasingly accurate market research, by antigay groups, and by GLBT consumers themselves.

CHAPTER 5

SELLING AMERICA'S MOST AFFLUENT MINORITY

Like the last chapter, this one looks at gay visibility and the marketing routines that produce it. Yet whereas chapter 4 addressed the routines marketers use to fabricate consumer appeals that are recognizably "gay," through product, image, or venue, here I look at how GLBT people are made visible as a target market. There are remarkable similarities in the routines of market segmentation across different consumer groups, as chapter 2 shows. Like the African American market, for example, the gay market is not a preexisting entity but must be brought into existence through the assumptions and technologies of market segmentation. The gay market illustrates the ideological transformations required to turn a disparate and suspect population—in this case people who (sometimes) identify as "gay"—into a coherent and desirable market. Yet gay marketing routines produce not only consuming subjects but sexually specific ones as well. As media scholar Ien Ang writes, "If it is true that consumers must be made, rather than found in order to create a market, so too are the citizens that form a public not naturally there, but must be produced and invented, made and made up."[1] The mechanisms of market segmentation, then, have implications not only in the realm of consumer institutions (advertising, public relations, distribution channels) but have broader political implications for how GLBT subjects are situated in the public sphere. What assumptions about market segments, as well as about sexuality, do marketers bring to the construction of the gay market? How do the routines of market segmentation, especially market research, produce the very thing they aim to discover (here, the gay market)? What view of the ideal gay consumer do these assumptions and routines construct?

Earlier, I discussed marketers' efforts to educate advertisers about the desirability of courting gay consumers. By acknowledging these efforts, some interviewees tacitly recognized the constructive work required to prepare the ground for marketing to gay people. Yet my interviewees did not talk in terms of constructing a gay market for advertisers, but took for granted a preexisting segment of gay consumers that they simply had to deliver to corporations in a palatable and profitable way. In his talk to the Boston Ad Club, *Advocate* publisher Joe Landry played down the magazine's long history of cultivating the gay market through research, talking to the press, approaching advertisers, and so on.[2] He announced, "The [gay market] category really comes to life in 1992," as though the gay market were a sleeping beauty simply waiting to be roused by an advertiser's kiss. By playing down marketers' efforts in cultivating consumer segments, Landry reflects the prevailing belief in niche segmentation that marketers merely reveal a preformed and clearly defined consumer group. Yet the history of market segmentation shows that marketers have responded to changes in manufacturing, distribution, and media technologies to create increasingly segmented consumer markets. Consumption historian Richard Tedlow argues that there have been three dominant stages in marketing in the United States. The first, pre–twentieth-century phase was marked by local, regionally fragmented markets, where large geographical distances, poor transportation, and slow communication systems made unfeasible the formation of an integrated nationwide market.[3] The second phase, which dominated the first half of the twentieth century, was characterized by the voluminous production of consumer goods, the spread of a sophisticated transcontinental network of transportation and distribution routes, and the beginnings of mass media. These developments allowed for the first time a national audience for advertising and a national market for goods. But industrialization also produced a crisis of overproduction, and the new marketing industries developed strategies to research, reach, and appeal to consumers in order to promote consumption. In Tedlow's third phase, beginning after World War II, marketers used increasingly sophisticated techniques, including demographic and psychographic research methods, to appeal to consumers with claims to lifestyle or identity affiliation. These techniques allowed marketers to differentiate otherwise similar products by linking them to specific niches, and to "value price" (i.e., charge more for) merchandise by associating products with upscale consumers.

The beginnings of market segmentation originated at least as far back as the turn of the twentieth century: Kathy Peiss, Andrew Heinze, Marilyn Kern-Foxworth, and Robert Weems show that marketers already appealed in distinct ways to women, Jewish immigrants, and people of color.[4] After World War II, however, increasingly sophisticated market research built upon teen culture and the visibility of the new social movements of the 1950s through the 1970s to divide populations into ever more narrowly defined demographic and psychographic groups.[5] By the early 1980s, *Advertising Age* could rather apocalyptically describe the U.S. consumer terrain as "split asunder into innumerable special interests—gray power, gay power, red power, black power, Sunbelt and frostbelt, environmentalists and industrialists . . . all more aware of their claims on society."[6] Joseph Turow identifies three factors that facilitated market segmentation. First, computers offered marketers access to unprecedented quantities of consumer information that could be manipulated by infinite demographic variables: age, gender, race, income, region, education, marital status, and so on. Second, computer technology augmented increasingly sophisticated market research techniques that clustered consumers according to psychographic characteristics that bore some, but not necessarily much, relation to demographic data: attitudes, opinions, behaviors, and lifestyles. Third, the development of psychographic profiles was facilitated by the rise in increasingly visible identity groups in the 1960s.[7] Marketers realized that demographics alone could predict only some consumer behavior, and that appealing to identity and attitudes, collected and manipulated as psychographic data, offered a much more nuanced approach to encouraging consumption. By the early 1970s, then, when the gay liberation movement brought gay people into the national media with unprecedented visibility, marketers already possessed both the strategies and the technologies necessary to organize this group into a recognizable market.

Market segmentation involves the transformation of social groups, loosely organized around contingent identifying characteristics, into consumer niches, where those characteristics are assumed to be stable, measurable, and powerful in predicting consumer behavior. Like market research, audience research assumes that disparate individuals constitute a natural group, a "taxonomic collective," that is united by a single characteristic—in the case of television audiences, the activity of watching television.[8] Ien Ang distinguishes the "social world of actual audiences" as "infinite, contradictory, dispersed and dynamic" from the "television audience" as a discursive construct (13). She problematizes the assumption upon which audience research is based: that there *is* a "television audience" that is measurable, knowable, and assimilable within television programmers' (and advertisers') main purpose—the organization of mass audiences for greatest profit. Quoting British cultural studies scholar Raymond Williams, she notes that "masses are illusory totalities: there are no masses, 'only ways of seeing people as masses'" (2). Yet even if the "television audience" can only ever be a fiction, it is a necessary one. Whatever its epistemological limitations, audience research is "institutionally enabling" (35): as long as media and advertising executives believe that television ratings offer meaningful data, they can continue to agree to set advertising rates and make programming decisions based on these data.

Television audiences and market segments are not the same, of course; the defining characteristics through which audiences are organized as collectives are different from those that organize consumers as markets. Yet audience and market research share the underlying aim of transforming subjects into taxonomic collectives for reasons of profit. They also share institutions: although Nielsen Media Research is most well known for its television ratings, the majority of its market research work looks at product use across different demographic groups. Just as "the television audience" is fabricated from data on people who watch television, so too is "the gay market" produced from market research data offered by gay (sometimes lesbian, bisexual, and transgender) people. Market research does not, then, simply offer a window onto a world of gay consumption, but selectively and strategically gathers, manipulates, and reports data gleaned from that world. Ang notes that critics of audience research tend to focus on its methodological limitations, rather than questioning the epistemological assumptions that underlie audience research measurement: what constitutes an "audience" or a "viewer," what it means to "watch" television, and ultimately, how the television audience is produced by acts of definition and measurement. Similarly, most discussions of the gay market either take for granted that market research figures are reliable, or wish for better methods to access and measure elusive gay consumers. Few marketers consider how markets, like audiences, are produced by the very technologies that purport to simply measure them.

Landry's description of the gay market as "com[ing] to life" is consistent with the dominant model of market research that assumes preformed markets are simply waiting to be roused. This model assumes not only that there is a preexisting gay market, but that sexual identification functions as an incontrovertible marker to distinguish a taxonomic collective of gay consumers from their heterosexual counterparts. This assumption reflects the prevailing view of sexuality: most people are naturally heterosexual, while others are naturally gay, a view in which bisexual and transgender people can only be seen as taxonomic problems. Contrary to this perspective, philosopher and historian Michel Foucault famously argues that sexualities do not reside in the body, in a set of behaviors, or even in desires, but in the discourses that transform bodies, behaviors, and desires into a "truth" of human sexuality. Foucault investigates the dominant discursive institutions that shaped sexuality in nineteenth-century France: law, religion, education, and medicine. Yet across so-called developed nations since the early twentieth century, the role these institutions have played in identity formation has been displaced, albeit unevenly, by institutions of consumption: advertising, marketing, public relations, and commercial media. If confession was a primary mode of producing knowledge about the subject in nineteenth-century institutions, market research—requiring a kind of consumer confession—was the quintessential discursive technology of the twentieth century. Market research not only generates knowledge about consumer practices, then, but also about subjects. In the case of the gay market, marketing data shape not only the segment but the very idea of homosexuality that distinguishes it.

Just as audience research attempts to separate the television audience from the nonaudience, market research technologies aim to parse gay consumers from their heterosexual peers. Queer theorist Eve Kosofsky Sedgwick argues that the distinction between people who are heterosexual and those who are homosexual is the primary organizing principle of the twentieth century, buoyed by other, lesser binaries such as "secrecy/disclosure, knowledge/ignorance, private/public, masculine/feminine, [and] majority/minority."[9] It is not necessary to agree with Sedgwick that the homo/hetero distinction trumps all others to acknowledge that a great deal of cultural investment goes into maintaining the boundary between homosexuality and heterosexuality. She argues that the dominant model of homosexuality, the "minoritizing" view, holds that there are people who for reasons of nature or nurture are fundamentally and unequivocally homosexual, and are thus categorically different from heterosexuals. She contrasts this with a less popular perspective, the "universalizing" view, which argues that heterosexually identified people do experience same-sex desire, even if they work hard to disavow it, just as homosexually identified people experience other-sex attractions.[10] Sedgwick looks at the quotidian efforts to maintain distinctions between "real" gay people and "real" heterosexuals, efforts that betray by their everydayness the commonplace slippage between same- and other-sex eroticism. Both because market segmentation relies upon an idea of markets as discrete conglomerations of stable identifiers that predict consumer behavior, and because the minoritized view dominates liberal discourses about sexuality, assumptions about the gay market tend to reproduce assumptions about sexuality: that there are people who are "really gay," are distinct in significant ways from "real" heterosexuals, and can be marketed to as such.

Gay marketers are confident both about their ability to reliably target gay consumers and that those consumers really are gay; as a direct mail flyer asserts, the *Advocate* is "the magazine *you* were *born* to read." Yet the gay market is thus produced from two fictions: the fiction of market segmentation and the fiction of an essentialized gay identity. Gay market segmentation deploys many of the same assumptions and technologies as those involved in other market segments. Yet the production of the gay market is also distinct from that of other markets, because nonnormative sexuality is its distinguishing feature. How are the technologies of market segmentation applied to the gay market, and what are the challenges of doing market research on gay-identified consumers? What assumptions underpin the constructions of markets, and how does the case of the gay market reveal some of the limits of those assumptions? Marketers claim that their efforts to sell the gay market is merely a matter of business. The technologies and assumptions that make market construction possible, however, are built upon ideological foundations and have political consequences, not least because they make visible a fictive entity called "the gay market" in a history of cultural invisibility and homophobia. Queer theorist Sally Munt writes that "lived identities are complicated fictions essential to our social function."[11] Both the fiction of sexual identity and the fiction of market segmentation are necessary fictions—one for the negotiation of social life, the other for the workings of marketing. That both are indispensable is not to suggest that either is free of the demand for analysis, for as the fiction of the gay market and the fiction of gay identity become ever more entwined, what it means to be gay becomes increasingly articulated through what it means to be a gay consumer.

A Quality, Not Quantity, Buy: Market Research

Market research is the primary weapon in the arsenal of consumer segmentation, offering one of a number of "market feedback technologies" that marketing and media industries developed throughout the twentieth century to anticipate and influence mass consumption.[12] Gathering data on consumers' demographic profiles, attitudes, lifestyles, and product usage is crucial in campaign strategy development. Market research makes gay consumers visible to national advertisers, provides publications with data on consumer tastes with which to tempt corporations to buy advertising space, and legitimates corporations' decisions to enter the market. But the formation of the gay market from a small and controversial social group means that marketers have to work particularly hard to court advertisers. National corporate advertisers' doubts about the size and profitability of the gay market and enduring squeamishness over homosexuality require that gay marketers present the gay market as distinct in highly desirable ways—as, in *Out*'s advertising director Kurt DeMars's words, a "a quality, not quantity, buy."[13]

Ang argues that without audience research, there is no such thing as the television audience. Likewise, as the history of African American and gay market segments suggest, without market research there can be no markets. The marketers I spoke to emphasized the central role of market research in cultivating the gay market. Marketing and public relations consultant Stephanie Blackwood commented:

> Until [national advertisers] can see us, until they know something about us (i.e., research), they're not going to spend money on us. And as we have become willing to be known, and as we have become willing to answer the marketers in question about who we are, what we buy, what we spend our money [on], that's why they're willing to invest in us, because they can see how we stack up against the other segments.[14]

This view was verified by Megan Ishler who, as director of advertising at the lesbian pornography magazine *On Our Backs*, struggled to gain national advertisers because of a lack of reliable data on her readers, or even on lesbian porn readers more generally:

> Advertisers who can afford to advertise with us—who can [pay for] full-page cover positions, for example—rely on market data that we can't possibly provide. There is no such thing as statistical analyses of women pornography consumers, lesbian pornography consumers. . . . And the sex industry, some are comfortable with us because of the name recognition—because of the earlier incarnation of *On Our Backs*—but many of them feel like they already know what the market will do if they are advertising with straight men. They don't know what will happen if they are advertising to lesbian women.[15]

Both Blackwood and Ishler emphasized the central importance of market research data in the cultivation of advertiser interest in the gay and lesbian market. But the knowledge that market research data affords is neither objective nor unmotivated. As Ohmann argues, "Market and audience research belong to the twentieth-century politics of knowing: who can look at whom with what instruments, who studies whom and with what ends, who becomes part of whose knowledge."[16] The business of gay market research is political, both in terms of the assumptions of market segmentation (on what criteria populations can be measured and divided into markets) and its effects.

In order to construct the gay market as a "quality buy," market researchers have tended to emphasize certain demographic and psychographic characteristics that have long been associated with gay men and that cast them as ideal consumers: they are affluent, educated, childless, tasteful, trendsetting, and loyal to advertisers who appeal to them. The *Advocate*'s surveys in the late 1960s and 1970s found their readers to be more affluent and educated than the general population, allowing publishers such as *Blueboy*'s Donald Embinder to brag in *Advertising Age*: "Now you can reach America's most affluent minority . . . the male homosexual."[17] This image has been reinforced in market research by Overlooked Opinions, Greenfield Online, and OpusComm since the late 1980s. Greenfield Online and Spare Parts' 1998 Internet survey, for example, found that lesbian and gay respondents' average annual household income was $57,300, compared with $52,000 for Internet users overall. Further, 89 percent of GLBT respondents reported some college education and 23 percent some postgraduate education, "making this group better educated than the Internet population in general."[18] OpusComm's 2002 "Gay/Lesbian Consumer On-line Census" found respondents' average household income to be $65,000, but did not offer a national average for comparison. This affluent, freespending image is enhanced by the perception that gay people are "DINKs" (Double Income, No Kids). Kurt DeMars summarized: "We're not putting Junior through college, we're not buying the wife shoes, and supporting the household, in most cases. . . . Even though we've got more income than the average U.S. adult, that income also goes further because—I always compare it to pretax and after tax—we don't pay taxes, basically!"[19] Although DeMars here intended to describe *Out*'s readers, at the time 70 percent male, 30 percent female, his reference to wives and children as a "tax" burden reveals whom he has in mind: the ideal gay consumer here is implicitly male, probably single, and certainly childless.

The elevated affluence and education levels used to describe the gay market are extrapolated to a psychographic profile of gays as tasteful, trendsetting, and loyal consumers. As account supervisor Patrick Sullivan suggests, the ideal image of the gay consumer invokes class- and gay-specific tastes:

> the average 21-to-29-year-old gay male beer drinker is a lot different in his mental makeup than the 21-to-29-year-old blue-collar beer drinker. This is a much more sensitive, much more well-educated, much more savvy, more intellectual person, so your advertising is going to reflect that. It's more high—it looks more like liquor ads than it does like beer. Because beer is usually—across the board, and this is generalizing—the beer ads are probably more like a sitcom than a PBS show.[20]

According to Sullivan, the company's targets are either sitcom-watching blue-collar drinkers or PBS-watching, affluent, educated, gay drinkers, but cannot be both blue-collar and gay. This class-specific subcultural capital is reflected in assumptions about gay men's taste and power to set trends. *Out*'s former editor in chief James Collard said, "Gay men have the taste level and the money to buy Prada, but also to buy Dockers, Gap, and Nautica."[21] Blackwood commented on how successful some alcohol advertisers have been at "creating a sense of 'you've got to drink [Absolut] to be a trendsetter' and that has great appeal for this market. It's one of the things we do, [and that] is we do set trends."[22] Not all marketers uncritically repeated this image of gay consumers, however. Marketing and PR consultant Bob Witeck commented, "Companies tend to think of gay people—especially those who are really consumer-identified—as being younger and hipper, and all of us are not. God knows I'm not!"[23]

Gay consumers are also perceived to be very loyal to companies that advertise to them and that are seen to "support" the gay community. Opus-Comm found that 82 percent of respondents said they were more likely to purchase products or services from companies they thought were gay friendly. As Sullivan asserted, "Loyalty is huge in this marketplace. If they believe that you stand by them, then they are there for you. I mean, look at Subaru—it's just an incredible loyalty that gays and lesbians have for Subaru."[24] Joe Landry explained why gay consumers might feel particularly invested in companies that market to them:

> You have a socially repressed consumer segment that's now identifiable and marketable. An ad from a corporation is seen as an affirmation that the company is interested in [gay] business. [Consumers feel] good about supporting companies that support their publications—there's an emotional connection to the product.[25]

Marketers are invested in promoting repeated use as evidence of gay consumers' loyalty to a product, rather than simply as habit. Within the logic of market segmentation, which hopes to create "emotional connections" between products and consumers, loyalty brings with it a sense of emotional commitment that habit does not.

Market research thus presents the gay market as a "quality" buy, packaging an attractive image of gay consumers that is both politically and economically expedient. Yet this image emerges from distortions inherent in market research, which are compounded by the ongoing stigma and homophobia that many GLBT-identified people suffer. The challenges of gaining access to openly GLBT-identified consumers and of achieving large enough representative samples have dogged gay market research. These challenges are not unique to the gay market, however; even the census, the only survey that aims to poll every U.S. household, underrepresents some constituencies, including people who are homeless or transient, who have difficulties reading or understanding the census form, and who are not legal residents.[26] Because market research usually requires respondents' voluntary participation, studies are often skewed toward the attitudes and demographics of those people who have both the time and motivation to contribute.

Gay market research also skews toward people who can afford to be open about their sexual identity. *POZ* publisher and direct marketer Sean Strub suggested that one reason that the gay market is so dominated by the image of the affluent, white gay man is that this was historically the most visible member of the gay community. Until the late 1980s,

> Coming out of the closet was primarily a function of affluence. The only people who could come out were the people who were financially secure enough, and I don't just mean rich people or people who were comparatively wealthy, but people who earned their income in a way that was protected when they came out, or people at the other end of the spectrum who had absolutely nothing to lose—you know, the homeless drag queen, or whatever. It was those extremes that could come out. We did not create something that enabled a Ford Motor Company factory worker to come out, and we barely have today.[27]

Representative gay market research would require that all potential respondents feel equally safe disclosing their sexuality, no matter what their socioeconomic level. Currently, however, openly GLBT-identified respondents to marketing surveys tend to come disproportionately from those segments of the GLBT community who are protected by wealth or an independent means of income, and whose willingness to participate is thus influenced by the very factors that market research aims to measure.

Marketers have responded to the problem of recruiting GLBT-identified research participants by gaining access to them in venues where their sexual identity can be taken for granted; gay and lesbian publications regularly poll their subscribers; Overlooked Opinions based its study on sign-up sheets from the 1993 gay March on Washington and gay bookstore mailing lists; and Simmons Market Research Bureau with Mulryan/Nash ad agency surveyed people on the mailing lists of GLBT political organizations, a gay mail-order catalog, and a gay credit card. Economist Lee Badgett notes that in gay and lesbian market research, "People with higher income levels are more likely to be surveyed, because they are more likely to read newspapers and magazines, they are more likely to join organizations, and they are more likely to be able to afford travel to events such as the March on Washington."[28] Thus not all gay-identified people are equally available for marketers to measure; even if peo-

ple are willing to come out to market researchers as gay, if they are not readers of gay magazines, donors to gay causes, Internet users, or otherwise on gay
mailing lists, they are hard to find and to survey. Blackwood summarized the
limits of this approach to sampling as "the problem of how you find the gay
person who isn't hooked into anything—magazines, gay organizations, or
even the Internet."[29]

Badgett acknowledges that readership surveys have some value, in terms of
telling publishers and advertisers something about readers of a particular magazine. Marketer and journalist Grant Lukenbill said, "I think for a marketer
who wants to target—officially target—gay and lesbian consumers, the best
research for them, for the most part, is probably still going to be the readership surveys of the magazines, because they're going to have to go to those gay
and lesbian magazines in order to sell the product."[30] Yet limited survey data
are interpreted beyond the population of the survey, in two ways. First, market research from a particular publication is assumed to describe GLBT people in general. As Strub commented:

> When somebody does a readers survey, well that's not describing the gay
> and lesbian community overall, it's describing those readers. But very
> often in the press reports that's misconstrued—"*Out* magazine says the
> average gay household has three CD players" or whatever. Well, no, it's
> not what *Out* magazine is saying; they are saying that this is their read-
> ership, and their readership varies from *Genre's*, or *Gay Community
> News's*, or the *New York Blade's*.[31]

Second, when marketers and journalists project readership data to describe
the GLBT population as a whole, they must guess the size of that population;
estimates range from the more conservative 3 percent to Kinsey's legendary
figure of 10 percent of the adult U.S. population. The tendency to overrepre-
sent affluent gays becomes compounded by the underreporting of gay people
in the general population. When inflated income figures are boosted by generous assessments of the size of the GLBT population, the gay market looks
enormously attractive. One infamous estimate by gay market researchers
Overlooked Opinions set the annual purchasing power of the gay market at
$514 billion in the early 1990s. Even the *Advocate's* then publisher, Niles Mer-
ton, who might have been most invested in circulating the myth of gay wealth,
called this figure "ludicrous."[32]

Not just gay magazine market research but all readership surveys tend to
exaggerate the affluence of their subscribers. Lee Badgett compares demographic data from gay and lesbian publications with those for readers of *USA*

Today, Ebony, Jet, and *Essence,* finding that all had household income averages much higher than those of the general population. She contends that "no legitimate economist would ever use data from national publications to study the general economic status of Americans; likewise, it would not be appropriate to describe all gay men and lesbians based on readers of the *Advocate* or the *Washington Blade,* two popular weekly gay publications."[33] In an *Advertising Age* article Howard Buford criticized the Simmons and Mulryan/Nash agency that surveyed political and direct mail lists as well as magazine readers, saying, "They positioned this as 'this is the gay market' rather than as a segment."[34] In response, a spokeswoman from Simmons attempted to justify their methods, saying, "This is not meant to be political or social research . . . there is no question this is a difficult market to sample."[35] Her defense suggests that less rigorous research standards apply to marketing studies than to "political or social research," a laxity that ignores the very real political and social consequences of any research, within the marketing domain and beyond.

Some market researchers, however, *have* positioned their research as having political and social effects, and many GLBT participants respond to it as such. Although some potential respondents may be too nervous to disclose their sexuality to researchers, others see their participation as a form of political activism in which coming out in the survey is empowering. For example, one person who had completed the OpusComm online consumer survey enthused: "Thanks for the offer of being heard!!! We as Gay/Lesbian community need to let our Brothers and Sisters know we ALL COUNT!!! Every single last one of us!!! Spread Love Not Hate!!! Keep our Voices Loud And Proud!!! Peace And Love To You All!!!"[36] OpusComm framed the impulse toward consumer visibility within the context of political participation; its Web site exhorted visitors to "Stand up and be counted," that is, to complete their marketing questionnaire. The desire to be made visible to national corporations explains, at least in part, the enthusiasm with which gay consumers participate in market research studies. Of a survey commissioned by *Out* magazine, advertising director DeMars recalled:

> The MRI subscriber study is maybe an 8-to-12-page survey that we send to our readers, to know what water they drink, how much, what kinds of car they drive, what fashions they wear. Everything about them. And we were expecting maybe 50 out of a thousand [to be returned], a typical response. We got over 700. So that's unheard of. . . . We know how responsive our readers are.[37]

Gay respondents' willingness to be measured suggests that some sections of the audience, at least, have a vested interest in marketers' research attentions as part of a struggle toward gay visibility. The marketers I interviewed assumed that this enthusiasm reflected an eagerness of gay populations to claim a position as consumers, yet completing marketing questionnaires may simply reflect, as for African American consumers decades earlier, a bid for visibility in whatever limited means currently available.[38]

There have been some efforts to overcome the problems of sampling, access, and extrapolation in market research surveys. These studies aim to solve the dual problems of self-identification and gaining access to GLBT respondents by designing relatively safe methods to communicate sexual identification or by selecting self-identified gay respondents from larger, random samples. Yankelovich Partners undertook a study in 1994 that included a question on whether the respondent was "gay/homosexual/lesbian," but omitted bisexuals.[39] Yankelovich researchers aimed to diminish respondents' potential anxiety about being identified as gay by using an interview technique that protected respondents' confidentiality: subjects did not disclose their sexuality directly to the interviewer, but by means of a number on a card. This study found that, contrary to the popular stereotype, gay men earned a little *less* on average than their heterosexual counterparts (annual 1993 individual income for gay men: $21,000; for heterosexual men: $22,500), and that lesbians earned about the same as heterosexual women ($13,300 and $13,200 respectively).

Lee Badgett compared market research data with information on GLBT participants in social science and health surveys: the 1990 Census, the Coronary Artery Risk Development in Young Adults longitudinal survey, the General Social Survey, a Human Rights Campaign random phone poll, voter exit polls from 1992 and 1996, and the Yankelovich Monitor 1994 study.[40] In contrast to the stereotype of the gay market as affluent, educated, and childless, she concludes, "gay, lesbian, and bisexual people do not earn more than heterosexual people; gay, lesbian, and bisexual people do not live in more affluent households than heterosexual people; two studies show that gay men earn less than similarly qualified heterosexual men; [and] gay, lesbian, and bisexual people are found throughout the spectrum of income distribution: some are poor, a few are rich, and most are somewhere in the middle, along with most heterosexual people."[41] The "Double Income, No Kids" stereotype of gay male affluence reflects gender inequalities in household income, not higher-than-average incomes of single gay men. Gender differences in earnings, where women earn on average only 74 percent of male incomes, are compounded in household incomes: gay male and heterosexual couples earn about the same, whereas lesbian couples earn 18 to 20 percent less. Badgett also found that many lesbian couples have children under 18 years old living in their household (31 percent of lesbians, compared with 37 percent of heterosexual women), while gay men are significantly less likely than heterosexual men to have children (23 percent of gay men compared with 33 percent of heterosexual men). The DINK stereotype, then, applies only to some gay men living in domestic partnerships.

Market researchers have attempted to gain more representative data on gay income and spending patterns by turning to the Internet. Scott Seitz, partner at Spare Parts marketing firm, said of a collaborative research project on gay and lesbian Internet users with Greenfield Online in 1998, "Many lesbians and gays prefer not to self-identify for a variety of reasons, but this study has shown dramatically that our community is out of the cybercloset in large numbers."[42] Researchers maintain that the Internet offers two advantages over readership surveys: they can poll large populations of GLBT respondents who are not on gay magazine, fund-raising, or political mailing lists; and they can reach users who see the Internet as a safer place than a magazine survey to disclose their sexual identification.[43] Yet even with these advantages, Internet surveys do not necessarily offer a truly representative sample of the GLBT population. Although Internet researchers can compare gay with nongay online respondents, the Internet is far more likely to offer access to younger and more affluent gays who have both the technology and the skill to navigate the Web.

Witeck-Combs Communications marketing consultancy and Harris Interactive, a market research group that bought Yankelovich Monitor in 2001, combined the access advantages of the Internet with new statistical techniques to correct sampling biases. Harris Interactive has a multimillion-member panel of whom approximately 6 percent consistently self-identify as gay, lesbian, or bisexual, and about 1 percent identify as transgender. Harris adjusts the data set to accommodate the biases inherent in sampling online populations. This approach has proven very reliable in tests, such as predicting the presidential, senate, and governor's races in the 2000 election.[44] The Harris/Witeck-Combs research has found, for example, that although GLBT respondents are somewhat more likely to appear in income brackets over $75,000 (25 percent of GLBT respondents, compared with 22 percent of total U.S. population), they are also more likely to be overrepresented in the lowest income bracket (41 percent of the GLBT respondents earned less than $35,000, compared with 31 percent of heterosexual respondents).[45] Education levels between the groups are remarkably similar: 17 percent of GLBT respondents and 16 percent of the total U.S. population reported completing a college degree, with

5 percent for both groups completing graduate school.[46] Further, similar to Badgett's survey, Witeck-Combs Communications and Harris Interactive's research found that a large number of GLBT respondents took care of children, though fewer than the heterosexual respondents: 24 percent of GLBT respondents had children living in their households, compared with 39 percent of the total U.S. population.[47] As the most representative data on GLBT people to date, Witeck-Combs's work with Harris Interactive dispels the lingering myth of the affluent gay DINK consumer that has historically dominated discussion of the gay market.

Witeck-Combs Communications' market research and Badgett's social science studies offer a much more accurate picture of GLBT demographics than other readership and Internet surveys have done. Increased accuracy suggests that marketers are coming ever closer to solving the methodological problems of representative sampling to bring them nearer the "truth" of the gay market. Yet despite the seemingly ravenous hunger for market research data, marketers collect and use these data selectively. They privilege demographic, psychographic, and product choice information from market research surveys over consumers' responses to advertising campaigns. The advertising executives I talked to expressed contempt for campaign testing with focus groups: Liz Gumbiner, for example, said that focus groups cannot "tell us that this is the right campaign or not, because people don't know: we're the advertising experts, they are not the experts."[48] After campaigns have been launched, marketers are happy to tout letters from grateful consumers, like this spokesperson from Hiram Walker to a gay-themed campaign: "I have never before in my life seen [such a] response. I have a file of letters an inch or two thick from gay consumers thanking us and vowing their loyalty."[49] Yet marketers invest little or no time in systematically gauging the response to campaigns, beyond the crude measurement of changes in sales volumes. Market research technologies therefore seek the "truth" of a market segment in information *about* consumers, not in feedback *from* them.

Further, even as market research offers an increasingly accurate (if narrowly focused) view of GLBT consumers, the trade and popular press continue to circulate a distorted image of the gay market as affluent, educated DINKs. This suggests that journalists strategically use market research data to promote the most expedient image of the gay market, rather than an accurate one. They may believe that the news that GLBT people are very similar to non-GLBT people isn't considered to be news, making for a flat story. Further, like marketers, journalists may be personally and professionally committed to promoting the gay market as viable and desirable, and so will prefer research that represents gay people as ideal consumers.

As market research shows that GLBT people are more like the general population than the affluent, educated, trendsetting ideal image of the gay consumer suggests, marketers and journalists must work harder to shore up a distinct and desirable image of the gay market. The role of market research data in constructing the gay market is therefore similar to other market segments: data do not reveal the "truth" of a population but function as an instrumental convenience in the circulation of goods. Like the television executives in Ang's study who used ratings data strategically to bolster programming hunches and to justify prejudices, but ignored ratings when they were inconvenient to their argument, marketers and journalists use market research data selectively to continue to portray the gay market as a "quality, not quantity, buy."

The *Crème de la Crème*: Skimming Off the Ideal Gay Consumer

More accurate market research data is inconvenient to marketers not only because it challenges the ideal image of the gay market, but because it undermines the notion of the taxonomic collective upon which market segmentation rests. In contrast to actual social groups that are necessarily contingently organized, ill-defined, and unruly, taxonomic collectives are the product of institutional efforts to organize a population according to a single defining characteristic that can be subjected to statistical measurement. Yet improved audience and market research reveals that collectives such as the "television audience" or the "gay market" are organized not according to a natural characteristic— "television viewing" or "gayness"—but by assumptions about what it means to watch television or to be gay. Gay market research is scrutinized most intensely for the representativeness of how a sample was selected and how respondents were asked to identify their sexual identification. Yet underlying these questions is a deeper set of beliefs about gay identity and its relation to consumption; gayness is an absolute, definable, fixed demographic attribute that has a knowable effect on consumer behavior. As with all market segments, the gay market is predicated upon three interconnected assumptions: the assumption of homogeneity, the assumption of separation, and the assumption of essence.

The Assumption of Homogeneity Taxonomic collectives are assumed to share one defining characteristic that renders all other differences within the group unimportant. In terms of market segmentation, all those who belong to a market, by virtue of a given characteristic, are assumed to count equally; simply identifying as gay places one in the gay market, making all other identities irrelevant. Market segmentation therefore has a homogenizing effect, privileging gayness as the unique qualifier of the gay market. Yet some marketers, such as the former publisher and editor in chief of a gay marketing newsletter, Dan Baker, admitted that talking about a homogeneous gay market was in some ways "nonsensical": "It is in fact obviously very, very diverse . . . it's made up of men and women of totally different ages, of totally different income groups, totally different education levels, totally different geographical locations, and so forth, so it's enormously split."[50] Similarly, journalist Grant Lukenbill acknowledged that "there's no average gay consumer. [There] is a gay and lesbian marketplace, a panorama of markets."[51]

Newer research that emphasizes the economic diversity of gay populations challenges the homogeneous ideal of the affluent gay consumer. Marketers tended to employ three distinct strategies to compensate for this increasing complexity. The first, expressed by Rivendell's Todd Evans and others, recommended diminishing the emphasis on the affluence of the gay market and stressing instead its size, loyalty, and the effectiveness of gay-specific venues for targeting gay consumers. He suggested that even a modest estimate of GLBT people as constituting 5 percent of the population would yield more than ten million gay consumers nationwide. In his view, neglecting this sizable group was simply an unthinking marketing approach: "If you wanted to reach all of North America, would you ignore Canada?"[52] Canadians might respond that they are, indeed, frequently overlooked by the behemoth of the U.S. media system, but Evans's point is well taken. In contrast to Kurt DeMars, Evans wants to put forward the gay market as a "quantity," not necessarily "quality," buy.

Others responded to the increasingly diverse image of the gay market by suggesting that advertisers expand their view of gay people's consumption patterns. Michael Wilke cites the Greenfield Online and Spare Parts' survey which found that GLBT people are not as wealthy as previously thought: "Long considered more affluent than the mainstream, the gay market has been pursued by high-end brands such as Gucci fashion, Waterford Crystal, and Movado watches. New research suggests those consumers may be closer to average incomes."[53] Wilke recommends that because gay consumers share more "average" incomes with their heterosexual counterparts, manufacturers of more "average" goods should appeal to the gay market. This is another reversal of the "quality, not quantity" view of the gay market: gays buy mass-produced packaged goods as well as high-end image products.

Wilke's suggestion is contested by the third strategy for accommodating the economic diversity of gay populations. This approach reaffirms the "quality" of the gay market by sectioning off the most wealthy gays from the rest. In a curt response to Wilke's argument for advertising packaged goods to gays, *Out*'s president Henry Scott countered: "There's an error in the central premise of the article 'Fewer Gays Are Wealthy, Data Says.'.... Brands such as Gucci and Waterford are not pursuing the 'gay market' any more than they're pursuing the heterosexual market. The truth is those brands are in logical pursuit of only the most affluent segment of the gay market."[54] Scott quotes a 1997 *Out* survey that found that its readers had an average annual household income of $77,100, compared with the Greenfield Online figure of $57,300; although gays overall might not be hugely wealthy, *Out* can deliver a wealthy segment of them. Employing a telling range of food metaphors, *Out*'s Kurt DeMars described social stratification among gay consumers: "I think the gay market is like any other market: you've got your burger-flippers down here and your pie-in-the-sky up here. So [*Out*'s readers are] definitely that upper echelon, the *crème de la crème*."[55] It is perhaps no surprise that DeMars employs food as a metaphorical hierarchy, given the close alignment of culinary and more expressly "cultural" tastes.[56]

Although marketers, sometimes begrudgingly, acknowledged taste differences and income distributions among their intended consumers, they almost never talked expressly about class. Class differences were displaced onto gender, employment, and regional differences. New York account executive Andrew Beaver said, "Don't think for a second that what I want as a consumer is similar to what Cheryl who lives in Des Moines, who is 22 and a lesbian and is going to work as a veterinary assistant [wants]. You know, we are not the same people."[57] Marketers commonly contrasted geographical regions to account for class differences among GLBT people across the United States, yet such a contrast displaces economic factors with regional factors in problematic ways. Although these claims may be based in part on marketers' hunches that there are real economic disparities between gays in smaller towns and cities compared with metropolitan areas, these assertions may also reflect the class and taste hierarchies of marketers' own milieus. The ideal image of the gay consumer as wealthy, savvy, and trendsetting more accurately reflects white, professional, gay marketers in New York or Los Angeles than it does the hypothetical lesbian veterinary assistant in Des Moines. Further, differences in region can account for taste differences without needing to explicitly acknowledge the economic conditions that underlie these; in the context of the United States' cultural resistance to talking about class, framing taste differences as regional rather than economic in origin deflects the otherwise troubling disparities between wealthy and poorer GLBT people.

The assumption of the homogeneity of the gay market is also challenged by the racial diversity of GLBT communities. Witeck-Combs Communications and Harris Interactive found in 2000 that GLBT respondents' racial and ethnic identifications approximately reflect those of the total U.S. population

(with, for example, 15 percent compared with 11 percent identifying as Hispanic, and 16 percent compared with 12 percent as black/African American,
respectively), yet gay market research in general has tended to ignore race as a
significant variable in gay consumption.[58] Media kits for advertisers from the
Advocate, *Q San Francisco*, and PlanetOut Partners list their readers' gender, age,
household income, and lifestyle preferences, but none includes race. Similarly,
Mulryan/Nash's publicity material—"Reaching the Gay Market"—showed a
"dynamic demographic profile" of "the typical gay consumer" as affluent and
highly educated, with no reference to race. I asked Howard Buford what this
elision suggested about the ways marketers think about people of color within
the gay market. He responded: "I don't think [marketers] think about them at
all."[59]

The idea of the gay market as a white market may have in part arisen from
a history of white-dominated portrayals of gays in advertising, which have
only recently become somewhat diversified. In our discussion of his role as
creative director of the 1994 gay-themed Ikea television commercial, I asked
Patrick O'Neil whether he had considered representing an interracial gay
couple. He explained that he cast two white men

> to keep the issue focused. . . . We tried in general, in the whole [Ikea]
> campaign, to pick people that felt diverse without that being the over-
> riding theme: "it's all about diversity" [*said in a campy, trivializing voice*].
> I mean there is going too far, doing it too much, so it sometimes can get
> in the way of their message. . . . Because I think also that [diversity] has
> suffered a little bit of a backlash. . . . I think there's a Gen X thing where
> it's like, give me a break, what the hell, diversity . . . like a PC back-
> lash. . . . So I am careful not to position things based on an ethnic quota
> about a spot. . . . But the two white guys, yeah, I felt a little bit like we
> could have maybe [cast a man of color], but I think if we had done that,
> that maybe would have lessened the impact of the whole idea of a gay
> couple. It would have been more about a black and a white guy, or
> something. I think: keep the minority pure! [*Laughs*] If that makes any
> sense at all.[60]

For O'Neil, "keep[ing] the issue focused" on gay matters requires the somewhat chilling strategy of "keep[ing] the minority pure," ostensibly to avoid
anti-"politically correct" backlash or token casting. His laughter and remark
about whether his statement "makes any sense" suggest that O'Neil is aware
of the awkwardness of exploring sexual diversity in the commercial while narrowing its racial diversity. Some of this awkwardness is beyond O'Neil's con-

trol, insofar as the routines of marketing leave little space for producers to expand beyond one dimension of diversity at a time, at least in mainstream television commercials.[61]

The white-dominated image of gay advertising has become tempered in gay and lesbian print media in recent years, however. An ad count of three issues each of the *Advocate*, *Curve*, *Girlfriends*, and *Out* magazines from the fall and winter of 2002–2003 show that 26 percent of ads that portray people include at least one person of color.[62] Yet there is a peculiar disconnect between the images in gay- and lesbian-themed advertising and how gay marketers think about the gay market: although print images now appear quite racially diverse, the portrayal of the market in press kits and articles about the market does little to complicate the prevailing belief that the gay market is a white market. Howard Buford's agency, Prime Access, serves clients who want to reach gay, Latina/o, and African American consumers, and is the only agency that explicitly refers to all these groups in its marketing publicity. Buford did not see these consumers as distinct target markets, but as situated in a complex and potentially overlapping network of identities:

> I think our vision of who [the gay market] is is different from anywhere else, anyone else who's doing this marketing. Because we very much think of people of color being very much part of the gay market, very much think of Spanish-speaking people being part of the gay market, and I don't think that's true anywhere else. It's not automatically true of clients—we have to have that conversation. We don't think of it as exclusively blond, circuit-party, blue-eyed white boys in T-shirts jumping up and down on gunboats, who are making $50,000 plus. I think that's really insulting.[63]

Buford's perception of the interrelationship of racial and sexual diversity led in turn to his sense of responsibility to diversify the public's view of gayness by including a wider range of representations in his ads: "One of our missions was not to let that image of the gay market, of kind of young, athletic, wealthy, white boys be the image of the gay market when people think of it in their minds. Both in the [gay] community and outside the community. So if you look at our advertising, none of it allows you to think that."[64]

One of Prime Access's major clients is a pharmaceutical company that produces a protease inhibitor for treating HIV infection. Buford discussed a print ad his agency produced for this medication that showed a racially diverse group of one woman and three men hiking to a mountain's summit. Although Sean Strub and others shared Buford's emphatic assertion that "we are very clear that the HIV market is not the gay market," HIV pharmaceutical ads frequently appear in gay publications, and commonly portray people of color.[65] Michael Wilke noted that HIV and AIDS pharmaceutical advertisers have "made an effort to create a multicultural picture of AIDS [and] will show a diversity of faces, but not everyone is supposed to be gay, so it's rather ambiguous as to whose sexuality is supposed to be [what]."[66] Even a casual count of HIV drug ads bore this assertion out. Of six pharmaceutical ads that featured models in the October 1998 issue of POZ, all portrayed people of color, or people whose race was not identifiable, and none showed only recognizably white models (see fig. 5.1, for example). Out's Henry Scott acknowledged that the greater range of racial diversity in HIV drug ads reflected advertisers' understanding "that the epidemic reaches different target populations and they are very consciously saying 'we can't just market to a white audience.'"[67] Yet the racial diversity in drug ads contrasts with ads for viatical companies: in the same issue of POZ, of eleven life insurance financial companies, five had photos of racially identifiable models, all of whom were white men (see fig. 5.2, for example).[68] This cursory comparison of pharmaceutical and viatical ads suggests that the high proportion of African Americans in HIV drug advertising does not simply reflect the demographic of the target population, where people of color have been disproportionately impacted by HIV and AIDS.[69] The contrast in images shows a complex interaction between ideas of race and class, where "health" is connoted by the bodies of black people, and "wealth" by the bodies of whites. For it is not just that black people are represented in HIV medication ads; these models are shown as hyperathletic, a picture of radiant health. As an article in POZ critiqued:

> Ads for HIV drugs are not so different from commercials for those no-drowsiness allergy meds, such as Allegra. . . . [Yet] while Allegra merely promises sneeze-free days of blue skies and green fields, the pitch for protease inhibitors makes a far more ambitious offer. These drugs won't just make you feel better; if you believe the hype, they can change your life.[70]

The African American male body is densely resonant with connotations of "health" as a result of long-held cultural stereotypes of black athleticism. Pharmaceutical companies consciously or otherwise invoke this image of the hyperathletic black male to respond to early representations of the dead AIDS "victim" in news and fictional narratives as "humiliated, thrown around in zip-up plastic bags, fumigated, denied burial."[71] As combination therapies have slowed the rate of AIDS deaths, the association of power, strength, and virile

FIGURE 5.1   A PICTURE OF HEALTH IN THE ZERIT MAN (*POZ*, OCTOBER 1998).

healthiness with black bodies can be deployed in opposition to the patholo-gized, enervated image of the white man with AIDS that dominated the media in the late 1980s and early 1990s.[72] At the same time, however, some of the unsightly and uncomfortable side-effects of HIV treatments can be con-veniently ignored: *POZ* journalist Richard Goldstein notes with irony that the struggle to portray people with AIDS (PWAs) as "vital, active citizens—people *living* with AIDS—should fold so easily into a strategy for plugging pharmaceutical products."[73] Given the logic of a pharmaceutical industry that prefers individual, medicated responses to the epidemic over community-based, activist ones,

No one should be surprised to see the once-militant image of the PWA evolve into that of the serenely confident Zerit man, the ubiquitous, all-inclusive icon who is certainly black but not necessarily gay. If his sexu-ality is ambiguous, though, the state of his health is not. Like the rest of

The advertisement reads:

Worried
about money?

If you have a life-threatening illness and money has become a concern, you can sell your **life insurance policy** for cash. Viatical Benefits Foundation coordinates the entire process and is committed to obtaining the absolute *highest* cash value for your policy.

Your illness is your business and we keep your private information in the strictest confidence. Viatical Benefits Foundation handles all insurance policies including individual, term, whole life, group, federal employees (FEGLI), and converted veterans (VGLI).

This means no more financial worries for you.

1-800-871-9440
Nationwide 24-hour confidential consultation

FIGURE 5.2 A PICTURE OF (FUTURE) WEALTH IN THE VIATICAL BENEFITS FOUNDATION MAN (*POZ*, OCTOBER 1998).

the combo chorus, he shows no signs of side effects: no fever, nausea, headache, no liver or kidney problems, no high triglycerides, no protease paunch or puppet-face deformities.[74]

As Peter Jackson argues in his analysis of black men in British advertising, "If sports and music are acceptable domains for the public expression of black male performativity—especially where the audience is white—sexuality is much more carefully circumscribed."[75] Showing fit, strong, healthy-looking African American men in HIV drug ads taps into the positive association of black athleticism while playing down what might be a troubling sexuality. As cultural critics Kobena Mercer and Isaac Julien describe, both blackness and male gayness have been associated with a dangerous hypersexuality.[76] The figure of the "disciplined" black athlete may be one way of employing the virile physicality associated with blackness while distancing the product from a dangerous and contagious sexuality. HIV drug ads that show African American men are a welcome relief both from the tradition of casting white models in gay ads and from the popular image of the diseased AIDS victim, and reflect Buford's and others' commitment to complicating the dominant image of the gay market as necessarily white. Yet the frequent occurrence of people of color in HIV drug ads also plays into racially stereotyped projections of physical strength and power.

Further, in 2001 these pharmaceutical ads came under attack for offering too "desirable" an image of people with HIV. Research by the San Francisco Public Health Department claimed that men who had seen the ads were less likely to practice safe sex; the department assumed a causal relationship between these respondents' lower vigilance about safe sex and the 50 percent increase in new HIV infection rates in 2000.[77] San Francisco considered a ban on billboard ads that showed hyperathletic images of HIV-positive people, and the U.S. Food and Drug Administration ordered Merck and others to withdraw ads "featuring robust young men heaving javelins, riding bikes and crewing on sailboats."[78] This example offers an interesting dilemma in the struggle for "positive images" of a racially diverse GLBT community. On one hand, readers of the gay press might welcome attractive portrayals of people of color. On the other, however, that these portrayals suggest that being HIV positive is not a life-threatening condition, nor even a particularly debilitating one, could ultimately have a negative effect on safe sex practices.[79]

Of all advertising in the gay press, HIV pharmaceutical ads have gone furthest to portray people of color, although again, HIV-positive consumers are not necessarily also part of the gay market. For the most part, however, most marketers implicitly or otherwise assume the gay market is racially homoge-

neous; because whiteness is the dominant category, marketers' lack of acknowledgment of people of color within the market leaves its whiteness un-
challenged. Market segmentation assumes a single meaningful characteristic to
distinguish a population and homogenizes diversity within that population. To
acknowledge racial and economic diversity among GLBT-identified populations complicates that homogeneity; marketers respond, on one hand, by rendering GLBT people of color largely invisible in market research and, on the
other, by producing a hierarchy of legitimacy in which only those most affluent, with sufficient cultural capital to prefer Gucci over Wal-Mart, are worthy
of marketers' attention. Within the increasing segmentation of target niches,
marketers must carve out and display only the subpopulations of the market
most desirable to advertisers and publishers. They do so by resisting the challenge that more representative market research data pose to the myth of the
affluent, white, gay consumer.

   The Assumption of Separation As Turow notes, market segmentation allows media executives to promise a specific audience to advertisers by appealing to the "claim of efficient separation."[80] By signaling to media consumers
that they are, or are not, part of the desired target market, niche media aim to
"deliver a desired group to advertisers without making them pay for audiences
they [do] not want."[81] In order to efficiently separate desirable from undesirable consumers, marketers must assume that there is a stable, identifiable, and
discrete characteristic that identifies people in the target group—gender, age,
region, and so on. The logic of gay market segmentation assumes that consumers within the gay market can be distinguished from those outside it by a
knowable boundary; you are either gay or you aren't. Yet the uncertain status
of bisexual and transgender people within the gay market challenges this idea
of sexual coherence and, by extension, the assumption of efficient separation.
This assumption does violence to a nuanced and shifting view of sexual identity that more accurately reflects many GLBT people's experience.

   Strikingly, in the course of interviewing for this project the nomenclature
has shifted from "the gay market" to "the GLBT market." For example, when
I asked Ginny Schofield in 1999 about her company's "GLBT employee
group," she clarified that it was a "gay and lesbian group: . . . no Bs, no Ts."[82]
By 2002, marketers regularly referred to the *GLBT* market. According to participants at a recent panel on "queer" marketing, the shift in terminology took
place to reflect GLBT activists' efforts to make the gay movement more inclusive, and to acknowledge that the homo/hetero divide was insufficiently nuanced to describe a range of nondominant sexual and gender identifications.[83]
Yet although this shift reflects a laudable acknowledgment of a more expansive
view of gender and sexuality among marketers, in reality bisexuals and trans-

gender people remain largely invisible both in the routines of market formation and in the image of the gay market these routines help to produce.

Until recently, market research has either omitted bisexuals entirely from
questions of sexual identification or have lumped bisexuals in with gays, lesbians, and transgender people, rendering them invisible as a distinct group.
One of the few market research projects that distinguished bisexuals from the
usual "GLBT" category, by Witeck-Combs Communications and Harris Interactive, found that the proportion of people identifying as bisexual is far
larger than is routinely imagined. In a survey of 533 gay, lesbian, and bisexual
respondents, 39 percent identified as bisexual, with women being more likely
to do so than men (60 percent and 40 percent, respectively).[84] Yet none of my
interviewees volunteered information about bisexuals as consumers, with the
exception of Dan Mullen, publisher of the bisexual magazine *Anything That
Moves*. When I asked, marketers tended to describe bisexuals either as constituting a distinct market that is uninterested in gay-themed ads but too small
to warrant much attention, or as part of a larger gay market and positively dis-
posed toward gay-themed appeals.

Dan Baker suggested that a bisexual market should be considered separate
from a gay one, because he assumed that "bisexual people would not respond
to something that was . . . specifically designed for the gay community. . . . I
would think that if you define yourself as a bisexual you would see yourself as
a separate community, you would not want to be perceived as being just gay."[85]
Baker was in the minority, however. When I asked *New York Times* columnist
Stuart Elliott if he thought there was a distinct bisexual market, he responded:

> Oh jeez, no! I think that's slicing the baloney a little too thin at this
> point! It's going to take a long time for that, like the transgender mar-
> ket. . . . It's probably too narrow a niche for even the most ardent mar-
> keter who's seeking new frontiers to cross. I think that's probably a little
> too narrowly focused even in this era of specialized media.[86]

So even if bisexuals might appreciate being specifically appealed to, marketers
may not invest in a bisexual market, or indeed a transsexual one, for reasons of
size. It is possible that Witeck-Combs Communications' findings will encourage marketers to consider making appeals to bisexuals in the future.

Although Elliott imagined bisexuals as a distinct market, others saw gay and
lesbian appeals as potentially including bisexuals. *Advocate* publisher Joe Landry
admitted, "I am not sure if there is a need for . . . bisexual information that's
not being disseminated through other [gay] media."[87] *Curve*'s publisher Frances

Stevens commented that "we see bisexual women as a secondary market [to the lesbian market]. We treat bisexual issues in the magazine as part of our community. We try and highlight as many lesbians as we can, but we don't really feel that [bisexual women] are out of the market."[88] *Curve* was one of the few publications that included a question about sexual identification in their readership surveys. According to Stevens, bisexual-identified women constituted approximately 7 percent of its readers.

Marketers offered a range of reasons for the underdeveloped bisexual market. Both Stuart Elliott and Catherine Draper, director of advertising at *Girlfriends* and *On Our Backs*, suggested that advertisers' disinterest in bisexuals resulted from the scarcity of national bisexual-specific publications and the paucity of bisexual market coverage in the trade press. Referring to the post-Stonewall gay movement, Stephanie Blackwood observed that "if the gay market has only really been defined within the past ten years, after a preceding twenty years of history, the bisexual movement, as such, is in its infancy."[89] This "natural lifecycle" model of niche marketing assumes an inevitable progression between the consolidation of political movements and corresponding marketing interest, a progression that obscures the active participation of marketers and publishers in garnering such interest. In particular, it obscures the conundrum of publications in general: to win lucrative advertising accounts, publications must both be nationally distributed and, as important, already have national advertising, a catch-22 that bisexual—as well as lesbian and erotic—publications struggle with.

The lack of attention to bisexual consumers also reflects a widespread ambivalence toward bisexuality. *Q San Francisco's* publisher Don Tuthill commented that although bisexuals are periodically of interest in *Newsweek* and on talk shows, bisexuality nevertheless remains a "touchy topic" for both gays and heterosexuals.[90] Describing the difficulty of wooing national advertisers to *Anything That Moves*, Dan Mullen recalled,

> During the entire AIDS crisis a lot of strong bisexual men in the movement put their heads down when they were the lightening rod for "You are the reason that this is happening [i.e., transmitting HIV to the heterosexual population]." So I think our community suffered a major setback then. . . . I think now there's a lot more organizing, there's a lot more people who want to recognize "Yes, there is a bisexual community." I think it's very threatening for people to come out [as bisexual] because of the underlying biphobia that runs through not only the straight community but also the gay and lesbian community.[91]

Some biphobia also reflects the belief that bisexuality is somehow not "real." According to Mullen, bisexuality is commonly misunderstood as a detour en route to fully acknowledging one is gay or lesbian, or as a denial that one is "really" gay or lesbian.

The ignorant suspicion with which many marketers view bisexuals is magnified with transgender people. With the exception of Witeck-Combs Communications and Harris Interactive's research, market researchers and gay publications' media kits all but ignore transgender people within the universe of the gay market. This may be in part for reasons of size: of Harris's sample of 533 GLBT people, only 1 percent identified as transgender. Yet transvestism and transsexuality are frequent jokes in mainstream ads and commonly serve to reinstate normative gender boundaries. For example, in a television commercial for Clothestime, a women's apparel company, a gorgeous, sexy, "woman" strips to reveal a man's chest and flexing biceps, accompanied by the tagline, "If Clothestime can make Paul look this good, imagine what we can do for *real* women." The discourse of realness was reflected by Stephanie Blackwood during a conversation about an ad for an upscale women's clothes store in which the apparently heterosexual model Linda Evangelista wore men's clothes. Although Blackwood enjoyed Evangelista's playful cross-dressing, she lamented that "in the lesbian community drag kings are becoming an increasingly popular phenomenon, even here in New York. I guess the whole thing about drag doesn't work for me [*laughs*] at all! I just don't get it, I mean—can we all just be who we are?"[92] Blackwood here suggests that drag king performances are a facade, a disavowal of being "who we are." Within this framework, she naturalizes a gender-normative lesbian sexuality as who we *really* are, refusing the potential of gender boundary-play to demonstrate the constructedness of gender and sexual identifications.[93]

The idea of a transgender market is further complicated by the range of positions that transgender identity might represent. Some, like transgender activist and writer Kate Bornstein, do their political work precisely on the cusp between masculine and feminine identifications in order to challenge people's normative ideas of gender.[94] Others, however, have far less investment in transgender visibility. As Sarah Siegel related in her experience as director of IBM's GLBT sales and talent program: "As far as transgender people I have met, plenty of them—the majority, in my experience—both IBMers and customers I've met are really: 'Thank you very much, I am a woman now, [or] I am a man now; I always was but now it's irrefutable and I don't want to identify as transgender because that was then, and now I am what I was always meant to be.' "[95] The low transgender presence in market research may reflect a reluctance of many transgender people to identify as transgender, preferring instead to identify as their chosen gender. In contrast to bisexuals, who make up a large part of the GLBT community and are rarely represented, transgender people are a small part of the community and get represented relatively often, but less as a target market than as an object of anxiety or derision.

Attention to bisexual and transgender consumers has not followed gay marketing in part because of their later visibility as social movements, their lack of flagship national publications, and the biphobia and transphobia that permeate the gay and lesbian, as well as the heterosexual, communities. Yet both identifications also test the assumption of separation upon which market segmentation rests. Marketers must assume, first, that there *is* a meaningful separation between who is "in" the gay market and who is not, and second, that gender and sexual identifications are sufficiently categorical criteria upon which to effect such a separation. As scholar Judith Halberstam remarks, gender ambiguity stages a crisis for categorical sexual difference, and is therefore "inevitably transformed into deviance, thirdness, or a blurred vision of either male or female."[96] Transgender people challenge the assumption of separation because they violate an essentialist view of gender and sexuality that assumes there are "real" men and women whose bodies are the baseline from which to determine sexual identity. Bisexuals also challenge the assumption of separation because they fit neither entirely within the category of "gay" nor outside it; they blur the either/or distinction between men and women upon which gay and lesbian identity rests. As Marjorie Garber asserts, bisexuality is "an identity that is also *not* an identity, a sign of the certainty of ambiguity, the stability of instability, a category that defies and defeats categorization."[97] With this discussion, I do not intend to collapse bisexuals and transgender people into a single category, not least since their experiences of visibility and stigma are very different. However, the ambiguities of both bisexual and transgender identities present an epistemological crisis for a coherent notion of the gay market insofar as they complicate the discrete boundaries of a stable, gendered sexuality upon which the separation of markets depends. Marketers have not engaged with bisexual and transgender consumers in part because of the epistemological anxieties these identities produce. These anxieties take form as derision ("slicing the baloney a little too thin"), distrust (bisexuality as "just a phase"), or erasure (bisexuals and transgender people as simply part of the dominant lesbian and gay market). The indeterminacy of gender and sexuality that transgender and bisexual people represent fundamentally violates the niche marketing demand for distinctive categorization, meaning that the shift toward addressing the GLBT market is an inclusion marked more by name than by concerted efforts to research, represent, and appeal to bisexual and transgender people.

The Assumption of Essence The third assumption upon which market segmentation rests is the assumption of essence: that marketers can identify with epistemological certainty a characteristic that meaningfully distinguishes those within the market from those outside it. The assumption of essence functions for all markets: segmentation only works if marketers can take for granted that "women" or "Latinos" or "18-to-49-year-olds" consume in predictable ways meaningful to gender, race, or age characteristics. From this perspective, bisexual and transgender people might be irritants on the boundary of the gay market, but there remains a significant number of people whose gay identity unequivocally places them within the gay market. Just as Ang demonstrates that the television audience is a fictional construct organized around the characteristic of watching television, so is the gay market a fictional construct organized around the characteristic of gayness.

A few marketers observed that "the gay market" is built upon the problematic assumption of an essential gayness. Dan Baker, for example, asserted that the question "What is the gay market?" was "nonsensical" because

> nobody can ever agree on what the definition [of gayness] is. To me it's a question of self-identification, but self-identification under what circumstances, and how? . . . If there are two middle-aged women living in what used to be called a Boston marriage, but have never had any contact with gay people, they don't belong to gay organizations, are those people part of the gay market? Is a 16-year-old person growing up on a farm who's beginning to realize [his or her] sexuality and does it with boys and girls—are *they* gay? I mean they may eventually self-identify as gay. Do people, men—I can only speak because of personal experience—there are men who live in the suburbs who come into town to have sex with men, but that's it. They don't know the people they [have sex with], they don't have any contact as gay, they don't go to gay bars, they go to the toilet to pick up some guy to have sex. Is *that* a gay person? How do you define that?[98]

Baker's nuanced view of sexual categories may be shared by other marketers, but gay marketing in general cannot afford to truly consider the challenges to the idea of a discrete, knowable, essentialized sexual identity that such a view presents.

Social scientists and market researchers have employed different strategies to attempt to identify gay people. In her overview of GLBT demographics taken from social and health surveys, Lee Badgett found that in only three of her six surveys were respondents asked to explicitly self-identify as gay, lesbian,

bisexual, or heterosexual.[99] In the remaining studies she was forced to extrap-
olate sexual identity information from other data available: in the U.S. census
gay identification was measured by counting a same-sex "unmarried partner"
of the householder, and in both the Coronary Artery Risk Development in
Young Adults and the General Social Survey research subjects were asked the
sex of their partners throughout their lives, leaving Badgett to assume that
"sexual orientation can be measured by identifying people with same-sex
partners."[100] Yet counting only those GLBT people who are living with a
partner leaves out significant numbers of single people and noncohabiting
couples, and, as Baker observed, the sex of one's partners does not reliably indicate one's sexual identification. The result of this necessary reading between
the lines means that each of these surveys underrepresents the actual numbers
of GLBT-identified people in the population as a whole.

With Harris Interactive, Bob Witeck developed a five-part assessment of
sexual identity: they asked respondents to indicate their sexual orientation (the
options were "gay," "lesbian," "bisexual," "transgender," "other," and "not
sure"), the gender of their current or most recent partner, their degree of at-
traction to same- and other-gender people, their participation in GLBT community events, and their consumption of GLBT print and online media. He
said that he had considered computing what I called a "gayness quotient" to
convey how strongly respondents identified as gay, lesbian, bisexual, or heterosexual, but acknowledged that the value of this quotient depended on the
context in which it would be used. For example, for more social science—
based studies, sexual orientation, gender of current or last partner, and attrac-
tion would probably be most meaningful. But for consumer-oriented research, degree of participation in GLBT events and media readership are more
relevant, because potential advertisers need to know how to reach GLBT-
identified people, no matter what the gender of their actual partners might be.

Further, Witeck said that he had been confused by the 15 percent of GLBT
respondents who identified themselves as "married" (one option among "single, never married," "living with partner," "divorced," "separated," and "wid-
owed").[101] When I asked whether perhaps people had chosen the "married"
category who were ceremonially but not legally married, such as registering
as domestic partners or forming a civil union, Witeck responded,

> On the number of marrieds . . . I think it begs more questions about
> how people choose to state their status, and I suspect there are numer-
> ous answers—including some who feel "married" but are not indeed
> legally married, and because many actually still are married lawfully to
> someone of the opposite sex. I think there are boundless packages today

for human relationships, and I feel ever more the investigator and never the judge.[102]

Witeck's comment about being "ever more the investigator" suggests that the more deeply he becomes involved in the details of researching GLBT identifications and behavior, the less able he is to categorize or criticize them; Witeck regularly acknowledged to me that some of the data he collected left more questions than they answered.

Witeck's engagement with the vagaries of what it means to be gay brings us back to why the question "What is the gay market?" is "nonsensical." When marketers assume that a market segment is distinguished by an essential characteristic, they must also assume that this characteristic has a meaningful relation to consumption. Yet even if it were possible to accurately quantify the numbers of GLBT people, such demographic data guarantees no equivalent group of gay consumers. A number of interviewees commented that it was not enough for someone to have sex with people of the same gender to be considered part of the "gay market." Mulryan/Nash partner David Mulryan explained: "We are not going to find the person who's closeted. . . . I cannot help you with those people, . . . because if you are not self-identified, if you are not confident enough that you can be openly gay, you cannot respond to advertising that is targeted at you."[103] Stuart Elliott echoed this sentiment when he said, "By definition, the people who subscribe to a gay magazine or who go to a gay event are going to be a different kind of a person than somebody who's getting their *Out* magazine in a plain envelope."[104] The presumption here is that you must be socially open as gay in order to be psychologically open to gay-specific appeals.

Even for relatively openly gay people, there is no necessary correspondence between this identity and purchasing behavior. Elliott continued, "Some people buy gay, and some people don't, and some are in the closet and some are out, and some go out of their way to buy products that they see advertised in gay publications and others couldn't care less."[105] Grant Lukenbill concurred: "I think there's still a lot of gays and lesbians making their purchasing decisions completely by default on a whole range of ideas and motivations that the company is completely oblivious to, is not even clicking into."[106] As Bob Witeck explained, GLBT people

also are Episcopalians, or middle class, or they're lawyers—they are all these other things too. So consumer behaviors are predicated on a mix of all those things. Being gay is very profound, it's probably one of the deeper needs or thoughts that affect your life, so therefore it's rather central to your identity, but nonetheless it's also bouncing off all those other things. . . . In fact, [if] there's one thing that's going to dictate—more than anything else—what you do in your kitchen or in your life, it's probably what your mother did.[107]

These considerations reveal increasingly complex levels of qualification of what constitutes "the gay market." Contrary to the assumption that a market can be defined by an essential characteristic, and that gayness *is* such a characteristic, marketers recognize that gay people can only be organized and appealed to insofar as they self-identify as gay, are openly identified as such, and are more receptive to gay-themed purchasing appeals than to others.

Quoting Michel Foucault, Ien Ang writes, "Truth is not a universal absolute that exists outside certain historical conditions, but is an institutionally produced category which refers to 'the ensemble of rules according to which the true and the false are separated.'"[108] Like the television audience, the gay market is an institutionally produced category of persons organized according to an "ensemble of rules" or assumptions, according to which some persons, the "truly gay," are separable from others. The constitution of "the 'television audience' [as] a separate category of people, objectively distinguishable from the nonaudience" requires "purging from it the unpredictable, the capricious."[109] Likewise, in the process of market-formation, the three assumptions required for market segmentation—homogeneity, separation, and essence—consolidate an essentialized view of sexuality and purge all those GLBT-identified people who undermine the idea of a distinct and coherent gay market including, but not limited to, the closeted, the "Bs," the "Ts," poorer gays, and people of color.

Identity Politics and the Politics of Knowing

The processes of market segmentation, therefore, do not innocently represent preexisting identity groups to interested advertisers, but shape them in particular ways in order to make them representable and sellable. The technologies and assumptions put to work in this formation produce not only a target market but also package the characteristics by which that target market is distinguished. Both markets in general and a particular idea of gayness are shaped through the three assumptions that make market segmentation possible: that markets are defined by a homogeneous, boundaried, and essential characteristic, and that gayness is such a characteristic. To think of the gay market not as a real thing but as a taxonomic collective organized around a set of assumptions for the purposes of selling goods reveals that the process of constructing markets does violence to those who don't belong by making them invisible or laughable, by depriving them of revenues for publications, and by making their presence less legitimate in the public domain. Yet it also does violence to those who appear to fit the idealized stereotype of the white, affluent, gay male consumer by essentializing gayness to a reified fact and thereby negating an expansive view of sexuality and desire. Processes of constructing sexuality have been a focus for Eve Sedgwick, who distinguishes the debates between essentialist and constructivist ideas about sexuality, on one hand, from what she terms minoritizing and universalizing views, on the other.[110] According to Sedgwick, the essentialist/constructivist debate is primarily concerned with causes: are people "really gay" (the essentialist view) or is gayness a product of discourses applied to certain behaviors and desires within a particular geographical and historical context (the constructivist view)? In contrast, the minoritizing/universalizing debate asks, "In whose lives is homo/heterosexual definition an issue of continuing centrality and difficulty?"[111] The minoritizing perspective is that homosexuality is of concern only to homosexuals, whereas the universalizing view acknowledges the complicated, slippery, ambivalent realities of people's erotic lives across the sexual spectrum.

Although Sedgwick finds most productive the minoritizing/universalizing perspectives on sexual identity, I find both this and the essentialist/constructivist debate useful in understanding how assumptions about market segmentation structure a narrow view of gayness. Gay market segmentation strategies are essentializing because they assume a fixed and measurable characteristic— "gayness"—within the bodies or psyches of some people. Such strategies disavow the social construction of sexuality and gender. Attempts to improve the methodological reliability of market research focus on increasingly accurate means to find and measure "real" gays, and deny that such methods produce the very thing they aim to find. But gay market segmentation strategies are also minoritizing, because they assume an absolute separation between heterosexual and homosexual consumers. This separation affirms the distinctiveness of the gay market and plays down the potential for erotic slippage between homo- and heterosexual desires. Thus, while the essentialist model is useful to address how market segmentation represses the constructedness of sexuality, the minoritizing view highlights those marketing strategies that reaffirm the fiction of an unequivocal distinction between homo- and heterosexuality. Although some advertisements flirt with the boundary between gay and straight desire, the dominant view of the gay market tends not to. A few marketers that I spoke to were aware of some of the assumptions that go into constructing the gay market, but nevertheless had to minimize the implications of these in order to construct a model of gayness that functions efficiently within the logic of niche marketing.

The gay market, then, fulfills the requirements of niche marketing, insofar as it is constructed from Ang's "invisible fictions" into a discrete, measurable, segment. Although these fictions operate with all consumer groups, each niche is shaped from particular contours, in response to historical circumstances and stereotypes, and has varying ideological effects. The distinctive features of "the gay market"—affluent, freespending, trendsetting, and loyal—respond to the earlier invisibility and stereotyping of silly queens, sad young men, and hypersexual perverts. Yet the "gay market" is not fact but rather represents a set of methods for organizing a group of gay-identified and identifiable, respectable, privileged people—methods that perpetuate the myth of normalcy of professional-managerial class life. Although this image of gays in marketing may come as a relief from some of the most egregious stereotypes, it erases both the real diversity and the political potential of queer lives. Anthropologist Esther Newton writes, "There is an anthropological axiom that says that if people believe a thing to be real, that belief has real consequences."[112] Fictions have a tendency to have material effects, particularly when the ideal image of the gay consumer is disseminated in a culture that offers only limited GLBT visibility. Although market researchers might not have in mind the political or social consequences of their survey data, they cannot control how it will be used. Sean Strub linked marketers' circulation of specious market research data to an amendment to Colorado's constitution that would have prevented the state's agencies or schools from enacting nondiscrimination laws to protect gays, lesbians, and bisexuals: "Politically, it's terrifying. There were brochures in Amendment 2 in Colorado that were specifically citing numbers from one firm's [research] as *proof* that gay people are already economically privileged . . . and that's where the gasoline that fires the 'special rights' engine is coming from, as much as anything else."[113] The fiction of the affluent gay consumer has been used to fight against gay civil rights in contexts—legislatures, workplaces—far beyond the realm of consumption. Market research data are used selectively and strategically not only by gay marketers who wish to see greater cultural acceptance of GLBT people but also by people working against such acceptance. Identity politics has therefore been transformed by the "politics of knowing" of market research, structuring the contemporary image of the GLBT community as "America's most affluent minority." The relationship between identity politics and consumer markets is particularly fraught in the case of the lesbian market; the problems of finding and appealing to lesbian consumers are compounded by negative associations with a politicized lesbian feminism to thwart marketers' efforts to construct a viable lesbian market. This is the topic of the following chapter.

CHAPTER 6

NEITHER FISH NOR FOWL

What is it that a lesbian market wants?
—HENRY SCOTT, former *Out* president[1]

The question of the lesbian consumer market pitches marketers pell-mell into the conundrum of femininity. Echoing Freud's plaintive query—"What does a woman want?"—put to Marie Bonaparte,[2] Henry Scott's question about lesbian consumers suggests that although lesbians may *want*, identifying the object of their desire is notoriously tricky. According to *Out*'s founding editor in chief, Sarah Pettit, in their efforts to attract national advertisers lesbian publications face a neither "'fish nor fowl' dilemma . . . people won't take them seriously as women's books, but won't take them seriously as gay books either."[3] Heterosexual women are stereotyped as exemplary consumers, either as housewives or as femmes fatales, and are not feminists. Gay men are assumed to be affluent, trendsetting, and oblivious to political critiques of consumption. Yet lesbians and, especially, lesbian feminists are not easily allied with either image of consumption; imagined to be hostile to the family and to fashion, they are neither the "fish" of heterosexual women, nor the "fowl" of gay men. In contrast to the gay male market, in which gay men's political visibility was transformed into marketing visibility, the struggle to create a lesbian market demonstrates how both business and political conditions can hinder the formation of a viable target niche. The marketing routines that shape new markets have not proven successful in organizing a dispersed and elusive group of lesbian consumers, and lesbian feminist critiques of consumer culture have not offered marketers a receptive environment for their appeals.

Even before the explosion of consumer culture in the early twentieth century, women were seen as the embodiment of consumer desire: female archetypes have long connoted luxury, decadence, and the perils of consumption. As historian Joyce Appleby writes, "If represented graphically luxury, of course, is a woman—sometimes a powerful evoker of desire, carrying the comb and mirror of cupidity and self-love; at other times an abject naked woman under attack from toads and snakes."[4] Victoria de Grazia, also a historian, argues that not just the image of consumption but consumer practices were feminized as a consequence of early capitalism and the development of an industrial economy.[5] First, as nineteenth-century, newly middle-class men wished to differentiate themselves from dissolute, effete aristocrats of both genders, consumption (especially of luxury goods) was disparaged as "feminine" in favor of a virile, production-oriented masculinity. Second, as the division of industrialized labor took men from the home to workplaces, women were left with the responsibilities of childcare and home management, including purchasing for the household. Third, as the availability of goods became increasingly diversified, "needs" became dichotomized between products that were seen as luxurious, irrational, and superfluous, and thus feminine, and those that were rational, functional, necessary, and hence masculine. These historical processes together produced two sometimes conflicting images of the female consumer: the housewife, "Mrs. Consumer," whose quotidian provisioning holds the fabric of domestic life together,[6] and the femme fatale, whose seductive femininity is fabricated through luxurious, trivial, deceptive consumption.

If heterosexual women have long been seen as archetypal consumers, more recently gay men have also been successfully constructed as a desirable target market, as I document elsewhere in this book. The image of the gay male market as wealthy, tasteful, and trendsetting is in marked contrast to the dominant image of lesbians. As one journalist noted,

> Marketers have gone after gay men because the stereotype is so attractive: affluent, brand-conscious, interested in fashion and style, creating trends that straight men will follow. That's the marketing antithesis of the stereotypical lesbian who supposedly wears a lumberjack shirt, sandals and no makeup and who does not set trends for straight women.[7]

Gay marketers have successfully capitalized on the reputation that gay men have as consumers, selling their attractive image back to advertisers to consolidate the gay market. The different associations with gay male and lesbian consumption is reflected in two ads for Bridgestone tires that appeared in the gay and lesbian press in 2003 (figs. 6.1 and 6.2): text on the ad showing two men together reassures readers that gay men "know how to accessorize . . . your entire life" (ellipsis in original). For the ad with two women, however, Bridge-

FIGURE 6.1 THE ACCESSORIZING POTENTIAL OF BRIDGESTONE TIRES FOR MEN (*ADVOCATE*, MARCH 4, 2003).

FIGURE 6.2 THE LIBERATORY POTENTIAL OF BRIDGESTONE TIRES FOR WOMEN (*ADVOCATE*, APRIL 15, 2003).

stone asserts: "Your ideas about liberation . . . are part of your identity" (ellipses in original). Whereas the gay male appeal prompts readers to consider tires as a fashion accessory, the appeal to lesbians associates the freedom of the road with the far more worthy goal of political liberation.

In contrast to the strong associations with effective, even compulsive, consumption that both heterosexual women and gay men invoke, the idea of a specifically lesbian market remains remarkably underdeveloped. When trade press journalists mention lesbians at all, it is usually to wonder about their absence in or alongside the gay market. In 1982 one journalist wrote that lesbians "are discounted so completely, when it comes to consumer power, that most people who talk about the 'gay market' make the implicit assumption that it is a male market."[8] As the putatively male gay market rapidly built momentum throughout the 1990s, journalists reported that "Economics Holds Back the Lesbian Ad Market," and "Lesbian Publications Struggle for Survival in a Market Dominated by Gay Males."[9] *New York Times* advertising columnist Stuart Elliott commented that "except [for] the small number of quote-unquote 'lipstick lesbians,' the average lesbian may not be the intended perfect consumer."[10] And in 2002 one journalist wrote that the gay market remained a "men's club," asking why marketers continue to "ignore lesbian consumers."[11]

This struggle to imagine the lesbian consumer plays out in contradictory ways in advertising in the gay and lesbian press. At first glance, there seems to be a discrepancy between marketers' sense of the lesbian market as underdeveloped and a relatively visible presence of women in ads in the gay and lesbian press. In ad counts of three recent issues each of two mixed gay and lesbian magazines (*Out* and the *Advocate*) and of two lesbian magazines (*Girlfriends* and *Curve*), women appear relatively often: in the lesbian publications, all the ads that showed people included women, as did 39 percent of ads in the mixed gay and lesbian titles.[12] Although the percentage is lower for ads in the mixed than the lesbian publications, women are still better represented in *Out*'s and the *Advocate*'s advertising than in their circulation figures (15 percent of *Out*'s and 27 percent of the *Advocate*'s readers are women). However, it would be simplistic to assume that these ad counts suggest a concerted effort to court lesbian consumers. Few of the ads, especially those from mainstream companies, appear to be produced specifically for lesbian consumers.[13] Some of the women in ads in lesbian and gay venues are clearly meant to be read as lesbians because, for example, they appear in couples with other women. But by no means can all the women that appear in ads in gay and lesbian media be construed as lesbian; some take on a "lesbian" connotation simply because of the venue, but many of these images read as straight-looking women, and some even appear in heterosexual scenarios with men. A better sense of the

underdeveloped lesbian market comes from looking at the amount of advertising in lesbian publications compared with mixed titles: lesbian magazines
survive on far fewer ad pages than do the mixed magazines (advertising occupied 25 percent of pages in *Girlfriends* and *Curve*, compared with 43 percent of
pages in the *Advocate* and *Out*). Further, the number of prestigious ads from
national corporations in lesbian publications is very small: only 15 national ads
appeared in three issues each of *Girlfriends* and *Curve*, compared with 158 national ads in three issues each of the *Advocate* and *Out*.

There is a similarly contradictory relationship between images of women
of color in the lesbian and gay press and a lack of recognition of a racially diverse lesbian market. In trade press articles, interviews, and publications' media
kits, marketers give a view of the gay niche as implicitly white: media kits describing the demographics of readers of the *Advocate* and *Q San Francisco* magazines and of online members of PlanetOut and gay.com Web sites list gender,
age, household income, and lifestyle preferences, but do not include racial
identity. Yet women of color appear relatively frequently in ads in gay and lesbian publications. In the three issues of the *Advocate*, *Curve*, *Girlfriends*, and *Out*,
17 percent of all ads that showed people included at least one woman of color.
The lesbian publications were more likely than the mixed gay and lesbian titles to include ads with women of color (39 percent of ads in the lesbian publications, compared with 12 percent of the mixed publications). Further, one
third of all ads that showed women included at least one woman of color. Although ads in mixed gay and lesbian publications are more likely to perpetuate the stereotype that the ideal gay consumer is white, the lesbian press offers
a much more racially diverse impression of lesbians as consumers. The scarcity
of advertising in the lesbian press, however, suggests that advertising images
represent less a commitment to cultivating an inclusive lesbian market than a
liberal impulse toward gender and racial diversity in advertising.

The lack of advertiser support for lesbian publications reflects the struggle
to construct a viable lesbian market, a struggle that involves both the routines
of marketing and the stereotypes that lesbianism, feminism, and female consumption invoke. If women are considered expert shoppers, and if gay men are
seen as stylish and enthusiastic consumers, it should follow that lesbians are
doubly endowed with a flair for consumption. Yet the lesbian market remains
elusive, partly for pragmatic reasons: communication scholar Danae Clark observes that in order for a group to be constituted as a market segment, it must
be identifiable, measurable, accessible, and profitable.[14] Marketers wrestle with
the formation of a lesbian market on all fronts: lesbians are seen as hard to
reach and to appeal to, as unprofitable and resistant to advertising. The challenges to the routines of market formation are compounded by stereotypes

and misunderstandings about lesbians, about feminists and, more broadly, about women's desires. Clark notes that "the beginning of the Second Wave of feminist politics and scholarship was marked by a hostility toward fashion, perceiving it as a patriarchal codification and commodification of femininity that enslaved women and placed their bodies on display."[15] The dominant strain of lesbian feminism that emerged in the 1970s dislocated women from both consumer and sexual economies by rejecting the traditional family structures and the sexual availability that Mrs. Consumer and the femme fatale imply. If these are the dominant models for female consumption, what place is there, if any, for lesbian consuming desire? If they are not producing themselves as objects of male desire, can women be seen as having any desire at all?

Through the metaphor of the gaze, feminist film theory offers a vocabulary for investigating the problem of autonomous female desire that both sexual agency and consumption require. Theorists such as Laura Mulvey and E. Ann Kaplan analyze the patriarchal modes of looking that are structured within Hollywood movies, in which the woman on screen is subject to the voyeuristic gaze of both the male characters in the film and the men in the audience, inevitably "tied to her place as bearer, not maker, of meaning."[16] As E. Ann Kaplan explains,

> Assigned the place of object (since she lacks the phallus, the symbol of the signifier), [woman] is the recipient of male desire, the passive recipient of [the male spectator's] gaze. If she is to have sexual pleasure, it can only be constructed around her objectification; it cannot be a pleasure that comes from desire for the other (a subject position)—that is, *her desire is to be desired.*[17]

Women in the audience can only experience pleasure either by identifying with the woman-as-spectacle on screen, or by identifying with male spectators. From this perspective, men are possessors of the gaze, and therefore of desire, which poses a problem for an autonomous female sexual agency. Within patriarchal modes of looking, the "lesbian" is, according to film scholar Teresa de Lauretis, an impossibility, because the same-sex eroticism suggested by "homosexuality" is displaced by the demands of male desire, the "homme," producing a relation between women that French theorist Luce Irigaray calls "hommo-sexuality."[18]

The institutional demands and routines of representation are clearly distinct between movies and marketing, but feminist film theory nevertheless offers a number of fruitful points of entry into an analysis of the underdeveloped lesbian market. First, feminist film theorists assume that femininity is not a natural, preexisting essence, but is constructed, in part through display: "woman" is produced through fabrication and adornment, represented within visual and narrative structures.[19] The critique of adornment and display that has characterized some strands of lesbian feminism since the 1970s troubles the relationship between femininity and consumption, and presents challenges to advertisers interested in wooing a potentially cynical target market. On what basis can marketers appeal to lesbian consumers, if not through the frames of heterosexual courtship or domestic efficiency? Second, film theorists address the "problem" of an autonomous female sexual agency within patriarchal systems: if women's primary "desire is to be desired," can lesbians be imagined to have desire for each other, for things? Third, in film as in marketing, "hommosexual" representations of women's desire for each other tend to function less to seduce lesbians than to appeal to heterosexual men. Given the dominance of the eroticized girl-girl motif in heterosexual men's pornography and in women's fashion magazines, how might marketers represent an "authentic" lesbian desire?

Finally, film scholars observe that although, theoretically, "woman" is imaginable only as bearer of the look, women in the audience clearly experience visual pleasure, and not necessarily by adopting a masculine position, or by masochistically identifying with the woman on screen. Film scholar Jackie Stacey attempts to theorize a relationship between the psychic and the social spectator: it is "only by combining theories of the psychic dimensions of cinematic spectatorship with analyses that are socially located that the full complexity of the pleasures of the cinema can be understood."[20] Andrea Weiss argues that although dominant cinematic codes have long worked to

> contain the most threatening aspects of women's sexuality, . . . lesbian spectators have been able to appropriate cinematic moments which seem to offer resistance to the dominant patriarchal ideology, and to use these points of resistance and the shared language of gossip and rumour to, in some measure, define and empower themselves.[21]

By extension, even if marketers find it hard to imagine lesbians as desiring consumers, studies of lesbian subcultures reveal that lesbians nevertheless do desire, and do consume. What might such studies reveal to marketers about lesbians' consumer practices outside dominant discourses of femininity?

Historians and critics of consumer culture have noted the associations between consumer and sexual desire: the very title of William Leach's history of department stores, *Land of Desire*, conflates consumption with other exotic, erotic longings,[22] and the typically female kleptomaniac replaces sexual desire with illicit consumer compulsions.[23] Yet the subject of this erotic-acquisitive desire is always assumed to be essentially feminine, naturally heterosexual. Clark writes, "Perhaps because . . . 'consumer culture thrives on heterosexuality and its institutions by taking its cues from heterosexual "norms,"' theories *about* consumerism fall prey to the same normalizing tendencies."[24] The heterosexualizing tendencies of consumption scholarship render the lesbian invisible, obscured by a fishy dyad—the hyperdesirous femme fatale and the pragmatic Mrs. Consumer. She is also, however, eclipsed by the fowl—the affluent, trendsetting, gay male peacock. It is the conflict between gender and sexuality upon which the problem of the lesbian market founders: lesbians are neither "real" women nor "really" gay. Scott's question—"What is it that a lesbian market wants?"—indicates the confusion that surrounds what lesbians might want as consumers, whether they are indeed capable of consumer desire, and what it means to imagine lesbian desire outside phallocentric consumer and sexual economies.

Where Are They?:
The Pragmatics of Producing the Lesbian Market

As I outlined in chapter 5, markets are shaped from the combined effects of marketers' assumptions about consumers and technologies of market segmentation. Like heterosexual women, gay men are seen as an identifiable, measurable, accessible, and profitable market, where their distinguishing characteristic, their "gayness," is imagined to have a meaningful impact on their consuming behavior. These assumptions appear to be gender- and sexuality-specific, however; characteristics attributed to both heterosexual women and gay men make them ideal targets for appeals. In contrast, both the image of lesbian consumers and the pragmatics of reaching them pose challenges for gay marketers. Some of my interviewees observed that marketers had not made much effort to even imagine a lesbian market. Henry Scott at *Out* magazine said,

> There has not been much effort so far to understand the female audience, to understand the lesbian audience and its purchasing patterns and what lesbians are interested in. . . . And I guess I've come to the point that what we are probably going to have to do is do some of this ourselves; nobody else is going to be out there doing the hard work of saying "what is it that a lesbian market (or markets) wants?"[25]

Part of the lack of interest in lesbian consumers reflects the gender distributions among gay marketing professionals. Gay men have been instrumental in the formation of the gay market by encouraging, educating, and offering their gay subcultural expertise to national, corporate marketers. In contrast, there has not been an equivalent group of lesbian professionals to champion the cause of a lesbian market. Stephanie Blackwood suggested that the lack of attention to lesbian consumers was attributable in part to male journalists' failure to identify and report on moments of lesbian appeal. She discussed a campaign by a women's clothing store:

> This fall they released a campaign. The most striking image was Linda Evangelista, two images of her, same photograph, one in drag, one not, looking at each other. . . . Her in a men's undershirt! With her hair slicked back, looking like a really handsome young Italian boy. Or her in a necktie. . . . I didn't see any press about it. And I would have thought, with Linda Evangelista—but then I say to myself, "Hey, it's about lesbians, why *would* you write about it, Mike Wilke?"[26]

Blackwood's question suggests that while actively covering the gay market for *Advertising Age* between 1995 and 1999, journalist Michael Wilke was more attuned to gay male appeals than to flirty, sexy, butch-femme appeals to women. The development of both the African American market and the gay male market shows that trade press coverage is crucial in the construction of a niche; before marketers can begin to target lesbians, publishers and journalists must foster the idea that lesbians are a potential niche to consider.

Even when marketers' interest in lesbian consumers is piqued by press coverage, marketers are faced with the challenge of gaining access to them, both for research purposes and to make advertising appeals. Interviewees lamented that doing market research with lesbians proved a formidable task because lesbians are less likely to read gay media, visit gay Web sites, attend gay events, and be on gay and lesbian direct mail lists. As Blackwood commented, "Why would you even think about advertising to lesbians if you can't *find* them? Where are they? It's a real challenge."[27] Lesbian publications are stuck in a vicious circle: in order to get prestigious national advertising they need to commission credible readership surveys from companies such as Simmons or MRI, yet to do that they need the funds that advertising can provide. *On Our Backs'* ad director Megan Ishler described the dearth of market research data on lesbians, and especially on readers of lesbian pornography:

> Everyone knows what a white, upper-middle-class, male readership is, no matter who they are sleeping with. And we know that that is a market that can be approached and will purchase, [but] I think that advertisers don't know what a lesbian market is. . . . It's the combination that I'm talking to them about advertising not in a women's magazine that's

just a women's magazine, but in a lesbian magazine—that's one strike already—and then to add on top of this, it's actually a naked lady lesbian magazine—nobody knows what I'm talking about![28]

The challenge of finding lesbian survey respondents prefigures the difficulty of locating lesbians as potential targets of advertising campaigns. One public relations consultant claimed that lesbians "have great [income] numbers. But it's a question of how do we find them? [Advertisers] are so used to seeing gay press that is so male-dominated."[29] Circulation numbers for lesbian publications are low and unaudited: *Curve's* circulation is 68,000, *Girlfriends* is 35,000, and *On Our Backs* is 25,000.[30] This is compared with *Out's* and the *Advocate's* circulations of 113,000 and 103,000, respectively. Further, Todd Evans from Rivendell, a marketing company that sells ad space in local gay and lesbian publications, commented that there are declining numbers of local publications exclusively or predominantly oriented toward lesbians; the number of local lesbian publications that Rivendell represents dropped from eleven in 1994 to three in 2002.[31]

In publications aimed at least nominally at both lesbians and gay men, readership surveys suggest that the proportions of women readers tend to be far lower than men: women make up only 27 percent of the *Advocate's* readers and 15 percent of *Out's*.[32] Henry Scott talked about struggles at *Out* to produce content that satisfied both lesbian and gay readers; although some topics (such as finances or adoption laws) might be of similar relevance, others (fashion, grooming) may be less so. Stephanie Blackwood concurred: "It's a very difficult proposition to attract gay men and lesbians to the same location. After all, we don't dress alike, we don't date alike, we don't mate alike, we don't have a take alike, so having a publication that covers . . . those very different realities is very difficult."[33] The low female readership of mixed gay and lesbian publications does not encourage advertisers to court lesbian consumers through those media. As Blackwood argued, because lesbians are such a small proportion of *Out's* readership, "you could get more lesbians by putting an ad in *Entertainment Weekly*, or advertising on *Ellen*, for God's sake. Right there, in a week you get as many viewers as you probably get in a whole year of *Out* readership. Not dissing on *Out*, but you know, it's just not much."[34] Even *Out's* president Henry Scott asked why advertisers would pay the cost of advertising to women in *Out* when they would be paying to advertise to a "lost 70 percent" of its readers (i.e., men), whom he perceived to be uninterested in ads directed toward lesbians.

Lesbians seem to be hard to reach in other venues as well. According to PlanetOut Partners' media kit, in 2001 only 15 percent of PlanetOut and gay.com members were women. Journalist Karla Solheim reports that gay.com has four times the number of chat rooms for men as for women, and only an estimated 15 to 20 percent of online chatters overall are women. Because people who chat spend longer online than people who surf content, lesbians spend less time online per visit than do men.[35] These figures suggest that the Internet does not offer greater access to lesbian consumers than do mixed gay and lesbian publications.

Lesbians are also less likely to be reached by event sponsorship efforts. *Out's* director of marketing, John Finco, suggested that the lesbian market is

> a harder audience to reach than men are; definitely men have a tendency to have more of a social structure around them. And the affluent lesbian population is much more insular. It doesn't mean that they don't talk to each other. There are ways to reach them, it's just much more difficult.[36]

In general, lesbians are believed to be less concentrated in urban environments, less likely to socialize at gay bars or events, and more oriented toward private social and entertainment patterns.[37] As ad agency head Howard Buford put it, "There are just hundreds of thousands, millions of lesbians who are paired off, living together, who are living quiet lives on the edge of the woods or in the heart of the city or wherever, that . . . are very hard to reach. And a lot of them don't necessarily want to be reached."[38] Although Buford may be reproducing a stereotype more than describing a real insularity among lesbians, this view nevertheless discourages marketers from making sponsorship appeals to lesbians.

Perhaps the biggest obstacle to the vitality of a lesbian market, however, is marketers' low expectations of its profitability. In contrast to the stereotype of gay men as affluent, well-educated "DINKs" (Double Income, No Kids), lesbians are seen as having lower disposable incomes and as less willing to part with their money. According to the Bureau of Labor Statistics, in 2002 women working full time made on average only 77.5 percent of the income of their male counterparts;[39] Lee Badgett reports that lesbian households tend to earn 18 to 20 percent less than both gay male and heterosexual couples because gendered wage differentials are compounded in households with two female incomes.[40] Marketers also believe that lesbians are more likely to have children than are gay men, further reducing their disposable income. This hunch is again borne out by research: Badgett found that 31 percent of lesbians, compared with 23 percent of gay men, had children under 18 years of age living at home. Badgett concludes that contrary to the myth of the affluent gay DINK, "gender is at least as important as sexual orientation in determining a person's economic position."[41]

Lesbians' lower average household income contributes to their reputation as frugal and as unresponsive to marketing appeals. According to Catherine Draper, ad director for *On Our Backs* and *Girlfriends*, "There's a general feeling that lesbians are not spending money, and are not consumers."[42] Direct marketer Sean Strub related that although he produced separate "cardpacks" (packages of advertising cards and coupons mailed to names on gay mailing lists) for both gay men and lesbians, the packs mailed to women, "Sapphile," "never made any money, but I always liked the parallel track concept."[43] Strub's company produced only three editions of Sapphile before deciding it was an unprofitable enterprise.

Some marketers have attempted to address the challenges of reaching large numbers of lesbians by treating them as part of a larger women's market. Deutsch's creative director Liz Gumbiner recalled that a cosmetics manufacturer was not "going after lesbians specifically, but they had a big sponsorship of Lilith Fair; you know, they will go where women are."[44] Stephanie Blackwood agreed: "It's a well-known fact that if you want to reach lesbians you advertise in women's publications first because lesbians tend to identify as *women* first."[45] Similarly, Deborah Isherwood, promotions manager at a large pharmaceutical company, assumed that lesbians use lube for the same reasons as other women: to compensate for reduced self-lubrication as a result of menopause. Somewhat as an afterthought, she added that lesbians might use lubricant with sex "toys, tools, whatever."[46] Although her company saw gay men as a distinct niche for its sexual lubricant and had plentiful market research data for this group, she had no equivalent data on lesbian use. The assumption that lesbians can be appealed to above all as women suggests that some marketers believe it is lesbians' femaleness, more than their sexuality, that shapes their consumer interests and needs.

Other marketers have addressed the obstacles to reaching lesbians by appealing to them as part of the gay market. As writer and activist Sarah Schulman comments, "While marketers are primarily focused on extracting consumer dollars from gay men, they *believe* that they are also marketing to gay women."[47] *Curve* publisher Frances Stevens commented that advertisers "who go into the mixed publications [such as *Out* and the *Advocate*] are really marketing toward the men, and the women are just sort of a perk, I guess."[48] Thus, although appeals to lesbians in mixed lesbian and gay publications are perceived to be uneconomical because of the "lost 70 percent" of male readers, the converse is not the case: rather than being the "lost 30 percent," lesbians are assumed to also respond to gay male appeals. Given the difficulties of reaching a prof-

itable market through lesbian-targeted media and venues, then, marketers hope
to court lesbian consumers in their appeals to both heterosexual women and
gay men.

From Lesbian Feminists to Lipstick Lesbians

Marketers who are optimistic that lesbian consumers come as a "perk" with
their appeals to heterosexual women and gay men overlook the more general
belief that lesbians are "neither fish nor fowl": for reasons of sexuality and gender politics they cannot be fully incorporated into either the straight women's
or the gay men's target markets. In the 1970s, lesbians' responses to consumer
culture were shaped as much by the women's movement as by the burgeoning
gay rights movement. The feminist critique of consumer culture meant that, as
Badgett summarizes, "for political reasons, lesbian feminists did not pursue the
kind of commodified sexual world of gay men."[49] Although commercial establishments flourished as part of the early gay rights movement, lesbians
tended to be suspicious of the capitalist underpinnings of these, preferring to
explore sexual freedom outside the commercial realm. Lesbian feminist critiques of capitalism combined with arguments against the beauty and fashion
industries, gaining lesbian feminists a remarkably tenacious reputation that, in
one marketer's words, they "have no sense of fashion, or are all nudists."[50] Henry
Scott observed, "There's a huge stereotype that lesbians aren't interested in style
and fashion, and as with all stereotypes there's some truth in it."[51]

   Although both gay men and lesbians rejected the dominant sexual economy of heterosexuality, lesbian feminists' rejection of conventional femininity,
articulated in part through consumption, made them far less redeemable than
gay men within a capitalist economy. Lesbian feminism thus separated lesbians
from their gay male peers, whom they saw as invested only in the hedonistic
here and now of an increasingly open public sexual culture. But lesbian feminism also separated lesbians from the ideal of the heterosexual woman consumer: lesbian feminists could be imagined neither as housewives nor as
femmes fatales. Sandra Lee Bartky observes, "Feminists are widely regarded as
enemies of the family; we are also seen as enemies of the stiletto heel and the
beauty parlor, in a word, as enemies of glamour."[52] The media representation
firm Rivendell Marketing used to have a sales representative who specialized
in working with advertisers of traditionally "women's" products. She struggled
unsuccessfully to sell ad space in lesbian publications to makeup, apparel, and
perfume companies because they believed that lesbians were not interested in
their products. That lesbians are antifashion is a stereotype circulated by lesbian marketers as well: Stephanie Blackwood advised marketers to be patient

when courting lesbians who have been "conditioned based on twenty-five years of the women's movement" not to consume in traditionally feminine ways.[53]

If lesbian feminists are viewed as the enemies of glamour, resisting the femme fatale consumer role, so too are they imagined as hostile to domestic life (the lesbian "gayby boom" notwithstanding), and are thus not redeemed by the image of Mrs. Consumer. Commenting on products traditionally sold to women, *Advertising Age* journalist Michael Wilke said, "There are ad nauseam amounts of ads selling laundry detergent and perfumes [in women's magazines], but lesbians suffer from being completely misunderstood and stereotyped in most people's minds" as not domestic and thus not attractive to advertisers of household products.[54] Ad agency partner David Mulryan suggested that not just a feminist antifamily attitude but also an antimale sentiment alienates potential advertisers from lesbian publications:

> If you look at a lot of the female gay press, we've got this rabid, left-handed, lesbian feminist representation, and "the world hates us" rhetoric that goes on, and that scares advertisers, you know? And the lesbian element of the gay press has absolutely politicized *everything*, down to where you put the dot on the page, and frankly my advertisers aren't interested in that nonsense. . . . A lot of these lesbians are very antimale— I mean they come off as being antimale—rightly so, but that's not going to get you very far. And they are perceived as being extremely hostile. And they have a right to be hostile, but you know, you've gotta play the game.[55]

Here Mulryan pays lip service to "understanding" what he perceives to be lesbian feminist hostility to men as in part justified, while actually trivializing this position as "nonsense" and as bad business practice. With his misogynistic characterization of the rabid, antimale lesbian feminist that underpins some gay men's perspectives on the lesbian market, Mulryan fails to consider the costs for lesbian publications of "play[ing] the game." Mulryan's comments prompt a consideration of how lesbian publications should "play the game" of the gay market. For some, playing the game means not only that publications should temper their overtly feminist politics, but also that they should offer more conventionally feminine images of lesbians. Such images became widely available in the early 1990s: the 1992 film *Basic Instinct* starring Sharon Stone has been heralded by some as kicking off the era of the "lipstick lesbian," followed in 1993 by lesbian cover stories in *New York* and *Newsweek* (fig. 6.3). *Vanity Fair* showed a less conventional image of femininity in its infamous cover photo of

k. d. lang getting a close shave from Cindy Crawford (fig. 6.4). Numerous other media references in the same year to "lesbian chic" and "lipstick lesbians"[56] proved that lesbians were no longer "the erotic equivalent to a Russian tractor,"[57] since "a girlfriend has replaced a baby as the woman's ultimate fashion statement."[58] As Kara Swisher invited, "America, come say hello to lesbians—they're hot! sexy! out there! Many gay women, who have long watched their lives minimized and distorted, can hardly contain themselves over the newfound attention."[59]

Marketers and critics alike have tended to characterize the lipstick lesbian as the newer, apolitical or postfeminist lesbian consumer, contrasting this image with the older, feminist, anticonsumption stereotype. David Mulryan, already tired of antimale lesbian feminists, doesn't approve of lipstick lesbians either: "These younger women that have classically defined themselves as 'lipstick' and everything, let's think about that: it may be good for lesbians but it's really antifeminist, isn't it?"[60] This sentiment is echoed by critic Arlene Stein, who dismisses lipstick lesbians as more concerned with lifestyle than with politics: "When lesbian feminists see young femmes strutting around in makeup and panty hose, they may see women intent on fitting in, assimilating into the straight world, shedding their anger, and forgetting their roots."[61] Marguerite Moritz is less concerned with sisterly sellouts than with the exploitation of lesbian chic for ultimately heteronormative purposes. Although she acknowledges that media attention to lesbians in the early 1990s was "long overdue and in some senses gratifying," she is suspicious of the mainstream media's seizure of lesbians as a hot cultural commodity.[62] Moritz comments that images of lesbian chic merely reproduce dominant structures of class and race, in which media attention is given "either to celebrity or to white, upper-middle-class, professional, fashionable, affluent urbanites who can be constructed as chic."[63] Further, she contends that the lesbian chic image represents lesbians "in the same sexualized and sexist ways that women in general have been formulated," a claim later echoed by activist and critic Alexandra Chasin.[64]

The lipstick lesbian may have been more a boon for mainstream media than for advertising in lesbian and mixed gay and lesbian publications. As Michael Wilke commented, "The whole lesbian chic thing has really not made its way over ultimately to marketing to lesbians. It's been largely a media event rather than a reality, when it comes right down to it."[65] Lesbian publications in particular find it hard to garner ads from large corporations, and those ads that do appear tend to be generic rather than deploy specifically lesbian signifiers. In contrast, some advertisers use lesbian themes less to appeal to lesbians than to connote diversity or a sexy glamour in mainstream media. Disaronno Amaretto profiled an ambiguously lesbian couple in a television commercial

FIRE AWAY: PLAYING COP IN SOMALIA AND BOSNIA

Newsweek

June 21, 1993 : $2.95

LESBIANS

Coming Out
Strong

What Are the
Limits of
Tolerance?

FIGURES 6.3 AND 6.4 "LIPSTICK LESBIANS" AND "LESBIAN CHIC" AT THE CUTTING EDGE (*NEWSWEEK*, JUNE 21, 1993, AND *VANITY FAIR*, AUGUST 1993).

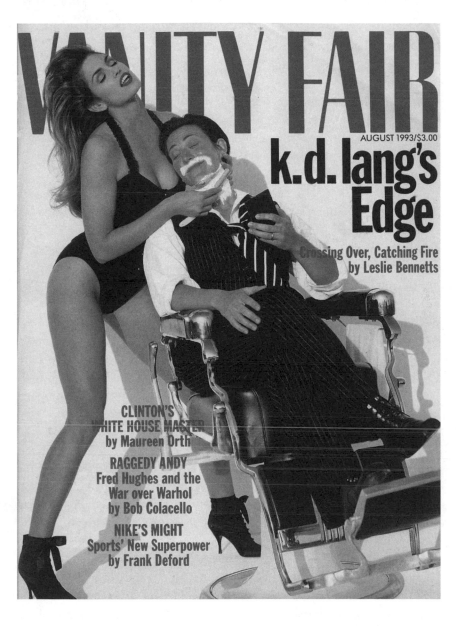

VANITY FAIR

AUGUST 1993/$3.00

k.d. lang's Edge

Crossing Over, Catching Fire
by Leslie Bennetts

CLINTON'S
WHITE HOUSE MASTER
by Maureen Orth

RAGGEDY ANDY
Fred Hughes and the
War over Warhol
by Bob Colacello

NIKE'S MIGHT
Sports' New Superpower
by Frank Deford

that ran in Canada and in one of three print ads that appeared in magazines in both Canada and the United States (fig. 6.5). Account supervisor Rachel Fox described the campaign strategy:

> Our core desire for Disaronno was to make women or men feel glam-orous, desirable, the center of attention. And our selling idea was that Di-saronno causes the consumer to feel alluring at any time. So that's our sell-ing strategy. So taking that brief and giving that to the creative teams, . . . it's quite easy to come up with something very sexy and sensual.[66]

The television commercial and one print ad showed an erotic exchange be-tween two feminine, flirty women that the agency hoped would lend a "sexy, classy, approachable, contemporary" flavor to their campaign. Fox declined to say whether the campaign was designed to appeal specifically to lesbians; the placement of the lesbian-themed print ad in a range of publications, from *Girl-friends* to *Playboy*, suggests that lesbian representations are available for the pleasure of diverse audiences. Fox wanted the ad to be "very attractive for both men and women, heterosexual or homosexual."

Some interviewees commented that if advertisers want to represent same-sex couples to connote "diversity," images of lesbians are an "easier pill to swal-low"[67] than are images of gay men together. As agency creative Liz Gumbiner explained of her decision to cast two women in a Mistic beverages television commercial,

> It's very easy for men to say, "Oh homosexuality is horrible, but give me two chicks together anytime." So we also knew we had that in our favor, that men are turned on by the idea of two women together, so we can get away with more [by showing lesbians] with men who are so inse-cure in themselves that two men together really disturbs them.[68]

Gumbiner wanted to include one gay-themed commercial as part of Mistic's diversity-emblematic, "Show Your Colors" campaign. Given this, portraying lesbians was a safer bet than gay men, since girl-girl couples are less likely to alienate heterosexual men. Gumbiner's statement suggests that although she is aware (and critical) of the cultural homophobia that influenced her decision to cast two women, she is prepared to capitalize on it: the Mistic ad can signal "diversity" while avoiding the "horror" of male homosexuality.

In both lesbian and mainstream publications, the lipstick lesbian offered marketers a way to show lesbians (real or imagined) in a "positive" light. Howard Buford was optimistic about a future increase in numbers of appeals

FIGURE 6.5 DISARONNO COUPLES TWO WOMEN TO APPEAL TO DIVERSE AUDIENCES (*ADVOCATE*, JUNE 8, 1999).

to women: "Most of our [gay] celebrities now are women and quite frankly lesbians are less threatening than gay men to straight executives. . . . A lot of it has to do with social acceptance, and advertising is never at the leading edge on that."[69] Yet the presence of high-profile, openly lesbian celebrities such as Martina Navratilova, k. d. lang, Melissa Etheridge, Ellen DeGeneres, and Rosie O'Donnell simply has not "produced" a lesbian market, suggesting that media visibility and a lesbian market exist in only a partially dependent relationship. Further, neither lesbian celebrities nor the lipstick lesbian stereotype has displaced the vilified image of the lesbian feminist. As Sue O'Sullivan comments, "Two images of lesbianism exist at the same time, one young and provocatively attractive and fashionable, the second older, dowdy, prescriptive and overtly political. Both images are fantastical; neither image corresponds any more to the multilayered realities of lesbians' lives than other media caricatures of women do."[70] The popular view does not imagine lipstick lesbians to be political or critical, and their joyous seizure of feminine accoutrements is taken as evidence that the lesbian feminist critique of women's images is simply outdated.

Where Is It? In Search of Lesbian Desire

Jane Gaines comments that when the "post-1982 pro-sex moment" produced for lesbian as well as heterosexual feminists "a climate in which it was possible to confess a taste for pornography, it also became possible to declare an interest in and even to confess a serious passion for clothes."[71] Yet among marketers the dominant view of lesbians as antisex and antishopping endures. The scourge of feminism compounds the pragmatic problems of imagining, measuring, and reaching a profitable lesbian market, and not only for the overtly political reason that lesbian feminism has traditionally been hostile to the commodification of femininity. That the implicitly postfeminist lipstick lesbian has not been welcomed as a new ideal consumer suggests that the dislocation of femininity from heterosexuality profoundly disrupts marketers' assumptions about female consumption: Does a lesbian want? Can a lesbian want? And, if so, *what* does a lesbian want, if it is not to get and keep a man?

In her memoir of the lesbian and gay movements of the 1970s, Karla Jay notes that the image of lesbians as sexless was an inadvertent consequence of early activists' choice "to downplay our sexuality because our primary goal was to make a political point, and back then the vision of a lesbian in bed conjured up an image of perversion, not radicalism."[72] Yet this desexualized image of the lesbian also reinforced existing beliefs about women's lack of sexual agency. Theories of female desire offered by feminist film theory help to make sense of the problem of female sexual agency and its relation to consumer desire and, by extension, to gay marketers' mystification about the lesbian market. Feminist film theory denaturalizes the association between femaleness and femininity, offering insight into why lesbians have been so hard to imagine as a consumer market. Just as there is nothing natural about femininity, there is nothing natural about women as consumers: women are imagined to be good consumers as a product of their position within heterosexual femininity. When lesbians, and especially lesbian feminists, detach themselves from heterosexual femininity, their desires and motivations become unimaginable.

If within dominant narratives women's "desire is to be desired," representing lesbian desire is impossible.[73] Some of the ads in both mainstream and gay and lesbian contexts suggest that advertisers have found a way to represent lipstick lesbians as desir*able*, in contrast to the stereotype of the ugly lesbian feminist, but the lack of trade press interest in lesbian consumers and low advertising revenues for lesbian publications suggest that marketers cannot imagine a lesbian audience as sufficiently desir*ing* to respond to their appeals. De Lauretis' discussion of "hommo-sexuality," in which women's desire for each other is reworked in the service of male desire, is useful in understanding how eroticized images of women together function less to appeal to a lesbian market than for the pleasure of heterosexual men and women. Canadian journalist Stephanie Nolen reviews lesbian kisses in popular media, including in ads for Parasuco Jeans, Hard Rock Las Vegas, and Disaronno.[74] She quotes a Toronto sex columnist who complained, "It's totally straight-looking women with no stereotypical lesbian trappings. It's male titillation—what men have always thought about when they think about lesbians. They think about themselves. Men think about threesomes."[75] Such "hommo-sexual" mainstream marketing images of feminine women in quasi-erotic scenarios seem more available to the male gaze than to lesbian pleasure. The appearance of lesbian images in putatively heterosexual women's fashion magazines also taps into the male titillation factor: straight women readers can vicariously fantasize the cachet that toying with girl-girl sex would afford them with the boys. In studies of audiences' responses to mainstream images of women in eroticized couples, however, lesbians commonly articulate ambivalence about these images when they perceive them to reinforce heteronormative sexual dynamics or to be for the benefit of heterosexual men.[76] As Danae Clark asserts, lesbian readers "know that they are not the primary audience for mainstream advertising, that androgyny is a fashionable and profitable commodity, and that the fashion models in these ads [with a "lesbian" aesthetic] are quite probably heterosexual."[77]

This is not to argue that lesbians do not enjoy seeing straight-looking or -identified women kiss. Lesbians find pleasure even in the most heterosexual-seeming manifestations of consumer culture by appropriating ad images for their own erotic satisfaction, by reworking styles in ways not intended by clothes designers, and by "shopping with their female lovers or partners, sharing the physical and erotic space of the dressing room."[78] These strategies yield pleasures not necessarily consciously offered by mainstream consumer culture, but that are, in cultural studies scholar Michel de Certeau's term, "poached" from that culture.[79] The pleasures of poaching lie in the subversion of the intended meanings of cultural forms, and in the illicit use of these forms in ways not intended by their producers.

How, then, can marketers represent lesbians in ads, especially when lesbians often perceive images of women together as inauthentic, as "for men"? De Lauretis argues that butchness offers possibly the most direct route for lesbians out of "hommo-sexuality" because the lesbian remains invisible "unless . . . she enters the frame of vision *as or with* a lesbian in male body drag."[80] Thus while the lipstick lesbian can be rendered invisible as an agent of desire by patriarchal modes of looking, the butch stands outside these modes and can function as an autonomously desiring subject. She is less recuperable within the girl-girl porn fantasy, and can be more easily credited with an active, assertive (because masculine) desire. Yet the butch has not been taken up by gay marketers as the icon of lesbian consumption, with one notable exception. According to journalist Frank DeCaro, the "hottest face in fashion" in 1994 was openly lesbian, Asian American model Jenny Shimizu (fig. 6.6).[81] As a *Curve* cover story describes,

> In a time when the tough-tender look is in and androgyny is all the rage, Jenny Shimizu has become a superstar. She has become the most talked-about face in fashion not only because she is the first Asian supermodel, a mechanic, and an out and proud lesbian, . . . but also because of her famous tattoos [one of] which runs down her right shoulder to her elbow and is of a scantily clad woman straddling a wrench. In place of the brand name "Snap-On," it reads "Strap-On."[82]

Shimizu was exoticized as an "anti-model" whose "ethnicity is a big asset way beyond the United Colors of Benetton."[83] But she was also eroticized because she was butch: her "androgynous" look, tattoos, and devil-may-care attitude were heralded as a relief at a time when the polished, feminine, English-model look was (momentarily) under attack. Yet Shimizu's later comments suggest that she ultimately felt bitter about being taken up as an exotic plaything by the fashion world, only to be discarded when the appeal of Asian androgyny had passed.

FIGURE 6.6 JENNY SHIMIZU (*CROUCHING*) POSES AS A CHIC BUTCH IN THIS ANDROGYNOUS cK ONE AD (*COSMOPOLITAN*, NOVEMBER 1994).

Despite Shimizu's blaze of fame, masculine women tend not to be popular representatives for lesbian consumption. Butches have not historically been imagined as attractive: a long-held stereotype has cast the bulldagger as a swaggering, overweight, domineering, predatory menace.[84] This stereotype may be changing, as illustrated by the Wachowski brothers' 1996 neo-noir film *Bound*, which recast the butch-femme couple as both subjects and objects of desire, and by the evolving popularity of the playful, assertive, gender-performative drag king scene. Although butches may be representable as desiring agents, they do not conform to the two dominant modes of consumption—that is, as housewife or as hyperdesirous feminine shopper. That butches have in fact long been keen and expert shoppers, however, is evidenced by Elizabeth Lapovsky Kennedy and Madeline Davis's study of lesbian communities in Buffalo, New York. These authors found that working-class African American and white butches dressed in men's clothing and "remember devoting a great deal of care—not to mention time and money—to their dress when preparing to step out on a Saturday night in the 1940s."[85]

When lesbian marketers are prepared to produce appeals to lesbians, they may be resistant to including a butch aesthetic in their work. As I mention in chapter 5, Blackwood lamented that the drag king "phenomenon . . . doesn't work for me at all," and asked, "can we all just be who we are?"[86] This suggests that some gay and lesbian marketers believe in essentialized ideas of sexuality and gender, where "being who we are" presumes that lesbians are naturally feminine. In their concern to offer the most "positive" images of lesbians and gays to compensate for years of invisibility and stereotyping, marketers may be invested in producing "appropriately" or "naturally" feminine images as the most flattering face of lesbianism.

Butchness tends to be articulated with working-class culture, at least historically, further distancing masculine women from the ideal model of consumption. Kennedy and Davis, for example, found that white, professional lesbians in Buffalo were less likely than African American and white working-class lesbians to adopt distinctively masculine dress. Indeed, it was not only Jenny Shimizu's racial and sexual exoticism that made her so popular but also her class position, suggested by frequent references to her tattoos and her "greasemonkey" beginnings as an auto mechanic. Although this may have increased her exotic capital as a model, the association between female masculinity and working-class pay rates may again place butches outside the bracket of the desirable consumer, this time for reasons of income. The few other examples of masculine women in advertising tend to be celebrities, and thus apparently wealthy: k. d. lang, who appeared wearing MAC cosmetics, and Martina Navratilova, a spokesperson for the Rainbow credit card and for Subaru.

For both business and political reasons, marketers have not yet produced a viable lesbian market. Dislocated from the glamorous world of the heterosexual femme fatale, and from Mrs. Consumer's nuclear family, lesbians are hard to figure as real women. Yet they do not belong in the imagined world of affluent tastefulness of gay men, either. Lesbian income levels, media and consumption habits, and social patterns mitigate against the formation of a lesbian market. But the politics of lesbian feminism is also an obstacle to imagining a lesbian niche. A political orientation is not necessarily a barrier to successful market-formation, however: gay men became increasingly desirable as a target market after their political activism in response to the AIDS epidemic brought them much media visibility. Lesbians are also seen as political, but the difference is that they politicized consumption. The early post-Stonewall gay male

liberation movement was critical of capitalism and its influence on homophobia, but in the later, more accommodationist stage of the movement, reflected in David Goodstein's post-1974 *Advocate*, consumption was not incompatible with gay liberation. On the contrary, many gay men felt that an
openly gay consumer culture was the route to liberation. In contrast, feminism, and especially lesbian feminism, has historically been much more skep-
tical about the liberatory potential of consumption and consumer visibility. By
drawing attention to how femininity is constructed through consumption,
feminism disrupted the convenient marriage of capitalism and patriarchy, and
disqualified lesbians from the criteria necessary to be considered a market.

Even recent incarnations of feminism that are pro-sex, pro-glamour, and
pro-shopping offer little comfort to marketers. When lesbians consume, they
can do so playfully and with pleasure, performing gender as a masquerade,
rather than unthinkingly conforming to normative standards of femininity.
The critical distance from these normative standards that feminism affords
does nothing to reassure advertisers as to the complicity of lesbian shoppers,
and offers little guidance about how to produce "authentically" lesbian appeals. Advertisers have adeptly folded the positive stereotypes of gay men and
heterosexual women into evolving images of consumption, but are baffled by
lesbians who borrow lipstick from an otherwise rejected system of heterosexual femininity for the purposes of lesbian erotic masquerade.

The dearth of marketing attention may come as a relief to some lesbians
who would prefer to remain unnoticed by advertising's judgmental, conform-
ist gaze. Yet the lack of a developed lesbian market on a national scale means
that lesbians are less likely to benefit from the advantages of gay marketing visibility. Scarce advertising in lesbian publications such as *Curve*, *Girlfriends*, and
On Our Backs leave these venues underfunded, and without more marketing
attention to lesbians, mixed gay and lesbian publications have little reason to
boost female readership by offering more lesbian-specific content. Further, the
partial and uncertain efforts to imagine lesbians as consumers perpetuates the
narrow view that lesbians are dowdy and sexless, and that women can only be
the recipients, not the initiators, of desire. In contrast to this image of desexualized lesbians, gay men are burdened with a stereotype of hypersexuality; if the
failure to imagine the lesbian consumer results from marketers' inability to
imagine lesbian desire, it may be the very possibility of imagining the gay man
as a sexually desiring agent that makes it possible to also imagine him as a consumer. However, the threat that gay male sexuality poses to the ideal of the respectable professional-managerial class gay consumer means that marketers
must work hard to contain the negative associations of gay sex. The production
and containment of queer sexuality is the subject of the following chapter.

CHAPTER 7

SEX SELLS

The stereotype of the dour, unsexy lesbian feminist has hindered the construction of a viable lesbian consumer segment. Yet whereas lesbians have been hard to imagine as agents of desire, gay men have long been regarded as sexual—indeed as hypersexual. Gay male sexual culture was fundamental in the formation of the gay niche, bringing gay men to marketers' attention in the 1970s. It is no coincidence that the first products from mainstream companies advertised in the gay press were for liquor and disco records, or that national gay magazines became profitable because of sexual advertising—classified ads, ads for pornography and, later, phone sex ads. The relation between gay men's sexual culture and commerce was not an easy one for national advertisers, however; no matter how attractive the image of the affluent, freespending gay man was in the 1970s, the taint of gay sex meant that most mainstream corporations avoided advertising in the gay press. Negative associations with gay men's sexuality only proliferated in the 1980s as the AIDS epidemic was characterized as "the gay plague."[1] Gay marketers were thus faced with a conundrum: on one hand, gay men's sexual culture helped to promote the idea of gay men as good consumers; on the other, it was precisely gay men's sexual culture that impeded the construction of the gay market on a national scale. Gay media publishers and marketers addressed the constraints that queer sex posed to a flourishing gay market by sequestering or banning explicit sexuality in advertising and editorial content.[2] Such sexual containment, however, exists in an uneasy relationship with the common sense of advertising, that "sex sells." The assumption that "sex sells" masks the relationship between sexuality and commerce, discourages analysis of the particular *ways* that sex is articulated to marketing, and ignores the limits placed upon visible manifestations of sexuality in advertising and commercial media. To put this another way, when might sex *not* sell? If "sex sells," why must gay sex be so contained? How must marketers construct the gay market if not through its sexuality, and with what consequences for queer sex and politics? The closeting of gay sexuality thus produces an interesting paradox: a market that is constituted as distinct through the nondominant sexuality of its constituency could be brought into being only through the effacement of that sexuality.

Richard Ohmann looks at how family magazines such as *Munsey's* and the *Ladies' Home Journal* cultivated late-nineteenth-century audiences drawn from the nascent professional-managerial class and sold them to advertisers.[3] These magazines offered training in "socially correct participation" to readers who were unfamiliar with the expectations of a new and somewhat plastic class position.[4] Part of this training concerned the appropriate place of sexuality: Ohmann finds that "sex could be thematized in these magazines if (a) it was framed as Art; (b) it was a vice of the lower orders; or (c) it was brought under moral censure."[5] Sexual content was not banished then, but was contained by aesthetic tastefulness or was portrayed as a class-based example against which "respectable" families could favorably compare themselves. Sexuality was thus deployed to clarify new formations of social stratification; a respectable professional-managerial identity was distinguished both from the "rude" classes and from a degenerate social elite in part through the training in sexual decorum that family magazines offered. Although Ohmann is concerned with a specific historical period and medium, his research suggests how the containment of sexuality helps produce a class-specific identity among readers, and prompts a consideration of the relationship between sexual content and social position in gay and lesbian media.

In her influential essay "Thinking Sex," Gayle Rubin offers a model with which to analyze the intersections between social and sexual stratification. She outlines the sexual practices that are legitimized in the "charmed circle" of sex:

> Sexuality that is "good," "normal," and "natural" should ideally be heterosexual, marital, monogamous, reproductive, and non-commercial. It should be coupled, relational, in the same generation, and occur at home. It should not involve pornography, fetish objects, sex toys of any sort, or roles other than male or female. Any sex that violates these rules is "bad," "abnormal," or "unnatural."[6]

Rubin's model suggests a process through which nonnormative sex is ejected from the charmed circle, and in which some delegitimized practices are subject to even tighter constraints than others, with queer sex requiring specific restrictions. She acknowledges that "some forms of homosexuality are moving in the direction of respectability"—that is, those that are vanilla, coupled, and monogamous—but that "most homosexuality is still on the bad side of the line."[7] In the production of the gay market and its personification of the ideal gay consumer, marketers struggled with the abject stereotypes of the hypersexual, promiscuous gay man, replacing these with "charmed" (or at least, less abject) manifestations of homosexuality as the public face of gayness.

Laura Kipnis looks at the relationship between social and sexual stratification in her study of pornography. She argues that the condemning discourses that surround porn reveal deeper anxieties about the relationship between sexuality and the social order:

> Control over the body has long been considered essential to producing an orderly work force, a docile populace, a passive law-abiding citizenry. Just consider how many actual laws are on the books regulating *how* bodies may be seen and what parts may not, *what* you may do with your body in public *and* in private, and it begins to make more sense that the out-of-control, unmannerly body is precisely what threatens the orderly operation of the status quo.[8]

The representation of sex, therefore, has ramifications beyond the display of desire and pleasure: it reveals deeper structures of power and control. Kipnis emphasizes that not all porn is equally challenging; publications that refuse to contain sexual explicitness in broader aesthetic or gender-normative codes (by showing obese or transsexual models, for example), or those that are deliberately class antagonistic (such as *Hustler* magazine), receive even greater censure than others. Kipnis's work helps to make sense of how sexual content is treated differently in gay and in putatively heterosexual magazines; there is no absolute boundary between acceptable and unacceptable sexual content, but such content is positioned in a "hierarchy of legitimacies,"[9] depending on what kind of sexual content is presented (gay, straight, commercial, arty, images, words, etc.) and in what context (gay and lesbian glossy magazines versus general-market magazines or local gay papers).

Kipnis also demonstrates how pornography's hierarchy of legitimacies is produced through taste; the most antagonistic images are not only those that transgress gender boundaries but those that blur class distinctions as well. As I have discussed elsewhere, French sociologist Pierre Bourdieu discusses how tastes, far from being arbitrary, simultaneously manifest and reassert cultural hierarchies.[10] For Bourdieu, taste includes both culinary dimensions (certain foods taste "good" or "bad") and aesthetic ones (classical music is "better" than pop). Given how centrally he positions the body in taste cultures, however, it is striking that he does not include sexual decorum as a third sense of taste, since sexual tastefulness is surely as embodied, naturalized, and yet ultimately cultural as culinary and aesthetic preferences. I extend Bourdieu's analysis to include a consideration of sexual tastefulness and its role in producing a desirable—that is, "respectable"—image of the ideal gay consumer. Hierarchies of food, art, and sex function semiautonomously from each other, although aesthetic valuation features strongly in judgments of sexual decorum (as in the distinction commonly made between "artful" erotica and "sleazy" pornography). Further, each sense has an intricate relationship with social hierarchies, including class, race, gender, and sexuality. Only through recognizing the role of sexual taste in these hierarchies can we understand how gay marketers use claims of "good taste" to distinguish acceptable from offensive manifestations of queer sex in different media.

Bourdieu's work, with some adaptations, is thus indispensable as a starting point to analyze sexual content in gay and lesbian media. First, he discusses taste in its aesthetic and culinary senses; I also apply it to sexual propriety, looking at the distinctions between "decorum" and "tastelessness." Second, he takes occupation, education, and gender as the dominant variables in the formation of taste; I argue that practices and sensibilities are also organized around other social positions and identifications, including sexuality. Third, while Bourdieu's concern is how taste functions in the stratification of classes (irrespective of sexuality), I look at how sexual and other taste hierarchies produce gay subcultural capital in gay and lesbian cultural contexts. Fourth, Bourdieu sees the family and schools as primary transmitters of cultural capital. I suggest that media, marketing, and popular culture also have a profound role to play, especially with respect to gay subcultural capital, which is not likely to be inculcated through dominant social institutions hostile to, or ignorant of, gay tastes and mores. How are the taste hierarchies manifested through sexual content and aesthetics articulated with gay subcultural capital to produce a class-specific ideal gay consumer?

Upgrading People's Impression of Gays

> Spend some time browsing at your local newsstand, and you are likely to see gay magazines displayed not alongside pornography, but alongside men's magazines or the ethnic press. It's *Playboy* and *Penthouse* that now come in plastic envelopes, not their mainstream gay counterparts.[11]

Most marketers take it for granted that a visible, commercial gay sexuality is incompatible with mainstream advertising; as advertising agency president Jack Sansolo asked, "You think I'd tell clients to advertise next to a 900 number? Give me a break."[12] This commonly held belief is reflected in the removal of sexual content and advertising from the gay press since the 1970s. *Advocate* publisher David Goodstein commented that the magazine was "being desleazified" in the mid-1970s to court mainstream advertisers, largely by sequestering sexually explicit content and classifieds at the back of the magazine.[13] Sex ads were gradually eliminated altogether from the *Advocate*, first into a pullout section (the "Pink Pages"), and in 1992 into a separate, mail-order publication (the *Advocate Classifieds*, later called *Unzipped*).

Most of the new gay and lesbian media that flourished in the 1980s and 1990s debuted without sex ads or dropped them in early issues. Advertisers and publishers, directing their opprobrium especially at phone sex advertisers, claimed that sex ads created an inhospitable environment for national goods and services. One article announcing a new Miami-based gay magazine, *miamigo*, boasted it "dumps smut, keeps flair, aims for upscale."[14] Journalist Dana Calvo quoted the publisher's reason for refusing sex ads: "We're still a very sexual, artsy magazine but not in advertising with triple XXX ads . . . we want to upgrade people's impression [of gays]."[15] Calvo's article makes explicit the inverse relationship between elevated cultural tastes (upgrading to the highbrow) and a debased advertising genre (XXX sex ads), and shows how the class position of gay men is made precarious, in part, by public evidence of their sexual culture.

How the incompatibility between sexual content and national advertising is negotiated differs among gay and lesbian media. Like *miamigo*, other glossy magazines such as the *Advocate*, *Out*, and *Curve* refuse sex ads altogether. Publishers of local gay and lesbian newspapers, however, tend to be more relaxed about sexual content. Because of their modest circulation, monochrome printing, and low-quality stock, most local papers do not expect to win many lucrative national advertisers. Further, because many are free publications and thus survive on ad income alone, they tend to remain dependent on sex-related advertising. To encourage national advertisers in the earlier pages, most shunt the sex ads to the back. However, the presence of sex ads at all is a barrier to increased national and "respectable" advertising in these publications. In order to attract "Mom and Pop businesses in Du Pont Circle" that might be squeamish about appearing next to sex ads, the *Washington Blade* reportedly made it "difficult" for sex-oriented businesses to advertise.[16]

The gay and lesbian consumer medium most stringently monitored for sexual material is the Internet. Web sites such as PlanetOut and gay.com have distanced themselves from sexual advertising; as a gay.com spokesperson explained, "'That's not the business we're going to be in. We're in the business of community, news' and other services."[17] Given the almost unlimited inter-

connectivity of the Internet, marketers for gay and lesbian Web sites obsessively revisit the question of whether visitors to gay portals will click their way
through linked sites to "adult content." Gfn.com's president and chief operating officer, Jeffrey Newman, commented that some advertisers "are still fearful of being associated with any adult content . . . they are still concerned at
how close to adult content we might be, or the site that [users] are going to
do business with is."[18] He emphasized, "We have a strict policy: we don't have
any [links] with adult content sites and we do everything to make sure people
can't get through at least three or four clicks from our site to adult content.
We are very, very careful about that issue."[19] As IBM advertising account executive Jim Consolantis explained, "The concern that most major advertisers
have, like IBM, is making sure that they don't get linked to any site that has
high sexual content."[20] The pressure that large advertisers can bring to bear on
Internet sites has produced an environment of hypervigilance. As *Advocate*
owner Liberation Publications, Inc., negotiated to merge with PlanetOut in
the summer of 2000, it sold *Unzipped* and at least two other pornography magazines to Specialty Publications, a company also owned by LPI's owner.

The most important single reason marketers gave for taking sex out of advertising was that they wanted to contradict the stereotype that gay men, in
particular, were hypersexual and/or pedophilic. Commenting on a gfn.com
campaign that appeared in mainstream as well as in gay and lesbian media,
CEO Walter Schubert said, "The ad campaign was not only something that
was meant to be tongue-in-cheek and cute to the gay community, but it was
also something that would show corporate America and the straight community that we're really not all sex fiends and monsters."[21] Yet counteracting this
stereotype was rarely given as a rationale for the removal of sexual advertising
and editorial content. Far more often publishers commented that they refused
sex ads because they alienate national advertisers. As Michael Shively, former
associate publisher at the *Advocate*, recalled,

> There was always this internal dialogue about the embarrassment of the
> [sex] ads, and when push came to shove [national advertisers] always
> said, "Well, because of the sexual content we can't put an ad in your
> magazine." No matter how far it went, once you got through to the
> decision-makers, they would say, "Well, you've got a great vehicle, and
> we would love to do this, but you have all these sex ads."[22]

Sex ads were perceived to reduce the quality of gay and lesbian media, making them appear sleazy and less viable as mainstream marketing vehicles.[23]
Michael Kaminer, *Out*'s original director of public relations, explained that the

publisher's decision to refuse sex ads was "a gamble, but it's a simple fact of life that you're not going to attract major advertisers with [sex ads] in your magazine. . . . The ads are lucrative, but there's no way you are going to get the big names."[24] Dan Baker concurred, noting that among lesbian and gay glossy magazine publishers in the early 1990s,

> There was a feeling that there were never going to be "mainstream"—
> and every time I use mainstream I put it in quotes—advertisers in gay
> publications as long as there was sex connected, and that was a signifi-
> cant step forward, or at least in their *minds* it was, when they decided that
> the only way to do it was to have a "general interest" gay magazine that
> then would get "general interest" ads.[25]

Another pressure on magazine publishers is distribution: some interviewees mentioned that sex ads restricted where magazines can be sold or given away. According to publisher Sean Strub, large numbers of *POZ* issues are distributed free through HIV/AIDS clinics, social services, health services, and so on: "I think that if we had sexually related advertising, or ads that were more sex-related, we would limit where the magazine could go, in terms of schools and AIDS educators and a lot of community-based organizations."[26] Some publishers were also concerned about international distribution. Frances Stevens, publisher and editor in chief of *Curve*, said that the magazine "service[s] a large Canadian distribution so . . . we want all the women who want to get the magazine to be able to get it."[27] Stevens was worried that including sexual advertising may put the magazine at risk of seizure by Canadian customs. This anxiety may be overstated: as the marketing director of the lesbian porn magazine *On Our Backs* commented, while the lesbian SM magazine *Bad Attitude* "saw a lot of problems with the Canadian distribution, we haven't had any problems with [foreign distribution] yet."[28] Representations of fetish, kinky, and SM sex are more at risk of seizure than what Kipnis calls "run-of-mill 'fuck and suck' pornography."[29]

In addition to advertisers and customs officials, marketers and readers may not want to see sex ads. Don Tuthill decided to exclude them from *Genre* and, more recently, *Q San Francisco* less because he wanted to court national advertisers than because he himself disliked gay publications that were "full of sex" and that "you can't have on your coffee table for your mother to read."[30] Henry Scott attributed *Out*'s rejection of sex ads to readers' wishes: "What people say is 'Sex is important in my life, and I can buy a magazine oriented to sex'—again it's a segmentation thing—'[but] that's not what I buy *Out* for.' "[31] Scott claimed that many of his readers may be interested in sexual content, but not in a general-interest gay and lesbian magazine.

Some interviewees attributed the removal of sex ads to a desire to broaden a magazine's gender appeal. Marketing consultant and freelance journalist Grant Lukenbill and the *Advocate*'s publisher Joe Landry both claimed that lesbians do not want to see evidence of gay men's sexuality in gay and lesbian publications. For example, Landry said, "When we did the redesign six years ago and took the sex advertising out of the [*Advocate*] and changed the title to the 'National Gay *and Lesbian* Magazine,' the readership went from 2 percent female to 25 percent, and between the last two readership surveys that we've done it's been constant at 27 percent."[32] He echoed the stereotype that lesbians are antisex in general and are repelled by male erotic activity in particular; by removing sex ads the *Advocate* became a more "lesbian-friendly" environment. He justified the magazine's national advertising-friendly policy in terms of a more "ethical" framework—protecting dour, sexless lesbian feminists from male sexuality or, indeed, *any* sexuality.

The containment of a public, commercial queer sexuality also conforms to the most respectable aims of the gay civil rights movement. Patrick Califia, who wrote a sex advice column for the *Advocate* for many years as Pat Califia, reported that the removal of the sex ads and his column from the *Advocate* "was largely driven by marketing, but the marketing was also backed up by a certain kind of understanding of what gay politics should be about, what the agenda should be, who should be in the movement, what we should tell straight people about ourselves."[33] These concerns produced a desexualized, class-respectable venue for national advertisers and, in turn, offered mainstream culture more broadly an image of a sexually discreet group of gay and lesbian readers and consumers.

The different institutional positions occupied by my interviewees may suggest some friction between them on the topic of sexual containment in gay-themed advertising and publications. Yet there was remarkably little dissent: most interviewees assumed that explicit sexual content in national magazines and on Internet sites precluded national advertising, and that sex ads tainted local publications. There were two notable exceptions to this view, however. First, staff at the pornography publication *On Our Backs* criticized the double standard that allowed national advertising in heterosexual-targeted pornography magazines but not in lesbian porn. Second, Shively, who sold advertising for the *Advocate* from 1980 to 1990, described a contentious debate about what could and couldn't be permitted in the magazine. One of his roles as associate publisher was to be

> the general of the penis police. There was this whole thing in the *Advocate* that our line was that you could not show a penis. So then it was, like, how much of a penis could you show when it's not a penis, right?

We're talking about hot debates in the production room when it's supposed to be going to the printers! And taking the X-Acto knife and
shaving an eighth of an inch off the bottom of a halftone to make it
penisless. And so it was like you could show pubes and then you could
show just the very top of the penis. And of course the advertisers are always arguing that sex sells, and they would send photographs of people
totally nude. And so back and forth it went.[34]

Shively described himself and Robert McQueen, then editor in chief, as "very
pro-sex" and caught in a dilemma about exactly how explicit representations
of sexuality could be in the *Advocate*. There were "screaming, yelling fights"
between production and advertising staff while the courier waited in the reception area to take the magazine to the printers.[35] Yet Shively reflected that
"what you see in the pages does not reflect what formed [the content]. It is
impossible to infer the process from the result." Although the process invoked
competing demands to be sex-positive and to win national advertisers, the
outcome reflected the more conservative argument: business demands won
out over sexual politics.

Thus even if magazine staff held different personal positions on the acceptability, or indeed the desirability, of sexual content in their publication, and
even if the line between acceptable and unacceptable is constantly negotiated,
the commonsense view that sex is incompatible with national advertising usually prevailed. Interviewees commonly faulted someone else for this: magazine
publishers blamed customs officials and others responsible for regulating distribution; magazine and Internet publishers blamed national advertisers for
pulling out if sex ads appeared in those venues; publishers protected readers—
both gay men and lesbians—from coming into contact with "offensive" material; and some marketers had an overriding concern to negate the stereotype
that gay people are all "sex fiends and monsters." Ad agencies, often positioned
as the most conservative force, in turn blamed clients for their unwillingness
to transgress sexual boundaries, and distribution channels for limiting what
can be shown. Liz Gumbiner recalled the fine lines drawn between what was
and wasn't acceptable during the shoot for the Mistic ad showing a lesbian
couple:

We had lingerie just hanging out to dry in the bathroom, and it would
have been just the quickest shot, but it implied intimacy, and so we
couldn't show that. And it's so funny, that we could have a woman [say]
"here's the person I want to spend the rest of my life with," but we
couldn't show their lingerie hanging in the bathroom. But if it was a

husband and wife? Sure, of course you could show a slip or something. . . . We thought it would be good to have a really quick flash of
them kissing at one point, but [our lawyer] was, like, "No way, no way!
It'll never get on the air."[36]

By attributing sexual conservatism to other elements in the production and
distribution process, most interviewees suggested that they would like to be
less sexually conservative, whether in the creation or in the acceptance of ads,
but that their hands were tied by prudish others on whom they depended for
business.

Respectability, the need to be taken seriously by mainstream advertisers,
ease of distribution, and the providing of a comfortable environment for
women and men readers (and their mothers) are some of the reasons marketers gave for banishing sexual advertising from or limiting it in gay and lesbian media. Yet interviewees such as Joe Landry emphasized that removing sex
ads alone was not sufficient to court national advertisers. Another effort has
been to emphasize the desirable demographics of the *Advocate*'s readers and the
high quality of the magazine's editorial content. Indeed, Landry's linking of
desirable demographics and high-quality editorial content with the desexualized environment suggests that the former can be produced only in a sex-free
context.

Being Friendly to Mainstream Advertisers

Both the trade press and my interviewees took it for granted that the presence
of sex ads in lesbian and gay media precludes mainstream advertising. The ads
and content of a range of lesbian and gay magazines called this assumption into
question, however. For although the publishers of these magazines emphasized
that they refused "sex ads," they evidently had accepted ads for sex stores,
books, catalogs, toys, and lubricants. How could these ads slip in under the
radar of rules against sex ads? What is it about them that allowed them a place
in gay glossy magazines that supposedly eschew explicit sexual references?
What, in turn, is the relationship between sexual editorial material and the
presence of national advertising?

From the testimony of magazine publishers, it appeared that there is a great
deal of ambiguity about what constitutes a sex ad. Although *On Our Backs* and
Girlfriends are published by the same company, the latter aims to be a lesbian
"lifestyle" magazine and, by rejecting sex ads, is "friendlier to mainstream
advertisers" than is the pornographic *On Our Backs*.[37] It does, though, take
ads from a women's sex store—Good Vibrations—which Draper saw as "more

like a new age music store, . . . a very wholesome . . . sex store for the nineteen" (fig. 7.1).[38] At the same time, *Girlfriends* turns down ads for pornographic videos and phone sex lines even though, as Draper put it, "It kills me to turn down money." She explained that they don't print phone sex ads because already nervous mainstream advertisers see this category as sleazy; in contrast, GoodVibrations does not pose such a threat. Similarly, although both *Out* and the *Advocate* turn down "sex ads," they do accept ads for lubricants and condoms (fig. 7.2).[39] Scott said his main concern was with ads for phone sex and escort services. Stevens said that at *Curve* they "do not carry 900 or sex-based ads," but she agreed that they would carry ads for sex toys and the Good Vibrations store; they accept ads on "a case-by-case basis . . . depend[ing] on the explicit nature of the ad."[40] This contradiction in gay and

FIGURE 7.1 DISCOVERING THE SECRETS OF LESBIAN SEXUALITY WITH GOOD VIBRATIONS (*GIRLFRIENDS*, OCTOBER 2002).

FIGURE 7.2 WHEN IT'S RAINING MEN, LIFESTYLES HELPS YOU WEATHER THE STORM (*ADVOCATE*, JUNE 10, 2003).

lesbian print media is mirrored by online Web sites: although PlanetOut Partners rejects sex ads, it does include an "adult" section of its Kleptomaniac microsite, which offers pornographic videos, sexual lubricants, and other sex-related products for sale.

Advertisers of erotic products are extremely careful to err on the side of respectability. Deborah Isherwood, promotions manager for a well-known sexual lubricant, explained that her company began to advertise in gay and lesbian publications because its share of the lubricant market had slipped as newer brands began to target gay men exclusively.[41] Isherwood was careful to emphasize that her company's marketing approach treated gay men as "just another demographic group"; its ads were neither gender- nor sexuality-specific, so they could be placed in a range of publications. Although its advertising strategy did not single out gay men as a distinct market, the company downplayed the sexual connotations of the product, and the name of the parent company was kept separate from that of the lubricant lest the product's sexual purpose taint the company's association with babies and children. Further, Isherwood explained that the company's advertising and sponsorship campaign attempted to link the lubricant to health (including safe sex) rather than to sex per se, aiming for "a professional manner and not promoting sexuality." This strategy minimized the product's sexual uses to maintain the conservative image of the parent company as well as to render its ads sufficiently tasteful to appear in gay and lesbian magazines.

In contrast to the sterile images in lubricant ads, some of the sexiest images in gay publications are for products that have little to do with sex, or even with sexual identity. Ads for Calvin Klein, Abercrombie & Fitch, and Gap portray handsome, boyish young men enjoying sexually ambiguous, athletic intimacy. Images that may appeal to gay men only covertly when they appear in other magazines convey at least an implicitly homoerotic message in gay publications. For example, Abercrombie & Fitch's fall 1999 "magalogue" explores the theme of "college wrestling." The campaign's creative director, Sam Shahid, talked frankly about the sexual connotations of the images as being "in the eye of the beholder. . . . Gays love it; straights love it; girls love it."[42] This wrestling campaign played with a familiar tension between the homosocial and the homoerotic;[43] what has changed is how readily the Abercrombie & Fitch agency and head office acknowledged the range of its appeal.

It is clear, then, that the much-touted refusal of sex ads applies to a narrow range of services—900-number phone sex lines and escorts. Although publishers may protest that they refuse sex ads, some sex-related products and stores do advertise, and some degree of generalized sexiness is accepted, even welcomed. What distinguishes banned sex ads from other sex-related and sexy advertising is their offer of an explicitly commercial sexual exchange that is likely to occur between strangers. Phone sex and escort services are thus positioned outside Rubin's charmed circle, while ads for sex products that can be used in an established, private, noncommercial sexual relationship (sex toys, videos) can be somewhat redeemed in the inner circle. Further, the increasing willingness of advertisers to acknowledge the homoerotic potential of fashion advertising suggests that sexiness has not been phased out of gay and lesbian publications but, rather, has been shifted from sexual services and products to more generalized, homosocial, arty scenarios. The Abercrombie & Fitch ads, like all "image advertising," sell the fantasy that the product's sexy attributes will be bestowed on the consumer; they do not sell the real possibility of sexual exchange, as sex ads do. So although gay and lesbian publishers ban explicit ads for commercial sexual services and allow only oblique references between sexual practices and products (lubricants, sex stores), they nevertheless encourage a tasteful sexiness in ads that are not expressly sex-related.

The relation between commercial sexuality and mainstream advertising becomes even more strained in pornographic media. Since the relaunch of *On Our Backs* in June 1998, most of the magazine's advertising has come from the sex industry, and the publishers have found it a real challenge to get national advertising. Advertising director Megan Ishler courted alcohol and cigarette companies as most likely to advertise in "sophisticate" titles such as *On Our Backs*, but they had yet to take the plunge. Ishler had tried a variety of strategies:

> I've asked advertisers who are in *Girlfriends* to [advertise in *On Our Backs*] dirt cheap or free—to bundle in the back cover of *On Our Backs* at half price, if they come in as part of their *Girlfriends* contract. I've been told "no" for that. I've been told "no" to try it for free one time, and then we can talk about a contract. . . . [Or] as part of an incentive for marketing: "If you sponsor this event, Alizé, . . . we'll give you the back cover of the magazine," [and] they said "no" because they did not want to appear on the back cover of our publication.[44]

Ishler was keen to give space away for free because a good response from free advertising was likely to induce them to pay for space in the future. More important perhaps, once one national advertiser in a given category enters a publication, others tend to follow. Yet mainstream advertisers have proven recalcitrant, for several reasons: *On Our Backs* has an unaudited circulation of 25,000, a small market by many magazines' standards; it is monochrome printed on low-quality stock; and it lacks significant market research data on lesbians generally and readers of lesbian pornography in particular. Further, many adver-tisers are squeamish about an association with lesbian sex, despite the cachet of girl-girl sex in mainstream pornography, and they may be worried about backlash from other consumers.

A preliminary review of a range of pornographic magazines revealed large differences in their advertising, which suggests the more or less scrupulous maintenance of boundaries between some categories of ads. In counting the types of ads in single issues of a variety of porn magazines,[45] I found an in-verse relationship between the presence of sex industry ads and the amount of national, mainstream, non-sex-related advertising. The majority of *Playboy*'s full-page ads were for alcoholic beverages (twenty-seven pages) and tobacco products (twenty-three pages); electronics, nonporn media, and apparel ads also appeared, including a wholesome Tommy Hilfiger ad on the back cover. The magazine had only one ad for an explicitly sex-related product (an erotic video for couples) that did not bear the *Playboy* brand. *Penthouse* had fewer al-cohol and tobacco ads (two and five full-page ads, respectively) and far more sex ads (twenty pages) than *Playboy*, mostly for 900-number phone sex lines and videos. *Hustler* had only sex-related advertising: in addition to two full-page ads for penis enlargers, it offered forty-five pages of phone sex and porn video ads. With pornographic magazines marketed to straight women, gay men, and lesbians, the picture is more complicated: *Playgirl*, ostensibly directed at heterosexual women readers, had only sex ads (seventeen pages);[46] the gay men's pornographic magazine *Blueboy* also had only sex ads (thirteen pages); *On Our Backs* had eight pages of sex ads, in addition to three ads for non-sex-related products; and the lesbian SM magazine *Bad Attitude* had three pages of sex and lesbian information ads.

In pornography directed at heterosexual men, then, more sex ads mean less national advertising. The presence of national, nonsex advertising reflects in part Kipnis's hierarchy of taste among magazines: *Playboy*'s and *Penthouse*'s "high-class" image wins national ads, whereas *Hustler* gets only sex ads. The class implications of this contrast was affirmed by a *Playboy* advertising repre-sentative, who explained that it was a "corporate decision," in keeping with the "upscale image of the magazine," not to accept "chat room, sex toys, or other [sex] ads."[47] This suggests that *Playboy*'s publisher, like lesbian and gay glossy magazine publishers, has chosen to avoid the sleazy image of sex ads. Yet the cultural legitimization that national advertising offers is less available to heterosexual women and queer women and men. Although *Playgirl* contains less explicitly sexual images than say, *Penthouse*, and interpellates readers as members of—or as aspiring to—the professional classes, it does not contain national advertising. *Playgirl*'s and *On Our Backs*' comparatively small circulations, lower-quality stock, and lack of market research data may contribute to mainstream advertisers' reluctance to buy space in them, as Ishler explained, yet the very presence of sex ads (in the absence of ads for other products) may perpetuate these magazines' image as less "respectable" than their "high-class" cousins.

Judgments about sex, class, and advertising also determine editorial content in nonpornographic magazines. Advertisers expressed anxiety about being associated not just with sex ads but also with "racy" editorial content. David Mulryan, partner at a gay-specific ad agency, explained his reservations about placing ads for a national advertiser—in this case Chase Manhattan Bank—in some gay and lesbian publications, including *Girlfriends*:

> Some of that editorial is pretty hot, right? And again, we do not want to hand all of the detractors at Chase a weapon to sink us with, you know? Because what does that help? So it's very tough. We are caught between the proverbial rock and a hard place. On the one hand, we have these rabid publications, and then we have this conservative bank, and frankly, I have to side with the conservative bank. They are writing the check, right?[48]

This comment suggests that when publishers are concerned about printing sexual content in their magazines, they are not being overly paranoid: advertisers and agency executives do indeed monitor gay and lesbian publications for editorial content that is "pretty hot." Yet publishers' caution challenges journalists' long-held commitment to uphold editorial decisions independent of advertising. Asked if there was a relationship between advertising and editorial content, *Out*'s Kurt DeMars responded, "Church and state. We need to keep the integrity of the magazine solid, and believe you me if we had a choice we would plaster our advertisers all over the editorial, but you can't really do that and keep a good product."[49] Draper told me that at *Girlfriends* "the editorial department can write anything, including stuff that is hurtful [to advertisers], if it's necessary and relevant."[50]

Further discussion with DeMars and Draper suggests that the "church and state" separation goes only so far, however. In its early days *Girlfriends* dropped its sexy centerfold after the magazine's editor in chief, Heather Findlay, bought *On Our Backs*. Moneka Hewlett, marketing director of both magazines, explained that removing the centerfold helped to differentiate the two publications and to segment their audiences. When Findlay purchased *On Our Backs*, "It made perfect sense to have all the sexual content be covered in that publication and have *Girlfriends* as more reflective of entertainment, politics, and culture."[51] Draper added that a centerfold "doesn't fly with mainstream advertisers." She recalled that when the Quality Paperback Book Club began to advertise in *Girlfriends,* a senior executive "freaked out" because of the centerfold and canceled future ads. Draper hoped that QPB would reconsider advertising in *Girlfriends* now that the centerfold was gone. This example suggests that appealing to national advertisers does affect editorial content in *Girlfriends,* even if the removal of the centerfold was also motivated by the need to diversify titles and readerships.

The boundaries of church and state—advertising and editorial—also broke down for *Out*'s publisher and editors. DeMars stressed that "editorial would never do anything that would jeopardize the value of a particular advertiser's message. . . . [For example,] we wouldn't have someone having sex in the book. We try to make things sexy, our fashion spreads have changed over the last few years. Now they are very sexy. . . . I guess we wouldn't write about these kinds of things, but it's all in how you present it: it's just got to be tasteful."[52] DeMars's comments affirmed that editorial is indeed responsive to the demands of advertisers. His statement that "it's just got to be tasteful" indicated that judgments of taste, rather than a cut-and-dried distinction between the sexual and the decent, ultimately determine what is acceptable. Although the magazine's publishing staff will not "plaster" advertisers' messages throughout the editorial content, the separation of church and state is not upheld when it comes to protecting advertisers from explicitly erotic or otherwise "tasteless" content.

Publishers and marketers believe that there are different sexual standards for gay and general-market publications, standards that reflect the enduring stereotype of the hypersexual gay man, in particular. Gay and lesbian magazines have to be much more scrupulous about sexual content than others do, and what might be construed as sexy playfulness elsewhere may be seen as controversial in gay magazines. Todd Evans, president of Rivendell Marketing, said that he understood publishers' motives when they were accused of "whitewashing" gay culture to get national advertising, because showing a bare-chested man in *Out* has very different implications from showing one in, for example, *Newsweek*.[53] As one journalist recalled, *Ten Percent*'s art director "once pulled a heavily beefcaked cover at the last minute because 'what works for *Vanity Fair* is too sexual for us. This is a new market for advertisers, and we're fighting a misconception that this group is obsessed with sex.'"[54] The different standards of appropriateness in gay versus apparently heterosexual magazines mirrors other ways in which taste is not an absolute measure of degrees of eroticism but depends on the interaction of gender, sexuality, race, and class. What is in the bounds of good taste in *Vanity Fair* exceeds those bounds in *Out*. What is possible in a gay or lesbian magazine's editorial is inappropriate in advertising. What is appropriate advertising in straight men's pornography has yet to make its way into women's and gay porn. But how do marketers decide and maintain the boundaries of what is acceptable, and in what contexts? How do appeals to taste determine representations of sex in gay and lesbian consumer venues?

Sexy or Sleazy? The Dimensions of Taste

Out editor in chief James Collard asserted that "most good magazines have got some kind of sex appeal, and that goes for everyone from *Vogue* to *Wallpaper*. A gay magazine can be sexy without being sleazy."[55] This suggests a commonsense distinction between "sexy" and "sleazy." How do marketers negotiate the boundary between these? If publishers refuse sex ads while allowing some sexual advertising and other content, how do they arbitrate between the permissible and the offensive? When they discussed sex ads and sexual content more generally, many publishers both explicitly and implicitly appealed to standards of taste. Yet taste is not measured against an absolute standard of sexual explicitness, but is under constant negotiation. How, then, do gay marketers use taste to protect publications, advertisers, and the public image of gayness from contamination by a vulgar, commercial, public sexuality, and how, in turn, do such measures simultaneously produce other forms of gay sexual culture?

Most marketers who appealed to standards of taste to justify their banning sexual content did not, or could not, articulate how they arrived at these standards. One exception was *Out*'s Henry Scott, who described adjudicating between more and less acceptable images according to "dimensions of taste."[56] He invoked three overlapping criteria of tastefulness: aesthetics (art versus pornography), erotic discretion (homosociality versus explicit homosexuality), and value or necessity (essential information versus gratuitous lasciviousness). With respect to aesthetics, Scott explained: "We have calculated lapses of taste on the editorial side and so we do things that we think are sexual and provocative, but tasteful at the same time. And usually our own rationale is there's something artistic about the presentation. . . . You know, what's the difference between Michelangelo's *David* and a still from a porn film?"[57] "Lapses of taste" are recuperable when they are "artistically" presented, which suggests a commonsense division between what is aesthetic and what is not, even in the absence of a reliable language with which to describe this distinction.

As for erotic discretion, Scott contrasted Bruce Weber's Abercrombie & Fitch ads, characterized by "innocence and playfulness" and taken by a famous commercial photographer, with ads for gay-specific products "where you also have men who don't have clothes on, but there's a sense of grimness about them that makes it look like it was filmed in a sex club as opposed to some guys playing football together." In the implied eroticism of Weber's series of ads, sexuality is circumscribed in the charming, playful homosociality of young men's sports.

With Scott's third dimension of taste, sexual or intimate bodily references were permissible if they were essential for conveying an important message. Scott compared a "tasteful" ad for a sexual lubricant with the "gratuitous taste-lessness" of an ad for an HIV-related nutritional supplement which declared, "Your mom doesn't know dick about nutrition": *Out* declined to run this ad. As long as they were tastefully rendered, Scott would accept ads related to safe sex or sexual health, but not ads that sold commercial sexual exchange or made "gratuitous" references to sex or genitals.

Scott's dimensions of taste confirm that the presence of sexual editorial and advertising has less to do with absolute markers of sexual explicitness than with how sex appears and how it is contained through aesthetic and other judgments. Beneath Scott's and other publishers' claims that sexual content is antithetical to respectability and mainstream advertising, marketers made subtle distinctions between taste and vulgarity; between private, domestic sexual consumption and public, commercial sexual exchange; between explicit sex and arty sexiness; between open homosexuality and sexually charged homosociality; and between editorial content and advertising.

Knowing Which Tastes to Cultivate

According to an ad for Dewar's whisky that appeared in *Out* in 1995, "The trick is knowing which tastes to cultivate" (fig. 7.3). The ad addresses a familiar dilemma, if an often less than conscious one: how do we know which tastes to cultivate? What do our tastes communicate about our standing in the world? On what grounds—educational, economic, aesthetic, familial, idiosyncratic—do we prefer some cultural practices and tastes over others? In order to produce a desirable gay market on a national scale, marketers had to contain images of commercial gay sexuality and did so through a framework of erotic and aesthetic tastefulness. The use of taste to contain queer sex reveals the class specificity of this containment: tastes are hierarchical and bear much relation to social privilege. By "knowing which tastes to cultivate" in their readers, marketers and publishers have both facilitated and limited a visible gay sexuality within gay publications, Web sites, and other venues, and have deployed "taste" in the pursuit of a sexually discreet, respectable, public gay cul-

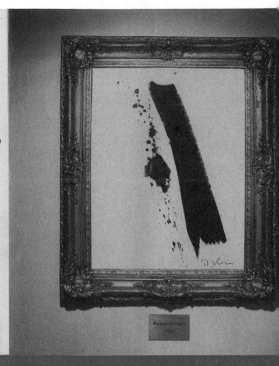

The trick is
owing which tastes
to cultivate.

Dewar's

FIGURE 7.3 DEWAR'S WHISKEY TEACHES CONSUMERS WHICH TASTES TO
CULTIVATE (*OUT*, JUNE 1995).

ture. This image of gay culture served both marketers' business needs by encouraging mainstream advertisers to appeal to gay consumers, and some gay
activists' political aims to offer the most "acceptable" face of gayness in the
pursuit of GLBT civil rights.

The finely calibrated distinctions between sexual decorum and sleaze serve
a prophylactic function, prompting inquiry into exactly what such boundaries
protect lesbian and gay media, their publishers, other advertisers, and their
readers from. Containing explicit, commercial sexuality in gay and lesbian
media "desleazifies" these media, their advertising, and the image of gay people more generally. Yet the class dimensions of taste and cultural capital
brought to bear on manifestations of public gay sexuality demonstrate that the
relationship between sex, sexuality, and social position is not fixed but oper-
ates in constant tension.

The containment of sex in gay media protects gender boundaries by
shielding lesbians, perceived as "naturally" less sexual (indeed, as antisex), from

the risk of confrontation with gay male sex. The constraints historically placed on women's sexual expression have been naturalized to appear as a consequence of (particularly white, upper-class) women's low sex drive, prudery, attachment to monogamy, and sexual vulnerability. Female sexual reserve is invoked to contain public, commercial sexuality in gay media in a number of ways: publishers such as Lukenbill and Landry see lesbian readers as needing protection from evidence of gay male commercial sex; serially monogamous lesbian relationships are posited as a standard for promiscuous gay men to emulate;[58] and lesbians are cast as sexual conservatives. The stereotype of the desexualized lesbian is thus used as a moral standard against which professional-class gay male sexuality must measure itself. Women's supposed sexual reticence justifies the desexing of gay and lesbian media, a process that reinscribes a vulnerable female sexuality, strengthens the division between the erotic lives of lesbians and those of gay men, and continues to burden women's sexuality with the role of preserving a respectable—that is, professional-managerial—manifestation of gay sexuality. In light of this, it makes sense that publishers solve the "problem" that an overt gay male sexuality poses to women by banning it rather than by working to increase the presence of a complementary, overt lesbian sexuality. Removing all sex ads (rather than, say, increasing sexual content for women) is seen as a remedy for the lack of interpellation of lesbian readers.

The protective functions of sexual containment may be most scrupulously applied to people of color. As cultural critic Richard Fung, scholars and artists Kobena Mercer and Isaac Julien, and historian Siobhan Somerville all argue, both gay men and black people tend to be stereotyped as endowed with an excessive sexuality.[59] In addition to marketers being less interested in queer consumers of color for reasons of lower market size and less disposable income, advertisers may shy away from casting African American men, in particular, for fear of epitomizing the stereotype of the hypersexual gay man. In an ad count of three 2002–2003 issues each of *Curve*, *Girlfriends*, the *Advocate*, and *Out*, only 10 percent of national ads that showed people included men of color.[60] Similarly, only 8.5 percent of national ads that showed people included women of color. This can be compared with much higher proportions of people of color in the general population: about 25 percent in 2000, according to the U.S. Census.[61] The reasons for the underrepresentation of women of color in ads may be very different than those for the underrepresentation of men of color, since this lack of visibility is the product of multiple factors which include market size, perceived affluence, and gay and lesbian media readership figures. Nevertheless, the additional threat to the image of the respectable gay consumer that the stereotype of the hypersexual African American or Latina/o poses may in part explain the relative scarcity of people of color in national advertising to gay consumers.

The containment of sexuality also protects the class borders of a privileged gay elite. As part of a more general public sexual commerce, sex ads facilitate interclass and interracial sexual contact, which Samuel R. Delany argues threatens the class-bound structures of professional social networks, families, and neighborhoods.[62] Rubin argues that sexual stratification is not simply mapped onto, but interacts with, other forms of social stratification: "The system of sexual oppression cuts across other modes of social inequality. . . . It is not reducible to, or understandable in terms of, class, race, ethnicity, or gender. Wealth, white skin, male gender, and ethnic privileges can mitigate the effects of sexual stratification."[63] Although there are no natural correspondences between Rubin's charmed circle of sex and a respectable, professional-managerial sexuality, critics of pornographic sleaze represent practices outside this circle as not only sexually offensive but as offensive to dominant class values as well. The term *sleaze*, as class coded as it is sexually coded, evokes a debased class position as much as a lack of sexual propriety. As a judgment on tastelessness, it demonstrates the extent to which sexual stratification is imbricated with economic and cultural capital.

Rubin's model of the charmed circle of sex, delineated by contaminated outer limits, works productively with Bourdieu's model of cultural hierarchies. It suggests that a further dimension of capital, *moral* capital, works in combination with other forms of capital—cultural, social, and so on—to structure power relations between groups. Moral capital is a symbolic resource accumulated through charmed sexual tastes and practices. These endow people with cultural privilege, which ranges from relative freedom from legal, psychological, or familial scrutiny to acknowledgment and celebration of one's sexuality by the media. In contrast, those activities and representations that breach the charmed circle bring low moral capital to their practitioners: people selling or buying pornography, queer people, nonmonogamous people, and people who participate in group, intergenerational, kinky, or SM sex all occupy positions of low moral capital and, as a result, risk censure. Sex ads, in particular, operate at the outer limits by placing sex in a public, commercial context; by offering low-commitment, relatively anonymous sex; and by extending an opportunity to heterosexually identified people to make forays into queer sex.

Just as different types of capital are interdependent for Bourdieu—such that high cultural capital, manifested in "good taste," is likely to be produced by and to reproduce economic, social, and educational capital—so moral capital is reciprocally dependent on other hierarchies. Occupying Rubin's charmed circle increases one's moral capital, which is likely, in turn, to afford privileged access to economic, legal, educational, and familial resources. The stakes in having a deviant sexuality are higher for working-class people, people of color, women, and queers because race, gender, and sexuality are reciprocally dependent on moral capital. For example, while many people work in the sex industry because they have limited economic and educational capital, their access to legal, economic, and other resources is further restricted by their trade.[64] Whereas those who are already socially privileged can afford to indulge in greater sexual transgression, others may be more invested in a respectable sexuality, both because their sexuality is more closely scrutinized (sexual privacy is proportional to social power) and because sexual transgression tends to be a barrier to upward social mobility. Stigmatized social groups may attempt to raise their social position with high moral capital; marketers (and others invested in producing "positive images" of lesbians and gays) are particularly invested in a desexualized image of gayness to compensate for the fact that both queer and commercial forms of sexuality occur outside the charmed circle. Because an openly homosexual identity already puts GLBT people on the outer limits, conforming to the inner circle in other respects—practicing monogamous, coupled, noncommercial, at-home, private, same-generation, vanilla sex—may recoup some moral capital for them, potentially gaining them broader social acceptance, access to economic and other resources, and protection from harassment.

Sex ads are viewed as such not necessarily because they portray erotic products, but because they situate queer sex in an expressly commercial, potentially public sphere, inviting a morally debased form of sexual exchange. In the distinction marketers draw between sex ads and other sexual content, however, some manifestations of sex are redeemable, particularly when tastefully rendered: the risk of low moral capital that sex poses may be mitigated by tethering sex to other forms of capital, such as cultural capital. Yet rather than reveal its social and cultural origins, taste "present[s] itself in the guise of an innate disposition";[65] like other hierarchies of legitimacy, sexual tastefulness is naturalized when its ideological roots are exnominated. A primary method of naturalizing sexual decorum is to appeal to aesthetics: marketers monitor representations through aesthetic hierarchies that stand in for sexual ones (Michelangelo's *David* in lieu of a porn film). Moral capital is thus mediated in part through cultural capital: aesthetics protects the genteel classes from a contaminating association with a vulgar (explicit, nonaesthetic, commercial) sexuality. By means of aesthetic judgments, sexual appropriateness is hitched to legitimized cultural capital. This relationship between moral and cultural capital structures the relationships among taste, art, the privileged sexuality of

Rubin's charmed circle, and their combined influence in maintaining cultural hierarchies.

The containment of sexuality in gay and lesbian media protects readers, publishers, and advertisers not just from the stereotype of the hypersexual gay man but from its sleazy impact on the ideal image of the professional-managerial gay consumer. Insofar as this image has become the dominant characterization of gayness both in gay and lesbian and in mainstream media, sexual containment protects the respectability of the newly visible gay and lesbian professional-managerial classes. Further, the construction of a sexually discreet, ideal consumer aids marketers both professionally and personally, especially those who are gay-identified. This image offers gay marketers a desirable image of gayness to sell to potentially homophobic advertising executives, corporate marketers, and journalists. Because gay-identified marketers are also likely to be readers of gay and lesbian publications, they can enjoy the aspirational or reassuring sense of the ideal gay consumer as an upstanding member of the professional-managerial class, tasteful and sexually discreet—an ideal "like them."[66]

Just as Bourdieu's approach shows how Rubin's model of sexual stratification is imbricated with social stratification, so Rubin offers Bourdieu a nuanced analysis of how sexual hierarchies function in the distribution of social and cultural resources. I do not want to imply, however, that class, race, and gender hierarchies map directly onto hierarchies of moral capital, because the greater one's social marginalization, the higher the stakes of sexual respectability. Nor am I suggesting that low moral capital automatically corresponds to low cultural capital, because, for example, the threat of sleaze produced by explicit sexuality can be redeemed by cultural capital, in the form of aesthetics. What I am suggesting is that the reputation of an openly gay group of professional marketers and, more broadly, of professional-managerial gay readers and consumers depends on a more vigilant level of sexual decorum than the reputation of heterosexual or closeted professional-managerial groups, because public manifestations of queer sex, in particular, threaten their movement into or their membership in this class. At a time when increasing numbers of professional gays and lesbians are coming out at work, the containment of sexual content, and especially "sleazy" sex ads, helps improve the public image of gayness. By banning sex ads and ensuring the aesthetic quality of other sexual content, publishers and marketers facilitate the accommodation of an emergent, openly gay professional-managerial class in both mainstream media and occupational environments.

The sexually respectable class image of gayness thus protects the reputations of the ideal gay consumer, actual gay consumers interested in a sexually respectable model of gayness, and marketers and publishers who wish to be both professionally successful and openly gay. Yet the prophylactic operations of taste can never be fully achieved. Michel Foucault critiques the "repressive hypothesis" of sexuality, the commonly held belief that sexual topics were eliminated from polite discourse in nineteenth-century France by a prudish, bourgeois society. He describes the processes whereby the containment of sexuality in some quarters, such as polite conversation, was accompanied by the proliferation of discourses about (deviant) sexuality in other areas, including medicine and pedagogy.[67] Foucault's argument applies to a specific historical period and region, but a similar process is evident in advertising-supported gay media, where strategies of sexual containment do not produce a total repression of queer sex so much as a proliferation of sexual deviance and pleasures. Although the boundary-work of taste is at one level *protective* of both "polite" gay and lesbian subcultures and a sexually insecure dominant culture, at another level it is also sexually *productive* in gay subcultural and mainstream spheres. In gay commercial culture, taste-based strategies of containment facilitate the multiplication of pleasures through diversified, segmented media and reinvoke the image of the hypersexual gay male.

Paradoxically, increasing scrutiny and production of discourses about the risks of gay public sex encourage the diversification of gay publications. As Scott mentioned, his readers consider sex important but "that's not what [they] buy *Out* for." Sexual containment fosters media and market segmentation, with the result that the gay and lesbian glossy magazine *Out* and the gay porn publication *Jock* meet some different—and some of the same—readers' needs. Segmentation also meets advertisers' and publishers' needs: Shively recalled that when the *Advocate* started to publish *Advocate Men*, a pornographic magazine, the senior staff told advertisers, " 'You can run one ad in the [*Advocate*] *Classifieds* . . . and you can run the same ad, only with full-frontal nudity, in *Advocate Men*.' And that made them very happy and, of course, we got double revenue."[68]

When the *Advocate* abandoned sex ads altogether in 1992, the independent publication, the *Advocate Classifieds*, rapidly became overtly pornographic, with images of nude men with erections, erotic short stories, phone sex and solicitation ads, and Califia's "Sex Adviser" column. Califia relates,

> I was told that my column couldn't remain in the main book because letters about foreskins did not belong in a serious newsmagazine. . . . The *Advocate* proper still runs advice columns—about AIDS. It seems that the only way we can legitimately talk about our sexuality is under the rubric of death and disease. We can't celebrate, defend, or describe

queer pleasure even though it was the quest for pleasure that made so many of us HIV-positive. This hypocrisy and prissiness robs the gay press of much of its old feistiness, earthiness, and power to rock the world.[69]

The segmentation of sexual advice—AIDS from foreskins—suggests the precision with which gay male sexuality is segmented, by offering a reticent (if diseased) image of queer sex in "serious newsmagazine[s]" while profiting from a diversification of pornographic publications. The distancing of respectable gay and lesbian publications from sexual content fits neatly with the logic of niche marketing: by segmenting gay and lesbian "lifestyle" content from pornography, readers subscribe to more publications and media publishers reap greater profits.

If one consequence of the containment of sex is the proliferation of gay sex through segmented media, another principal effect is the "incitement to speak." Foucault argues,

> More important [than the proliferation of illicit discourses] was the multiplication of discourses concerning sex in the field of exercise of power itself: an institutional incitement to speak about it, and to do so more and more; a determination on the part of the agencies of power to hear it spoken about, and to cause *it* to speak through explicit articulation and endlessly accumulated detail.[70]

Marketers' constant invocation of the risk of sexual contagion somewhat undermines their attempts to construct an assimilable, desexualized public face of gayness. Almost every article and public presentation about the gay market reminds readers and listeners of the risk of coming into contact with pornography, sleaze, or "adult content." Ironically, constant references to public manifestations of gay sex emphasize that adult content is part of many gay men's lives—if you pay attention to all this anxiety, gay men seem to seek out adult content more than any other. In the incitement to speak about gay sex, and in their efforts to produce a newly respectable gay and lesbian consumer, gay marketers reinscribe the stereotype of the hypersexual gay man: we cannot think about the gay market without being reminded of the risk of contamination by pornography. Attempts to limit gay sex produce, then, the very image of the hypersexual queer that marketers struggle so hard to avoid.

Does sex sell? In national lesbian and gay glossy magazines, on many Internet sites, and in some local papers, sex does not sell nonnormative sexualities, nor does it sell commercial sexual products and services. In certain aesthetic and informational contexts, sex may sell, but selling sex itself risks a lowering of moral capital and the alienation of national advertisers. The stereotype of the hypersexual gay man, the fear of queer sex, the AIDS epidemic, and the associations between explicit sexuality, low moral capital, and sleaze mean that in ad-supported gay and lesbian media, the ban on selling sex desexualizes both the image of the market and actual consumers. To the extent that sex can sell in gay and lesbian media, it must be contained by being distanced from an explicitly queer sexuality through appeals to aesthetic tastefulness. Ironically then, marketers expel the very quality that makes the gay market distinct—its sexuality—and pour into the vacuum other means to differentiate the gay niche. What replaces the ideal gay consumer's sexual specificity is his class-specific, gay subcultural capital, marked by good taste and sexual discretion. Yet if the homosexual is a person produced by same-sex desire, what does it mean to be gay, lesbian, or bisexual if that identity is dissociated from queer sex? What are the consequences of being interpellated—"Hey, you're gay!"—by media vehicles in which sexual identification is emptied of an open, lusty, joyous acknowledgment of queer desire? And how does sexual containment shape the political terrain upon which gay civil rights battles are to be fought?

CHAPTER 8

JUST LIKE YOU

On the eve of the 2000 GLBT Millennium March on Washington, D.C., journalist Hank Stuever crankily wrote, "The Love That Dared Not Speak Its Name now yawns and checks its watch as being gay becomes more market niche than rebellion."[1] As corporate sponsors flocked to the march in pursuit of the gay market, Stuever expressed concerns shared by many that year: greater gay market visibility had precipitated a decrease in political activism, and gayness had become more a consumer lifestyle than a sexual identity. Twenty-eight years after the first mention of gay-related consumption in the advertising trade press, the gay market had matured to a point where openly gay marketing professionals had easy access to representatives from many Fortune 500 companies, where commercially funded media were profitable enterprises, and where gay and lesbian characters were increasingly incorporated into gay-specific advertising and mainstream television shows. But as the concerns over corporate sponsorship of the Millennium March also revealed, the maturing of the gay market had not come without contestation, and GLBT commentators asked what this newfound visibility might portend for the gay civil rights movement. Activist and writer Alexandra Chasin summarized the march as "an occasion for economic maneuvers cloaked in the guise of politics," adding that, "it was the very paradigm of intersection between the gay and lesbian niche market and the gay and lesbian political movement."[2] Another critic protested, "We are harkened to D.C. as consumers, no worse, as commodities. We have been sold to the highest bidders."[3] The march catalyzed anxieties not just about institutionalized gay politics and the role of marketers therein but also about the changing relationship between gay communities and the mainstream, between identity and politics, and between freedom and co-optation. In considering the role of marketing in these relationships, the relevant question is not whether gay marketing is a matter of business or politics, but how the business of gay marketing shapes the politics of GLBT sexuality.

Debates about gay marketing tend to posit an opposition between the benefits of gay visibility and the costs of gay assimilation. The 2003 landmark U.S. Supreme Court decision *Lawrence vs. Texas*, which overturned all the remaining antisodomy legislation in thirteen states, was seen by many as reflecting a greater level of tolerance, if not acceptance, of homosexuality. This tolerance has been attributed in part to a greater awareness of gay issues among heterosexual Americans, facilitated by gay visibility in the media and marketing. For example, journalists Moni Basu and Catherine Shoichet quote army veteran Danny Ingram, who helped to organize Atlanta's Pride parade: "*Will & Grace* will have more to do with [social change] than this decision by the Supreme Court will. . . . Gay and lesbian people are becoming more accepted in society. And as that continues it will become less and less of an issue . . . for society at large."[4] Within this discourse of social progress, visibility is assumed to have an inevitably positive effect for GLBT people.

Some GLBT critics, however, are suspicious that this greater visibility encourages assimilation into the heterosexual mainstream, at a cost for GLBT subcultures. Briefly summarized, debates about assimilation ask whether gay political activism should work to integrate gays fairly and equitably into existing laws, social structures, and cultural norms (the assimilationist view) or should instead work to change those laws, structures, and norms to produce a different culture altogether (the anti-assimilationist view). Queer theorist Michael Warner asserts that homophobia makes assimilation very appealing for many gay people: "Like most stigmatized groups, gays and lesbians were always tempted to believe that the way to overcome stigma was to win acceptance by the dominant culture, rather than to change the self-understanding of that culture."[5] Gay writer Michael Bronski warns about the limits of such acceptance, arguing that assimilationist aspirations are "anchored in the belief that homosexuality is a minor human differentiation, and that if gay people were less publicly demonstrative, or obvious, in their social or sexual affect— less publicly homosexual—they would be accepted by heterosexuals."[6] Debates about the value of assimilation for broad social change are extensive and beyond the domain of this study.[7] Here I consider the charge of assimilationism as it has been applied to gay marketing, and question whether assimilation is the most productive frame through which to understand the value and limits of gay consumer visibility.

Critics who see gay marketing as inevitably assimilationist tend to argue that gay marketing is normalizing in intent and depoliticizing in effect. From this perspective, marketing routines affirm only those lesbians and gays who fit easily within the standards of the heterosexual mainstream in terms of elevated social position, sexual decorum, and polite politics, while ostracizing all others. In his book on the politics of pleasure in gay male culture, Bronski writes that "the assimilationist position is predicated on a deeply held belief in the worth of such basic, social structures as traditional sexual morality, monogamous marriage, accepted gender roles, and the nuclear family."[8] Author Sarah Schulman is alarmed by what she sees as a marketing tendency to bolster the acceptability of homosexuality by showing gays consuming the same goods in the same kinds of ways as monogamous, heterosexual, nuclear families do. She argues that marketing images render "homosexuality into more socially acceptable, privatized family units on the reproductive model, instead of the current community-based culture."[9] Chasin adds that the kind of assimilation that gay marketing encourages demands a particularly normative version of gender: "The assertion that gay men and lesbians are just like straight people means not only that the subcultural community is willing and able to Americanize, but that the sexual orientations—gay and lesbian—that once seemed to bear the threat of gender subversion can indeed present themselves as men and women, in the same way that straight people are men and women, masculine and feminine, respectively."[10] Although dominant American ideology holds that assimilation is, in Bronski's words, a "positive, culturally unifying mechanism," only certain kinds of people, and limited subcultural practices, are assimilable.[11] He observes that strict limits are placed on what mainstream culture welcomes from racial, ethnic, and sexual subcultures. "The elements of subcultures that manifest themselves in dominant culture after 'assimilation' are those that are most likely to give pleasure: food, theater, music, inventive and original language, humor, clothing, even the more elusive notions of 'style' and 'fashion.'"[12] That many of his examples of welcomed practices are related to consumption shows how far the politics of culture are played out on the material-symbolic terrain of the habitus.

Critics concerned with assimilation also argue that gay marketing seduces GLBT people into the naive view that as long as they can consume like everyone else, they have the same rights as everyone else. Schulman sees gay consumers as enticed by the promise of consumption in an assimilationist package, and sees a demise of grassroots activism and agitation as a result: "It is very seductive for gay people to confuse the presence of limited gay images in advertising with some kind of social equity, but it is entirely illusory. There is no corollary between appearing in advertising and social or political power."[13] Chasin is critical of ads that suggest that gay liberation is possible through consumption. She writes, "I would not worry so much about an ad that dramatizes the idea that assimilation is a cause of liberation and enfranchisement an effect of consumption if I did not see these ideas at work in the movement."[14] From this perspective, gay marketing has had a depoliticizing effect on gay people who are assumed to be more concerned with their next purchase than with civil rights progress.

Chasin also links corporate advertising and sponsorship with a narrowing of the priorities, concerns, and representativeness of gay and lesbian organizations on a national scale. As civil rights groups such as the Human Rights Campaign have become increasingly successful at courting large corporate sponsors, so have their political agendas focused on the most "acceptable" issues in queer politics, such as gays in the military and gay marriage. Chasin quotes the HRC's executive director, Elizabeth Birch, who expressly acknowledged the relationship between gay activism and marketing. In 1998 Birch told a reporter, "In the 1990s there had to be a meeting of minds between raw activist spirit and the communications and marketing techniques that define a new voice for gay America."[15] Chasin is concerned that allowing corporate voices to speak for "gay America" establishes a political agenda that favors the concerns of those gays already otherwise privileged.

I join the critics of gay assimilation in some of their concerns over the normalizing tendencies within gay marketing. However, their critiques sometimes obscure more than they clarify; the relationships between gay subcultures and the putatively heterosexual mainstream are far more complex and contradictory than the charge of assimilation can accommodate. Assimilationist critiques of gay marketing tend to posit a relation between an authentic gay subculture and a corrupting mainstream that is strikingly reminiscent of classic high-culture vs. mass-culture debates. Herbert Gans summarizes two centuries of these debates thus: mass culture is aesthetically vulgar, whereas high culture has artistic merit; mass culture is corrupted by its commercial imperatives, while high culture is not compromised by the need to make money; mass culture has a negative effect on high culture, adopting and polluting the latter's forms and luring potential high-culture producers into producing mass products; and mass culture has a negative effect on audiences and society more generally, lowering the levels of "taste" and producing media that " 'narcotize' and 'atomize' people, . . . render[ing] them susceptible to techniques of mass persuasion that skilled demagogues can use to abrogate democracy."[16] Gans counters each of these suppositions with examples to the contrary, arguing that there are no absolute, definable boundaries between high and low culture, tastes, or audiences, but that these distinctions are created to protect the interests of elite social groups.

By exchanging "mass" with "mainstream" and "high culture" with "gay subcultures," the pervasiveness of the mass-culture perspective in assimilationist critiques of gay marketing becomes apparent. Some critics argue that by entering the mainstream, all that is unique, authentic, and valued in gay subcultures is debased or lost. As gay columnist Dan Savage declared, "Gay culture is boring because gay culture is going away . . . and gay culture is going away because the oppression is going away. I think that's a pretty fair trade."[17] Similarly, self-avowed assimilationist Daniel Harris expresses an ambivalent attitude toward assimilation and the threat posed to the gay highbrow by niche marketing. On one hand, he welcomes assimilation, a time when "my society is as indifferent to—indeed stultifyingly bored by—my sexual orientation as I am."[18] Yet on the other, he laments the loss of a fabulous, stylish, aesthetic taste culture that closeted gays produced: "Gay visibility necessarily entails the disappearance of gay culture, which depends for its survival precisely on our invisibility, on our marginalization, which once led us to use the aristocratic ideals of aestheticism and conspicuous displays of our own exquisiteness to achieve an alternative, artistic form of respectability in a society that had denied us moral respectability." According to Harris, the very circumstance he desires, where "society is as indifferent to . . . [his] sexual orientation" as he is, has led to the downfall of a distinctly gay "ethnic identity." His version of the mass-culture critique posits a mainstream against which he nostalgically laments the demise of a marginalized gay taste elite, leading him to conclude that "assimilation is good for gay people but bad for gay culture."[19]

As cultural studies research indicates, however, mainstream institutions, on one hand, and subcultures, on the other, are complexly interlinked. In her research on American hip-hop cultures, for example, scholar Tricia Rose counters critiques that rap and graffiti have become commodified.[20] She points out that to argue for a pure, precommercial hip-hop culture is to ignore that graffiti artists have long incorporated characters and symbols from popular culture into their work, and that DJs and rap artists have incorporated prerecorded, copyrighted work by other musicians into their own music. She concludes, "It would be naive to think that breakers, rappers, DJs and writers were never interested in monetary compensation for their work."[21] The important shift in hip-hop's relation to mainstream culture since the 1970s has not been from pleasure to profits, "from precommodity to commodity, but the shift in control over the scope and direction of the profit-making process, out of the hands of local black and Hispanic entrepreneurs and into the hands of larger white-owned, multinational businesses."[22] This shift in control has not produced a passive, acquiescent, hip-hop culture, but one where African American, Latin, and white producers and listeners continue to struggle (with very unequal resources) over rap's production, distribution, and meanings.

Like hip-hop, as gay subcultures have become the focus of corporate interest the balance of power has shifted, particularly in terms of who has control over cultural definitions and who reaps profits. Yet in contrast to Daniel Harris's assumption that there was a precommodified aesthetic gay subculture untainted by any connection with the mainstream, gay cultural historians show, in industrial-era urban environments at least, that gay subcultures have always engaged with both mainstream and increasingly openly gay-owned commerce.[23] They have also used apparently heterosexual texts as a means of identification, community-building, and pleasure, as well as opposition.[24] Conversely, "straight" culture has long adopted aspects of queerness for entertainment and other purposes. Both when producers build gay subcultural references into mainstream texts (knowingly or otherwise) and when gay fans adopt texts (with or without the intention of producers), the boundaries between a corrupting mainstream and a pure gay subculture become impossible to support.

Mass-culture critics assume that the culture industries lure talent away from high-culture pursuits. Similarly, some GLBT commentators argue that gay professionals have simply been co-opted by mainstream corporations to inject a gay sensibility into advertising campaigns. Sarah Schulman claims that gay-identified marketers have been hired by corporate America to entice gay consumers with the fantasy of assimilation and upward mobility: "Most seductively, the presence of these individuals in the industry allows their previously overlooked or excluded community a veneer of normalcy by the fact of being represented in the marketplace."[25] The assimilationist critique assumes that gay cultural workers' queer sensibility can only ever be absorbed into the mainstream, robbing it of its distinctiveness and prostituting it in the service of corporate profits. However, gay marketing professionals navigate a complex set of demands placed upon them by their sexual identification, on one hand, and their professional roles, on the other. Media scholar Ien Ang's argument for reimagining television audiences is applicable to producers, as well: "Rather than conceiving viewers as having a unified individuality that is consistent across circumstances, they should be seen as inhabiting multiple and mobile identities that fluctuate from situation to situation."[26] Similarly, marketers' roles in various institutions and positions of power are likely to produce multiple and mobile identifications, challenging simplistic ideas of their relation to mainstream culture or, for that matter, to gay subcultures. As cultural studies scholar Janice Radway argues, dominant ideologies are not necessarily consistent, but allow "interstices in the social fabric where individuals or groups might manage to address the reality of their social situation in ways that do not work completely against their own interests."[27] Marketing texts, as well as marketers' class, professional, and sexual identifications, offer many ideological seams through which both gay consumers and marketers themselves can experience identity, politics, and community in contradictory ways.

The belief that mass culture has a negative effect on audiences by producing a narcotized, apolitical society is also echoed in the assimilationist critique that holds gay consumption accountable for a lamentable demise in gay activism.[28] Yet allegations that assimilationist messages depoliticize GLBT people discredit audiences in the same way that mass-culture critiques do: both assume that readers of ads simply absorb their messages wholesale. Cultural studies scholars have shown that audiences negotiate dominant texts in all sorts of unanticipated ways, taking from them what they need and expressing ambivalence over the more oppressive messages.[29] Similarly, GLBT people have resisted some of the normative aspects of gay marketing, both collectively and individually. As queer theorists Lauren Berlant and Elizabeth Freeman document, Queer Nation, an affiliation of local activist groups that emerged from ACT UP in 1990, engaged with the very epicenters of consumer culture, and not to simply endorse the value of consumption for gays. Queer Nation chapters chanted "We're here, we're queer, we're not going shopping!" in downtown sections of Gay Pride marches.[30] Queer Nation hoped to disrupt consumer culture contexts, reminding straight consumers of the constant presence of GLBT people. According to Berlant and Freeman, "Queer Nation tactically uses the hyper-spaces created by the corporeal trademark, the metropolitan parade, the shopping mall, print media, and finally advertising, to recognize and take advantage of the consumer's pleasure in vicarious identification . . . to reveal to the consumer desires he/she didn't know he/she had, to make his/her identification with the product 'homosexuality' both an unsettling and a pleasurable experience."[31] Such actions suggest ways in which at least consumer sites, and possibly consumption as well, offer the chance not only to fit in but to radically assert both the constructedness of sexuality and the specificity of queer difference. However, Queer Nation's narrowly youthful membership and short life span suggests that its deconstructive agenda did not have broad or enduring appeal to GLBT people more generally.

More recently, groups associated under the umbrella of Gay Shame have articulated resistance to what they consider to be the commodification of GLBT identity. As the San Francisco group's Web site explains:

> Gay Shame is the radical alternative to consumerist "pride" crap. We are committed to a queer extravaganza that brings direct action to astound-

ing levels of theatricality in order to expose the evildoers who use the
sham of gay "pride" as a cover-up for their greed and misdeeds. We seek
nothing less than a new queer activism that addresses issues of race, class,
gender, and sexuality, to counter the self-serving "values" of the gay
mainstream. We are dedicated to fighting the rabid assimilationist mon-
ster of corporate gay "pride" with a devastating mobilization of queer
brilliance.[32]

According to journalist Tommi Avicolli Mecca, Gay Shame is "an outgrowth
of a younger generation's disgust with over-commercialized pride celebrations
that are more about corporate sponsorships, celebrity grand marshals, and
consumerism, than about the radicalism that gave birth to our post-Stonewall
gay-liberation movement."[33] One strategy the San Francisco group has advocated is shaming companies, organizations, and individuals whom they see as
betraying GLBT people. Nominations for the 2003 Gay Shame awards included PlanetOut, for "consistently marketing our identities to the highest
bidder," GLAAD, for "shill[ing] for any company that advertises in the gay
press," and Mary Cheney, Vice President Dick Cheney's daughter, for "acting
as a liaison between the Gay and Lesbian Community and none other than
Coors, one of the most right-wing corporations serving our nation."[34] Gay
Shame thus turns the routines of gay pride upside down by an ironic awarding of "honors" to capitalist homophobes and gay turncoats.

Resistance to the normalizing tendencies of the gay market is also enacted
by individuals. As I discuss in chapter 6, communication scholar Danae Clark
argues that lesbian readers are not necessarily interpellated by fashion magazines' coyly lesbian appeals, but may enact their own, lesbian-inflected "guer-
rilla warfare" in spaces of consumption.[35] Shopping has "provided a homosocial space for women . . . to interact and bond. Lesbians have been able to
extend this pleasure by shopping with their female lovers or partners, sharing
the physical and erotic space of the dressing room, and afterwards wearing/ex-
changing the fashion commodities they purchase."[36] Gay men and lesbians
also have a long history of using consumer practices to undermine gender
norms, through drag and masquerade. English professor Carole-Anne Tyler
summarizes the view that drag and butch/femme roles reveal the artifice of
sexual difference: "Butch, like fem, role-playing de-natures identity and sexuality, confronting heterosexist essentialism with the artifices of gender and the
errant play of desire."[37] She continues that although male camp suggests a hy-
perfemininity, "even macho masculinity is read as camp."[38] Feminist film
scholar Jane Gaines elaborates a spectrum of female masquerade in cinema,
from "a femininity which knows it is excessive but uses its own overload par-
odically" to a "masquerade in which actresses are disguised as men."[39]

Consumption figures centrally in camp and masquerade. As columnist Lisa Montanarelli declares in the queer magazine *Black Sheets*, "I bought slut drag at Toys 'R' Us." She advises:

> If you're tired of braving high prices and long shopping lines at your favorite trendy fetish stores, Toys 'R' Us now offers a new collection of slutwear for little girls—or bigger girls and boys who want some extra-tight girlie drag. When my daddy (not my biological one) took me to Toys 'R' Us for my birthday, we discovered that this reputable toy store now stocks strapless, sequin, off-the-shoulder tops, feather boas, marabou shirts and skirts, high-heel training shoes and countless other fashion items guaranteed to precipitate the onset of puberty.[40]

Concerns about the assimilationist impulses of gay marketing allow little space for a campy interpretation of consumer culture that allows gays and lesbians to aggressively reappropriate stereotypes and to pervert normative sexual roles. The assimilationist critique cannot accommodate the myriad ways in which GLBT-identified people negotiate the specificities of their desires, incomes, and habitus in part through their consumption.

To assert that there is sufficient evidence from readership and audience studies to posit at least a degree of reader autonomy from even the most hegemonic cultural texts does not imply, however, an unhinged relativism or infinitely polysemous universe of consumer culture. Nor is consumption inevitably resistive, or gender play subversive. In her discussion of gendered consumption, cultural theorist Rita Felski notes that, "If anything, the celebration of the resistive agency of the female consumer is currently in danger of becoming a new orthodoxy, which often pays scant attention to the limited alternatives available to many women as well as the economic, racial, and geopolitical constraints determining the nature and extent of their access to commodities."[41] While it would be premature to argue that a celebration of resistive gay consumers is the new orthodoxy, Felski's point is well taken: consumers may be able to consume resistively, playfully, kinkily, and campily only insofar as they have the material and symbolic resources to do so.

Film scholar Jackie Stacey warns that "there is nothing inherently radical about pleasure" and cautions against "the dangers of embracing the pleasures of the popular too readily."[42] Audience pleasure has been conflated with activity, and activity in turn is assumed to be ideologically resistant, at least in opposition to the stereotype of audience *in*activity. Further, just because camp performances parody gender roles does not guarantee a critique of them. When GLBT people resistively read ads, perform gender masquerade, and willfully pervert mass-manufactured goods, these strategies do not necessarily challenge the dominant view of either sexuality or gender, even if they may afford their practitioners some space within dominant culture for alternative identifications.

I do not wish to imply in this overview that there is a direct analogy between the mass-culture critique and the argument that gay marketing is inevitably assimilationist. The high culture that mass-culture critics attempt to protect has a different relation to the mainstream than gay culture does, and the threats to high culture from absorption into mass culture are perceived differently from the threats to gay culture of assimilation into a heterosexual mainstream. Conversely, the potential gains for high culture of mixing with mass culture are less obvious than the potential gains that gay assimilation might afford (some) GLBT people. The value of the analogy is less to argue that high and gay culture occupy the same relation to the mainstream than to demonstrate that underlying both critiques is a profound distrust of commercialized culture and an investment in distinguishing from it an unsullied high culture or a pure gay culture. As Sarah Thornton shows, people involved in rave scenes invoke "the mainstream," and especially mainstream media, to distinguish their subcultures. She asserts: "Like the mainstream, '*the* media' is . . . a vague monolith against which subcultural credibilities are measured."[43] Similarly, both critics of gay assimilation and gay marketers posit a heterosexual mainstream to differentiate gay subcultures, although with different criteria and for different purposes.

The threat that gay marketing poses to gay culture is commonly assumed to come from assimilation. I argue, instead, that gay marketing is troubling not because it is assimilationist but because it promotes particular kinds of distinction. Gayness is not absorbed by the mainstream so much as it is shaped in opposition to that mainstream, but still within dominant conventions of an essentialized sexuality marked by privilege and good taste. The routines of market segmentation brought to bear on any market assume an essential characteristic that is unique to the group, is measurable, and that is relevant in consumption practices. In the case of the gay market, these routines affirm a minoritized distinction between "really" gay people and "really" heterosexual people both for market segmentation purposes (to target gays as a distinct group) and for the comfort of non-gay-identified people (to reassure them of their categorical difference from gay people).

The minoritized view of sexuality upon which gay market segmentation rests also bolsters gay- and lesbian-identified professionals' expertise. Far from hankering after the mainstream, most marketers are invested in a nonassimilated, identifiable gay subculture that is distinct from a similarly identifiable straight mainstream. Just as Thornton's club workers invoked the mainstream to champion their subcultural capital, gay- and lesbian-identified marketers distance their work from that of their heterosexual colleagues in order to assert both the specificity of a distinctly gay niche and the value of their own sexual identity and related subcultural capital. Because these marketers are employed precisely for a rarefied, gay-inflected taste that their professional position and sexual identity afford, the assimilation of gay subcultures into the heterosexual mainstream would destroy the very niche that underpins their employment and professional expertise.

Gay marketing not only promotes a minoritized view of gayness but, with other media practices, further differentiates privileged, sexually discreet, gender-normative gays from everyone else. This limited view of the ideal gay consumer is in part a product of the norms of marketing in which people of color, older people, poor and working-class people, and a host of other less privileged sectors of society are underrepresented or invisible. The life worth emulating in mainstream marketing is the affluent life, irrespective of sexuality. But the narrow image of the gay consumer is also a product of the history of gay visibility. Given that gay representations in mainstream media have until recently been either invisible or scapegoated, the best-intentioned media workers have struggled to produce positive images of gay and lesbian characters. Like articles that appeared in the trade press to advise white advertisers how to represent African Americans in ads in the 1940s,[44] Mike Wilke offers advertising guidelines on his Commercial Closet Web site. He warns prospective advertisers that characterizations of "feminine gay men and deceitful/ scary transgender people are clichés that alienate many, and [images of] 'lipstick lesbians' alone are limiting."[45] Ideally, more positive images increase heterosexuals' tolerance toward GLBT people and offer respite to GLBT audiences in need of representations with which they can gladly identify. At the intersection of these cultural conditions—marketing norms and the history of gay representations—it comes as no surprise that the kind of differentiation that gay marketing produces is a privileged and sexually respectable one.

The kinds of images that have been circulated in gay marketing risk producing a gay version of the "model minority" stereotype, however. The myth of the model minority has historically been applied to Asian Americans, who are "believed to enjoy extraordinary achievements in education, upward mobility, rising income, and [to be] problem-free in mental health and crime," according to sociologists Paul Wong, Chienping Faith Lai, Richard Nagasawa, and Teiming Lin.[46] The model minority myth is perceived by many Asian Americans and non-Asians as a preferable alternative to earlier portrayals of "Orientals" as the "Yellow Peril." But some scholars have argued that the myth simultaneously has at least three negative consequences: it obscures the plight of those Asian Americans who are not "making it"—who are not academically successful, wealthy, and psychologically well-balanced; it endorses conformism to the dominant American values of upward mobility and political docility; and it implies that racism is no longer a structuring factor in the life chances of nonwhite Americans.[47] This last point is especially pernicious because it pits the stereotyped success of one racial minority against the equally stereotyped failures of others: if Asian Americans can be successful, then poor and struggling blacks and Latina/os must simply not be working hard enough and only have themselves to blame for their difficulties.

The very distinct histories of Asian and GLBT stereotyping warns against too simplistic a comparison between the two versions of model minority, but a comparison is nonetheless instructive. The myth of the ideal gay consumer as affluent, educated, apolitical, and tasteful displaces demonized or trivial images of homosexuals with images of GLBT people as a model sexual minority. This myth obscures the ongoing fact of antigay discrimination in law, employment, and cultural life that mean, for example, that gay men earn less on average than heterosexual men, as do lesbians and heterosexual women, and that only a dozen states protect employees from discrimination based on sexual identification. The myth of the ideal gay consumer encourages conformity to normative sexual, family, and social standards, and assumes that the checkout line and the voting booth, but not the street, are the appropriate places for political activism. And the model sexual minority myth pits the visible success of a narrow class of privileged gays against those less well off to suggest that institutional discrimination plays no part in the life chances of GLBT Americans.

Marketers reproduce the image of a model sexual minority to maintain the distinctiveness of the gay market while reassuring the heterosexual majority that the market is unthreatening to dominant norms. They do so, paradoxically, by emphasizing the similarity between (but not the sameness of) gay and heterosexual consumers. A press release from Spare Parts proclaimed that "lesbians and gay men, according to a new, nationwide study conducted over the Internet, are surprisingly settled, apolitical, and want to be portrayed as 'no different than anybody else,'" a portrayal that marketers are happy to offer.[48] Gay consumers are also represented as just like the heterosexual mainstream in terms of values. According to marketing consultant Grant Lukenbill, "Americans of homosexual orientation feel all the same emotions about life, God, and country as Americans of heterosexual orientation [do]."[49] Marketer Stephanie Blackwood surmised that the gender of one's partner is "the significant difference [between homosexuals and heterosexuals]. It really is the only difference, isn't it?"[50] Similarly, advertising executive Andrew Beaver initially minimized the difference between gay and heterosexual consumers, saying that gay consumers "are just like everybody else: they breathe the same air, they live in the same world, they deal with the same problems and they just happen to have—you know, their sexual orientation is different. And that's that." He modified this by adding, "I shouldn't say that. . . . There are other challenges that gay people have that straight people don't have to have."[51]

The "just like you" claim sets up a false equivalence between economically privileged gays and socially, legally, and economically privileged heterosexuals, minimizing the very real differences between these groups in terms of interpersonal and institutionalized discrimination. By emphasizing the similarities between privileged GLBT and heterosexual people, the "just like you" claim simultaneously undermines the shared experiences of homophobia across classes, genders, and racial groups within GLBT populations. Yet this claim nevertheless protects the heterosexual mainstream from any real threat of slippage between gay and straight, because the "just like you" argument, while appearing to emphasize the similarities with the heterosexual majority, in fact reinstates a minoritized view of gayness. Market segmentation requires an absolute break between homosexuality and heterosexuality, reasserting their fundamental discontinuity. When marketers claim that gays are "just like" the heterosexual majority, they preserve the gay market as distinct but not in threatening ways. By adopting heterosexual, professional-class norms of respectability, affluent gays and lesbians can construct a habitus somewhat protected from the more vilified associations with (particularly male) homosexuality, and gain access to elite groups of all sorts and sexualities. The taste culture that gay marketing helps to produce allows privileged gays to unhitch along lines of sexual solidarity, and express class solidarity with heterosexual professionals instead.

Because national gay media tend to reproduce the habitus, tastes, and mores of privileged urban gays, this view becomes what is most easily recognized as "gay culture." *Advocate* columnist Patrick Califia expressed concern about the narrow view of gay life represented in magazines such as *Out* and the *Advocate*: "I think that there's an inherent tension between the desire to mainstream so you can attract advertisers, and actually serving the needs of an audience that's a minority. . . . What the *Advocate* and *Out* both market is the illusion that there's no more oppression to worry about and that if you just have a good enough job and live in a big city you are okey-dokey."[52] In addition to reassuring advertisers and readers alike that homophobia is a thing of the past, this ad-friendly strategy also eclipses sexually and politically provocative queer cultures. As Michael Warner writes,

> The queer ethos is currently thriving in urban scenes, in pockets of alternative culture in the suburbs, among younger queers, in drag culture,

among black and Latino cultures, in club scenes and the arts, on Web sites and in queer zines, among all kinds of people in the least likely places. For all this vitality, it is no longer the public face of the lesbian and gay movement. . . . . This immense network, in which so many people are working to bring a queer world into being, is less and less what people have in mind when they think of the lesbian and gay movement.[53]

Commercially supported gay media have neither removed the need for alternative queer cultures, nor have they effectively suppressed them. However, the visibility offered by gay marketing increasingly shapes the agenda for gay civil rights pursued in the pages of the commercially supported gay press and by corporate-sponsored national gay civil rights groups.

The "business, not politics" refrain suggests that it is possible to separate out the experience of GLBT lives from their political circumstances, that gays are just another identity or lifestyle group, like golfers. Yet the gay market was constituted in part through the political marginalization of GLBT people. As ad agency executive Howard Buford said, if GLBT people "weren't marginalized, then they would be part of the mainstream, and there would be no need to appeal to them as a distinct group."[54] Gay marketing visibility complements an already-existing political visibility, it does not produce it. For as long as homosexuality remains politically and socially contested, any visibility that marketing affords cannot help but both rest upon and reproduce a view of GLBT people as in part politically constituted. Thus however much companies prefer that their gay marketing appears purely motivated by the pursuit of profits, their "business, not politics" distinction is clearly untenable.

But the demand for "politics, not business" of some GLBT critics is also unsustainable. To imagine that political battles can only be fought in a pristine gay world outside the consumer sphere is as unrealistic as it is limiting. This position ignores the opportunities for civil rights gains that corporate interest in profit-making offers: increased media visibility as television pursues high audience ratings, GLBT employee rights as companies find ways to retain valued workers, sponsorship funds to gay rights groups as corporations enhance their public reputations, and so on. More fundamentally, given how far consumption is involved in the production and articulation of identity, GLBT people's most intimate identifications—necessarily political—cannot help but be imbricated with the world of business, as are heterosexuals'. It is not that business interests and political concerns are absolutely incompatible, but that the logics of niche segmentation as they are applied to a controversial social group produces a contained visibility. Contained visibility can only ever yield conditional acceptance.

In the introduction to their anthology of writings about public sex, the Dangerous Bedfellows editors ask, "Who will be privileged to speak on behalf of whom, through what venues, and with whose approval? How will the mainstream media be allowed to frame discourse on public sex? How will the 'gay community' be defined: who will be included, who will assign blame, who will make decisions?"[55] The dominant voices of gay and lesbian media argue that the fundamental goal of the gay rights movement should be fought in Gayle Rubin's charmed circle of sex: the right to have married, monogamous, coupled, private, vanilla sex. Gay men and lesbians stepping outside that circle into the realm of dangerous, commercialized, sleazy sexuality—whether in magazines, in stores, in theaters, or on the streets—are on their own, since the legitimate goals and principles of gay communities lie elsewhere.

Gay marketing has been fundamental to the cultural transformation that has taken place since the 1970s, including a move from gay invisibility and negative stereotyping toward increasingly positive images, greater dialogue between the supposedly heterosexual mainstream and gay subcultures, and shifts in allegiances based on class affinities as well as sexuality. This transformation demands a more nuanced approach to GLBT politics and representation than the assimilationist argument can accommodate. Even while gay marketing represents a narrow version of gayness, it also offers GLBT people increasing opportunities to see, identify with, and shop as GLBT people. And although gay marketing endorses the most normative impulses of the heterosexual mainstream, it also brings revenues to gay publications, Web sites, and groups that do not only pursue the most normative agendas. Beyond the pages of commercially supported media, queer cultures abound in zines, independent film, pornography, and local commercial establishments, reflecting a less well-funded but more interesting scene than that of the sexually decorous, class-structured view of gayness offered by national advertisers. It remains to be seen what impact gay marketing has had on GLBT people's ability to imagine alternatives to the dominant gay habitus of gay consumer culture. An ad from AT&T is not evidence that the battle for gays rights is won, but nor does it herald the end of a gay fighting spirit. Gay readers engage with advertising thoughtfully and with multiple commitments and desires, even if it is impossible to know what the range of those commitments and desires may be.

Gay marketing is a matter of business *and* politics, and is sometimes too the business *of* politics. Yet the politics of gay and lesbian marketing visibility is far from straightforward: visibility yields some beneficial effects and some troubling ones. I do not concur with the most apocalyptic predictions from some GLBT critics about the consequences of gay marketing, nor do I see those occasional images of gays and lesbians in marketing as the sea change that others optimistically forecast. Gay marketing images are often fun, sometimes inter-esting, and occasionally gratifying. The significance of corporate investment in underwriting gay and lesbian media and civil rights campaigning is not to be underestimated. But it is inherently frustrating to put faith in the consumer sphere as the route to acceptance; for all its pleasures, to hope for political gains in the increasingly desperate attempts of corporate America to court gays and lesbians is to put trust in a fickle creature. Real and important changes in the lives of GLBT people are taking place outside the consumer sphere, even as GLBT consumers might also welcome interest from corporate America. The distinction between "business and politics" is bogus: marketing images of and to GBLT people must necessarily involve both. Yet gay marketing requires that GLBT politics be desexualized, and that GLBT sexuality, when it appears at all, be depoliticized. Considerations of the value of gay marketing must prior-itize queer sexuality in sexual identification, turning from the question of whether gay appeals are a matter of "business or politics" to ask if GLBT pol-itics are a matter of "business or pleasure." The answer, again, must be "Both."

PITCHING THE GAY MARKET

This study is not ethnography in the classic sense of the term, but takes an ethnographic approach to the construction of the gay market. Broadly speaking, ethnography is the practice of writing about cultures from researchers' detailed and ongoing involvement with those cultures. Sociologists Martyn Hammersley and Paul Atkinson write, "In its most characteristic form, [ethnographic research] involves the ethnographer participating, overtly or covertly, in people's daily lives for an extended period of time, watching what happens, listening to what is said, asking questions—in fact, collecting whatever data are available to throw light on the issues that are the focus of the research."[1] Much ethnographic work has been done in recent years on the production of cultural goods, including fine and popular art, television, radio, film, magazines, and books.[2] Largely using participant observation, cultural production ethnographies offer a framework to look at such issues as how routines reproduce some ideologies more easily than others; what constraints are placed upon media producers, texts, and distribution; how audiences are considered in the production process; and the role of media researchers as themselves cultural producers. I adopted alternative methods to approach the field of gay marketing, yet the spirit of these ethnographies is present in this study, most especially in my respect for the productive aspects of marketing processes at all stages of formation, distribution, and reception, and my focus on marketers' professional culture as an important factor in how the gay market is produced.

Whereas much scholarly research on advertising concentrates on ad texts, Michael Arlen, Randall Rothenberg, Karen Shapiro, and Don Slater used participant observation in advertising agencies to look at the complexities of the advertising process.[3] Arlen and Rothenberg each focused on a single campaign (AT&T and Subaru commercials, respectively); Slater and Shapiro both compared advertising processes between a small number of agencies and products. Using advertising ethnographies as a starting point, I designed this project to investigate the processes of constructing and maintaining the gay market from a broader perspective than either textual analysis or a participant observation study of a few agencies or campaigns could offer. Through interviews, presentations, and a variety of documents, I hoped to tap into the working practices of marketing professionals to investigate the production of the gay market in a range of venues. This combination of approaches yielded a diverse range of data from which I could draw out both the continuities and the disparities between campaigns, venues, agencies, and sites.

As this research progressed, I became increasingly aware of how deeply my subject of study, marketing, determined the very means of getting and analyzing my data. Marketing "pitch" was an underlying frame for my research; it structured many interactions with my subjects, and could also be applied to my own strategies for getting and analyzing information. "The pitch" describes, most typically, the process whereby ad creatives introduce a new campaign to clients—selling ideas to sell products. But marketers, publishers, and journalists are all involved in promoting the idea of the gay market, and their product as somehow useful in gay marketing, whether this product is market research data, the readership of a magazine, the idea of gays as loyal and affluent, and so on. Considering the ways in which different data and my approaches to them were structured by this pitch helped me step back from a fruitless debate between whether data are "true" or "false," to consider again how they are shaped, contained, obscured, and elided in their production and analysis. In her study of the production of a public radio show based on the book club format, Lisa Henderson observes that "*Storyline*, like other call-in radio programs, is a highly managed form of public discourse."[4] As a woman-centered project, such management had high stakes, not least the containment of the negative associations with the term *feminism*. Similarly, gay marketing pitch bears an additional burden over general-market discourse because of the contested status of a visible gay consumer culture.

Cultural production ethnographies have encouraged diverse approaches to collecting data, especially if access to participant observation is limited. My data for this project included both spoken materials and documents that I began collecting in the fall of 1997. Between January 1998 and April 2003, I interviewed forty-five professionals who worked, or had formerly worked, in gay marketing. I carried out follow-up interviews with thirteen of these participants, and continued with occasional phone calls and e-mails with others to get updates or check information. I contacted potential interviewees in two ways. Most effective was "snowball sampling":[5] Jason Heffner, deputy director of the Gay and Lesbian Alliance Against Defamation (GLAAD) gave me the names and contact information for my first five interviewees who, in turn, recommended that I talk to people they knew. Many were generous in their suggestions, offers of contact information, and willingness to let me use their names in correspondence with other possible interviewees. Some, however, were reluctant to pass on information about colleagues involved in gay marketing. Such gatekeeping was particularly apparent between national corporations and advertising agencies; employees in both types of institutions protected their counterparts in the other. Caitlin Hume, sales representative at *Out* magazine, suggested why there may be some nervousness about passing colleagues' information on to me. Advertising agents may be protective because "the client pays and [agency executives] are petrified of you going to the client and potentially criticizing their campaign. And the client needs to be defensive because they want to handle how their image is protected, they want to keep it in-house."[6] Other areas of marketing such as public relations, market research, and journalism function through active networking and information sharing; marketers in these fields tended to be more willing to pass on information.

Snowball sampling has the advantage of deploying an already established relationship to make new contacts. Prospective interviewees were more likely to agree to an interview if someone they knew had already talked to me. Yet this sampling method also has its limits, most obviously that all possibly helpful interviewees did not know each other. It was striking how small I found the gay marketing world—in New York, at least: after only a few conversations interviewees suggested I talk to the same group of people. As a result I also used cold-calling to contact additional subjects, although as Gamson and others have found, this yielded much lower rates of response than did snowball sampling.[7] Cold-calling did, however, allow me some access to companies and professionals who were not integrated in the gay market milieus concentrated in New York and San Francisco. I used magazine mastheads, trade and popular press articles, presentations on the gay market, and the membership directory of the New York Advertising and Communications Network (now Out Professionals) to identify and locate further potential interviewees.

In most cases I first wrote a letter or an e-mail to prospective interviewees, mentioning who had suggested that I contact them, outlining my project, and explaining why they, in particular, would be an invaluable source of information. A week or so after I sent each letter I called or e-mailed the marketer to set a time for an interview. Of sixty-five requests I was ultimately granted interviews with forty-five gay marketers.

Interview relations depend a great deal on the power differentials between interviewee and researcher. Political scientist Lewis Anthony Dexter recommends that researchers spare themselves some measure of indebtedness by recognizing that interviewees are also gaining something from the exchange. He suggests that people in elite and specialized roles enjoy being interviewed because it arouses their curiosity, offers them the enjoyment of telling or teaching someone something, grants them the attention of an "understanding stranger," and presents an opportunity for pleasurable "self-analysis."[8] For my project, I would add that many of my interviewees may have believed that both the discussion and the results of my project would feed back into their work by, for example, offering another perspective on gay marketing or raising their profile as gay marketers. As such, the interview itself could have been a marketing opportunity. Others expressed an interest in GLBT politics and may have seen my project as aligned with their often-articulated investments in gay visibility.

The reasons some contacts refused or did not reply to repeated requests for an interview may have been numerous. Laura Nader observes that the powerful often resist being observed, making research that involves "studying up" challenging.[9] Joshua Gamson acknowledges that gaining access is particularly hard in those contexts where proprietary information is produced and circulated, making media elites difficult to reach.[10] Professionals tend to be busy, and people working in advertising, public relations, and marketing commonly work within a system of billable hours, which do not easily offer the flexibility of taking time out of a workday for an interview. Some interviewees accommodated this by agreeing to talk to me in the evening or on the weekend. Others may have been unwilling to trust a researcher with the details of campaigns; in addition to the general anxiety that advertising ideas and strategies will be stolen is the concern that gay people and issues are so often misrepresented that marketers are not willing to offer information that may be misleadingly used. One interviewee was initially very reluctant to talk to me and expressed concern about being quoted out of context, as had happened to him in the past. When he did agree, he was not comfortable with being audiotaped and did not send me a media kit. In a couple of cases contacts had moved on to other jobs, positions, or projects. For example, when I made contact with Mark Malinowski, Levi Strauss's representative for the Dockers advertorial in *Out* magazine, he was already working on a subsequent campaign and was reluctant to revisit what seemed to him a long-past experience. Some contacts may have been suspicious of my request for an interview out of a belief that academic research is irrelevant (compared, for example, with market research), and because much scholarly work in this area has been highly critical of the industry. I used this last critique as a point of leverage with reluctant interviewees, however, suggesting to them that because much academic research had not dealt adequately with marketers' points of view this was their chance to have their say. In some cases where I was not able to interview a subject, I attempted to get an overview from them (or from someone else in a similar role) in public presentations, or gleaned at least part of their story from news articles and Web sites.

The forty-five interviewees can be categorized as follows: twenty-six interviewees were men, eighteen were women, and one was transgender. Thirty-four identified as gay, lesbian, or bisexual, four identified themselves as heterosexual, and seven did not disclose their sexual identity. In many cases subjects explicitly identified their sexuality, as in Andrew Beaver's comment that "of the many things that I am, gay is one of them," or Hume's, "I think it helps sometimes that I'm not gay."[11] In cases where interviewees did not identify themselves as gay in the interview, I subsequently asked them to do so by e-mail (as "Gay/Lesbian/Bisexual," "Heterosexual," or "Not disclosed"). Only one interviewee, Howard Buford, identified himself to me as a person of color.[12] They worked as magazine publishers, ad directors, marketers, sales representatives, and editors; advertising agency creatives and account executives; corporate marketers; market researchers and public relations consultants; and journalists covering the gay market beat. Twenty-three subjects were based in New York, with five others elsewhere on the East Coast. Eight worked in San Francisco, and three more were elsewhere in California. Two were based in a Colorado city, one in a Texas city, and two in Toronto, Canada. I did not know one interviewee's location (for details on each interview see appendix 2).

I conducted seventeen of the initial interviews in person, usually in subjects' offices, sometimes in cafes or restaurants, and once in a subject's home. One subject agreed to answer questions only on e-mail. The remaining initial interviews I conducted by phone. Four follow-up interviews were conducted in person, ten by phone, and six by e-mail. Spoken interviews ranged in length from fifteen minutes to two hours. I audiotaped all but one of the in-person interviews, with permission from each subject (the exception took place in a restaurant too noisy to trust a tape-recording). I also audiotaped twenty-five of the thirty-three phone interviews, using a recording device attached to the phone and again asking each subject's permission. Some interviewees preferred not to be taped for confidentiality reasons, and in one instance recording equipment was not available at the time of the interview. Some subjects would talk to me only if their identities and their companies remained confidential; I agreed to change their names and to disguise their locations, companies, products, and campaign information in any public discussion of the project.

I began my early interviews with broad questions, following Dexter's advice to start with "questions where the key words are quite vague and ambiguous, so the interviewee can interpret them in his own terms, and out of his own experience."[13] I also asked open-ended questions to encourage a "quasi-monologue":[14] for example, I usually began interviews by asking subjects to describe their role in the company and elaborate upon what they do. As the interview progressed, I asked subjects' opinions on various issues in gay marketing, including what the ideal gay consumer looked like, whether lesbians were considered part of the gay market, whether publications and Web sites that included sex ads were likely to get national advertising, and so on. I was interested in concrete descriptions of what they actually did, as well as a more abstracted understanding of the gay market. I tailored these questions according to what I knew about interviewees. For example, as a longtime critic of advertising, Stuart Elliott was particularly well-informed about the history of gay marketing; however, not being an agency executive, he could not tell me about the particular phases of specific campaign development.

As the interview period progressed, my questions became increasingly focused and I stopped asking about topics that had begun to produce redundant information, a process Shapiro calls the "accumulating interview."[15] Following her advice, I continued to ask the same question for only as long as the particularities of a specific ad, campaign, venue, or professional role were unique; where previous answers were unclear; when comparing cases across ads, campaigns, venues, or roles; when earlier sources seemed unreliable; when the question elicited different responses from different kinds of people (across gender or professional roles, for example); and when the question was one of opinion, rather than fact—although even here much redundancy still emerged.

Over time I became more adept at anticipating what people might and could tell me. Subjects related a great deal about their professional experience, expertise, and political and activist commitments. They offered much factual information about their tasks and responsibilities, their publications' or companies' marketing or readership data, their market share, and so on. They also offered opinions from marketing, political, and analytic perspectives: some were knowledgeable of contemporary cultural theory and volunteered responses that problematized, for example, essentialized views of the gay market (Dan Baker), and narrowly pragmatic explanations of the lack of interest in lesbian consumers (Megan Ishler). Interviewees also generously offered networking information, sharing names and contact details of professional and personal acquaintances for future interviews and possible field sites.

There were also limits to what subjects could, or would, tell me. In some cases I asked questions that they simply didn't know the answer to. Some subjects were prevented from imparting some details of their work by nondisclosure agreements or a more general need to protect their companies' or clients' proprietary information. Others were not willing to disclose their companies' financial information. Magazine publishers, for example, proved reticent in telling me the proportion of revenue earned from advertising compared with subscriptions and sales. Both what is said and what is not said offer useful data, however. Howard Becker argues that informants' speech can be taken as evidence of events about which the subject has had the opportunity to gather reliable information and has no reason to misrepresent the issue or mislead the researcher.[16] Yet even when an interviewee's statement does not seem to be accurate, "It may still provide useful evidence for a different kind of conclusion. Accepting the sociological proposition that an individual's statements and descriptions of events are made from a perspective which is a function of his position in the group, the observer can interpret such statements and descriptions as indications of the individual's perspective on the point involved."[17] Questionable, inaccurate, selective, biased, or withheld information from participants is thus grist for the research mill if treated according to Becker's second principle, as evidence of an ideologically constructed social world.

Public presentations on gay marketing were a useful supplement to the interviews. I gained access to individuals whom I had not otherwise interviewed, witnessed marketers' shaping the gay market for different audiences, and participated in gay market–oriented conversations before and during the events. I gathered data from the following presentations: Michael Wilke's overview of gay, lesbian, bisexual, and transgender images in television commercials to the Philadelphia chapter of the National Lesbian and Gay Journalists' Association (NLGJA, February 22, 1998); Joe Landry's and Steve Watson's presentations to the Boston Ad Club (January 20, 1999); *Out* magazine and the *New York Times*'s "*Times* Talks" panel on the gay market, "Advertising to Gay America" (April 8, 1999); the *New York Times*'s "*Times* Talks" panel on gay commerce on the Internet, "The Boys in the Bandwidth" (February 29, 2000); a PrideFest 2002 panel, "Marketing to the GLBT Consumer" (May 4, 2002); two NLGJA conference panels, "Gay Demographics: The Rocky Road to Research" and "Gay Cable Channel: Ghetto or Liberated Zone?" (both September 14, 2002); The New York LGBT Center's panel "The 10% Market Share: The Ins and Outs of Queer Marketing" (March 20, 2003); and the Equality Forum panel "International Gay Media" (May 1, 2003). See appendix 2 for a list of presentations. The presentations differed from interviews most significantly in terms of the audience. In interviews, I was the primary and immediate audience, whereas in presentations the audience was made up of the organizing group's members and an interested public. The panels allowed me to see marketers working in a professional milieu and, specifically, how marketers pitch their work, companies, campaigns, or products to other marketers as well as to an interested lay public.

The documents I assembled for analysis came from different stages in the marketing process. I reviewed ads directed (or possibly directed) toward gay consumers and appearing in both gay and general-market media since 1958, including in the *Advocate* magazine (periodically since 1967; every issue since October 1998), *Out* (some issues since 1992; every issue since February 1997), *Deneuve*, later *Curve* (some since 1991; every issue since September 1998), *Girlfriends* (since September 1998), *Philadelphia Gay News* (since June 2000), *On Our Backs* (since its relaunch in June 1998), and *Bad Attitude* (1999). I also looked at occasional issues from a range of other gay, lesbian, bisexual, and queer national, local, and pornographic publications including *Alternative Family* (August–September 1998), *Anything That Moves* (Fall 1998), *Black Sheets* (issue 16, 2000), *Blueboy* (December 1999), *Clikque* (March 2000), *Drummer* (issue 211, 1998), *Lesbian News* (May 1998), *Metrosource* (Summer 1998), and *Q San Francisco* (November 1998). I have also looked at two issues of *POZ* (September and October 1998). I frequently reviewed ads and content on two Internet gay affinity sites, PlanetOut and gay.com, as well as on the gay financial site, gfn.com. Both in publications and on Web sites I was particularly interested in ads (products, images, and placement), discussions of marketing or consumption, the appearance of sexual ads and content, the gender distribution of ads and content, political coverage, and if and how the reader was expressly addressed as a consumer.

I analyzed examples of catalogs from 1994 from Shocking Gray, Tzabaco, Girls and Company, M2M, 10% Productions, Greenwood/Cooper, Alternative Creations, International Male, and the National AIDS Awareness campaign. Although not all of these were expressly or exclusively directed to gay consumers, they nevertheless included gay-coded products (such as rainbow items in the National AIDS Awareness campaign). I also have four cardpacks from Our Tribe and Community Cardpacks which contain postcard-sized ads from *Out, POZ*, and other magazines, travel agencies, credit cards, dating services, phone sex lines and pornography, only one of which is dated ("Pride '96").[18] With the ads, catalogs, and cardpacks I was particularly interested in the products being advertised, the advertised companies, the codes used in ads to connote gayness, and in which media or venues the ads appeared.

In addition to seeing how magazines and Web sites position ads and make appeals to gay consumers, I was interested in how their marketers packaged readers and gay consumers more generally for potential advertisers. I collected paper and Web-based press kits for the *Advocate, Out, Q San Francisco, POZ, Curve, Passport*, PlanetOut, and gay.com. I also looked at trade press and popular press articles in which journalists circulate information and opinion about gay consumers. These included articles in *Advertising Age, Adweek*, the *New York Times*, the *Washington Post*, the *Wall Street Journal*, the *Los Angeles Times*, the *San Francisco Chronicle*, the *Boston Globe, Newsweek*, and other general-interest, national and local papers and magazines. I located these materials through hard copies of the publications, the Lexis/Nexis database, citations in other work on the gay market, and the kind contributions of colleagues and friends.

I monitored print, e-mail, and Web site documents concerning gay marketing from GLBT organizations. These included press releases from the Gay and Lesbian Alliance Against Defamation (GLAAD), its *Images* newsletter, and annual GLAAD Media Awards lists of nominees and winners; e-mails from the New York Advertising and Communications Network's (NYACN, now Out Professionals), its *Newsbreaks* newsletter and membership directory; and e-mails from the National Gay and Lesbian Journalists Association (NLGJA) and its *Alternatives* newsletter. These sources provided examples to supplement interview data, highlighted aspects of gay marketers' professional culture, and were useful in locating potential interviewees.

Documents suggesting how advertising agencies and other marketers package the gay market for prospective clients included both print and Web site press kits for Prime Access, Mulryan/Nash, Rivendell Marketing, and Spare Parts. I examined one large market survey report by Overlooked Opinions (*Report* 3.2 [1992]), other market research by Witeck-Combs Communications with Harris Interactive, and by OpusComm. I also looked at all six issues of *Quotient*, a newsletter for marketers interested in reaching gay consumers (December 1994 to May 1995). I received a number of corporate documents concerning the Dockers advertorial in *Out* magazine including memos, faxes, notes, lists of role models, and the summary section of an in-house report of the project.

The "gay consumer" is produced through printed and, in recent years, Web-based texts more than in any other context. Documents are the primary medium in which marketers produce and circulate knowledge, data, and opinions about, as well as images of, gay consumers. Documents require different analytic considerations from spoken data: they are neither more nor less valid than material collected in face-to-face interviews, for example, but perform different functions and are subject to different constraints than spoken data. Hammersley and Atkinson assert that documents are "not necessarily to be read at face value, as accurate representations of social reality, but can suggest themes, images, or metaphors."[19] Further, the range of documents I collected function differently in the constitution of the gay market; ads are evidence of "the gay market" in ways different from, say, gay market research surveys, and thus require distinct approaches to their respective themes, images, and metaphors.

Together, then, written and spoken data combine to offer many access points to gay marketing, including how marketers pitch gay consumption and consumers to each other, to clients, and to gay consumers; how gay marketing is produced in a variety of venues; and how gay marketers reflect upon their professional practices. Pursuing interview, documentary, and historical data afforded me a view that could account for changes over time and consider the role of a range of institutions in constructing the gay market.

In analyzing these data I borrowed a question from Henry Kingsbury: "What is at issue here?"[20] If the gay market is not a material entity but a construction always in process, what is being constructed? In what ways? On the basis of what assumptions? With what consequences? I tried to remain aware of the multiple and contradictory investments among sources and to resist assuming seamless ideological positions among different kinds of data.[21] Sources offered both information and opinion; both are ideologically structured but function differently, as Becker observed. In considering different sources I treated each with their use in mind, especially in terms of how marketing pitch might operate for each source and to whom such pitches were made. Rather than the interviewees offering responses that were either transparent or opaque, I increasingly understood that they shared some knowledge, packaged in particular ways, under some circumstances. For example, Andrew Beaver was concerned to downplay the distinctiveness of the gay market in the context of some specific campaigns he had overseen. He said, "It doesn't have to be a gay and lesbian thing for a gay and lesbian person to get it, and to find themselves in the brand. You know what I mean? We're not simply gay and lesbian, we are just unique people, we are just people, you know?"[22] By the end of our interview I felt I had been the recipient more of a marketing pitch than Beaver's genuine perceptions of the gay market, perhaps a pitch he was working with in a current campaign. Yet I began to realize that in some senses all my interviews involved some degree of marketing pitch, in that everyone I spoke to inevitably had some investments in the credibility of the gay market; their agencies, companies, or publications; their own professional image or career development; or simply their impression management in front of a researcher. Realizing that pitching underlay all the interviews allowed me to treat their content not as fact versus opinion, but as facts and opinions carefully, if not consciously, prepared for presentation.

If the interviews were at some level a pitch, the public presentations were much more expressly so: presenters were aware that audience members may also be future customers. For example, Joe Landry based his overview of the gay market for the Boston Ad Club on figures from the *Advocate*'s press kit, offering readership information as descriptive of gay consumers as a whole and using that information to counter the myths that have discouraged appeals to gay consumers in the past. In a couple of instances, the pitch function of presentations was self-reflexively and humorously acknowledged. For instance, Amy Simmons, advertising director of gay.com, responded to a question about the efficacy of Web advertising from a marketer of a large hotel chain with "Can I talk to you after this?" to audience laughter and applause.[23] In presentations marketers were pitching their products, companies, and expertise not only to me but to other marketers and potential clients.

When I considered how pitching functioned in texts, I was initially tempted to see some, like ads, as expressly marketing texts, and others, like trade and popular press articles, as more objective. Yet all texts need to be treated as invested, if in different ways and with different ends in mind. As with interviews and presentations, journalists and other writers moved between disclosure and concealment, offering some data and not others and blurring the boundaries between samples (gay readership surveys, market research surveys) and a broader notion of the "gay community." Some writers expressed greater commitment to representativeness. For example, Dan Baker told me that in the gay market newsletter *Quotient* he attempted to circulate more accurate data about gay consumers' affluence and spending power (from Yankelovich and other sources) than earlier market research. However, other market researchers deflected criticisms of unrepresentative market research data, protesting that the gay market is particularly difficult to sample.[24] Despite these differences, *Quotient*, Simmons, and *Advertising Age* all had a vested interest in pitching the gay market as viable, valuable, and lucrative. Further, the professionals involved—Baker, the Simmons spokeswoman, *Advertising Age's* Michael Wilke, and others—were each involved in constructing their own professional image as credible, their publications or companies as advertiser-worthy, and/or their research as valid. As a result, I consider all primary documents on gay marketing as themselves marketing documents; indeed, given the public circulation of many of these documents, the pitch may structure documents even more than interviews in which marketers might have felt they could express more conditional, ambivalent, or personal responses.

The question of pitch did not only frame my data, then, but also the field relations in which those data were gathered. Radway and other cultural production ethnographers have acknowledged similarities between their own professional identities and the productive aspects of their work and those of their subjects.[25] In her study of television talk shows, Laura Grindstaff compares her research to television producers' processes of eliciting, selecting, condensing, editing, and presenting personal experience for a television audience.[26] She argues that to position herself as an objective, honest researcher in opposition to duplicitous, exploitative talk show staff (not a comparison she endorses) is untenable, given the similarities between each role's strategies (sometimes deceptive) and output (always selective). Just as the marketers I spoke to packaged the presentation of information and their professional identities in sometimes motivated and self-interested ways, so too did I. In order to complete this project I needed to pitch myself as credible and my project as valuable to gain access to interviewees, documents, and other data. Not only did my interviewees pitch themselves as professionals through their gay marketing knowledge and expertise, but I too produced myself as a scholar through my own field of knowledge and expertise. Whatever my discomfort or frustration with the ways in which some interviewees shaped their discourse for maximum gain, I too shaped what

I told them, asked them, and did with their words. This is not to suggest that either they or I were duplicitous in our presentations of our selves and our work, but rather to acknowledge that all such presentations are not transparent but invested.

Recognizing the ways in which I have shaped this project raises questions of my accountability as a researcher working with a particular constituency, as a lesbian, and as a feminist. I hope that this work does justice to the commitments, as well as the contradictions, of many gay marketers. But I also hope that my criticisms meet the demands of my political commitments to resisting a closure of what is imaginable as gayness, to reasserting the radical potential of queer sexuality for disrupting gender and other hierarchies, and to offering another cultural frame (marketing) in which to consider the constructedness of sexuality. Just as I am both professionally and politically accountable as a scholar in constructing this project, I also hold gay marketers similarly accountable, if to a differently constituted audience, for their work in constructing the gay market. I hope, ultimately, that this book may be helpful in an ongoing debate about the meanings of different manifestations of nonnormative sexuality within an increasingly marketing-dominated cultural space.

The Gay Marketers

Job titles were correct at the time of the interviews: many interviewees have since changed jobs and/or employers.

Artigas, Justo. Male, sexuality not disclosed. Director of public relations, Dolce & Gabanna, New York. Phone interview, February 19, 1999.

Baker, Dan. Gay male. Former publisher and editor in chief of *Quotient* newsletter, New York. In-person interview, September 17, 1998.

Beaver, Andrew. Gay male. Executive vice president, Deutsch advertising agency, New York. In-person interview, February 23, 1998.

Blackwood, Stephanie. Lesbian. Partner, Spare Parts and, subsequently, Double Platinum public relations and marketing agencies, New York. In-person interview, January 19, 1998; phone interview, January 5, 1999; phone interview, May 1, 1999; phone interview, August 18, 2001.

Buford, Howard. Gay male. President, Prime Access, Inc., advertising agency, New York. In-person interview, February 13, 1998; in-person interview, November 14, 2001; phone interview, April 15, 2003.

Califia, Patrick. Female-to-male transsexual. Journalist, San Francisco. Phone interview, May 10, 2001.

Capossela, Donna. Female, sexuality not disclosed. Sales and marketing representative, and intern, *Out* magazine, New York. In-person interview, March 31, 1999.

Daly, Nancy (pseudonym). Lesbian. Sales executive for gay market, national brewing company. Phone interview, January 19, 1999.

DeMars, Kurt. Gay male. Advertising director, *Out* magazine, New York. In-person interview, April 1, 1999.

DiBruno, Steve (pseudonym). Gay male. Sales executive for gay market, national airline. Phone interview, October 7, 1998.

Draper, Catherine. Lesbian. Advertising director, *Girlfriends* and *On Our Backs* magazines, San Francisco. Phone interview, January 21, 1999.

Elliott, Stuart. Gay male. Advertising columnist, *New York Times*, New York. In-person interview, November 18, 1998; phone interview, December 16, 1998; phone interview, August 23, 2001.

Evans, Todd. Gay male. President, Rivendell Marketing Company, renamed Rivendell Media, Inc., in 2003, New York. Phone interview, September 17, 1999; e-mail, April 2, 2003.

Falk, Gene. Gay male. Senior Vice President, Showtime, New York. Phone interview, September 27, 2002; phone interview, October 4, 2002.

Farber, Matt. Gay male. Consultant, MTV Networks, New York. Phone interview, September 27, 2002; e-mail, September 30, 2002; phone interview May 17, 2003.

Fabrizio, Louis. Male, sexuality not disclosed. Former publisher, *Out* magazine, New York. E-mail, January 10, 2000.

Finco, John. Gay male. Director of marketing, *Out* magazine, New York. In-person interview, April 14, 1999.

Fine, Judith. Female, sexuality not disclosed. Owner, lingerie store, Northampton, Mass. In-person interview, August 8, 2001.

Fox, Rachel. Female, sexuality not disclosed. Account supervisor, McCann McLaren advertising agency, Toronto. Phone interview, February 18, 1999.

Gumbiner, Liz. Heterosexual female. Creative director, Deutsch advertising agency, New York. In-person interview, September 7, 1998.

Hewlett, Moneka. Lesbian. Marketing director, *On Our Backs* and *Girlfriends* magazines, San Francisco. Phone interview, October 23, 1998.

Hume, Caitlin. Heterosexual female. Sales and marketing representative, *Out* magazine, New York. In-person interview, February 2, 1999; in-person interview, March 31, 1999.

Isherwood, Deborah (pseudonym). Female, sexuality not disclosed. Promotion manager at pharmaceutical/health products company. Phone interview, September 23, 1998.

Ishler, Megan. Lesbian. Director of advertising, *On Our Backs* magazine, San Francisco. Phone interview, December 3, 1998; phone interview, December 11, 1998.

Landry, Joe. Gay male. Publisher, *Advocate* magazine, Los Angeles. Phone interview, January 5, 1999; phone interview, October 18, 2001.

Lukenbill, Grant. Gay male. Marketing consultant, journalist, New York. In-person interview, February 2, 1998.

McCusker, Anna. Heterosexual female. Vice President of marketing, PrideVision, Toronto. Phone interview, December 13, 2002.

Monat, Gail. Lesbian. Co-owner of women's sex store, Northampton, Mass. In-person interview, August 22, 2001.

Mullen, Dan. Gay male. Business manager, *Anything That Moves* magazine, San Francisco. Phone interview, March 18, 1999.

Mulryan, David. Gay male. Partner, Mulryan/Nash advertising agency, New York. Phone interview, January 24, 1999.

O'Neil, Patrick. Gay male. Art director, Deutsch advertising agency, New York. In-person interview, November 18, 1998.

Sarisky, Kara. Female, sexuality not disclosed. Advertising sales representative, *Playboy* magazine, city unknown. Phone interview, April 19, 2000.

Schlegal, Jack. Gay male. Board member, New York Advertising and Communications Network, editor of NYACN's *Newsbreaks* newsletter, New York. Phone interview, January 11, 1999.

Schofield, Ginny (pseudonym). Lesbian. Cochair of her high-tech company's Gay and Lesbian Task Force. Phone interview, February 22, 1999.

Schubert, Walter. Gay male. President and CEO, gfn.com, New York. Phone interview, August 24, 2001.

Scott, Henry. Gay male. President, *Out* magazine, New York. In-person interview, February 2, 1999.

Shively, Michael. Gay male. Formerly associate publisher, *Advocate* magazine, San Francisco area. Phone interview, August 21, 2001.

Smith, Megan. Lesbian. President and Director, board of directors for PlanetOut Partners, San Francisco. Phone interview, February 17, 2003.

Stevens, Frances. Lesbian. Publisher and editor in chief, *Curve* magazine, San Francisco. Phone interview, November 10, 1998.

Strub, Sean. Bisexual male. Publisher, *POZ* magazine; President, Strubco, New York. In-person interview, October 28, 1998; e-mail, August 19, 2001; e-mail, August 21, 2001; in-person interview, November 18, 2001; in-person interview, October 25, 2002; e-mail, November 12, 2002; e-mail, February 20, 2003.

Sullivan, Patrick. Heterosexual male. Account supervisor, Integer Group advertising agency, Denver. Phone interview, February 17, 1999.

Taylor, Kelly. Lesbian. Publisher and editor in chief, *Alternative Family* magazine, Van Nuys, Calif. Phone interview, January 27, 1999.

Tuthill, Don. Gay male. Publisher, *Q San Francisco* magazine, San Francisco. Phone interview, October 21, 1998; phone interview, August 14, 2001.

Wilke, Michael. Gay male. Journalist, *Advertising Age*, New York. In-person interview, January 19, 1998; e-mail, August 14, 2001.

Witeck, Bob. Gay male. Partner, Witeck-Combs public relations company, Washington, D.C. Phone interview, November 22, 1998; phone interview, August 14, 2001; e-mail, April 22, 2003, 8:55 A.M. and 4:50 P.M.

PRESENTATIONS

February 22, 1998: The Commercial Closet (Philadelphia). Michael Wilke. Presentation to the National Lesbian and Gay Journalists Association: Philadelphia chapter.

January 20, 1999: Boston Ad Club (Boston). Joe Landry, publisher, *Advocate* magazine; Steve Watson, marketing representative, Lotus Corporation.

April 8, 1999: "*Times* Talks—Advertising to Gay America" (New York City). Stephanie Blackwood, partner, Spare Parts; Howard Buford, president and CEO, Prime Access; Jim Consolantis, senior partner and worldwide creative director, Ogilvy and Mather; Stuart Elliott, advertising columnist, *New York Times*; Todd Evans, president, Rivendell Marketing Company; Mark Malinowski, senior marketing specialist, Levi Strauss.

February 29, 2000: "*Times* Talks—The Boys in the Bandwidth: The Growth of the Gay and Lesbian Online Marketplace" (New York City). Jim Dean, director of information services development, Greenfield Online; Stuart Elliott, advertising columnist, *New York Times*; Jeffrey Newman, president and COO of gfn.com, president and CEO of out.com; Evan Orenstein, executive vice president, global communications, Razorfish; Amy Simmons, director of advertising, Online Partners, gay.com.

May 4, 2002: "Marketing to the GLBT Consumer." PrideFest 2002 Panel (Philadelphia). Stephanie Blackwood, partner, Double Platinum; Wes Combs, President and co-founder, Witeck-Combs Communications; Keith Ferrazzi, CEO and president, YaYa Communications; Stephanie Gibbons, senior vice president of advertising, Showtime; Sarah Siegel, program director, GLBT sales and talent, IBM.

September 14, 2002: National Lesbian and Gay Journalists Association Annual Conference, "Gay Demographics—The Rocky Road to Research" (Philadelphia). Lee Badgett, associate professor of economics, University of Massachusetts-Amherst and research director, Institute for Gay and Lesbian Strategic Studies; John Bremer, research scientist, Harris Interactive; Kipp Cheng, senior journalist, DiversityInc.com; Amy Falkner, lead researcher, GL Census Partners; Jeffrey Garber, partner, Opus-Comm; Gary Gates, research associate, the Urban Institute; Bob Witeck, CEO, Witeck-Combs Communications.

September 14, 2002: National Lesbian and Gay Journalists Association Annual Conference, "Gay Cable Channel—Ghetto or Liberated Zone?" (Philadelphia). Gene Falk, senior vice president, Showtime; Matt Farber, consultant, MTV Networks; Larry Gross, professor, the Annenberg School for Communication, University of Pennsylvania; Charles Ignacio, executive producer, *In the Life*; Mark Lieber, senior vice president of programming, PrideVision; Katherine Sender, assistant professor, the Annenberg School for Communication, University of Pennsylvania.

March 20, 2003: "The 10% Market Share: The Ins and Outs of Queer Marketing." New York Lesbian, Gay, Bisexual, and Transgender Center (New York City). Todd Evans, president, Rivendell Marketing; Serge Gojkovich, consultant to the British Tourist Authority; Sarah Siegel, program director, GLBT sales and talent, IBM; Katherine Sender, assistant professor, the Annenberg School for Communication, University of Pennsylvania; Jake Stafford, strategist, Witeck-Combs Communications.

May 1, 2003: "International Gay Media." Equality Forum Panel (Philadelphia). Olaf Alp, publisher, *Sergej* and *Mate* (Germany); Chris Crain, chief operating officer, Windows Media; Joe Landry, publisher, Liberation Publications, Inc.; Katherine Sender, assistant professor, the Annenberg School for Communication, University of Pennsylvania.

NOTES

1. THE BUSINESS AND POLITICS OF GAY MARKETING

1. Martha T. Moore, "Courting the Gay Market," *USA Today*, April 23, 1993, 1B.
2. Adam Pertman, "Ads Target Big Dollars, Not Big Change," *Boston Globe*, February 4, 2001.
3. Riccardo A. Davis, "Marketers Game for Gay Events," *Advertising Age*, May 30, 1994, S1.
4. Antonio Gramsci, Quintin Hoare, and Geoffrey Nowell-Smith, *Selections from the Prison Notebooks of Antonio Gramsci*.
5. Don Slater, *Consumer Culture and Modernity*, 52.
6. Robert Kuttner, *Everything for Sale*, 32 (emphasis in original).
7. Lizbeth Cohen, *A Consumers' Republic: The Politics of Mass Consumption in Postwar America*.
8. Ibid., 115.
9. See Robert Weems, *Desegregating the Dollar*, for a history of the cultivation of the African American market.
10. Lisa Peñaloza, "We're Here, We're Queer, and We're Going Shopping!," 14.
11. Ibid., 16.
12. E-mail from gayadvocacy.com, July 24, 2003.
13. Alexandra Chasin, *Selling Out: The Gay and Lesbian Movement Goes to Market*, 92.
14. Olivia Travel Web site: *see* www.olivia.com (retrieved November 17, 1997).
15. George Chauncey, *Gay New York: Gender, Urban Culture, and the Making of the Gay Male World, 1890–1940*, 52
16. Elizabeth Lapovsky Kennedy and Madeline D. Davis, *Boots of Leather, Slippers of Gold: The History of a Lesbian Community*, 9.
17. Dan Baker, interview, September 17, 1998. For details of data collection and a list of interviewees, see appendixes 1 and 2.
18. Dan Baker, "A History in Ads: The Growth of the Gay and Lesbian Market," 20.

19. Grant Lukenbill, *Untold Millions: Positioning Your Business for the Gay and Lesbian Consumer Revolution*, 1.

20. According to GLAAD's press materials from 2000: "The GLAAD Media Awards presented by ABSOLUT VODKA honor individuals and projects in the media and entertainment industries for their balanced and accurate representations of lesbian, gay, bisexual, and transgender people and the issues that affect their lives."

21. Michael Bronski, *Culture Clash: The Making of Gay Sensibility*, 178.

22. Alexandra Chasin, "Selling Out: The Gay/Lesbian Market and the Construction of Gender," *Sojourner* (June 1997); Fred Fejes and Ron Lennon, "Defining the Lesbian/Gay Community? Market Research and the Lesbian/Gay Press," *Journal of Homosexuality* 39.1 (2000); Amy Gluckman and Betsy Reed, "The Gay Marketing Moment: Leaving Diversity in the Dust," *Dollars and Sense* (November/December 1993); Amy Gluckman and Betsy Reed, eds., *Homo Economics: Capitalism, Community, and Lesbian and Gay Life*; Peñaloza, "We're Here, We're Queer, and We're Going Shopping!"; Sarah Schulman, "The Making of a Market Niche," *Harvard Lesbian and Gay Review* (Winter 1998); Sarah Schulman, *Stagestruck: Theater, AIDS, and the Marketing of Gay America*.

23. Ruth Zeilberger, "Where the Boys Are, Where the Girls Are: Travel Industry Vying for GLBT Market," *DiversityInc.*, March 5, 2003.

24. M. V. Lee Badgett, "Beyond Biased Samples: Challenging the Myths on the Economic Status of Lesbians and Gay Men"; M.V. Lee Badgett, "Income Inflation: The Myth of Affluence Among Gay, Lesbian, and Bisexual Americans"; M.V. Lee Badgett, "The Myth of Gay and Lesbian Affluence," *The Gay and Lesbian Review* (Spring 2000).

25. Gluckman and Reed, "The Gay Marketing Moment." 17.

26. Quoted in Fejes and Lennon, "Defining the Lesbian/Gay Community?" 28.

27. Schulman, "The Making of a Market Niche" and *Stagestruck*. See also Gabriel Rotello, *Sexual Ecology: Aids and the Destiny of Gay Men*; Andrew Sullivan, *Virtually Normal: An Argument About Homosexuality*; Michael Warner, *Fear of a Queer Planet: Queer Politics and Social Theory* and *The Trouble with Normal: Sex, Politics, and the Ethics of Queer Life*.

28. Schulman, "The Making of a Market Niche," 18.

29. Fred Fejes and Kevin Petrich, "Invisibility, Homophobia, and Heterosexism: Lesbians, Gays, and the Media," 11. See also Katherine Sender, "Gay Readers, Consumers, and a Dominant Gay Habitus: Twenty-Five Years of the 'Advocate' Magazine."

30. Chasin, *Selling Out*, 9.

31. Ibid., 244. When she wrote this, Chasin was cochair of the International Gay and Lesbian Human Rights Committee, which was sponsored by American Airlines, among other companies.

32. Daniel Harris, "The Making of a Subculture," 25.

33. Daniel Mendelsohn, "We're Here! We're Queer! Let's Get Coffee!" 30.

34. Ibid., 31.

35. Suzanna Danuta Walters, *All the Rage: The Story of Gay Visibility in America*, 10.

36. Eric Clarke, "Queer Publicity and the Limits of Inclusion," 84.

37. Don Slater, "On the Wings of the Sign: Commodity Culture and Social Practice," 477.

38. Such as J. R. Dominick and G. E. Rausch, "The Image of Women in Network TV Commercials"; Erving Goffman, *Gender Advertisements*; L. T. Lovdal, "Sex Role Messages in Television Commercials: An Update"; A. S. R. Manstead and C. Mc-Culloch, "Sex-Role Stereotyping in British Television Advertisements"; L. Z. McArthur and B. G. Resko, "The Portrayal of Women and Men in American Television Commercials."

39. Judith Butler, "Imitation and Gender Subordination"; Danae Clark, "Commodity Lesbianism"; Victoria de Grazia and Ellen Furlough, *The Sex of Things: Gender and Consumption in Historical Perspective*; Teresa de Lauretis, "Sexual Difference and Lesbian Representation"; Michel Foucault, *The History of Sexuality*, vol. 1: *An Introduction*; bell hooks, *Black Looks: Race and Representation*; Kobena Mercer and Isaac Julien, "Race, Sexual Politics, and Black Masculinity: A Dossier"; Eve Kosofsky Sedgwick, *Epistemology of the Closet*; Warner, *Fear of a Queer Planet*.

40. Foucault, *The History of Sexuality*, vol. 1.

41. Sedgwick, *Epistemology of the Closet*.

42. Ibid., 85.

43. Gayle S. Rubin, "Thinking Sex: Notes for a Radical Theory of the Politics of Sexuality," 13.

44. Ibid., 15.

45. See, for example, Richard Dyer, "White"; hooks, *Black Looks*; Mercer and Julien, "Race, Sexual Politics, and Black Masculinity"; Siobhan B. Somerville, *Queering the Color Line: Race and the Invention of Homosexuality in American Culture*; Warner, *Fear of a Queer Planet*.

46. Stuart Hall, "Introduction: Who Needs Identity?," 5–6.

47. Pierre Bourdieu, *Distinction: A Social Critique of the Judgement of Taste*.

48. Sarah Thornton, *Club Cultures: Music, Media, and Subcultural Capital*, 10.

49. Richard Ohmann, *Selling Culture: Magazines, Markets, and Class at the Turn of the Century*, 245 (emphasis added). Barbara and John Ehrenreich define the professional-managerial class as "salaried mental workers who do not own the means of production and whose major function in the social division of labor may be described broadly as the reproduction of capitalist culture and capitalist class relations." These authors argue that the role of the professional-managerial class is to oil the administrative and ideological cogs between the owning class and the laboring classes. See Barbara Ehrenreich and John Ehrenreich, "The Professional-Managerial Class," 12.

50. Warren St. John, "Metrosexuals Come Out," *New York Times*, June 22, 2003, 1.

51. Thomas Frank, *The Conquest of Cool: Business Culture, Counterculture, and the Rise of Hip Consumerism*; Roland Marchand, *Advertising the American Dream: Making Way for Modernity, 1920–1940*.

52. Michael J. Arlen, *Thirty Seconds*; William Leiss, Stephen Kline, and Sut Jhally, *Social Communication in Advertising: Persons, Products, and Images of Well-Being*; Randall Rothenberg, *Where the Suckers Moon: An Advertising Story*; Karen Shapiro, "The Construction of Television Commercials: Four Cases of Interorganizational Problem Solving"; Don Slater, "Advertising as Commercial Practice: Business Strategy

and Social Theory"; Don Slater, "Corridors of Power"; Matthew Soar, "'The Children of Marx and Coca Cola': Advertising and Commercial Creativity."

53. Slater, "Corridors of Power," 127.

54. Shapiro, "The Construction of Television Commercials."

55. Janice Radway, "Ethnography Among Elites: Comparing Discourses of Power"; Janice Radway, *A Feeling for Books: The Book-of-the-Month Club, Literary Taste, and Middle-Class Desire.*

56. Ibid., 42–43.

57. See, for example, Catherine Lutz and Jane Lou Collins, *Reading National Geographic*; Ohmann, *Selling Culture*; Radway, *A Feeling for Books.*

58. Sender, "Gay Readers, Consumers, and a Dominant Gay Habitus."

59. Joshua Gamson, *Freaks Talk Back: Tabloid Talk Shows and Sexual Nonconformity.*

60. Judith Butler, "Merely Cultural," *Social Text*, 276.

61. Larry Gross, *Up from Invisibility: Lesbians, Gay Men, and the Media in America*, 233.

62. The follow-up interviews were conducted with marketers who openly self-identified as gay, lesbian, or bisexual, and who worked in an ongoing capacity within gay marketing, as gay-focused ad agency executives, gay marketing consultants, publishers, and public relations experts (rather than, for example, on a single campaign).

63. The *Advocate* (since 1967), *Alternative Family* (August–September 1998 only), *Anything That Moves* (Fall 1998 only), *Bad Attitude* (since 1997), *Black Sheets* (issue no. 16, 2000), *Blueboy* (December 1999 only), *Clikque* (March 2000), *Deneuve*, later *Curve* (some since 1991; every issue since September 1998), *Girlfriends* (since September 1998), *Drummer* (issue no. 211, 1998), *Hustler* (December 1999 only), *Lesbian News* (May 1998 only), *Men* (April 2001 only), *Metrosource* (Summer 1998 only), *On Our Backs* (since its relaunch in June 1998), *Out* (some issues since 1992; every issue since February 1997), *Penthouse* (November 1999 only), *Philadelphia Gay News* (June 16–22, 2000 only), *Playboy* (December 1999 only), *Playgirl* (November 1999 only), *POZ* (September and October 1998 only), and *Q San Francisco* (November 1998 only).

64. The *Advocate*: October 16, October 29, and November 26, 2003; *Curve*: November and December 2002, February 2003; *Girlfriends*: October, November, and December 2002; *Out*: October, November, and December 2002.

65. Gay.com; the gay financial site, gfn.com; and PlanetOut.

66. These included *Advertising Age*, *Adweek*, the *Boston Globe*, the *Los Angeles Times*, the *New York Times*, *Newsweek*, the *San Francisco Chronicle*, the *Wall Street Journal*, and the *Washington Post*, among others.

67. "Dimensions of taste" is Henry Scott's term (interview, February 2, 1999).

2. Evolution, Not Revolution

1. Lorraine Baltera, "No Gay Market Yet, Admen, Gays Agree," *Advertising Age*, August 28, 1972, 3.

2. Ibid., 3.

3. Viacom has since postponed the debut of the gay cable channel, largely because of the financial climate in the early 2000s, according to an inside source. At the time

of writing, the media conglomerate had announced a tentative launch date of spring 2005.

4. Ohmann, *Selling Culture*, 91.

5. Richard S. Tedlow, *New and Improved: The Story of Mass Marketing in America*; Joseph Turow, *Breaking Up America: Advertisers and the New Media World*.

6. John D'Emilio, "Capitalism and Gay Identity."

7. Chauncey, *Gay New York*; Kennedy and Davis, *Boots of Leather*.

8. For an excellent summary of gay consumption before 1970, see Blaine J. Branchik, "Out in the Market: A History of the Gay Market Segment in the United States."

9. Jeffrey Escoffier, "The Political Economy of the Closet."

10. Karla Jay, *Tales of the Lavender Menace: A Memoir of Liberation*.

11. *ONE vs. Oleson*, 355 U.S. 371 (January 13, 1958).

12. Thomas Waugh, *Hard to Imagine: Gay Male Eroticism in Photography and Film from Their Beginnings to Stonewall*.

13. Rodger Streitmatter, *Unspeakable: The Rise of the Gay and Lesbian Press in America*, 87.

14. Dick Michaels, "Happy Birthday to Us," 6.

15. Joe Landry, Boston Ad Club presentation, January 20, 1999. These figures include both display and classified ads.

16. Streitmatter, *Unspeakable*, 88.

17. See the June 1969 issue, p. 23.

18. Edward M. Alwood, *Straight News: Gays, Lesbians, and the News Media*; Lukenbill, *Untold Millions*.

19. For a history of the *Advocate*'s courting of national advertisers, see Sender, "Gay Readers, Consumers, and a Dominant Gay Habitus."

20. "Gay window ads" is Michael Bronski's phrase (see Bronski, *Culture Clash*), and "gay vague" is Michael Wilke's in various *Advertising Age* articles; see also Clark, "Commodity Lesbianism," and Katherine Sender, "Selling Sexual Subjectivities: Audiences Respond to Gay Window Advertising." A recent example of gay window advertising is the Volkswagen "da-da-da" ad that showed two young men driving aimlessly around a neighborhood: gay people tend to read these characters as a gay male couple, while heterosexual viewers are more likely to see them as roommates.

21. For this and many other examples I am indebted to Michael Wilke and his excellent archive of gay, lesbian, bisexual, and transgendered ads: www.commercialcloset.org.

22. John D'Emilio and Estelle Freedman, *Intimate Matters: A History of Sexuality in America*, 305.

23. David Allyn, *Make Love, Not War: The Sexual Revolution—An Unfettered History*.

24. Although the Stonewall riots tend to be seen as the beginning of the contemporary gay rights movement, this event occurred in the context of an already fertile pre-Stonewall gay publishing and activist community. The *Advocate*, for example, had been in production since 1967: see John D'Emilio, *Sexual Politics, Sexual Communities: The Making of a Homosexual Minority in the United States, 1940–1970*; and Streitmatter, *Unspeakable*.

25. Thomas Frank, *The Conquest of Cool*.

26. Alwood, *Straight News*.

27. Baltera, "No Gay Market Yet," 3.

28. Rich Wandel, president of the Gay Activist Alliance, quoted in Baltera, "No Gay Market Yet," 199.

29. The immature queer still haunted the gay market more than a decade later, when *Newsweek* quoted a gay computer business owner who declared, "We're sending a strong message to society that we aren't just silly queens—we're solid, responsible citizens." Quoted in Kim Foltz et al., "The Profit in Being Gay," *Newsweek*, November 12, 1984.

30. Alwood, *Straight News*.

31. Stuart Elliott, interview, November 18, 1998.

32. Streitmatter, *Unspeakable*, 183, 185.

33. David Goodstein, "Editorial," *Advocate*, January 29, 1975, 3.

34. Kenon Breazeale, "In Spite of Women: Esquire Magazine and the Construction of the Male Consumer," *Signs* 20.1 (1994): 1.

35. Hefner, quoted in Barbara Ehrenreich, *The Hearts of Men: American Dreams and the Flight from Commitment*, 44.

36. See the November 11, 1979, issue, p. 20.

37. See the February 12, 1975, issue.

38. N. R. Kleinfeld, "Homosexual Periodicals Are Proliferating," *New York Times*, August 1, 1978, D4.

39. Karen Stabiner, "Tapping the Homosexual Market," *New York Times Magazine*, May 2, 1982, 76.

40. Streitmatter, *Unspeakable*, 314.

41. *Business Week*, "Gays: A Major Force in the Marketplace" (September 3, 1979); Stabiner, "Tapping the Homosexual Market."

42. Stabiner, "Tapping the Homosexual Market," 74.

43. Frisch, quoted in ibid., 36.

44. Humphries, quoted in ibid., 85.

45. Stabiner, "Tapping the Homosexual Market," 74.

46. *Business Week*, "Gays: A Major Force in the Marketplace," 118.

47. See, for example, ibid.; Dougherty, "Homosexual Magazines in Bids"; Bradley Johnson, "Bowing to Mainstream, Advocate Sex Ads End," *Advertising Age*, August 24, 1992; Bradley Johnson, "The Gay Quandary," *Advertising Age*, January 18, 1993; Kleinfeld, "Homosexual Periodicals Are Proliferating"; Jennifer Pendleton, "National Marketers Beginning to Recognize Gays," *Advertising Age*, October 6, 1980.

48. Stabiner, "Tapping the Homosexual Market," 82.

49. Ibid.

50. Pendleton, "National Marketers Beginning to Recognize Gays," 84.

51. Elliott interview, November 18, 1998.

52. Jim Merrett, "A Gay Look at Advertising," *Advocate*, December 5, 1988.

53. See Fall 1987 issue.

54. Pertman, "Ads Target Big Dollars, Not Big Change," *Boston Globe*, February 4, 2001.

55. This list is not complete, nor are all of these publications still in print. In addition, Time Warner researched the viability of a new publication, *Tribe*, in 1994 (Keith J. Kelly, "Healthcare Fuels Magazine Growth," *Advertising Age*, May 30, 1994), and *Out* developed and then abandoned a fashion, sports, and fitness magazine for gay men, *PE*, in 1998.

56. Stuart Elliott, "As the Gay and Lesbian Market Grows, a Boom in Catalogs That Are 'Out, Loud and Proud,'" *New York Times*, September 10, 1993; Shannon Oberndorf, "The Gay '90s Fail to Deliver; Overhyped and Underachieving, Gay Catalogers Struggle to Survive," *Catalog Age*, November 1995.

57. David D. Kirkpatrick, "POZ Magazine Sponsors Trade Fair Aimed at Consumers with HIV," *Wall St. Journal*, May 30, 1996; Kim Painter, "Expo for HIV-Positive Carves Out a Niche for Education, Marketing," *USA Today*, September 9, 1997.

58. Michael Wilke, "Burgeoning Gay Web Sites Spark Advertiser Interest," *Advertising Age*, June 22, 1998; Michael Wilke, "Wired Lesbians/Gays Lure Marketers: 'Net Savvy Segment Draws Brand-Name Media, Advertisers," *Advertising Age*, December 11, 1995.

59. Elliott interview, November 18, 1998.

60. Stuart Elliott, "A Market That's Educated, Affluent, and Homosexual," *New York Times*, September 23, 1992, D27.

61. Stuart Elliott, "Advertisers Bypass Gay Market," *USA Today*, July 17, 1990, 1B.

62. See Badgett, "Income Inflation"; Ray Delgado, "Study Suggests Gays a Marketer's Dream; Group Willing to Show Brand Loyalty," *Houston Chronicle*, June 11, 1994; Lukenbill, *Untold Millions*.

63. See an *Advertising Age* special feature on the gay market in January 1993, as well as Jane Applegate, "From Videos to Greeting Cards, Gay Clout Abounds," *Washington Post*, May 3, 1993; Bruce Horovitz, "Alternative Approach: Finding New Ways to Appeal to Gays, Lesbians," *Los Angeles Times*, February 23, 1993; Moore, "Courting the Gay Market."

64. Horovitz, "Alternative Approach," D1.

65. Gary Levin, "Mainstream's Domino Effect," *Advertising Age*, January 18, 1993, 32.

66. Moore, "Courting the Gay Market," 1B.

67. Elliott interview, November 18, 1998.

68. Thomas A. Stewart, "Gay in Corporate America," *Fortune*, December 12, 1991. In May 2000, NYACN joined other professional groups to become Out Professionals.

69. Michael Wilke, "Seven Top Shops Disclose Policies on Gays," *Advertising Age*, October 27, 1997.

70. Lynn Jones, "AT&T Targets Gays and Lesbians, Direct Mail Campaign," *Direct* (August 1994); Nancy Coltun Webster, "Playing to Gay Segments Opens Doors to Marketers," *Advertising Age*, May 30, 1994; Michael Wilke, "Big Advertisers Join Move to Embrace Gay Market," *Advertising Age*, August 4, 1997.

71. Dan Baker, "So, Just How Big Is the Gay Market, Really?" *Quotient*, December 1994 3.

72. Henry Scott, interview, February 2, 1999.

73. Todd Evans, president of Rivendell Marketing, phone interview, September 17, 1999.

74. Michael Wilke, "Ad Survey Shows Appeal of Gay Themes," *Advertising Age*, May 6, 1996, 19.

75. Landry, Boston Ad Club presentation, January 20, 1999.

76. Wilke, "Big Advertisers Join Move to Embrace Gay Market," 10.

77. Caitlin Hume, interview, March 31, 1999.

78. Stuart Elliott, "Imaginative Supplements Help a Pair of Magazines Build Relationships with Marketers," *New York Times*, June 26, 1998, D4.

79. Johnson, "Bowing to Mainstream, Advocate Sex Ads End."

80. Streitmatter, *Unspeakable*, 309.

81. Christy Fisher, "Local Print Bumps into National Ad Walls," *Advertising Age*, May 30, 1994.

82. John Schwartz, "Online Gays Become a Market for Advertisers," *Washington Post*, May 22, 1999, E5.

83. Johnson, "The Gay Quandary," 29; Applegate, "From Videos to Greeting Cards," F10; Hazel Kahan and David Mulryan, "Out of the Closet," *American Demographics* (May 1995): 40, respectively.

84. Johnson, "The Gay Quandary," 29.

85. Michael Wilke, "Fewer Gays Are Wealthy, Data Says," *Advertising Age*, October 19, 1998.

86. Henry Scott, "Targeting Affluent Gays: Letter to the Editor," *Advertising Age*, November 2, 1998. In 1998, *Out*'s readers' reported an average household income of $77,000, compared with $57,000 for Greenfield Online's gay respondents.

87. Quoted in Horovitz, "Alternative Approach," B7.

88. Bradley Johnson, "Economics Holds Back the Lesbian Ad Market," *Advertising Age*, January 18, 1993.

89. Ibid., 34.

90. Michael Wilke, "Gay Print Media Ad Revenue Up 36%," *Advertising Age*, October 6, 1997, 26.

91. By including a discussion of HIV-positive people and people with AIDS in advertising I do not want to suggest that all people who appear in these ads are supposed to be read as gay. Yet because AIDS disproportionately affects the gay male community, and many HIV pharmaceutical ads appear in gay media, there is at least an implication that some of the people shown are intended to be read as gay.

92. Sean Strub, interview, October 28, 1998.

93. See, for example, Richard Goldstein, "Climb Every Mountain: The Art of Selling HIV Drugs," *POZ* (October 1998).

94. Jim Kirk, "Orbitz Effort Hopes to Land Gay Travelers," *Chicago Tribune*, June 19, 2002.

95. Joe Landry, phone interview, October 18, 2001.

96. Cliff Rothman, "A Welcome Mat for Gay Customers," *New York Times*, August 17, 2001, F1.

97. Theresa Howard, "John Hancock Ads Reflect Real Life; Firm Reaches Out to Diverse USA," *USA Today*, December 11, 2000, B6.

98. Elliott, phone interview, August 23, 2001.

99. OpusComm e-mail: July 9, 2002.

100. Amy Falkner, GL Census Partners, at the National Lesbian and Gay Journalists Association Annual Conference, "Gay Demographics—The Rocky Road to Research" (Philadelphia), September 14, 2002.

101. For example, Harris Interactive used online polling and propensity sampling techniques to correctly predict the popular vote in 36 of 38 states in the 2000 presidential election, as well as 27 senatorial and 7 governors' races: Research Business
Report, "Harris Interactive Uses Election 2000 to Prove Its Online MR Efficacy
and Accuracy" (November 2000).

102. PRNewswire, "PlanetOut Partners, Inc. Posts First Full Quarter of Positive Operating Income," October 9, 2002.

103. Peter Frieberg, " 'We Can Do This': Ethnic Gay Magazines Are on the Rise," *Press
Pass Q* (August 2002).

104. Kipp Cheng, "The Men's Club: Why Do Marketers Ignore Lesbian Consumers?"
(Web site: DiversityInc.com, April 12, 2002; retrieved April 15, 2002). Rivendell
Marketing changed its name to Rivendell Media in 2003.

105. For information on gay media mergers see Reed Abelson, "Out Magazine Acquired
by Key Rival," *New York Times*, February 21, 2000; Elinor Abreu, *Gay Portals Come
Out*; Dan Fost, "PlanetOut Expands Its Universe," *San Francisco Chronicle*, September 7, 2000; Carrie Kirby, "Gay Media Call Off Merger," *San Francisco Chronicle*,
March 9, 2001; Alex Kuczynski, "Merger to Link Gay Print and Internet Outlets,"
New York Times, March 23, 2000; Mary McNamara, "Will Mergers Quiet the Voice
of the Gay Press?" *Los Angeles Times*, April 13, 2002.

106. Scott, quoted in McNamara, "Will Mergers Quiet the Voice of Gay Press?" E4.

107. For press coverage of this announcement and subsequent debates about its import,
see: David Bauder, "Race on for 'Gay TV,'" *Associated Press*, April 30, 2002; Michael
Bronski, "Invisible Exposure: Two Media Powerhouses Have Announced Plans for
Gay-and-Lesbian Cable Channels. But Could Gay TV Mean the Death of Queer
Culture?" *Boston Phoenix*, January 31, 2002; Maureen Dowd, " 'Will & Will' 24/7,"
New York Times, January 13, 2002; Michael Giltz, "Will Gay Pay?" *New York Post*, Jan-
uary 13, 2002; David Goetzl, "Leading Edge: Showtime, MTV Gamble on Gay
Net," *Advertising Age*, January 14, 2002; Tim Goodman, "Channel for Gays? It's
About Time," *San Francisco Chronicle*, January 21, 2002; Gail Shister, "New Gay-
Lesbian Channel Is Work of Two Wharton Chums," *Philadelphia Inquirer*, January 15,
2002; Lewis Whittington, "Opening TV's Closet to Different Audience," *Philadel-
phia Inquirer*, January 16, 2002.

108. Landry, phone interview, January 5, 1999.

109. Elliott, phone interview, August 23, 2001.

110. Tedlow, *New and Improved*; Turow, *Breaking Up America*.

111. Dwight E. Brooks, "Consumer Markets and Consumer Magazines: Black America
and the Culture of Consumption, 1920–1960"; Kathy Peiss, *Hope in a Jar: The Making of America's Beauty Culture*; Weems, *Desegregating the Dollar*.

112. Sullivan, cited in Weems, *Desegregating the Dollar*, 32.

113. Marilyn Kern-Foxworth, *Aunt Jemima, Uncle Ben, and Rastus: Blacks in Advertising
Yesterday, Today, and Tomorrow*, 38.

114. John W. Ellis IV, "It's Not Enough to Throw Open the Shop's Doors," *Advertising Age*, February 16, 1998, 510. See also the rather anxious special feature on "diversity" in *Advertising Age* (ibid.), in which numerous journalists celebrate efforts by corporations to appeal to people of color, and bemoan agencies' difficulties in creating and retaining a racially diverse talent pool.

115. Turow, *Breaking Up America*, 82.

116. *Business Week*, "Gays: A Major Force in the Marketplace," 118.

117. Elliott interview, November 18, 1998.

118. Howard Buford, interview, February 13, 1998.

119. In Katherine Sender, *Off the Straight and Narrow: Lesbians, Gays, Bisexuals, and Television* (video, 63 min).

120. The stereotype of the obliging domestic continues to be embodied in the mascots Aunt Jemima and Uncle Ben, however. See Kern-Foxworth, *Aunt Jemima, Uncle Ben, and Rastus*; Weems, *Desegregating the Dollar*.

3. Professional Homosexuals

1. M. V. Lee Badgett, *Money, Myths, and Change: The Economic Lives of Lesbians and Gay Men*, 103.

2. Slater, *Consumer Culture and Modernity*, 188.

3. For a fascinating comparison of the diffusion of household appliances in Britain and the United States, see Sue Bowden and Avner Offer, "The Technological Revolution That Never Was: Gender, Class, and the Diffusion of Household Appliances in Interwar England," in de Grazia and Furlough, eds., *The Sex of Things*.

4. Leiss, Kline, and Jhally, *Social Communication in Advertising*; Marchand, *Advertising the American Dream*; Michael Schudson, *Advertising, the Uneasy Persuasion: Its Dubious Impact on American Society*.

5. Marchand, *Advertising the American Dream*, 8.

6. Frank, *The Conquest of Cool*, 35.

7. Ibid., 92.

8. Scott M. Cutlip, *The Unseen Power: Public Relations, a History*, 12; Stuart Ewen, *PR! A Social History of Spin*.

9. Cutlip, *The Unseen Power*, 764.

10. Ewen, *PR!*, 401.

11. Ohmann, *Selling Culture*, 25.

12. Ibid.

13. Ibid., 90.

14. Marchand, *Advertising the American Dream*, 29.

15. Ehrenreich and Ehrenreich, "The Professional-Managerial Class."

16. Bourdieu, *Distinction*, 153–54.

17. National Gay and Lesbian Task Force, "2001 Capital Gains and Losses," 18.

18. Badgett, *Money, Myths, and Change*, 37.

19. Annette Friskopp and Sharon Silverstein, *Straight Jobs, Gay Lives: Gay and Lesbian Professionals, the Harvard Business School, and the American Workplace*.

20. James D. Woods, *The Corporate Closet: The Professional Lives of Gay Men in America.*

21. Ibid., 172.

22. Ibid., 188.

23. Patrick Califia, phone interview, May 10, 2001.

24. Sean Strub, e-mail, August 19, 2001.

25. Matt Farber, e-mail, September 30, 2002.

26. Stuart Elliott, phone interview, August 23, 2001. Elliott refers here to *The Best Little Boy in the World* by Andrew Tobias (writing as John Reid) (New York: Putnam, 1973).

27. Joe Landry, phone interview, October 18, 2001.

28. Stephanie Blackwood, phone interview, August 18, 2001.

29. Friskopp and Silverstein, *Straight Jobs, Gay Lives*, 108–109.

30. Sean Strub, interview, November 18, 2001.

31. Don Tuthill, phone interview, October 21, 1998.

32. Landry, phone interview, October 18, 2001.

33. Michael Shively, phone interview, August 21, 2001.

34. Califia interview.

35. Strub interview, November 18, 2001.

36. Friskopp and Silverstein, *Straight Jobs, Gay Lives*, 309.

37. Ibid.

38. NYACN has since become Out Professionals, where the proportion of women has remained about the same. Of course, association membership does not necessarily reflect the actual proportion of lesbian-identified marketers across the board. Further, since my interview sampling largely employed the snowballing technique, my contacts may not have been aware of other lesbian marketers. Yet the limited presence of lesbians in associations and social-professional networks reflects gendered practices that structure professional and marketing cultures more generally.

39. Ivy Kazenoff and Anthony Vagnoni, "Babes in Boyland," *Creativity* (October 1997): 18–20. Subsequent page numbers are cited in the text.

40. Friskopp and Silverstein, quoting a closeted lesbian, in *Straight Jobs, Gay Lives*, 367.

41. Schulman, *Stagestruck*, 116.

42. Stephanie Blackwood, phone interview, May 1, 1999.

43. Friskopp and Silverstein, *Straight Jobs, Gay Lives*, 362.

44. Ibid.

45. Joe Landry, Boston Ad Club presentation, January 20, 1999.

46. Bob Witeck, phone interview, November 22, 1998.

47. Schulman, *Stagestruck*, 105–106.

48. Dan Baker, interview, September 17, 1998.

49. Ibid.

50. Kurt DeMars, interview, April 1, 1999.

51. Michael Wilke, interview, January 19, 1998.

52. Witeck, phone interview, November 22, 1998.

53. Thornton, *Club Cultures*, 11.

54. Caitlin Hume, interview, February 2, 1999.

55. Howard Buford, interview, February 13, 1998.

56. Marchand, *Advertising the American Dream*, 36.

57. Witeck, phone interview, November 22, 1998.

58. Stephanie Blackwood, "*Times* Talks—Advertising to Gay America" (New York City), April 8, 1999.

59. See *Newsbreaks* (May–June 1999).

60. Patrick Sullivan, phone interview, February 17, 1999.

61. Hume interview, February 2, 1999.

62. Alwood, *Straight News*, 301.

63. See Woods, *The Corporate Closet*, 196, for an overview of Levi Strauss's employee group genesis.

64. Ginny Schofield (pseudonym), phone interview, February 22, 1999.

65. Stephanie Blackwood, interview, January 19, 1998.

66. Schofield interview.

67. Thomas Frank, *The Conquest of Cool*; Woods, *The Corporate Closet*; Friskopp and Silverstein, *Straight Jobs, Gay Lives*, 350.

68. Betsy Sharkey, "The Way Out," *Adweek*, July 19, 1993, 24.

69. Ibid., 19.

70. Wilke interview, January 19, 1998.

71. Blackwood interview, January 19, 1998.

72. Wilke, "Seven Top Shops Disclose Policies on Gays," 22.

73. Howard Buford, interview, November 14, 2001.

74. Stewart, "Gay in Corporate America."

75. Ibid., 46.

76. Ibid.

77. Jack Schlegal, phone interview, January 11, 1999; see also Out Professionals' Web site (www.outprofessionals.org), retrieved February 25, 2003.

78. Articles appear, respectively, in *Newsbreaks* (February 2003): 1; *Newsbreaks* (January 2003): 1; and on NYACN's Web page, September 22, 1999.

79. Melissa Wolf, director-founder, Women's Studio Center, Inc.: Out Professionals' Web site (see note 77), retrieved February 25, 2003.

80. Pierre Bourdieu, *Language and Symbolic Power*.

81. Blackwood interview, August 18, 2001.

82. David Mulryan, phone interview, January 24, 1999.

83. *See* www.outprofessionals.org/history/html (retrieved February 2, 2003).

84. Sean Strub, e-mail, February 20, 2003.

85. Walter Schubert, phone interview, August 24, 2001.

86. Matt Farber, phone interview, September 27, 2002.

87. Patrick O'Neil, interview, November 18, 1998.

88. DeMars interview.

89. Hume interview, February 2, 1999.

90. DeMars interview.

91. Buford interview, February 13, 1998.

92. Stuart Elliott, interview, November 18, 1998.

93. Andrew Beaver, interview, February 23, 1998.

94. Blackwood interview, January 19, 1998.

95. Beaver interview.

96. Buford interview, February 13, 1998.

97. Liz Gumbiner, interview, September 7, 1998.

98. Strub interview, November 18, 2001.

99. Sean Strub, e-mail, November 12, 2002.

100. Strub interview, February 18, 2001.

101. Ibid.

102. Lisa Henderson, " 'Storyline' and the Multicultural Middlebrow: Reading Women's Culture on National Public Radio," *Critical Studies in Mass Communication* 16 (1999): 335.

103. Ibid., 336.

104. Stewart, "Gay in Corporate America," 46; Baltera, "No Gay Market Yet, Admen, Gays Agree"; and Mulryan interview, respectively.

4. How Gay Is Too Gay?

1. Leiss, Kline, and Jhally, *Social Communication in Advertising*.

2. Richard Dyer, "Seen to Be Believed: Some Problems in the Representation of Gay People as Typical," *Studies in Visual Communication* 9.2 (1983): 2.

3. Arlen, *Thirty Seconds*; Rothenberg, *Where the Suckers Moon*; Schudson, *Advertising, the Uneasy Persuasion*; Slater, "Advertising as Commercial Practice."

4. Gayle Tuchman, *Making News: A Study in the Construction of Reality*.

5. Walters, *All the Rage*, 28 (emphasis in original).

6. Clark, "Commodity Lesbianism," 195.

7. Ohmann, *Selling Culture*, 91.

8. Keith Ferrazzi, PrideFest 2002 panel: "Marketing to the Gay and Lesbian Consumer" (Philadelphia), May 4, 2002.

9. Roland Barthes and Stephen Heath, *Image, Music, Text*, 32–51.

10. Slater, *Consumer Culture and Modernity*, 31.

11. Henry Scott, interview, February 2, 1999.

12. Steve Rothaus, "Big Business Looks to the Rainbow," *Miami Herald*, August 26, 2002.

13. Joe Yonan, "Out on the High Seas," *Boston Globe*, September 22, 2002, M1.

14. Stuart Elliott, "The Showtime Network Prepares a $10 Million Campaign Blitz for Its 'Queer as Folk' Series," *New York Times*, November 28, 2000.

15. This magazine insert appeared in the *Advocate* and *Out* in the spring of 2003.

16. Christy Fisher, "Local Print Bumps into National Ad Walls," *Advertising Age*, May 30, 1994.

17. Grant Lukenbill, interview, February 2, 1998.

18. The Centers for Disease Control found that men who have sex with men make up the largest proportion (60 percent) of men diagnosed with AIDS in 1997, for example. See Centers for Disease Control, "The HIV/AIDS Epidemic in the United States, 1997–1998" (www.cdc.gov: 2000).

19. Sean Strub, interview, October 28, 1998.

20. Bob Witeck, phone interview, November 22, 1998.

21. Scott interview.

22. Rachel Fox, phone interview, February 19, 1999.

23. Fox interview.

24. Liz Gumbiner, interview, September 7, 1998.

25. Catherine Draper, phone interview, January 21, 1999.

26. Stuart Elliott, interview, November 18, 1998.

27. Joe Landry, Boston Ad Club presentation, January 20, 1999; see also Peñaloza, "We're Here, We're Queer, and We're Going Shopping!"

28. Dan Mullen, phone interview, March 18, 1999.

29. Michael Shively, phone interview, August 21, 2001.

30. Andrew Beaver, interview, February 23, 1998.

31. Joe Landry, phone interview, January 5, 1999.

32. Gordon Cramb, "Gay Games Prove Commercial Success," *Financial Times*, August 1, 1998, 2.

33. Scott interview.

34. Walter Schubert, phone interview, August 24, 2001.

35. Bob Adams, "Paying to Look Perfect," *Advocate*, September 3, 2002.

36. Howard Buford, interview, November 14, 2001.

37. Ibid.

38. Judith Williamson, *Decoding Advertisements: Ideology and Meaning in Advertising*.

39. Bronski, *Culture Clash*, 187.

40. Gumbiner interview.

41. Levin, "Mainstream's Domino Effect," 30.

42. Prime Access Inc. and Rivendell Marketing, "2002 Gay Press Report"; Wilke, "Gay Print Media Ad Revenue up 36%."

43. Don Tuthill, phone interview, October 21, 1998.

44. Landry interview, January 5, 1999.

45. John Finco, interview, April 14, 1999.

46. Scott interview.

47. Ibid.

48. Howard Buford, "*Times* Talks—Advertising to Gay America" (New York City), April 8, 1999.

49. Scott interview.

50. See, for example, Jennifer Gilbert, "Ad Spending Booming for Gay-Oriented Sites," *Advertising Age*, December 6, 1999; Kirk, "Orbitz Effort Hopes to Land Gay Travelers"; James C. Luh, "Truly Out for a Change," *Internet World*, March 1, 2000; Leslie J. Nicholson, "A Friendlier Financial World for Gays and Lesbians," *Philadelphia Inquirer*, March 24, 2000; PRNewswire, "PlanetOut Partners, Inc. Posts First Full Quarter of Positive Operating Income," October 9, 2002; Schwartz, "Online Gays Become a Market for Advertisers"; Bob Tedeschi, "More Companies Are Working to Attract Gay and Lesbian Customers," *New York Times*, August 26, 2002; Wilke, "Wired Lesbians/Gays Lure Marketers."

51. PRNewswire, "PlanetOut Partners."

52. *Advocate*, "Surfing an Online Tidal Wave," June 6, 2000.

53. PRNewswire, "PlanetOut Partners."

54. Stuart Elliott, "*Times* Talks—The Boys in the Bandwidth: The Growth of the Gay and Lesbian Online Marketplace" (New York City), February 29, 2000.

55. Jim Dean, "*Times* Talks—The Boys in the Bandwidth" (New York City), February 29, 2000.

56. Schwartz, "Online Gays Become a Market for Advertisers," E1.

57. Elliott interview, November 18, 1998.

58. Gilbert, "Ad Spending Booming for Gay-Oriented Sites," 58.

59. The Internet is not only a venue for appealing to gay consumers but for circulating information about them, too, in the form of Web-based press kits. See the following chapter.

60. John Campbell, "Consuming Pink Triangles: Privacy, Surveillance, Identity, and 'Gay Marketing'" (paper presented at the International Communication Association, San Diego, 2003).

61. Saul Hansell, "So Far, Big Brother Isn't Big Business," *New York Times*, May 7, 2000, C1.

62. Press release from the Gay and Lesbian Alliance Against Defamation (GLAAD-LINES), May 22, 2000.

63. Todd Evans, phone interview, September 17, 1999.

64. Wilke, "Gay Print Media Ad Revenue Up."

65. Evans interview.

66. Todd Evans, e-mail, April 2, 2003.

67. Fisher, "Local Print Bumps into National Ad Walls."

68. Evans interview.

69. Richard Roeper, "Falwell Brews Up a Tempest in Beer Stein Over 'Gay Ad,'" *Chicago Sun-Times*, May 5, 1999; Hanna Rosin, "Falwell Lights into Budweiser," *Washington Post*, May 12, 1999.

70. Roeper, "Falwell Brews Up a Tempest"; Rosin, "Falwell Lights into Budweiser."

71. However, rallying responses by GLAAD and other groups, as well as press attention to the Bud Light ad, may have increased gay consumers' awareness of the Anheuser-Busch's campaign, ironically making it more effective as a result of right-wing protestations.

72. Finco interview.

73. Rose Farley, "Straighten Up and Fly Right," *Dallas Observer*, April 16, 1998.

74. Stuart Elliott, "Absolut Customizes a Campaign to Salute the Gay and Lesbian Alliance Against Defamation," *New York Times*, February 22, 2001, C6.

75. Finco interview.

76. Strub interview, October 28, 1998.

77. Ibid.

78. Buford interview, February 13, 1998.

79. Strub interview, October 28, 1998.

80. Buford interview, February 13, 1998.

81. Sean Strub, e-mail, November 12, 2002.

82. Patrick O'Neil, interview, November 18, 1998.

83. Elliott interview, November 18, 1998.

84. Buford, "*Times* Talks—Advertising to Gay America" (New York City), April 8, 1999.

85. Stephanie Gibbons, "Marketing to the GLBT Consumer," PrideFest 2002 Panel (Philadelphia), May 4, 2002.

86. Gene Falk, phone interview, September 27, 2002.

87. Schubert interview.

88. Quoted by Jeffrey Newman, "*Times* Talks—The Boys in the Bandwidth" (New York City), February 29, 2000.

89. Schubert interview.

90. David Mulryan, phone interview, January 24, 1999.

91. "King of the Gay Airwaves," *Victory!* (June 1994).

92. Matthew Fraser, "Bad Deals, Bungling Hurt Pridevision," *Ontario (Can.) National Post*, December 25, 2002.

93. Yahoo! TV, "Canadian Gay TV Channel Pinkslips Staff," December 23, 2002.

94. Bill Carter, "MTV and Showtime Plan Cable Channel for Gay Viewers," *New York Times*, January 10, 2002. The undated memo appeared on the Web site Internalmemos.com (retrieved November 18, 2002).

95. Beaver interview.

96. Elliott interview, November 18, 1998.

97. Gumbiner interview.

98. Ibid.

99. O'Neil interview.

100. Scott interview; Tuthill interview, October 21, 1998.

101. Steve DiBruno (pseudonym), phone interview, October 7, 1998.

102. Buford interview, February 13, 1998.

103. Stuart Hall, "Encoding/Decoding," in S. Hall et al., eds., *Culture, Media, Language*.

104. Rothenberg, *Where the Suckers Moon*, 112; Karen Shapiro, "The Construction of Television Commercials."

105. Shapiro, "The Construction of Television Commercials," 263.

106. Ibid., 316.

107. Dyer, "Seen to Be Believed," 3.

108. Mulryan interview.

109. Richard Dyer, "Stereotyping," in R. Dyer, ed., *Gays and Film*.

110. Kurt DeMars, interview, April 1, 1999.

111. Buford interview, February 13, 1998.

112. O'Neil interview.

113. Ibid.

114. Stephanie Blackwood, interview, January 19, 1998; Michael Wilke, interview, January 19, 1998; Blackwood interview, January 19, 1998; and Elliott interview, November 18, 1998, respectively.

115. O'Neil interview.

116. Blackwood interview, January 19, 1998.

117. Wilke interview.

118. Heather Findlay, "Gay 101," *Out* (July–August 1994): 84.

119. Ibid., 85.

120. DiBruno interview.

121. Patrick Sullivan, phone interview, February 17, 1999.

122. Elliott interview, November 18, 1998.

123. Ibid.

124. Beaver interview.

125. Alexander Doty, *Making Things Perfectly Queer: Interpreting Mass Culture*, xi.

126. DeMars interview.

127. Memo from Mark Malinowski, July 17, 1998.

128. Caitlin Hume, interview, February 2, 1999.

129. Stuart Elliott, "Levi Strauss Begins a Far-Reaching Marketing Campaign to Reach Gay Men and Lesbians," *New York Times*, October 19, 1998.

130. George Raine, "Dockers Coming Out," *San Francisco Examiner*, October 21, 1998; and Mark Malinowski, "*Times* Talks—Advertising to Gay America" (New York City), April 8, 1999.

131. Stuart Elliott, "*Times* Talks—Advertising to Gay America" (New York City), April 8, 1999.

132. Malinowski, "*Times* Talks—Advertising to Gay America" (New York City), April 8, 1999.

133. Louis Fabrizio, e-mail, January 10, 2000.

134. Malinowski, "*Times* Talks—Advertising to Gay America" (New York City), April 8, 1999; and Malinowski, quoted in Elliott, "Levi Strauss Begins a Far-Reaching Marketing Campaign," C11.

135. Malinowski, in Elliott, "Levi Strauss Begins a Far-Reaching Marketing Campaign," C11.

136. Elliott, "Imaginative Supplements Help a Pair of Magazines Build Relationships with Marketers."

137. Malinowski, "*Times* Talks—Advertising to Gay America" (New York City), April 8, 1999.

138. Spare Parts and Greenfield Online, press release, October 14, 1998.

139. Elliott, "Levi Strauss Begins a Far-Reaching Marketing Campaign," C11.

140. Malinowski, "*Times* Talks—Advertising to Gay America" (New York City), April 8, 1999.

141. Elliott, "*Times* Talks—Advertising to Gay America" (New York City), April 8, 1999.

142. Fabrizio e-mail.

143. Hume interview, February 2, 1999.

144. Fabrizio e-mail.

145. Hume interview, February 2, 1999.

146. Ibid.

147. Ibid.

148. Ibid.

149. Dale, quoted in Elliott, "Levi Strauss Begins a Far-Reaching Marketing Campaign," C11.

150. Hayes, quoted in ibid.

151. Hume interview, February 2, 1999.

152. Elliott, "Levi Strauss Begins a Far-Reaching Marketing Campaign," C11.

153. DeMars interview.

154. Fabrizio e-mail.

155. Hume interview, February 2, 1999.

156. Malinowski, "*Times* Talks—Advertising to Gay America" (New York City), April 8, 1999.

157. Raine, "Dockers Coming Out," D4.

158. Thanks to Lisa Henderson for this term.

159. Raine, "Dockers Coming Out," D4.

160. Ibid.

5. Selling America's Most Affluent Minority

1. Ien Ang, *Desperately Seeking the Audience*, 32.

2. Joe Landry, Boston Ad Club presentation, January 20, 1999.

3. Tedlow, *New and Improved*.

4. Andrew R. Heinze, *Adapting to Abundance: Jewish Immigrants, Mass Consumption, and the Search for American Identity*; Kern-Foxworth, *Aunt Jemima, Uncle Ben, and Rastus*; Peiss, *Hope in a Jar*; Weems, *Desegregating the Dollar*.

5. Peñaloza, "We're Here, We're Queer, and We're Going Shopping!"; Turow, *Breaking Up America*.

6. Turow, *Breaking Up America*, 40.

7. Ibid., 43–44.

8. Ang, *Desperately Seeking the Audience*, 33. Subsequent page numbers are cited in the text.

9. Sedgwick, *Epistemology of the Closet*, 11.

10. Ibid., 85.

11. Sally Munt, *Heroic Desire: Lesbian Identity and Cultural Space*, 83.

12. Ang, *Desperately Seeking the Audience*, 7.

13. Kurt DeMars, interview, April 1, 1999.

14. Stephanie Blackwood, interview, January 19, 1998.

15. Megan Ishler, phone interview, December 3, 1998.

16. Ohmann, *Selling Culture*, 101.

17. Embinder, quoted in Dougherty, "Homosexual Magazines in Bids," 20.

18. Spare Parts and Greenfield Online, press release, October 14, 1998.

19. DeMars interview.

20. Patrick Sullivan, phone interview, February 17, 1999.

21. Stan Williams, "Securing the Out Post," *DNR*, April 24, 1998, 3.

22. Blackwood interview, January 19, 1998.

23. Bob Witeck, phone interview, November 22, 1998.

24. Sullivan interview.

25. Joe Landry, Boston Ad Club presentation, January 20, 1999.

26. See, for example, Don Boroughs, "Why This Census Sags in the Middle," *U.S. News and World Report*, April 23, 1990; Steve Brewer, "Asian-Americans Count on Cen-

sus: Nationwide, Minorities Are Underreported," *Houston Chronicle*, December 17, 1997; Knight Ridder Newspapers, "Population of U.S. Hispanics Underestimated, Report Says," *Seattle Times*, May 12, 2002; Cindy Rodriguez, "Census Bolsters Theory Illegal Immigrants Undercounted," *Boston Globe*, March 20, 2001; Barbara Vobejda, "Census Spotted Nearly 230,000 Homeless People: Critics, Agency Agree 1990 Count Made in One Night Found Only a Portion of the Total," *Washington Post*, April 13, 1991.

27. Sean Strub, interview, October 28, 1998.

28. Badgett, "Income Inflation," 7.

29. Blackwood, quoted in Ronald Alsop, "Are Gay People More Affluent Than Others?" *Wall Street Journal*, December 30, 1999, B3.

30. Grant Lukenbill, interview, February 2, 1998.

31. Strub interview, October 28, 1998.

32. Merton, quoted in Johnson, "The Gay Quandary," 29.

33. Badgett, *Money, Myths, and Change*, 25.

34. Buford, quoted in Michael Wilke, "Reliable Research Difficult to Gather, Analyze," *Advertising Age*, August 4, 1997, 11.

35. Quoted in ibid.

36. *See* www.glcensus.org/2002Commentary.htm (retrieved September 22, 2003).

37. DeMars interview.

38. See Weems, *Desegregating the Dollar*.

39. Lukenbill, *Untold Millions*, 73.

40. Badgett, "Income Inflation."

41. Ibid., 4.

42. Spare Parts and Greenfield Online, press release, October 14, 1998, 2.

43. Schwartz, "Online Gays Become a Market for Advertisers."

44. Research Business Report, "Harris Interactive Uses Election 2000 to Prove Its Online MR Efficacy and Accuracy."

45. Harris Interactive, "LGBT Voter Education and Research Project" (2000), 12. Figures for the total U.S. population come from the March 1999 *Current Population Statistics* report, quoted in the Harris Interactive 2000 report.

46. Ibid., 10.

47. Ibid., 13.

48. Liz Gumbiner, interview, September 7, 1998.

49. Quoted in Webster, "Playing to Gay Segments Opens Doors to Marketers," S6.

50. Dan Baker, interview, September 17, 1998.

51. Lukenbill interview.

52. Todd Evans, phone interview, September 17, 1999.

53. Wilke, "Fewer Gays Are Wealthy, Data Says," 58.

54. Scott, "Targeting Affluent Gays: Letter to the Editor," 24.

55. DeMars interview.

56. Bourdieu, *Distinction*, 99.

57. Andrew Beaver, interview, February 23, 1998.

58. Harris Interactive, "LGBT Voter Education and Research Project," 15.

59. Howard Buford, phone interview, April 15, 2003.

60. Patrick O'Neil, interview, November 18, 1998.

61. See Lisa Henderson's discussion of the limits of Rose Troche and Guinevere Turner's film *Go Fish* in dealing with complex intersections of sexual and racial difference. Lisa Henderson, "Simple Pleasures: Lesbian Community and 'Go Fish,'" *Signs* 25.1 (1999).

62. The *Advocate*: October 16, October 29, and November 26, 2003; *Curve*: November and December 2002, February 2003; *Girlfriends*: October, November, and December 2002; *Out*: October, November, and December 2002.

63. Howard Buford, interview, February 13, 1998.

64. Buford interview, February 13, 1998.

65. Ibid.

66. Michael Wilke, interview, January 19, 1998.

67. Henry Scott, interview, February 2, 1999.

68. Viatical companies buy life insurance policies from people who are terminally ill: the person gets a lump sum (often much less than the value of the policy) and the company collects the proceeds after the person's death. With the success of recent combination therapies for maintaining the health of many HIV-positive people, many viatical companies have yet to see a profit on their investment.

69. A Centers for Disease Control survey reported that "the 1998 rate of reported AIDS cases among African Americans was 66.4 per 100,000 population, more than 2 times greater than the rate for Hispanics and 8 times greater than the rate for whites." Although it is impossible to accurately determine the rates of HIV infection, researchers estimated that about 1 in 50 African American men and 1 in 160 African American women were HIV-positive. Estimates were not available for Latina/o populations. Centers for Disease Control, "HIV/AIDS Among African Americans" (www.cdc.gov: 2000); Centers for Disease Control, "HIV/AIDS Among Hispanics in the United States" (www.cdc.gov: 2000).

70. Goldstein, "Climb Every Mountain," 66.

71. Simon Watney, "The Spectacle of AIDS," in Abelove, Barale, and Halperin, eds., *The Lesbian and Gay Studies Reader*, 207.

72. Films appearing in the United States that addressed AIDS almost universally represented white men, whose ultimate demise was documented at length: see, for example, *An Early Frost* (1985), *Philadelphia* (1993), and *In the Gloaming* (1997).

73. Goldstein, "Climb Every Mountain," 66.

74. Ibid.

75. Peter Jackson, "Black Male: Advertising and the Cultural Politics of Masculinity," *Gender, Place, and Culture* 1.1 (1994): 55.

76. Mercer and Julien, "Race, Sexual Politics, and Black Masculinity."

77. John Ritter, "Ads Linked to Rise in Rate of HIV Infections. City Considers Ban on Drug Billboards," *USA Today*, April 6, 2001.

78. Jayson Blair, "Healthy Skepticism and the Marketing of AIDS," *New York Times*, August 5, 2001, D14. Although Blair's ignominious departure from the *New York Times* in 2003 might cast suspicion on this quote, other sources confirm the FDA's actions.

79. Howard Buford, whose agency Prime Access produced one of the withdrawn ads, questioned the reliability of the data upon which this policy decision was made (interview, November 14, 2001).

80. Turow, *Breaking Up America*, 55.

81. Ibid., 55—56.

82. Ginny Schofield, phone interview, February 22, 1999.

83. "The 10% Market Share: The Ins and Outs of Queer Marketing," New York Lesbian, Gay, Bisexual, and Transgender Center (New York City), March 20, 2003.

84. Bob Witeck, e-mail, April 22, 2003, 8:55 A.M. Figures are from a 2002 study.

85. Baker interview.

86. Stuart Elliott, interview, November 18, 1998.

87. Joe Landry, phone interview, January 5, 1999.

88. Frances Stevens, phone interview, November 10, 1998.

89. Stephanie Blackwood, phone interview, January 5, 1999.

90. Don Tuthill, phone interview, October 21, 1998.

91. Dan Mullen, phone interview, March 18, 1999.

92. Blackwood interview, January 19, 1998.

93. See Judith Butler on gender performativity, *Gender Trouble: Feminism and the Subversion of Identity (Thinking Gender)*, and Joshua Gamson's analysis of talk shows' scandalized treatment of bisexuality and transgenderism compared with their normalized representations of gayness, *Freaks Talk Back: Tabloid Talk Shows and Sexual Nonconformity*.

94. Kate Bornstein, *Gender Outlaw: On Men, Women, and the Rest of Us*.

95. Sarah Siegel, "Marketing to the GLBT Consumer," PrideFest 2002 Panel (Philadelphia), May 4, 2002.

96. Judith Halberstam, *Female Masculinity*, 20.

97. Marjorie B. Garber, *Vice Versa: Bisexuality and the Eroticism of Everyday Life*, 70.

98. Baker interview.

99. Badgett, "Income Inflation."

100. Ibid., 9.

101. Bob Witeck, e-mail, April 22, 2003, 8:55 A.M.

102. Bob Witeck, e-mail, April 22, 2003, 4:50 P.M.

103. David Mulryan, phone interview, January 24, 1999.

104. Elliott interview, November 18, 1998.

105. Ibid.

106. Lukenbill interview.

107. Witeck interview, November 22, 1998.

108. Ang, *Desperately Seeking the Audience*, 9.

109. Ibid., 36–37.

110. Sedgwick, *Epistemology of the Closet*.

111. Ibid., 40.

112. Esther Newton, "Of Yams, Grinders, and Gays," in Newton, ed., *Margaret Mead Made Me Gay*, 235.

113. Strub interview, October 28, 1998.

6. Neither Fish Nor Fowl

1. Henry Scott, interview, February 2, 1999.

2. Ernest Jones, *The Life and Work of Sigmund Freud* 2:421.

3. Pettit, quoted in Robin Pogrebin, "Lesbian Publications Struggle for Survival in a Market Dominated by Gay Males," *New York Times*, December 23, 1996, D7.

4. Joyce Appleby, "Consumption in Early Modern Thought," in Brewer and Porter, eds., *Consumption and the World of Goods*, 166.

5. Victoria de Grazia, "Introduction," in de Grazia and Furlough, *The Sex of Things*.

6. Victoria de Grazia, "Establishing the Modern Consumer Household," in de Grazia and Furlough, eds., *The Sex of Things*, 152.

7. Johnson, "Economics Holds Back the Lesbian Ad Market," 34. It is notable that this article's title suggests that it is lesbians' lower-than-average incomes that hinder the lesbian market, when the article's content focuses more on style issues.

8. Stabiner, "Tapping the Homosexual Market," 74.

9. Johnson, "Economics Holds Back the Lesbian Ad Market"; Pogrebin, "Lesbian Publications Struggle for Survival."

10. Stuart Elliott, interview, November 18, 1998.

11. Cheng, *The Men's Club* (Web site).

12. The *Advocate*: October 16, October 29, and November 26, 2003; *Curve*: November and December 2002, February 2003; *Girlfriends*: October, November, and December 2002; *Out*: October, November, and December 2002.

13. By "mainstream" I mean those companies that do not offer a specifically gay or lesbian product or service, but that include gays and, occasionally, lesbians, among a range of target markets. These companies include Subaru, Absolut vodka, and HBO, among others.

14. Clark, "Commodity Lesbianism," 187.

15. Ibid., 188.

16. Laura Mulvey, "Visual Pleasure and Narrative Cinema," in Thornham, ed., *Feminist Film Theory: A Reader*, 59.

17. E. Ann Kaplan, "Is the Gaze Male?" in Snitow, Stansell, and Thompson, eds., *Desire: The Politics of Sexuality*, 327 (emphasis added).

18. De Lauretis, "Sexual Difference and Lesbian Representation," 142.

19. Jane Gaines, "Introduction: Fabricating the Female Body," in Gaines and Herzog, eds., *Fabrications: Costume and the Female Body*.

20. Jackie Stacey, *Star Gazing: Hollywood Cinema and Female Spectatorship*, 33.

21. Andrea Weiss, "A Queer Feeling When I Look at You," in Gledhill, ed., *Stardom: Industry of Desire*, 297.

22. William Leach, *Land of Desire: Merchants, Power, and the Rise of a New American Culture*.

23. Rita Felski, "Imagined Pleasures: The Erotics and Aesthetics of Consumption," in Felski, ed., *The Gender of Modernity*.

24. Clark, "Commodity Lesbianism," 186, quoting Jane Gaines.

25. Scott interview.

26. Stephanie Blackwood, interview, January 19, 1998.

27. Blackwood interview, January 19, 1998.

28. Megan Ishler, interview, December 3, 1998.

29. Moore, "Courting the Gay Market," 1B.

30. Figures for 2002 and 2003.

31. Cheng, *The Men's Club* (Web site).

32. "International Gay Media," Equality Forum Panel (Philadelphia), May 1, 2003.

33. Stephanie Blackwood, "*Times* Talks—Advertising to Gay America" (New York City), April 8, 1999.

34. Blackwood interview, January 19, 1998.

35. Karla Solheim, "The Battle of the Queer Dot-Coms," *Girlfriends* (March 2000).

36. John Finco, interview, April 14, 1999.

37. As Angela McRobbie (1980) argues in her critique of early studies of working-class male youth subcultures, researchers often overlook female subcultures because these are more likely to be organized within and around domestic spaces, making them hard to reach and observe.

38. Howard Buford, interview, February 13, 1998.

39. David Leonhardt, "Gap Between Pay of Men and Women Smallest on Record," *New York Times*, February 17, 2003.

40. Badgett, "Income Inflation."

41. Badgett, *Money, Myths, and Change*, 3.

42. Catherine Draper, interview, January 21, 1999.

43. Sean Strub, e-mail, November 12, 2002.

44. Liz Gumbiner, interview, September 7, 1998.

45. Blackwood, "*Times* Talks—Advertising to Gay America" (New York City), April 8, 1999.

46. Deborah Isherwood, interview, September 23, 1998.

47. Schulman, "The Making of a Market Niche," 17.

48. Frances Stevens, interview, November 10, 1998.

49. Badgett, *Money, Myths, and Change*, 111.

50. Draper interview.

51. Scott interview.

52. Bartky, quoted in Gaines, "Introduction," 3.

53. Lukenbill, *Untold Millions*, 34.

54. Michael Wilke, interview, January 19, 1998.

55. David Mulryan, interview, January 24, 1999.

56. See, for example, J. Kasindorf, "Lesbian Chic: The Bold, Brave New World of Gay Women," *New York*, May 10, 1993; L. Bennetts, "k.d. lang Cuts It Close," *Vanity Fair* (August 1993); Sylvia Rubin, "The New Lesbian Chic: In Movies, TV, Music, Sports, Politics, Gay Women Find They're in Fashion," *San Francisco Chronicle*, June 22, 1993; E. Salholz, "Lesbians Coming Out Strong: The Power and the Pride," *Newsweek*, July 19, 1993; Elizabeth Snead, "Lesbians in the Limelight: Some Chafe at Media's Embrace," *USA Today*, July 13, 1993; Kara Swisher, "Targeting the Gay Market," *Washington Post*, April 25, 1993.

57. James Wolcott, "Lover Girls," *Vanity Fair* (June 1997).

58. John Harlow, "Cut It Out Girls: Thompson Pulls the Plug on Lesbian Chic," *London Sunday Times*, June 29, 1997.

59. Swisher, "Targeting the Gay Market," H1.

60. Mulryan interview.

61. Arlene Stein, "All Dressed Up, But No Place to Go? Style Wars and the New Lesbianism," in Creekmur and Doty, eds., *Out in Culture: Gay, Lesbian, and Queer Essays on Popular Culture*, 478.

62. Marguerite Moritz, "Lesbian Chic: Our Fifteen Minutes of Celebrity?" in Valdivia, ed., *Feminism, Multiculturalism, and the Media: Global Diversities*, 127.

63. Ibid., 136.

64. Ibid., 128; Chasin, *Selling Out: The Gay and Lesbian Movement Goes to Market* and "Selling Out: The Gay/Lesbian Market and the Construction of Gender."

65. Wilke interview.

66. Rachel Fox, interview, February 18, 1999.

67. Patrick O'Neil, interview, November 18, 1998.

68. Gumbiner interview.

69. Wilke, "Big Advertisers Join Move to Embrace Gay Market," 10.

70. Sue O'Sullivan, "Girls Who Kiss Girls and Who Cares?" in Hamer and Budge, eds., *The Good, the Bad, and the Gorgeous*, 92.

71. Gaines, "Introduction," 6.

72. Jay, *Tales of the Lavender Menace*, 141.

73. Kaplan, "Is the Gaze Male?" 327.

74. Stephanie Nolen, "Lipstick Vogue: Kissing Up to Another Taboo," *Toronto Globe and Mail*, August 28, 1999.

75. Ibid., C6.

76. Susan McKenna, "Television and the Search for the Postfeminist Body," paper presented at the ICA's 50th Annual Conference, Acapulco, June 1–5 (2000); Sender, "Selling Sexual Subjectivities."

77. Clark, "Commodity Lesbianism," 192.

78. Ibid., 198.

79. See Henry Jenkins, "Television Fans, Poachers, Nomads," in Gelder and Thornton, eds., *The Subcultures Reader*.

80. De Lauretis, "Sexual Difference and Lesbian Representation," 155 (emphasis in original).

81. Frank DeCaro, "She Has the Most Talked-About Face in Fashion," *Houston Chronicle*, June 4, 1994, 7.

82. Zélic Pollon, "Jenny Shimizu: From Greasemonkey to Supermodel," *Curve* (September 1996): 41.

83. DeCaro, "She Has the Most Talked-About Face in Fashion," 7.

84. Halberstam, *Female Masculinity*.

85. Kennedy and Davis, *Boots of Leather, Slippers of Gold*, 154.

86. Blackwood interview, January 19, 1998.

7. SEX SELLS

1. See, for example, Robin Marantz Henig, "AIDS: A New Disease's Deadly Odyssey." *New York Times*, February 6 1983.

2. Sender, "Gay Readers, Consumers, and a Dominant Gay Habitus."

3. See the Ehrenreichs' summary of the formation and effects of the professional-managerial class in the twentieth century: Ehrenreich and Ehrenreich, "The Professional-Managerial Class."

4. Ohmann, *Selling Culture*, 245.

5. Ibid., 253.

6. Gayle S. Rubin, "Thinking Sex," 13—14.

7. Ibid., 15.

8. Laura Kipnis, *Bound and Gagged: Pornography and the Politics of Fantasy in America*, 134.

9. P. Bourdieu et al., *Photography: A Middle-Brow Art*, 95.

10. Bourdieu, *Distinction*.

11. Joseph Hanania, "Closeted No Longer," *Los Angeles Times*, October 29, 1995, E1.

12. Sansolo, quoted in Thomas A. Stewart, "Gay in Corporate America," 56.

13. Goodstein, quoted in N. R. Kleinfeld, "Homosexual Periodicals Are Proliferating," D4.

14. Dana Calvo, "Sex Minus XXX," *South Florida Sun-Sentinel*, November 24, 1998, 10.

15. Ibid.

16. Fisher, "Local Print Bumps into National Ad Walls," S2.

17. Schwartz, "Online Gays Become a Market for Advertisers," E1.

18. Jeffrey Newman, presentation, "*Times* Talks—The Boys in the Bandwidth: The Growth of the Gay and Lesbian Online Marketplace" (New York City), February 29, 2000.

19. Ibid.

20. Jim Consolantis, presentation, "*Times* Talks—Advertising to Gay America" (New York City), April 8, 1999.

21. Walter Schubert, phone interview, August 24, 2001.

22. Michael Shively, phone interview, August 21, 2001.

23. Catherine Draper, phone interview, January 21, 1999.

24. Kaminer, quoted in Cyndee Miller, "Mainstream Marketers Decide Time Is Right to Target Gays," *Marketing News*, July 20, 1992, 15.

25. Dan Baker, interview, September 17, 1998.

26. Sean Strub, interview, October 28, 1998.

27. Frances Stevens, phone interview, November 10, 1998.

28. Moneka Hewlett, phone interview, October 23, 1998.

29. Kipnis, *Bound and Gagged*, 67. See also Janine Fuller and Stuart Buckley, *Restricted Entry: Censorship on Trial*; Neil Hartlen, "Out of the Courts and into the Press: An Analysis of Media Representations of *Little Sister's v. Canadian Customs*," *ParaDoxa* 2.2 (1996). Both offer overviews of Canadian customs policies and their differential application to some types of media as well as their intended destination: customs seizes more of the same publications destined for lesbian and gay bookstores than for general outlets.

30. Don Tuthill, phone interview, October 21, 1998.

31. Henry Scott, interview, February 2, 1999.

32. Joe Landry, phone interview, January 5, 1999.

33. Patrick Califia, phone interview, May 10, 2001.

34. Shively interview.

35. Ibid.

36. Liz Gumbiner, interview, September 7, 1998.

37. Draper interview.

38. Ibid.

39. Condom ads appeared in the national gay and lesbian press for the first time in the summer of 2003.

40. Stevens interview.

41. Isherwood, phone interview, September 23, 1998.

42. Shahid, quoted in Stuart Elliott, "Abercrombie & Fitch Extends a Print Campaign to TV," *New York Times*, August 6, 1999, C5.

43. Sedgwick, *Epistemology of the Closet*.

44. Megan Ishler, phone interview, December 3, 1998.

45. *Bad Attitude* 11.1 (1997), *Blueboy* (December 1999), *Hustler* (December 1999), *On Our Backs* (October-November 1999), *Penthouse* (November 1999), *Playboy* (December 1999), and *Playgirl* (November 1999).

46. The publishers have acknowledged their gay readership, however, and the magazine's ads reflect this. See Clare Harth, "Fan Male," *Out* (December 1999).

47. Kara Sarisky, phone interview, April 19, 2000.

48. David Mulryan, phone interview, January 24, 1999. Mulryan/Nash closed in early 2000.

49. Kurt DeMars, interview, April 1, 1999.

50. Draper interview.

51. Hewlett interview.

52. DeMars interview.

53. Todd Evans, phone interview, September 17, 1999.

54. Eve M. Khan, "The Glass Closet," *Print* (September–October 1994): 30.

55. James Collard, then editor in chief at *Out*, quoted in Williams, "Securing the Out Post," 3.

56. Scott interview.

57. Ibid.

58. See, for example, Rotello, *Sexual Ecology*.

59. Richard Fung, "Looking for My Penis: The Eroticized Asian in Gay Porn Video," in *How Do I Look? Queer Film and Video*, ed. Bad Object-Choices; Mercer and Julien, "Race, Sexual Politics, and Black Masculinity"; Somerville, *Queering the Color Line*. Yet, as Fung notes, this characterization is not shared by Asian men who tend to be seen as less sexual than white and African American men.

60. The *Advocate*: October 16, October 29, and November 26, 2003; *Curve*: November and December 2002, February 2003; *Girlfriends*: October, November, and December 2002; *Out*: October, November, and December 2002.

61. *See* www.census.gov/prod/2001pubs/c2kbr01-1.pdf, 3 (retrieved September 9, 2003).

62. Samuel R. Delany, *Times Square Red, Times Square Blue*.

63. Rubin, "Thinking Sex," 22.

64. Pat Califia, "When Sex Is a Job, Cops Come a-Knocking on Your Door," *Out* (April 1999): 54. As Pat Califia, Patrick Califia wrote a monthly column for *Out* from No-

vember 1998 to November 1999. He told me that his contract was not renewed, in part, because the magazine owners were "fluffing the magazine to be sold" (Califia interview). Further, his last column responded to Henry Scott's public claims that *Out* publishers and advertisers are only interested in their most affluent gay (and lesbian) readers (Pat Califia, "For Richer or for Poorer," *Out* [November 1999]). Califia criticized Scott and lesbian and gay publishing generally for reproducing the myth of affluence of lesbians and gays, and for ignoring the real concerns of queers across all socioeconomic classes. Califia suggested that his outspoken criticism of the class politics of the gay and lesbian glossy magazines, more than his sexual writing, was the ultimate reason for the nonrenewal of his contract. In the new incarnation of a "less PG-rated" *Out* magazine, Califia's sexual writing may have been welcome, but a discussion of class and affluence was more controversial. I don't know if Califia knew his days writing for *Out* were numbered when he concluded this article: "Like other queers from poor backgrounds, I don't belong here" (142).

65. Bourdieu, *Distinction*, 99.
66. When I asked advertising agency partner David Mulryan whom he had in mind as the audience for his ads, he explained that he saw them "like me: . . . gay, white, whatever, you know? That they have the same things that I want. That's what I assume. That they've had a tough time and they've re-created themselves and they live in New York" (Mulryan interview).
67. Foucault, *The History of Sexuality*, vol. 1, *An Introduction*.
68. Shively interview.
69. Pat Califia, *Public Sex: The Culture of Radical Sex*, 21.
70. Foucault, *The History of Sexuality* 1:18.

8. JUST LIKE YOU

1. Hank Stuever, "Straight Arrows in Gayville, USA," *Washington Post*, April 27, 2000, C1.
2. Chasin, *Selling Out*, 218.
3. Marla Erlien, "Moving Beyond the Millennium March: Diving into the Dangers of Freedom," *Gay Community News* (Summer 1999): 5.
4. Ingram, quoted in Moni Basu and Catherine E. Shoichet, "Society Shifted Before Court Did: Gays More Open Since Hardwick Case," *Atlanta Journal and Constitution*, June 29, 2003, 8A.
5. Warner, *The Trouble with Normal*, 50.
6. Michael Bronski, *The Pleasure Principle: Sex, Backlash, and the Struggle for Gay Freedom*, 3.
7. See, for example, Rotello, *Sexual Ecology*; Sullivan, *Virtually Normal*; Urvashi Vaid, *Virtual Equality: The Mainstreaming of Gay America*; Warner, *Fear of a Queer Planet*; Warner, *The Trouble with Normal*.
8. Bronski, *The Pleasure Principle*, 3.
9. Schulman, "The Making of a Market Niche," 17.
10. Chasin, *Selling Out*, 132–33.

11. Bronski, *The Pleasure Principle*, 37.

12. Ibid., 45.

13. Schulman, *Stagestruck*, 143.

14. Chasin, *Selling Out*, 141.

15. Ibid., 209.

16. Herbert Gans, *Popular Culture and High Culture*, 44.

17. Savage, quoted in Hank Stuever, "Straight Arrows in Gayville, USA," C3.

18. Harris, "The Making of a Subculture," 24.

19. Ibid., 24—25.

20. Tricia Rose, *Black Noise: Rap Music and Black Culture in Contemporary America*.

21. Ibid., 40.

22. Ibid.

23. Chauncey, *Gay New York*; D'Emilio, *Sexual Politics, Sexual Communities*; D'Emilio and Freedman, *Intimate Matters*; Kennedy and Davis, *Boots of Leather, Slippers of Gold*.

24. Bronski, *Culture Clash*; Bronski, *The Pleasure Principle*; Doty, *Making Things Perfectly Queer*; Richard Dyer, *Heavenly Bodies: Film Stars and Society*; Vito Russo, *The Celluloid Closet*.

25. Schulman, *Stagestruck*, 106.

26. Ang, *Desperately Seeking the Audience*, 162.

27. Janice Radway, "Identifying Ideological Seams: Mass Culture, Analytic Method, and Political Practice," *Communication* 9 (1986): 97.

28. Chasin, *Selling Out*; Chasin, "Selling Out: The Gay/Lesbian Market and the Construction of Gender"; Mendelsohn, "We're Here! We're Queer! Let's Get Coffee!" *New York*, September 30, 1996; Schulman, "The Making of a Market Niche"; Schulman, *Stagestruck*; Warner, *The Trouble with Normal*.

29. See, for example, Jacqueline Bobo, "*The Color Purple*: Black Women as Cultural Readers," in Pribham, ed., *Female Spectators: Looking at Film and Television*; Susan J. Douglas, *Where the Girls Are: Growing Up Female with the Mass Media*; Andrea Press, *Women Watching Television*; Janice Radway, *Reading the Romance: Women, Patriarchy, and Popular Literature*; Stacey, *Star Gazing*.

30. Lauren Berlant and Elizabeth Freeman, "Queer Nationality," in Warner, ed., *Fear of a Queer Planet*, 210.

31. Ibid., 208.

32. *See* www.gayshamesf.org/info.htm (retrieved February 8, 2003).

33. Tommi Avicolli Mecca, "Gay Shame." *Philadelphia Gay News*, June 6, 2002.

34. *See* www.gayshamesf.org/info.htm (retrieved February 8, 2003).

35. Clark, "Commodity Lesbianism," 198, using John Fiske's term.

36. Ibid., 198.

37. Carole-Anne Tyler, "Boys Will Be Girls: The Politics of Gay Drag," in Fuss, ed., *Inside/Out: Lesbian Theories, Gay Theories*, 32.

38. Ibid., 33.

39. Gaines, "Introduction: Fabricating the Female Body," 25.

40. Lisa Montanarelli, "I Bought Slut Drag at Toys 'R' Us," *Black Sheets* (2000): 30.

41. Felski, "Imagined Pleasures," 63.

42. Stacey, *Star Gazing*, 46.

43. Thornton, *Club Cultures*, 6.

44. Weems, *Desegregating the Dollar*, 32–33.

45. *See* www.commercialcloset.org (retrieved February 8, 2003).

46. Paul Wong et al., "Asian Americans as a Model Minority: Self-Perceptions and Perceptions by Other Racial Groups," *Sociological perspectives* 41.1 (1998): 95–96; see also Doobo Shim, "From Yellow Peril Through Model Minority to Renewed Yellow Peril: Asians in Popular Media—Constructing (Mis)Representations," *Journal of Communication Inquiry* 22.4 (1998).

47. Stacey J. Lee, *Unraveling the "Model Minority" Stereotype: Listening to Asian American Youth.*

48. Spare Parts and Greenfield Online, press release, October 14, 1998, 1.

49. Lukenbill, *Untold Millions*, 37.

50. Stephanie Blackwood, interview, January 19, 1998.

51. Andrew Beaver, interview, February 23, 1998.

52. Patrick Califia, phone interview, May 10, 2001.

53. Warner, *The Trouble with Normal*, 67.

54. Howard Buford, phone interview, April 15, 2003.

55. Dangerous Bedfellows, *Policing Public Sex: Queer Politics and the Future of Aids Activism*, 18.

APPENDIX 1: PITCHING THE GAY MARKET

1. Martyn Hammersley and Paul Atkinson, *Ethnography: Principles in Practice*, 1.

2. See, for example, Howard Becker, *Art Worlds*; Brenda Jo Bright and Elizabeth Bakewell, *Looking High and Low: Art and Cultural Identity*; Barry Dornfeld, *Producing Public Television, Producing Public Culture*; Paul Espinosa, "The Audience in the Text: Ethnographic Observations of a Hollywood Story Conference," *Media, Culture and Society* 4 (1982); Gamson, *Freaks Talk Back*; Michael Griffin, "Between Art and Industry: Amateur Photography and Middlebrow Culture," in Gross, ed., *On the Margins of Artworlds*; Lisa Henderson, "Directorial Intention and Persona in Film School," in Gross, ed., *On the Margins of Artworlds*; Henderson, " 'Storyline' and the Multicultural Middlebrow"; Henry Kingsbury, *Music, Talent, and Performance: A Conservatory Cultural System*; Lutz and Collins, *Reading National Geographic*; Janice Radway, *A Feeling for Books*; Roger Silverstone, *Framing Science: The Making of a BBC Documentary*; K. Warchol, "Artists Entering the Marketplace," in Gross, ed., *On the Margins of Art Worlds*.

3. Arlen, *Thirty Seconds*; Rothenberg, *Where the Suckers Moon*; Shapiro, "The Construction of Television Commercials"; Slater, "Advertising as Commercial Practice."

4. Henderson, " 'Storyline' and the Multicultural Middlebrow," 340.

5. See, for example, Gamson, *Freaks Talk Back*, 228.

6. Caitlin Hume, interview, February 2, 1999.

7. Gamson, *Freaks Talk Back*.

8. Lewis Anthony Dexter, *Elite and Specialized Interviewing*, 37–38.

9. Laura Nader, "Up the Anthropologist," in Hymes, ed., *Reinventing Anthropology*.

10. Gamson, *Freaks Talk Back*.

11. Andrew Beaver, interview, February 23, 1998; Hume interview, February 2, 1999.

12. Buford's status as the only African American interviewee reflects the low numbers of people of color in advertising generally: see *Advertising Age*'s special issue on "Diversity" (i.e., racial diversity), February 16, 1998.

13. Dexter, *Elite and Specialized Interviewing*, 55.

14. Ibid., 56.

15. Shapiro, "The Construction of Television Commercials," 470.

16. Howard Becker, *Sociological Work*.

17. Ibid., 29.

18. I would like to thank Michael Bronski for giving me his collection of catalogs and cardpacks for this project.

19. Hammersley and Atkinson, *Ethnography*, 161.

20. Kingsbury, *Music, Talent, and Performance*, 24.

21. Radway, "Identifying Ideological Seams."

22. Beaver, interview, February 23, 1998.

23. Amy Simmons, "*Times* Talks—The Boys in the Bandwidth: The Growth of the Gay and Lesbian Online Marketplace" (New York City), February 29, 2000.

24. Wilke, "Reliable Research Difficult to Gather, Analyze."

25. Radway, "Ethnography Among Elites."

26. Laura Grindstaff, *The Money Shot*.

WORKS CITED

Abelove, Henry, Michèle Aina Barale, and David M. Halperin, eds. *The Lesbian and Gay Studies Reader.* New York: Routledge, 1993.

Abelson, Reed. "Out Magazine Acquired by Key Rival." *New York Times*, February 21, 2000, C12.

Abreu, Elinor. *Gay Portals Come Out* (Industry Standard, 2000 [cited February 18, 2000]). Available from www.thestandard.com.

Adams, Bob. "Paying to Look Perfect." *Advocate*, September 3, 2002.

Advocate. "Surfing an Online Tidal Wave." June 6, 2000, 18.

Allyn, David. *Make Love, Not War: The Sexual Revolution—An Unfettered History.* New York: Routledge, 2001.

Alsop, Ronald. "Are Gay People More Affluent Than Others?" *Wall Street Journal*, December 30, 1999, B1, B3.

Alwood, Edward M. *Straight News: Gays, Lesbians, and the News Media.* New York: Columbia University Press, 1996.

Ang, Ien. *Desperately Seeking the Audience.* London and New York: Routledge, 1991.

Appleby, Joyce. "Consumption in Early Modern Thought." In John Brewer and Roy Porter, eds., *Consumption and the World of Goods*, 162–73. New York: Routledge, 1993.

Applegate, Jane. "From Videos to Greeting Cards, Gay Clout Abounds." *Washington Post*, May 3, 1993, F10.

Arlen, Michael J. *Thirty Seconds.* New York: Farrar, Straus, and Giroux, 1980.

Badgett, M. V. Lee. "Beyond Biased Samples: Challenging the Myths on the Economic Status of Lesbians and Gay Men." In Gluckman and Reed, eds., *Homo Economics*, 65–71.

——. "Income Inflation: The Myth of Affluence Among Gay, Lesbian, and Bisexual Americans," 23 pages. New York/Amherst, Mass.: Policy Institute of the National Gay and Lesbian Task Force *and* the Institute for Gay and Lesbian Strategic Studies, 1998.

——. *Money, Myths, and Change: The Economic Lives of Lesbians and Gay Men*. Chicago: University of Chicago Press, 2001.

——. "The Myth of Gay and Lesbian Affluence." *The Gay and Lesbian Review* (Spring 2000): 22–25.

Baker, Dan B. "A History in Ads: The Growth of the Gay and Lesbian Market." In Gluckman and Reed, eds., *Homo Economics*, 11–20.

——. "So, Just How Big Is the Gay Market, Really?" *Quotient* (December 1994): 3.

Baltera, Lorraine. "No Gay Market Yet, Admen, Gays Agree." *Advertising Age*, August 28, 1972, 3.

Barthes, Roland and Stephen Heath. *Image, Music, Text*. New York: Hill and Wang, 1977.

Basu, Moni and Catherine E. Shoichet. "Society Shifted Before Court Did: Gays More Open Since Hardwick Case." *Atlanta Journal and Constitution*, June 29, 2003, 8A.

Bauder, David. "Race on for 'Gay TV.'" *Associated Press*, April 30, 2002.

Becker, Howard. *Art Worlds*. Berkeley: University of California Press, 1982.

——. *Sociological Work*. New Brunswick, N.J.: Transaction Books, 1970.

Bennetts, L. "k. d. lang Cuts It Close." *Vanity Fair* (August 1993): 94–98, 142–46.

Berlant, Lauren and Elizabeth Freeman. "Queer Nationality." In Warner, ed., *Fear of a Queer Planet*, 193–229.

Blair, Jayson. "Healthy Skepticism and the Marketing of AIDS." *New York Times*, August 5, 2001, D14.

Bobo, Jacqueline. "*The Color Purple*: Black Women as Cultural Readers." In Deirdre Pribham, ed., *Female Spectators: Looking at Film and Television*, 90–109. New York: Verso, 1988.

Bornstein, Kate. *Gender Outlaw: On Men, Women, and the Rest of Us*. New York: Routledge, 1994.

Boroughs, Don. "Why This Census Sags in the Middle." *U.S. News and World Report*, April 23, 1990, 14.

Bourdieu, Pierre. *Distinction: A Social Critique of the Judgement of Taste*. Cambridge: Harvard University Press, 1984.

——. *Language and Symbolic Power*. Cambridge, Eng.: Polity, 1991.

Bourdieu, P., L. Boltanski, R. Castel, and J. C. Chamboredon. *Photography: A Middle-Brow Art*. Cambridge, Eng.: Polity, 1990.

Bowden, Sue and Avner Offer. "The Technological Revolution That Never Was: Gender, Class, and the Diffusion of Household Appliances in Interwar England." In de Grazia and Furlough, eds., *The Sex of Things*, 244–74.

Branchik, Blaine J. "Out in the Market: A History of the Gay Market Segment in the United States." *Journal of Macromarketing* 22.1 (2002): 86–97.

Breazeale, Kenon. "In Spite of Women: Esquire Magazine and the Construction of the Male Consumer." *Signs* 20.1 (1994): 1–22.

Brewer, Steve. "Asian-Americans Count on Census: Nationwide, Minorities Are Underreported." *Houston Chronicle*, December 17 1997, 38.

Bright, Brenda Jo and Elizabeth Bakewell. *Looking High and Low: Art and Cultural Identity*. Tucson: University of Arizona Press, 1995.

Bronski, Michael. *Culture Clash: The Making of Gay Sensibility*. Boston: South End Press, 1984.

———. "Invisible Exposure: Two Media Powerhouses Have Announced Plans for Gay-and-Lesbian Cable Channels. But Could Gay TV Mean the Death of Queer Culture?" *Boston Phoenix*, January 31, 2002.

———. *The Pleasure Principle: Sex, Backlash, and the Struggle for Gay Freedom*. New York: St. Martin's, 1998.

Brooks, Dwight E. "Consumer Markets and Consumer Magazines: Black America and the Culture of Consumption, 1920–1960." Ph.D. diss., University of Iowa, 1991.

Business Week. "Gays: A Major Force in the Marketplace" (September 3, 1979): 118.

Butler, Judith P. *Gender Trouble: Feminism and the Subversion of Identity*. New York: Routledge, 1990.

———. "Imitation and Gender Subordination." In Abelove, Barale, and Halperin, eds., *The Lesbian and Gay Studies Reader*, 307–320.

———. "Merely Cultural." *Social Text* 52–53.15(2–3) (1997): 265–77.

Califia, Pat. "For Richer or for Poorer." *Out* (November 1999): 66, 68, 142.

———. *Public Sex: The Culture of Radical Sex*. Pittsburgh: Cleis Press, 1994.

———. "When Sex Is a Job, Cops Come a-Knocking on Your Door." *Out* (April 1999): 54, 56.

Calvo, Dana. "Sex Minus XXX." *South Florida Sun-Sentinel*, November 24, 1998, 10, 80.

Campbell, John. "Consuming Pink Triangles: Privacy, Surveillance, Identity, and 'Gay Marketing.'" Paper presented at the International Communication Association, San Diego, May 2003.

Carter, Bill. "MTV and Showtime Plan Cable Channel for Gay Viewers." *New York Times*, January 10, 2002, C1, C5.

Centers for Disease Control. "HIV/AIDS Among African Americans." *See* www.cdc.gov, 2000.

———. "HIV/AIDS Among Hispanics in the United States." *See* www.cdc.gov, 2000.

———. "The HIV/AIDS Epidemic in the United States, 1997–1998." *See* www.cdc.gov, 2000.

Chasin, Alexandra. *Selling Out: The Gay and Lesbian Movement Goes to Market*. New York: St. Martin's, 2000.

———. "Selling Out: The Gay/Lesbian Market and the Construction of Gender." *Sojourner* (June 1997): 14–15.

Chauncey, George. *Gay New York: Gender, Urban Culture, and the Making of the Gay Male World, 1890–1940*. New York: Basic Books, 1994.

Cheng, Kipp. "The Men's Club: Why Do Marketers Ignore Lesbian Consumers?" (Web site: DiversityInc.com, April 12, 2002; retrieved April 15, 2002).

Clark, Danae. "Commodity Lesbianism." In Abelove, Barale, and Halperin, eds., *The Lesbian and Gay Studies Reader*, 186–201.

Clarke, Eric. "Queer Publicity and the Limits of Inclusion." *Gay and Lesbian Quarterly* 5.1 (1999): 84–89.

Cohen, Lizbeth. *A Consumers' Republic: The Politics of Mass Consumption in Postwar America*. New York: Knopf, 2003.

Cramb, Gordon. "Gay Games Prove Commercial Success." *Financial Times*, August 1, 1998, 2.

Cutlip, Scott M. *The Unseen Power: Public Relations, a History*. Hillsdale, N.J.: Lawrence Erlbaum, 1994.

Dangerous Bedfellows. *Policing Public Sex: Queer Politics and the Future of AIDS Activism*. Boston: South End Press, 1996.

Davis, Riccardo A. "Marketers Game for Gay Events." *Advertising Age*, May 30, 1994, S1, S5.

de Grazia, Victoria. "Establishing the Modern Consumer Household." In de Grazia and Furlough, eds., *The Sex of Things*, 151–61.

——. "Introduction." In de Grazia and Furlough, eds., *The Sex of Things*, 1–10.

de Grazia, Victoria and Ellen Furlough. *The Sex of Things: Gender and Consumption in Historical Perspective*. Berkeley: University of California Press, 1996.

de Lauretis, Teresa. "Sexual Difference and Lesbian Representation." In Abelove, Barale, and Halperin, eds., *The Lesbian and Gay Studies Reader*, 141–58.

DeCaro, Frank. "She Has the Most Talked-About Face in Fashion." *Houston Chronicle*, June 4, 1994, 7.

Delany, Samuel R. *Times Square Red, Times Square Blue*. New York: New York University Press, 1999.

Delgado, Ray. "Study Suggests Gays a Marketer's Dream; Group Willing to Show Brand Loyalty." *Houston Chronicle*, June 11, 1994, 1B–2B.

D'Emilio, John. "Capitalism and Gay Identity." In Abelove, Barale, and Halperin, eds., *The Lesbian and Gay Studies Reader*, 467–76.

——. *Sexual Politics, Sexual Communities: The Making of a Homosexual Minority in the United States, 1940–1970*. Chicago: University of Chicago Press, 1983.

D'Emilio, John and Estelle Freedman. *Intimate Matters: A History of Sexuality in America*. New York: Harper and Row, 1988.

Dexter, Lewis Anthony. *Elite and Specialized Interviewing*. Evanston, Ill.: Northwestern University Press, 1970.

Dominick, J. R. and G. E. Rausch. "The Image of Women in Network TV Commercials." *Journal of Broadcasting* 16 (1972): 259–65.

Dornfeld, Barry. *Producing Public Television, Producing Public Culture*. Princeton, N.J.: Princeton University Press, 1998.

Doty, Alexander. *Making Things Perfectly Queer: Interpreting Mass Culture*. Minneapolis: University of Minnesota Press, 1993.

Dougherty, Philip H. "Homosexual Magazines in Bids." *New York Times*, July 13, 1976, 20.

Douglas, Susan J. *Where the Girls Are: Growing Up Female with the Mass Media*. New York: Times Books, 1994.

Dowd, Maureen. " 'Will & Will' 24/7." *New York Times*, January 13, 2002.

Dyer, Richard. *Heavenly Bodies: Film Stars and Society*. Basingstoke, Eng.: Macmillan, 1986.

——. "Seen to Be Believed: Some Problems in the Representation of Gay People as Typical." *Studies in Visual Communication* 9.2 (1983): 2–19.

——. "Stereotyping." In R. Dyer, ed., *Gays and Film*, 27–39. London: British Film Institute, 1977.

——. "White." *Screen* 29.4 (1988): 44–64.

Ehrenreich, Barbara. *The Hearts of Men: American Dreams and the Flight from Commitment*. Garden City, N.Y.: Anchor Press/Doubleday, 1983.

Ehrenreich, Barbara and John Ehrenreich. "The Professional-Managerial Class." In Pat Walker, ed., *Between Labor and Capital*, 5–45. Boston: South End Press, 1979.

Elliott, Stuart. "Abercrombie & Fitch Extends a Print Campaign to TV." *New York Times*, August 6, 1999, C5.

——. "Absolut Customizes a Campaign to Salute the Gay and Lesbian Alliance Against Defamation." *New York Times*, February 22, 2001, C6.

——. "Advertisers Bypass Gay Market." *USA Today*, July 17, 1990, 1B–2B.

——. "As the Gay and Lesbian Market Grows, a Boom in Catalogs That Are 'Out, Loud and Proud.'" *New York Times*, September 10, 1993, D17.

——. "Imaginative Supplements Help a Pair of Magazines Build Relationships with Marketers." *New York Times*, June 26, 1998, D4.

——. "Levi Strauss Begins a Far-Reaching Marketing Campaign to Reach Gay Men and Lesbians." *New York Times*, October 19, 1998, C11.

——. "A Market That's Educated, Affluent, and Homosexual." *New York Times*, September 23, 1992, D27.

——. "The Showtime Network Prepares a $10 Million Campaign Blitz for Its 'Queer as Folk' Series." *New York Times*, November 28, 2000, C9.

Ellis, John W., IV. "It's Not Enough to Throw Open the Shop's Doors." *Advertising Age*, February 16, 1998, S10.

Erlien, Marla. "Moving Beyond the Millennium March: Diving into the Dangers of Freedom." *Gay Community News* (Summer 1999): 4–8.

Escoffier, Jeffrey. "The Political Economy of the Closet." In Gluckman and Reed, eds., *Homo Economics*, 123–34.

Espinosa, Paul. "The Audience in the Text: Ethnographic Observations of a Hollywood Story Conference." *Media, Culture and Society* 4 (1982): 77–86.

Ewen, Stuart. *PR! A Social History of Spin*. New York: Basic Books, 1996.

Farley, Rose. "Straighten Up and Fly Right." *Dallas Observer*, April 16, 1998, 17, 18, 20.

Fejes, Fred and Ron Lennon. "Defining the Lesbian/Gay Community? Market Research and the Lesbian/Gay Press." *Journal of Homosexuality* 39.1 (2000): 25–42.

Fejes, Fred and Kevin Petrich. "Invisibility, Homophobia, and Heterosexism: Lesbians, Gays, and the Media." *Critical Studies in Mass Communication* 10.4 (1993): 396–422.

Felski, Rita. "Imagined Pleasures: The Erotics and Aesthetics of Consumption." In Felski, ed., *The Gender of Modernity*, 61–90. Cambridge: Harvard University Press, 1995.

Findlay, Heather. "Gay 101." *Out* (July-August 1994): 84–85.

Fisher, Christy. "Local Print Bumps into National Ad Walls." *Advertising Age*, May 30, 1994, S2.

Foltz, Kim, George Raine, Lynda Wright, and David L. Gonzalez. "The Profit in Being Gay." *Newsweek*, November 12, 1984, 84, 89.

Fost, Dan. "PlanetOut Expands Its Universe." *San Francisco Chronicle*, September 7, 2000, C1.

Foucault, Michel. *The History of Sexuality*, vol. 1: *An Introduction*. Trans. Robert Hurley. London and New York: Penguin, 1978.

Frank, Lisa and Paul Smith. *Madonnarama: Essays on Sex and Popular Culture*. Pittsburgh: Cleis Press, 1993.

Frank, Thomas. *The Conquest of Cool: Business Culture, Counterculture, and the Rise of Hip Consumerism*. Chicago: University of Chicago Press, 1997.

Fraser, Matthew. "Bad Deals, Bungling Hurt Pridevision." *Ontario (Can.) National Post*, December 23, 2002.

Frieberg, Peter. " 'We Can Do This': Ethnic Gay Magazines Are on the Rise." *Press Pass Q* (August 2002).

Friskopp, Annette and Sharon Silverstein. *Straight Jobs, Gay Lives: Gay and Lesbian Professionals, the Harvard Business School, and the American Workplace*. New York: Scribner, 1995.

Fuller, Janine and Stuart Buckley. *Restricted Entry: Censorship on Trial*. Vancouver, Can.: Press Gang, 1995.

Fung, Richard. "Looking for My Penis: The Eroticized Asian in Gay Porn Video." In *How Do I Look? Queer Film and Video*, ed. Bad Object-Choices, 145–60. Seattle: Bay Press, 1991.

Gaines, Jane. "Introduction: Fabricating the Female Body." In Gaines and Charlotte Herzog, eds., *Fabrications: Costume and the Female Body*, 1–27. New York: Routledge, 1990.

Gamson, Joshua. *Freaks Talk Back: Tabloid Talk Shows and Sexual Nonconformity*. Chicago: University of Chicago Press, 1998.

Gans, Herbert. *Popular Culture and High Culture*. New York: Basic Books, 1974.

Garber, Marjorie B. *Vice Versa: Bisexuality and the Eroticism of Everyday Life*. New York: Simon and Schuster, 1995.

Gilbert, Jennifer. "Ad Spending Booming for Gay-Oriented Sites." *Advertising Age*, December 6, 1999, 58.

Giltz, Michael. "Will Gay Pay?" *New York Post*, January 13, 2002.

Gluckman, Amy and Betsy Reed. "The Gay Marketing Moment: Leaving Diversity in the Dust." *Dollars and Sense* (November/December 1993): 16–19, 34–35.

Gluckman, Amy and Betsy Reed, eds. *Homo Economics: Capitalism, Community, and Lesbian and Gay Life*. New York: Routledge, 1997.

Goetzl, David. "Leading Edge: Showtime, MTV Gamble on Gay Net." *Advertising Age*, January 14, 2002, 4.

Goffman, Erving. *Gender Advertisements*. New York: Harper and Row, 1979.

Goldstein, Richard. "Climb Every Mountain: The Art of Selling HIV Drugs." *POZ* (October 1998): 64–67.

Goodman, Tim. "Channel for Gays? It's About Time." *San Francisco Chronicle*, January 21, 2002.

Goodstein, David. "Editorial." *Advocate*, January 29, 1975, 3.

Gramsci, Antonio, Quintin Hoare, and Geoffrey Nowell-Smith. *Selections from the Prison Notebooks of Antonio Gramsci*. New York: International Publishers, 1971.

Griffin, Michael. "Between Art and Industry: Amateur Photography and Middlebrow Culture." In Larry Gross, ed., *On the Margins of Artworlds*, 183–205. Boulder, Colo.: Westview, 1995.

Grindstaff, Laura. *The Money Shot: Trash, Class, and the Making of TV Talk Shows*. Chicago: University of Chicago Press, 2002.

Gross, Larry. *Up from Invisibility: Lesbians, Gay Men, and the Media in America*. New York: Columbia University Press, 2001.

Halberstam, Judith. *Female Masculinity*. Durham, N.C.: Duke University Press, 1998.

Hall, Stuart. "Encoding/Decoding." In S. Hall, D. Hobson, A. Lowe, and P. Willis, eds., *Culture, Media, Language*, 128–39. London: Hutchinson, 1980.

——. "Introduction: Who Needs Identity?" In S. Hall and P. DuGuy, eds., *Questions of Cultural Identity*, 1–17. London: Sage, 1996.

Hammersley, Martyn and Paul Atkinson. *Ethnography: Principles in Practice*. 2d ed. London; New York: Routledge, 1995.

Hanania, Joseph. "Closeted No Longer." *Los Angeles Times*, October 29, 1995, E1–E4.

Hansell, Saul. "So Far, Big Brother Isn't Big Business." *New York Times*, May 7, 2000, C1, 13, 14.

Harlow, John. "Cut It Out Girls: Thompson Pulls the Plug on Lesbian Chic." *London Sunday Times*, June 29, 1997.

Harris, Daniel. "The Making of a Subculture." *Harvard Gay and Lesbian Review* (Winter 1998): 24–25.

Harris Interactive. "LGBT Voter Education and Research Project." 2000, 70 pages.

Harth, Clare. "Fan Male." *Out* (December 1999): 52.

Hartlen, Neil. "Out of the Courts and into the Press: An Analysis of Media Representations of *Little Sister's v. Canadian Customs*." *ParaDoxa* 2.2 (1996): 217–33.

Heinze, Andrew R. *Adapting to Abundance: Jewish Immigrants, Mass Consumption, and the Search for American Identity*. New York: Columbia University Press, 1990.

Henderson, Lisa. "Directorial Intention and Persona in Film School." In Larry Gross, ed., *On the Margins of Artworlds*, 149–66. Boulder, Colo: Westview, 1995.

——. "Simple Pleasures: Lesbian Community and 'Go Fish.'" *Signs* 25.1 (1999): 37–64.

——. "'Storyline' and the Multicultural Middlebrow: Reading Women's Culture on National Public Radio." *Critical Studies in Mass Communication* 16 (1999): 329–49.

Henig, Robin Marantz. "AIDS: A New Disease's Deadly Odyssey." *New York Times*, February 6, 1983, 28.

hooks, bell. *Black Looks: Race and Representation*. Boston: South End Press, 1992.

Horovitz, Bruce. "Alternative Approach: Finding New Ways to Appeal to Gays, Lesbians." *Los Angeles Times*, February 23, 1993, B7.

Howard, Theresa. "John Hancock Ads Reflect Real Life; Firm Reaches Out to Diverse USA." *USA Today*, December 11, 2000, B6.

Jackson, Peter. "Black Male: Advertising and the Cultural Politics of Masculinity." *Gender, Place, and Culture* 1.1 (1994): 49–59.

Jay, Karla. *Tales of the Lavender Menace: A Memoir of Liberation*. New York: Basic Books, 1999.

Jenkins, Henry. "Television Fans, Poachers, Nomads." In Ken Gelder and Sarah Thornton, eds., *The Subcultures Reader*, 506–522. New York: Routledge, 1997.

Johnson, Bradley. "Bowing to Mainstream, Advocate Sex Ads End." *Advertising Age*, August 24, 1992, 28.

——. "Economics Holds Back the Lesbian Ad Market." *Advertising Age*, January 18, 1993, 34, 37.

——. "The Gay Quandary." *Advertising Age*, January 18, 1993, 29, 35.

Jones, Ernest. *The Life and Work of Sigmund Freud.* Vol. 2. New York: Basic Books, 1953.

Jones, Lynn. "AT&T Targets Gays and Lesbians, Direct Mail Campaign." *Direct* (August 1994): 25.

Kahan, Hazel and David Mulryan. "Out of the Closet." *American Demographics* (May 1995): 40–47.

Kaplan, E. Ann. "Is the Gaze Male?" In Ann Snitow, Christine Stansell, and Sharon Thompson, eds., *Desire: The Politics of Sexuality*, 321–38. London: Virago, 1983.

Kasindorf, J. "Lesbian Chic: The Bold, Brave New World of Gay Women." *New York*, May 10, 1993, 31–37.

Kazenoff, Ivy and Anthony Vagnoni. "Babes in Boyland." *Creativity* (October 1997): 18–20.

Kelly, Keith J. "Healthcare Fuels Magazine Growth." *Advertising Age*, May 30, 1994, S4.

Kennedy, Elizabeth Lapovsky and Madeline D. Davis. *Boots of Leather, Slippers of Gold: The History of a Lesbian Community*. New York: Routledge, 1993.

Kern-Foxworth, Marilyn. *Aunt Jemima, Uncle Ben, and Rastus: Blacks in Advertising Yesterday, Today, and Tomorrow*. Westport, Conn.: Greenwood, 1994.

Khan, Eve M. "The Glass Closet." *Print* (September–October 1994): 21–31, 115.

"King of the Gay Airwaves." *Victory!* (June 1994): 12–13.

Kingsbury, Henry. *Music, Talent, and Performance: A Conservatory Cultural System*. Philadelphia: Temple University Press, 1988.

Kipnis, Laura. *Bound and Gagged: Pornography and the Politics of Fantasy in America*. Durham, N.C.: Duke University Press, 1999.

Kirby, Carrie. "Gay Media Call Off Merger." *San Francisco Chronicle*, March 9, 2001, B1.

Kirk, Jim. "Orbitz Effort Hopes to Land Gay Travelers." *Chicago Tribune*, June 19, 2002.

Kirkpatrick, David D. "POZ Magazine Sponsors Trade Fair Aimed at Consumers with HIV." *Wall St. Journal*, May 30, 1996, B10.

Kleinfeld, N. R. "Homosexual Periodicals Are Proliferating." *New York Times*, August 1, 1978, D4.

Knight Ridder Newspapers. "Population of U.S. Hispanics Underestimated, Report Says." *Seattle Times*, May 12, 2002, A8.

Kuczynski, Alex. "Merger to Link Gay Print and Internet Outlets." *New York Times*, March 23, 2000, C11.

Kuttner, Robert. *Everything for Sale: The Value and Limits of Markets*. New York: Knopf, 1997.

Leach, William. *Land of Desire: Merchants, Power, and the Rise of a New American Culture*. New York: Vintage, 1993.

Lee, Stacey J. *Unraveling the "Model Minority" Stereotype: Listening to Asian American Youth*. New York: Teachers College Press, 1996.

Leiss, William, Stephen Kline, and Sut Jhally. *Social Communication in Advertising: Persons, Products, and Images of Well-Being*. New York: Routledge, 1990.

Leonhardt, David. "Gap Between Pay of Men and Women Smallest on Record." *New York Times*, February 17, 2003, A1.

Levin, Gary. "Mainstream's Domino Effect." *Advertising Age*, January 18, 1993, 30, 32.

Lovdal, L.T. "Sex Role Messages in Television Commercials: An Update." *Sex Roles* 21.11–12 (1989): 715–24.

Luh, James C. "Truly Out for a Change." *Internet World*, March 1, 2000.

Lukenbill, Grant. *Untold Millions: Positioning Your Business for the Gay and Lesbian Consumer Revolution*. New York: Harper, 1995.

Lutz, Catherine and Jane Lou Collins. *Reading National Geographic*. Chicago: University of Chicago Press, 1993.

Manstead, A. S. R. and C. McCulloch. "Sex-Role Stereotyping in British Television Advertisements." *British Journal of Social Psychology* 20 (1981): 171–80.

Marchand, Roland. *Advertising the American Dream: Making Way for Modernity, 1920–1940*. Berkeley: University of California Press, 1985.

McArthur, L. Z. and B. G. Resko. "The Portrayal of Women and Men in American Television Commercials." *Journal of Social Psychology* 97 (1975): 209–20.

McKenna, Susan. "Television and the Search for the Postfeminist Body." Paper presented at the International Communication Association, 50th Annual Conference, Acapulco, June 1–5 (2000).

McNamara, Mary. "Will Mergers Quiet the Voice of Gay Press?" *Los Angeles Times*, April 13, 2002, E4.

McRobbie, Angela. "Settling Accounts with Subcultures." *Screen Education* 34 (1980): 37–49.

Mecca, Tommi Avicolli. "Gay Shame." *Philadelphia Gay News*, June 6, 2002.

Mendelsohn, Daniel. "We're Here! We're Queer! Let's Get Coffee!" *New York*, September 30, 1996, 24–31

Mercer, Kobena and Isaac Julien. "Race, Sexual Politics, and Black Masculinity: A Dossier." In R. Chapman and J. Rutherford, eds., *Male Order: Unwrapping Masculinity*, 97–164. London: Lawrence and Wishart, 1988.

Merrett, Jim. "A Gay Look at Advertising." *Advocate*, December 5, 1988, 42–44.

Michaels, Dick. "Happy Birthday to Us." *Los Angeles Advocate* (September 1967): 6.

Miller, Cyndee. "Mainstream Marketers Decide Time Is Right to Target Gays." *Marketing News*, July 20, 1992, 8–15.

Montanarelli, Lisa. "I Bought Slut Drag at Toys 'R' Us." *Black Sheets* (2000): 30.

Moore, Martha T. "Courting the Gay Market." *USA Today*, April 23, 1993, 1B.

Moritz, Marguerite. "Lesbian Chic: Our Fifteen Minutes of Celebrity?" In A. N. Valdivia, ed., *Feminism, Multiculturalism, and the Media: Global Diversities*, 127–44. Thousand Oaks, Calif.: Sage, 1995.

Mulvey, Laura. "Visual Pleasure and Narrative Cinema." In Sue Thornham, ed., *Feminist Film Theory: A Reader*, 58–69. New York: New York University Press, 1999.

Munt, Sally. *Heroic Desire: Lesbian Identity and Cultural Space*. New York: New York University Press, 1998.

Nader, Laura. "Up the Anthropologist." In D. Hymes, ed., *Reinventing Anthropology*, 284–311. New York: Random House, 1974.

National Gay and Lesbian Task Force (NGLTF). "2001 Capital Gains and Losses." Washington, D.C.: NGLTF, 2003.

Newton, Esther. "Of Yams, Grinders, and Gays." In Esther Newton, ed., *Margaret Mead Made Me Gay*, 229–37. Durham, N.C.: Duke University Press, 2000.

Nicholson, Leslie J. "A Friendlier Financial World for Gays and Lesbians." *Philadelphia Inquirer*, March 24, 2000, D1–D2.

Nolen, Stephanie. "Lipstick Vogue: Kissing Up to Another Taboo." *Toronto Globe and Mail*, August 28, 1999, C6.

Oberndorf, Shannon. "The Gay '90s Fail to Deliver; Overhyped and Underachieving, Gay Catalogers Struggle to Survive." *Catalog Age*, (November 1995): 1, 49, 50.

Ohmann, Richard. *Selling Culture: Magazines, Markets, and Class at the Turn of the Century.* New York: Verso, 1996.

O'Sullivan, Sue. "Girls Who Kiss Girls and Who Cares?" In Diane Hamer and Belinda Budge, eds., *The Good, the Bad, and the Gorgeous*, 78–95. San Francisco: Pandora, 1994.

Painter, Kim. "Expo for HIV-Positive Carves Out a Niche for Education, Marketing." *USA Today*, September 9, 1997.

Peiss, Kathy. *Hope in a Jar: The Making of America's Beauty Culture.* New York: Metropolitan Books/Henry Holt, 1998.

Peñaloza, Lisa. "We're Here, We're Queer, and We're Going Shopping! A Critical Perspective on the Accommodation of Gays and Lesbians in the Marketplace." *Journal of Homosexuality* 31.1–2 (1996): 9–41.

Pendleton, Jennifer. "National Marketers Beginning to Recognize Gays." *Advertising Age*, October 6, 1980, 84.

Pertman, Adam. "Ads Target Big Dollars, Not Big Change." *Boston Globe*, February 4, 2001, E1.

Pogrebin, Robin. "Lesbian Publications Struggle for Survival in a Market Dominated by Gay Males." *New York Times*, December 23, 1996, D7.

Pollon, Zélie. "Jenny Shimizu: From Greasemonkey to Supermodel." *Curve* (September 1996): 40–44.

Press, Andrea. *Women Watching Television.* Philadelphia: University of Pennsylvania Press, 1991.

Prime Access, Inc., and Rivendell Marketing. "2002 Gay Press Report," 23 pages. New York: 2002.

PRNewswire. "PlanetOut Partners, Inc. Posts First Full Quarter of Positive Operating Income," October 9, 2002.

Radway, Janice. "Ethnography Among Elites: Comparing Discourses of Power." *Journal of Communication Inquiry* 13.2 (1989): 3–11.

——. *A Feeling for Books: The Book-of-the-Month Club, Literary Taste, and Middle-Class Desire.* Chapel Hill: University of North Carolina Press, 1997.

——. "Identifying Ideological Seams: Mass Culture, Analytic Method, and Political Practice." *Communication* 9 (1986): 93–125.

——. *Reading the Romance: Women, Patriarchy, and Popular Literature.* Chapel Hill: University of North Carolina Press, 1984.

Raine, George. "Dockers Coming Out." *San Francisco Examiner*, October 21, 1998, D1, D4.

Reid, John (Andrew Tobias). *The Best Little Boy in the World.* New York: Ballantine Books, 1973.

Research Business Report. "Harris Interactive Uses Election 2000 to Prove Its Online MR Efficacy and Accuracy" (November 2000): n.p.

Ritter, John. "Ads Linked to Rise in Rate of HIV Infections. City Considers Ban on Drug Billboards." *USA Today*, April 6, 2001, 4A.

Rodriguez, Cindy. "Census Bolsters Theory Illegal Immigrants Undercounted." *Boston Globe*, March 20, 2001, A4.

Roeper, Richard. "Falwell Brews Up a Tempest in Beer Stein Over 'Gay Ad.'" *Chicago Sun-Times*, May 5, 1999, 11.

Rose, Tricia. *Black Noise: Rap Music and Black Culture in Contemporary America*. Hanover, N.H.: Wesleyan University Press, 1994.

Rosin, Hanna. "Falwell Lights into Budweiser." *Washington Post*, May 12, 1999, C1.

Rotello, Gabriel. *Sexual Ecology: AIDS and the Destiny of Gay Men*. New York: Dutton, 1997.

Rothaus, Steve. "Big Business Looks to the Rainbow." *Miami Herald*, August 26 2002.

Rothenberg, Randall. *Where the Suckers Moon: An Advertising Story*. New York: Knopf (distributed by Random House), 1994.

Rothman, Cliff. "A Welcome Mat for Gay Customers." *New York Times*, August 17, 2001, F1.

Rubin, Gayle S. "Thinking Sex: Notes for a Radical Theory of the Politics of Sexuality." In Abelove, Barale, and Halperin, eds., *The Lesbian and Gay Studies Reader*, 1–44.

Rubin, Sylvia. "The New Lesbian Chic: In Movies, TV, Music, Sports, Politics, Gay Women Find They're in Fashion." *San Francisco Chronicle*, June 22, 1993, B3–B4.

Russo, Vito. *The Celluloid Closet*. New York: HarperCollins, 1995.

Salholz, E. "Lesbians Coming Out Strong: The Power and the Pride." *Newsweek*, July 19, 1993, 54–60.

Schudson, Michael. *Advertising, the Uneasy Persuasion: Its Dubious Impact on American Society*. New York: Basic Books, 1984.

Schulman, Sarah. "The Making of a Market Niche." *Harvard Lesbian and Gay Review* (Winter 1998): 17–20.

———. *Stagestruck: Theater, AIDS, and the Marketing of Gay America*. Durham, N.C.: Duke University Press, 1998.

Schwartz, John. "Online Gays Become a Market for Advertisers." *Washington Post*, May 22, 1999, E1, E5.

Scott, Henry. "Targeting Affluent Gays: Letter to the Editor." *Advertising Age*, November 2, 1998, 24.

Sedgwick, Eve Kosofsky. *Epistemology of the Closet*. Berkeley: University of California Press, 1990.

Sender, Katherine. "Gay Readers, Consumers, and a Dominant Gay Habitus: Twenty-Five Years of the 'Advocate' Magazine." *Journal of Communication* 51.1 (2001): 73–99.

———. *Off the Straight and Narrow: Lesbians, Gays, Bisexuals, and Television*. Video (63 min). Northampton, Mass.: Media Education Foundation, 1998.

———. "Selling Sexual Subjectivities: Audiences Respond to Gay Window Advertising." *Critical Studies in Mass Communication* 16.2 (1999): 172–96.

Shapiro, Karen. "The Construction of Television Commercials: Four Cases of Interorganizational Problem Solving." Ph.D. diss., Stanford University, 1981.

Sharkey, Betsy. "The Way Out." *Adweek*, July 19, 1993, 2–31.

Shim, Doobo. "From Yellow Peril Through Model Minority to Renewed Yellow Peril: Asians in Popular Media—Constructing (Mis)Representations." *Journal of Communication Inquiry* 22.4 (1998): 385–409.

Shister, Gail. "New Gay-Lesbian Channel Is Work of Two Wharton Chums." *Philadelphia Inquirer*, January 15, 2002.

Silverstone, Roger. *Framing Science: The Making of a BBC Documentary*. London: British Film Institute, 1985.

Slater, Don. "Advertising as Commercial Practice: Business Strategy and Social Theory." Ph.D. diss., Cambridge University (U.K.), 1985.

——. *Consumer Culture and Modernity*. Cambridge, Eng.: Polity, 1997.

——. "Corridors of Power." In J. F. Gubrium and D. Silverman, eds., *The Politics of Field Research: Sociology Beyond Enlightenment*, 113–31. Newbury Park, Calif.: Sage, 1989.

——. "On the Wings of the Sign: Commodity Culture and Social Practice." *Media, Culture, and Society* 9 (1987): 457–580.

Snead, Elizabeth. "Lesbians in the Limelight: Some Chafe at Media's Embrace." *USA Today*, July 13, 1993, 1D.

Soar, Matthew. " 'The Children of Marx and Coca Cola': Advertising and Commercial Creativity." Master's thesis, Simon Fraser University, 1996.

Solheim, Karla. "The Battle of the Queer Dot-Coms." *Girlfriends* (March 2000): 26–31, 40.

Somerville, Siobhan B. *Queering the Color Line: Race and the Invention of Homosexuality in American Culture*. Durham, N.C.: Duke University Press, 2000.

Spare Parts and Greenfield Online. "New Internet Study Offers Insights About Gay Community Beliefs and Habits" (press release), October 14, 1998, 4 pages.

St. John, Warren. "Metrosexuals Come Out." *New York Times*, June 22, 2003, 1.

Stabiner, Karen. "Tapping the Homosexual Market." *New York Times Magazine*, May 2, 1982, 34–36, 74–85.

Stacey, Jackie. *Star Gazing: Hollywood Cinema and Female Spectatorship*. New York: Routledge, 1994.

Stein, Arlene. "All Dressed Up, But No Place to Go? Style Wars and the New Lesbianism." In Corey K. Creekmur and Alexander Doty, eds., *Out in Culture: Gay, Lesbian, and Queer Essays on Popular Culture*, 476–83. Durham, N.C.: Duke University Press, 1995.

Stewart, Thomas A. "Gay in Corporate America." *Fortune*, December 12, 1991, 42–56.

Streitmatter, Rodger. *Unspeakable: The Rise of the Gay and Lesbian Press in America*. Boston: Faber and Faber, 1995.

Stuever, Hank. "Straight Arrows in Gayville, USA." *Washington Post*, April 27, 2000, C1–C3.

Sullivan, Andrew. *Virtually Normal: An Argument About Homosexuality*. New York: Knopf, 1995.

Swisher, Kara. "Targeting the Gay Market." *Washington Post*, April 25, 1993, H1, H6.

Tedeschi, Bob. "More Companies Are Working to Attract Gay and Lesbian Customers." *New York Times*, August 26, 2002, C4.

Tedlow, Richard S. *New and Improved: The Story of Mass Marketing in America*. New York: Basic Books, 1990.

Thornton, Sarah. *Club Cultures: Music, Media, and Subcultural Capital*. Hanover, N.H.: Wesleyan University Press, 1996.

Tuchman, Gayle. *Making News: A Study in the Construction of Reality*. New York: Free Press, 1978.

Turow, Joseph. *Breaking Up America: Advertisers and the New Media World*. Chicago: University of Chicago Press, 1997.

Tyler, Carole-Anne. "Boys Will Be Girls: The Politics of Gay Drag." In Diana Fuss, ed., *Inside/Out: Lesbian Theories, Gay Theories*, 32–46. New York: Routledge, 1991.

Vaid, Urvashi. *Virtual Equality: The Mainstreaming of Gay America*. New York: Anchor Books, 1995.

Vobejda, Barbara. "Census Spotted Nearly 230,000 Homeless People: Critics, Agency Agree 1990 Count Made in One Night Found Only a Portion of the Total." *Washington Post*, April 13, 1991, A3.

Walters, Suzanna Danuta. *All the Rage: The Story of Gay Visibility in America*. Chicago: University of Chicago Press, 2001.

Warchol, K. "Artists Entering the Marketplace." In Larry Gross, ed., *On the Margins of Art Worlds*, 71–93. Boulder, Colo.: Westview, 1995.

Warner, Michael. *Fear of a Queer Planet: Queer Politics and Social Theory*. Minneapolis: University of Minnesota Press, 1993.

——. *The Trouble with Normal: Sex, Politics, and the Ethics of Queer Life*. New York: Free Press, 1999.

Watney, Simon. "The Spectacle of AIDS." In Abelove, Barale, and Halperin, eds., *The Lesbian and Gay Studies Reader*, 202–211.

Waugh, Thomas. *Hard to Imagine: Gay Male Eroticism in Photography and Film from Their Beginnings to Stonewall*. New York: Columbia University Press, 1996.

Webster, Nancy Coltun. "Playing to Gay Segments Opens Doors to Marketers." *Advertising Age*, May 30, 1994, S6.

Weems, Robert. *Desegregating the Dollar: African American Consumberism in the Twentieth Century*. New York: New York University Press, 1998.

Weiss, Andrea. "A Queer Feeling When I Look at You." In Christine Gledhill, ed., *Stardom: Industry of Desire*, 283–99. London: Routledge, 1991.

Whittington, Lewis. "Opening TV's Closet to Different Audience." *Philadelphia Inquirer*, January 16, 2002.

Wilke, Michael. "Ad Survey Shows Appeal of Gay Themes." *Advertising Age*, May 6, 1996, 19.

——. "Big Advertisers Join Move to Embrace Gay Market." *Advertising Age*, August 4, 1997, 1, 10.

——. "Burgeoning Gay Web Sites Spark Advertiser Interest." *Advertising Age*, June 22, 1998, 30.

——. "Fewer Gays Are Wealthy, Data Says." *Advertising Age*, October 19, 1998, 58.

——. "Gay Print Media Ad Revenue Up 36%." *Advertising Age*, October 6, 1997, 26.

——. "Reliable Research Difficult to Gather, Analyze." *Advertising Age*, August 4, 1997, 11.

——. "Seven Top Shops Disclose Policies on Gays." *Advertising Age*, October 27, 1997, 22.

——. "Wired Lesbians/Gays Lure Marketers: 'Net Savvy Segment Draws Brand-Name Media, Advertisers." *Advertising Age*, December 11, 1995, 33.

Williams, Stan. "Securing the Out Post." *DNR*, April 24, 1998, 3.

Williamson, Judith. *Decoding Advertisements: Ideology and Meaning in Advertising.* London: Boyars, 1978.

Wolcott, James. "Lover Girls." *Vanity Fair* (June 1997): 64–67.

Wong, Paul, Chienping Faith Lai, Richard Nagasawa, and Teiming Lin. "Asian Americans as a Model Minority: Self-Perceptions and Perceptions by Other Racial Groups." *Sociological perspectives* 41.1 (1998): 95–118.

Woods, James D. *The Corporate Closet: The Professional Lives of Gay Men in America.* New York: Free Press, 1993.

Yahoo! TV (*see* http://tv.yahoo.com/news). "Canadian Gay TV Channel Pinkslips Staff," December 23, 2002 (retrieved December 27, 2002).

Yonan, Joe. "Out on the High Seas." *Boston Globe*, September 22, 2002, M1, M8.

Zeilberger, Ruth. "Where the Boys Are, Where the Girls Are: Travel Industry Vying for GLBT Market." *DiversityInc.*, March 5, 2003.

Emma Donoghue, editor, *Poems Between Women: Four Centuries of Love, Romantic Friendship, and Desire*

James T. Sears and Walter L. Williams, editors, *Overcoming Heterosexism and Homophobia: Strategies That Work*

Patricia Juliana Smith, *Lesbian Panic: Homoeroticism in Modern British Women's Fiction*

Dwayne C. Turner, *Risky Sex: Gay Men and HIV Prevention*

Timothy F. Murphy, *Gay Science: The Ethics of Sexual Orientation Research*

Cameron McFarlane, *The Sodomite in Fiction and Satire, 1660-1750*

Lynda Hart, *Between the Body and the Flesh: Performing Sadomasochism*

Byrne R. S. Fone, editor, *The Columbia Anthology of Gay Literature: Readings from Western Antiquity to the Present Day*

Ellen Lewin, *Recognizing Ourselves: Ceremonies of Lesbian and Gay Commitment*

Ruthann Robson, *Sappho Goes to Law School: Fragments in Lesbian Legal Theory*

Jacquelyn Zita, *Body Talk: Philosophical Reflections on Sex and Gender*

Evelyn Blackwood and Saskia Wieringa, *Female Desires: Same-Sex Relations and Transgender Practices Across Cultures*

William L. Leap, ed., *Public Sex/Gay Space*

Larry Gross and James D. Woods, eds., *The Columbia Reader on Lesbians and Gay Men in Media, Society, and Politics*

Marilee Lindemann, *Willa Cather: Queering America*

George E. Haggerty, *Men in Love: Masculinity and Sexuality in the Eighteenth Century*

Andrew Elfenbein, *Romantic Genius: The Prehistory of a Homosexual Role*

Gilbert Herdt and Bruce Koff, *Something to Tell You: The Road Families Travel When a Child Is Gay*

Richard Canning, *Gay Fiction Speaks: Conversations with Gay Novelists*

Laura Doan, *Fashioning Sapphism: The Origins of a Modern English Lesbian Culture*

Mary Bernstein and Renate Reimann, eds., *Queer Families, Queer Politics: Challenging Culture and the State*

Richard R. Bozorth, *Auden's Games of Knowledge: Poetry and the Meanings of Homosexuality*

Larry Gross, *Up from Invisibility: Lesbians, Gay Men, and the Media in America*

Linda Garber, *Identity Poetics: Race, Class, and the Lesbian-Feminist Roots of Queer Theory*

Richard Canning, *Hear Us Out: Conversations with Gay Novelists*

David Bergman, *The Violet Hour: The Violet Quill and the Making of Gay Culture*

Alan Sinfield, *On Sexuality and Power*